Investment Advice Diploma (IAD)

# UK Regulation and Professional Integrity

Edition 6, May 2014

This learning manual relates to syllabus version 6.0 and will cover examinations from **21 August 2014 to 20 April 2015**

APPROVED WORKBOOK

Welcome to the Chartered Institute for Securities & Investment's UK Regulation and Professional Integrity study material.

This manual has been written to prepare you for the Chartered Institute for Securities & Investment's UK Regulation and Professional Integrity examination.

Published by:
Chartered Institute for Securities & Investment
© Chartered Institute for Securities & Investment 2014
8 Eastcheap
London
EC3M 1AE
Tel: +44 20 7645 0600
Fax: +44 20 7645 0601

Email: customersupport@cisi.org
www.cisi.org/qualifications

Author:
Phil Read, Chartered FCSI
Andrew Hall, Head of Professional Standards, CISI

Reviewers:
Lesley Chester BA (Hons), FCA, AMCT, Chartered FCSI
Dhaneswar Chooramun, Chartered MCSI

This is an educational manual only and Chartered Institute for Securities & Investment accepts no responsibility for persons undertaking trading or investments in whatever form.

While every effort has been made to ensure its accuracy, no responsibility for loss occasioned to any person acting or refraining from action as a result of any material in this publication can be accepted by the publisher or authors.

All rights reserved. No part of this publication may be reproduced, stored in a retrieval system, or transmitted, in any form or by any means, electronic, mechanical, photocopying, recording or otherwise without the prior permission of the copyright owner.

Warning: any unauthorised act in relation to all or any part of the material in this publication may result in both a civil claim for damages and criminal prosecution.

A learning map, which contains the full syllabus, appears at the end of this manual. The syllabus can also be viewed on cisi.org and is also available by contacting the Customer Support Centre on +44 20 7645 0777. Please note that the examination is based upon the syllabus. Candidates are reminded to check the Candidate Update area details (cisi.org/candidateupdate) on a regular basis for updates as a result of industry change(s) that could affect their examination.

The questions contained in this manual are designed as an aid to revision of different areas of the syllabus and to help you consolidate your learning chapter by chapter.

Learning manual version: 6.1 (May 2014)

## Learning and Professional Development with the CISI

The Chartered Institute for Securities & Investment is the leading professional body for those who work in, or aspire to work in, the investment sector, and we are passionately committed to enhancing knowledge, skills and integrity – the three pillars of professionalism at the heart of our Chartered body.

CISI examinations are used extensively by firms to meet the requirements of government regulators. Besides the regulators in the UK, where the CISI head office is based, CISI examinations are recognised by a wide range of governments and their regulators, from Singapore to Dubai and the US. Around 50,000 examinations are taken each year, and it is compulsory for candidates to use CISI learning manuals to prepare for CISI examinations so that they have the best chance of success. Our learning manuals are normally revised every year by experts who themselves work in the industry and also by our Accredited Training Providers, who offer training and elearning to help prepare candidates for the examinations. Information for candidates is also posted on a special area of our website: cisi.org/candidateupdate.

This learning manual not only provides a thorough preparation for the examination it refers to, it is also a valuable desktop reference for practitioners, and studying from it counts towards your Continuing Professional Development (CPD).

CISI examination candidates are automatically registered, without additional charge, as student members for one year (should they not be members of the CISI already), and this enables you to use a vast range of online resources, including CISI TV, free of any additional charge. The CISI has more than 40,000 members, and nearly half of them have already completed relevant qualifications and transferred to a core membership grade.

Completing a higher level examination enables you to progress even more quickly towards personal Chartered status, the pinnacle of professionalism in the CISI. You will find more information about the next steps for this at the end of this manual.

With best wishes for your studies.

Ruth Martin, Managing Director

| | |
|---|---|
| The Financial Services Industry | 1 |
| UK Financial Services and Consumer Relationships | 37 |
| UK Contract and Trust Legislation | 67 |
| Integrity and Ethics in Professional Practice | 89 |
| The Regulatory Infrastructure of the UK Financial Services | 119 |
| FCA and PRA Supervisory Objectives, Principles and Processes | 157 |
| FCA and PRA Authorisation of Firms and Individuals | 199 |
| The Regulatory Framework Relating to Financial Crime | 259 |
| Complaints and Redress | 321 |
| FCA Conduct of Business Fair Treatment and Client Money Protection | 335 |
| Glossary and Abbreviations | 407 |
| Syllabus Learning Map | 429 |

It is estimated that this manual will require approximately 80 hours of study time.

**What next?**
See the back of this book for details of CISI membership.

**Need more support to pass your exam?**
See our section on Accredited Training Providers.

**Want to leave feedback?**
Please email your comments to learningresources@cisi.org

# Chapter One
# The Financial Services Industry

| | |
|---|---|
| 1. The Role of the Government | 3 |
| 2. Financial Investment in the Economy | 7 |
| 3. Global Financial Services | 10 |
| 4. Government and Central Banks' Roles in Financial Markets | 19 |
| 5. Economic, Financial and Stock Market Cycles | 24 |
| 6. Global Trends and Their Impacts | 29 |

**This syllabus area will provide approximately 2 of the 80 examination questions**

The Financial Services Industry

In this chapter you will gain an understanding of:

- The role that the UK government plays in the economy, in particular its input to regulation, taxation and social welfare.
- The factors that influence the UK financial services industry and the role of financial investment in the economy.
- The role and structure of financial services and its key participants in the UK, Europe, North America and Asia.
- The role of governments and central banks in financial markets.
- The impact of global trends.

# 1. The Role of the Government

## Learning Objective

1.1     Understand the factors that influence the UK financial services industry:

1.1.1     The role of the government in the economy: policy, regulation, taxation and social welfare

# 1.1     General Economic Policy Aims

As well as providing a legal and regulatory framework for economic activity, the government plays a role directing and managing the economy. The key aims of a government's economic policy are to:

- Achieve **sustainable growth** in national income per head of population. Sustainable growth would imply an increase in national income in real terms – after stripping inflation. As the economy grows then so does national income – as a consequence the demand for goods and services increases. Sustainable growth gives the impression that major fluctuations in the business cycle (boom and bust cycles) are avoided, and that economic activity/output grows in an upward trend. This is seen as the key aim and outcome of the government's economic policy.
- **Control inflation** in prices – a key objective of the economic policy by many governments in recent years.
- **Full employment** – the achievement of full employment does not mean that everyone who wants a job will be employed, rather that there are low levels of unemployment and involuntary unemployment is a short term issue, not a long term trend.
- Manage the **balance of payments** – between exports and imports. The wealth of a country relative to others (ie, their ability to borrow) depends on the achievement of an external balance over time. Deficits in external trade, with imports exceeding exports, may also damage the prospects for economic growth and have an impact on the perceived **creditworthiness** of a country.

## 1.2 Fiscal Policy

This is a government policy on taxation, public borrowing and public spending.

- **Direct taxation** is the taxation of incomes on individuals and companies, as well as on wealth in the form of inheritance tax.
- **Indirect taxation** is the taxation of products and services that consumers/companies purchase and use, ie, value added tax (VAT).

The amount that government's borrow each year is now known as the **public sector net cash requirement (PSNCR)** in the UK. The PSNCR is the annual excess of spending over income for the entire public sector – not just for central government. → Deficy / surplus

A government can intervene in the economy by:

- spending more money and financing this expenditure by borrowing;
- collecting more in taxes without increasing spending (ie, increase tax levels/lower threshold levels);
- collecting more in taxes in order to increase spending, thus diverting income from one part of the economy to another.

As the government increases its spending, national income tends to rise – in real terms and of price affordability. Increasing the taxes raised without increasing spending indicates a **contractionary** fiscal stance. Governments may raise taxation just to take inflationary pressures from the economy. Collecting more in taxes in order to increase spending, thus diverting income from one part of the economy to another, indicates a broadly **neutral** fiscal stance.

If government raises taxes and spending by the same amount, there will be an increase in aggregate monetary demand. Taxpayers would have saved some of the money they pay in increased tax, but the government will spend all of the increased tax within the real economy. Therefore, the net effect is that more real money is spent. This effect is called the **balanced budget multiplier**.

As government spending or tax reductions may be inflationary, and the impact of higher domestic prices make imports relatively cheaper and exports less competitive in foreign markets, the government fiscal policy has important implications for the **balance of payments** (discussed later in Section 2.3).

Government fiscal policy is also used to **reduce unemployment** and stimulate employment. For example:

- increased government spending on capital projects, on which people are employed to work;
- government-funded training schemes;
- taxation of companies on the basis of the numbers and pay levels of employees.

Government spending, however, can create and increase inflationary pressures on the economy – which can lead to the creation of more unemployment. Fiscal policy, therefore must be used with great care, even if the aim is to create new jobs.

# The Financial Services Industry

The impact of changes to a government's fiscal policy is not always certain. The policy to pursue one aim (eg, lower inflation) can have a knock-on effect on the pursuit of other aims (eg, employment). The effects of fiscal changes can take a very long time to feed through to the economy – by which time other factors may have changed, complicating the overall outcome.

The Government balances how its fiscal policy will affect savers, investors and companies alike.

Companies are affected by tax rules on dividends and profits, and by tax breaks for certain activities.

A feature of a government's fiscal policy is that it needs to budget what it plans to spend, leading to how much it will therefore need to rise – through taxation or by borrowing.

The planning of a government's fiscal policy usually follows an annual cycle. In the UK, the most important statement of changes to policy is the 'budget', which takes place in the spring of each year. The Chancellor of the Exchequer will also deliver a pre-budget report in the autumn.

Because of the annual planning cycle of government finances, fiscal policy is not very responsive to shorter-term developments in the economy. Therefore, the Government will use monetary policy for shorter-term adjustments of the economy.

*Fiscal = Long term management*
*Monetary = Short Term*

## 1.3 Monetary Policy

Monetary policy is concerned with changes in the amount of money in circulation (the money supply) and with changes in the price of money – interest rates. These variables are linked with inflation in prices generally, and also with exchange rates – the price of the domestic currency in terms of other currencies.

Since 1997, the most important aspect of monetary policy in the UK has been the influence over interest rates exerted by the Bank of England (BOE), the central bank of the UK. The Monetary Policy Committee (MPC) of the BOE has the responsibility of setting interest rates, with the aim of meeting the government's inflation target of 2% based on the consumer prices index (CPI). The CPI is the name used in the UK for the harmonised index of consumer prices (HICP), a standard European-wide measure of inflation.

The MPC influences interest rates by deciding the short-term benchmark **repo rate** – the rate at which the BOE deals in the money markets. This is known as the BOE's **base lending rate**, or **base rate** for short.

The base rate affects the commercial rates, which financial institutions then set for the different financial instruments they offer or deal in (eg, mortgage and personal loan rates). Therefore, if the MPC changes the base rate, commercial banks will normally be expected to react quickly by changing their own deposit and lending rates accordingly.

## 1.3.1 Monetary Policy Committee (MPC) Meetings

The MPC meets every month to set the interest rate. Throughout the month, the MPC receives extensive briefing on the economy from BOE staff. This includes a half-day meeting – known as the pre-MPC meeting – which usually takes place on the Friday before the MPC's interest-rate-setting meeting. The nine members of the committee are made aware of all the latest data on the economy and hear explanations of recent trends and analysis of relevant issues. The committee is also told about business conditions around the UK from the Bank's agents. The agents' role is to talk directly to business to gain intelligence and insight into current and future economic developments and prospects.

The monthly MPC meeting is a two-day affair. The meeting starts with an update on the most recent economic data. A series of issues is then identified for discussion. On the following day, a summary of the previous day's discussion is provided and the MPC members individually explain their views on what policy should be. The governor then puts to the meeting the policy which he believes will command a majority and members of the MPC vote. Any member in a minority is asked to say what level of interest rates they would have preferred, and this is recorded in the minutes of the meeting. The interest rate decision is announced at 12 noon on the second day.

## 1.3.2 Public Accountability: Explaining Views and Decisions

Minutes of the MPC meetings are published two weeks after the interest rate decision. The minutes give a full account of the policy discussion, including differences of view. They also record the votes of the individual members of the committee. The committee has to explain its actions regularly to parliamentary committees, particularly the Treasury committee.

In addition to the monthly MPC minutes, the Bank publishes its inflation report every quarter. This report gives an analysis of the UK economy and the factors influencing policy decisions. The inflation report includes the MPC's latest forecasts for inflation and output growth. Because monetary policy operates with a time lag of about two years, it is necessary for the MPC to form judgments about the outlook for output and inflation.

The MPC uses a model of the economy to help produce its projections. The model provides a framework to organise thinking on how the economy works and how different economic developments may affect future inflation. But this is not a mechanical exercise. Given all the uncertainties and unknown factors of the future, the MPC's forecast has to involve a great deal of judgment about the economy.

See also Section 4.1, for more details on the membership of the MPC.

The Financial Services Industry

## 2. Financial Investment in the Economy

### Learning Objective

1.1     Understand the factors that influence the UK financial services industry:

1.1.2   The role of financial investment in the economy: primary markets; secondary markets; balance of payments; exchange rates

## 2.1 Primary Markets

The term primary market refers to the market for new issues of shares or other securities (for example, loan instruments).

Organisations such as companies and governments need capital in order to carry out their activities (for example, to buy premises and invest in machinery). In order to raise this capital they may issue securities such as shares or loan stock.

- **Shares** represent a share in the ownership of a company. Investors buy them in the hope of either capital appreciation of the value of the company, and therefore of the price of the share, or of income, if the company earns profits and pays them to its investors in the form of dividends.
- **Loan instruments** represent borrowings by the issuer, which would normally expect to be repaid at some time. They therefore have a capital repayment value to the investor and (usually) a coupon, which represents the interest that will be paid periodically to the investor. An example of a loan instrument issued by a company is a debenture; an example of a loan instrument issued by the UK government is a gilt.

In order to raise the money it needs, whether by way of share capital or loan capital, the issuer will offer the new securities on the primary market.

Primary markets are important both for new ventures – for example, a company that is just being established – and for existing ventures that are raising new capital, or which have been in existence for a while but are just introducing their existing shares to the public market for the first time.

For a new company, listing its shares for the first time, the London Stock Exchange (LSE) acts as the primary market in the UK: the market through which it reaches its initial investors and raises a new tranche of capital. The process of introducing shares or loan stock on to the market for the first time is known as **listing** them. So, for example, shares in UK public limited companies are likely to be listed on the LSE.

Issuers have to meet certain standards before they can list their securities on the market, such as:

- their size;
- the number of securities they are introducing to the market;
- the information they give potential investors, so that they can decide whether to invest or not;
- on an ongoing basis, the information they must disclose to the marketplace about themselves and the securities.

Shares can also be issued on overseas markets.

## 2.2 Secondary Markets

Once an investor has bought a holding in shares or loan instruments, however, he may not wish to hold them indefinitely. They may stop satisfying his needs because:

- his circumstances change (he needs his money back, or his investment objectives change); or
- the investment itself changes (it rises in value, so that the investor wants to sell it to capitalise on the gain. Alternatively, if the securities are shares, the company may have become less profitable and stopped paying worthwhile dividends; the investor wants to switch to an investment paying him better dividends).

The secondary markets offer a mechanism for him to sell or switch investments; they are the market in which investors sell shares that have already been introduced to the market. Thus, they offer an **exit route** for investors who want to sell their investments. They also offer a route for investors to buy securities which are already in existence from other investors.

As a place on which investors can, through their stockbrokers, trade in shares, loan stocks and other securities, the LSE acts as a secondary market in securities.

In the case of shares and loan instruments being dealt on the secondary market, the company raises no new money; cash travels via the market from the buying investor to the seller. It is only when securities are issued on the market for the first time (via the primary market) that the issuer (company) raises new money.

## 2.3 The Balance of Payments

The balance of payments in an economy measures the payments between that country and others. It is therefore made up of the country's exports and imports of goods and services and of transfers of financial capital. It thus measures all the payments received, and money owed, from overseas parties – less all the payments made, and debts owed, to people overseas.

### 2.3.1 Current and Capital Accounts

The accounts used to measure the UK's balance of payments are:

- the current account; and
- the capital and financial account.

The balance of payments figures also include a **balancing item** to correct any statistical errors and to make sure the accounts **balance**.

The **current account** measures flows in relation to trade in goods and services, income from investment and as compensation of employees, and current transfers (eg, private sector gifts to people overseas, or government aid to abroad). The current account balance is usually seen as the most important component of the balance of payments, because it has the greatest impact on other economic factors such as output and employment.

The **capital and financial account** measures flows in such things as overseas investment in the UK, UK private-sector investment abroad, foreign currency borrowing by, and deposits with, UK banks, and changes in official reserves.

The **balancing item** is included to deal with errors and omissions in the accounts: if more currency flows into the UK than is recorded in actual transactions, the balancing item will be positive, and vice versa.

## 2.4    Exchange Rates

The balance of payments between the UK and other countries is important for a number of reasons, not least the impact that it may have on UK exchange rates (and therefore on the competitiveness of UK exports and of imports into the UK economy).

A deficit on the current account means that the country is not matching its overseas expenditure with its current overseas income. How much this matters depends on the size of the deficit and on how persistent it is; a small negative balance, or one which only lasts for a short time, may not be regarded as too serious; it can be financed by the country running down its reserves somewhat, or by capital inflows. But one which lasts for longer has to be financed from somewhere – and a country's reserves are not infinite, so cannot be run down indefinitely. The alternative is to increase overseas borrowing, so as to finance the deficit; but to do this too much is not in the country's interests either, since the larger the UK's debts to the outside world, the greater the servicing requirements (repayment of interest and capital) on that debt.

One method of correcting a current account deficit is to allow sterling to fall in value against other currencies. This tends to make foreign goods and services more expensive for UK buyers and so encourages them to reduce imports and **buy British** instead. In addition, it makes UK goods and services cheaper for overseas customers, helping UK exports. Both these factors will help to restore a positive current account balance.

However, if the current account is also being financed by rising overseas debt, this can create concerns about the stability of the economy, which may lead to government action to raise interest rates (so as to prevent an outflow of investment funds). Higher interest rates can encourage foreign investors to invest in sterling assets – pushing up the exchange rate as they buy sterling to do so. Rising interest rates may well lead to a strengthening of the currency – which is clearly at odds with the strategy, discussed in the previous paragraph, of trying to manage the current account through a low exchange rate.

Thus, persistent surpluses and deficits on the balance of payments can create a considerable headache for a government and can impact on exchange rates, interest rates and consequently other activity in the economy.

# 3. Global Financial Services

**Learning Objective**

1.1 Understand the factors that influence the UK financial services industry:

1.1.3 The role and structure of the global financial services industry and its key participants: UK; Europe; North America; Asia

## 3.1 Financial Services in the UK

The structure of financial regulation is covered in detail in Chapter 5, where the relationship between Her Majesty's Treasury (HMT), the BOE, the Financial Policy Committee (FPC), the Financial Conduct Authority (FCA) and the Prudential Regulation Authority (PRA) is explained.

The Treasury is the UK's economics and finance ministry. It is responsible for formulating and implementing the government's financial and economic policy. Its aim is to raise the rate of sustainable growth, and achieve rising prosperity and a better quality of life with economic and employment opportunities for all.

## 3.2 Financial Services in Europe

The European Union (EU) was set up after the Second World War, with the aim of integrating the various countries and helping them rebuild their economies. The process of European integration was launched on 9 May 1950 when France officially proposed to create *'the first concrete foundation of a European federation'*.

The EU works towards single European markets in various trade sectors, finance being one of the most important. The aim is to remove barriers to inter-state trade by, among other things, ensuring that similar regulatory rules are in place. From a financial services perspective this should mean that, in terms of investor protection, it makes no difference to a customer whether he buys a financial product from a provider in his home state, or from another member state.

A single market in financial services has long been an objective of the EU. In a single market, financial institutions authorised to provide financial services in one member state are able to provide the same services throughout the EU, competing on a level playing field within a consistent regulatory environment. Such a single market in financial services will *'act as a catalyst for economic growth across all sectors of the economy, boost productivity and provide lower – cost and better – quality financial products for consumers, and enterprises'*.

However, the integration of financial markets in the EU has progressed much further and faster in wholesale than in retail financial services, with the latter still segmented largely on national lines.

The Financial Services Industry

### 3.2.1 The Lamfalussy Process

Given the scale of the task involved in adopting and implementing such a large programme of Financial Services Action Plan (FSAP) regulations and directives, the European Council of Finance Ministers (ECOFIN) decided in July 2000 to complete a single EU capital market by 2003. A committee of wise men chaired by Baron Alexandre Lamfalussy was appointed. The Lamfalussy committee recommended a new decision-making procedure for the adoption of EU legislation affecting the securities markets, which was endorsed by the Stockholm European Council in March 2001.

The Lamfalussy framework set out a fourfold approach to EU requirements. This approach applies to directives and regulations adopted prior to the entry into force of the Treaty of Lisbon. It will continue to apply until this legislation is amended and brought into line with the Treaty of Lisbon and the European system of financial supervision (ESFS).

In addition to the still operative pre-Lisbon Lamfalussy framework, there is a separate framework for post-Lisbon legislation.

The **European Insurance and Occupational Pensions Authority (EIOPA)** is an independent advisory body to the European Parliament and the Council of the EU. EIOPA's core responsibilities are to support the stability of the financial system, transparency of markets and financial products as well as the protection of insurance policyholders, pension scheme members and beneficiaries.

The **European Banking Authority (EBA)** is composed of high-level representatives from the banking supervisory authorities and central banks of the EU. Their role is to advise the Commission, either at its request, within a time limit which the Commission may lay down according to the urgency of the matter, or on the committee's own initiative, in particular as regards the preparation of draft-implementing measures in the field of banking activities; and to contribute to the consistent implementation of community directives and to the convergence of member states' supervisory practices throughout the community; and to enhance supervisory co-operation, including the exchange of information.

The **European Securities and Markets Authority (ESMA)** is an independent EU authority that contributes to safeguarding the stability of the EU's financial system by ensuring the integrity, transparency, efficiency and orderly functioning of securities markets, as well as enhancing investor protection. In particular, ESMA fosters supervisory convergence both amongst securities regulators, and across financial sectors by working closely with the other European Supervisory Authorities (ESAs) competent in the field of banking and EIOPA.

ESMA's work on securities legislation contributes to the development of a single rulebook in Europe. This serves two purposes: firstly, it ensures the consistent treatment of investors across the EU, enabling an adequate level of protection through effective regulation and supervision; secondly, it promotes equal conditions of competition for financial service providers, as well as ensuring the effectiveness and cost-efficiency of supervision for supervised companies. As part of its role in standard-setting and reducing the scope of regulatory arbitrage, ESMA strengthens international supervisory co-operation. Where requested in European law, ESMA undertakes the supervision of certain entities with pan-European reach.

Finally, ESMA also contributes to the financial stability of the EU, in the short, medium and long term, through its contribution to the work of the **European Systemic Risk Board (ESRB)**, which identifies potential risks to the financial system and provides advice to diminish possible threats to the financial stability of the EU. ESMA is also responsible for co-ordinating actions of securities supervisors and adopting emergency measures when a crisis situation arises.

A key change in the introduction of the ESMAs is that they, unlike their predecessor (CESR), have much stronger powers. Although they are sparsely staffed, they have the ability to bind the member states in ways that their predecessors did not. The trend is towards greater EU control. In the frequently asked questions (FAQs) section of its website, ESMA states *'ESMA's work on securities legislation contributes to the development of a single rule book in Europe…'*. The FAQs also state *'As part of its role in standard setting and reducing the scope of regulatory arbitrage, ESMA strengthens international supervisory co-operation. Where requested in European law, ESMA undertakes the supervision of certain entities with pan-European reach'*. All this goes further than the kind of supervisory co-operation which Lamfalussy had in mind.

Whilst ESMA is independent, there is full accountability in relation to the European Parliament, where it will appear before the relevant Committee, known as the Committee of Economic and Monetary Affairs (ECON), at its request for formal hearings. Full accountability in relation to the Council of the EU and the European Commission (EC) also exists. The authority reports on its activities regularly at meetings and also through an annual report.

## 3.2.2 The UK Regulators' (FCA and PRA) Priorities for Work in the EU and International Arena

The need for enhanced regulatory co-operation and co-ordination is particularly important in Europe, because of the considerable level of integration in the wholesale market and because the EU's single market legislation implies and requires high levels of co-operation and co-ordination. Within Europe, the regulator of the group, the regulator of the subsidiary, the regulator of the branch and the regulator in the country where the recipient of a service is based each have areas of exclusive responsibility and control, and areas where responsibilities overlap.

The following are the FCA's and PRA's key priorities in relation to EU and international regulation:

- Better regulation, ie, extensive consultation with stakeholders, consideration of the use of non-legislative tools, rigorous impact assessments of policy options, and subsequent review of measures to assess their actual impact.
- Continued commitment to a strengthened Lamfalussy structure.
- Enhanced supervisory co-operation in the EU and international context to improve oversight of firms operating on a cross-border basis.
- Promotion of principles-based and risk-based approaches in global fora, such as the sectoral committees and the Financial Stability Forum (FSF).

# The Financial Services Industry

### 3.2.3 The European Central Bank (ECB)

The ECB is the central bank for Europe's single currency, the euro. The ECB's main task is to maintain the euro's purchasing power and thus price stability in the euro area. The euro area comprises of the 17 EU countries who have adopted the euro since 1999.

The ECB and the national central banks together constitute the eurosystem, the central banking system of the euro area. The main objective of the eurosystem is to maintain price stability: safeguarding the value of the euro. The ECB is committed to performing all central bank tasks entrusted to it effectively. In doing so, it strives for the highest level of integrity, competence, efficiency and transparency.

### The European System of Central Banks (ESCB)

The ESCB is comprised of:

- the European Central Bank (ECB); and
- the national central banks (NCBs) of all 28 EU member states.

This means that the ESCB includes the national central banks of those EU member states that have not yet adopted the euro.

### Tasks of the ECB

The ECB only carries out a few operations. Instead, it focuses on formulating the policies and on ensuring that the decisions are implemented consistently by the NCBs.

In particular, the ECB is responsible for:

- defining eurosystem policies;
- deciding, co-ordinating and monitoring the monetary policy operations;
- adopting legal acts;
- authorising the issuance of bank notes;
- interventions in the foreign exchange (FX) markets;
- international and European co-operation.

Further, the ECB is responsible for:

- statutory reports;
- monitoring financial risks;
- fulfilling advisory functions to community institutions and national authorities;
- running the IT systems;
- strategic and tactical management of the ECB's foreign reserves.

## 3.3 Financial Services in the US

The regulatory structure is quite complicated, it is daunting and confusing, and it has its costs and complications. However, one great advantage of this complicated and duplicative system is that it gives someone with an innovative idea more than one place to turn; there is no monopoly regulator.

## 3.3.1 The Regulatory Agencies

- There are five federal regulators of depository institutions, as well as one or more regulators in each of the 50 states. The states also regulate lenders and mortgage originators that are not depositories.
- There is a separate federal agency that has the responsibility for regulating Federal Home Loan Mortgage Corporation (Fannie Mae), Federal National Mortgage Association (Freddie Mac), and the Federal Home Loan Bank System. (Fannie Mae and Freddie Mac are government-sponsored enterprises that provide a secondary market in home mortgages in the US. They purchase mortgages from the lenders who originate them; they hold some of these mortgages and some are securitised – sold in the form of securities, which they guarantee.)
- There are two federal regulators of the securities markets and financial instruments, as well as 50 state regulators (and 50 state attorney generals, who are prepared to bring lawsuits against securities firms on behalf of their respective states' citizens).
- The regulation of insurance companies is exclusively the domain of the 50 states.
- Pension funds are regulated by two federal agencies, and, again, the 50 states have a say.
- Consumer fraud in financial products can be the responsibility of yet another federal agency, as well as the 50 states.

There are overlapping responsibilities and jurisdictional disputes throughout this framework. For example, federal bank regulators and the 50 state bank regulators are constantly struggling for jurisdiction with respect to consumer protection issues. As another example of regulatory complexity, a commercial bank's holding company is usually regulated by the Federal Reserve, while the primary safety-and-soundness regulator for the bank itself is the federal Office of the Comptroller of the Currency (OCC), or one of the 50 state bank regulators. Until recently if the bank was a savings institution, the regulator of its holding company would have been the federal Office of Thrift Supervision (OTS). But since July 2011 the OCC assumed responsibility from the OTS for the ongoing examination, supervision, and regulation of federal savings associations and rule-making for all savings associations, state and federal. The OCC republished under its own name all the **previous** rules of the OTS so that firms would have consistency.

## 3.3.2 The Securities and Exchange Commission (SEC)

The mission of the US SEC is to protect investors, maintain fair, orderly and efficient markets, and facilitate capital formation.

The laws and rules that govern the securities industry in the US derive from a simple and straightforward concept: all investors, whether large institutions or private individuals, should have access to certain basic facts about an investment, prior to buying it, and so long as they hold it. To achieve this, the SEC requires public companies to disclose meaningful financial and other information to the public. This provides a common pool of knowledge for all investors to use to judge for themselves whether to buy, sell or hold a particular security. Only through the steady flow of timely, comprehensive and accurate information can people make sound investment decisions.

The SEC oversees the key participants in the securities world, including securities exchanges, securities brokers and dealers, investment advisers and mutual funds. The SEC is concerned primarily with promoting the disclosure of important market-related information, maintaining fair dealing, and protecting against fraud.

It is the responsibility of the SEC to:

- interpret federal securities laws;
- issue new, and amend existing, rules;
- oversee the inspection of securities firms, brokers, investment advisers, and ratings agencies;
- oversee private regulatory organisations in the securities, accounting, and auditing fields; and co-ordinate US securities regulation with federal, state and foreign authorities.

## Key Legislation

### Investment Company Act of 1940

This act regulates the organisation of companies, including mutual funds, that engage primarily in investing, reinvesting and trading in securities, and whose own securities are offered to the investing public. The regulation is designed to minimise conflicts of interest that arise in these complex operations.

### Investment Advisers Act of 1940

This law regulates investment advisers. With certain exceptions, this act requires that firms or sole practitioners compensated for advising others about securities investments, must register with the SEC and conform to regulations designed to protect investors.

### Sarbanes-Oxley Act of 2002

This act mandated a number of reforms to enhance corporate responsibility, enhance financial disclosures and combat corporate and accounting fraud, and created the Public Company Accounting Oversight Board (PCAOB), to oversee the activities of the auditing profession.

### Dodd-Frank Wall Street Reform and Consumer Protection Act

A compendium of federal regulations, primarily affecting financial institutions and their customers, that the Obama administration passed in 2010 in an attempt to prevent the recurrence of events which caused the 2008 financial crisis. The Dodd-Frank Wall Street Reform and Consumer Protection Act, commonly referred to as simply 'Dodd-Frank', is supposed to lower risk in various parts of the US financial system.

## 3.3.3   The Federal Reserve

Federal Reserve banks were established by Congress as the operating arms of the nation's central banking system. Many of the services provided by this network to depository institutions and the government are similar to services provided by banks and thrift institutions to business customers and individuals. Reserve banks hold the cash reserves of depository institutions and make loans to them. They move currency and coin into and out of circulation, and collect and process millions of cheques each day. They provide cheque accounts for the Treasury, issue and redeem government securities, and act in other ways as fiscal agents for the US government. They supervise and examine member banks for safety and soundness. The Reserve banks also participate in the activity that is the primary responsibility of the Federal Reserve system: the setting of monetary policy.

## 3.3.4 The Office of the Comptroller of the Currency (OCC)

The OCC charters, regulates and supervises all national banks. It also supervises the federal branches and agencies of foreign banks. Headquartered in Washington DC, the OCC has four district offices, plus an office in London to supervise the international activities of national banks.

The OCC's nationwide staff of examiners conducts on-site reviews of national banks and provides sustained supervision of bank operations. The agency issues rules, legal interpretations and corporate decisions concerning banking, bank investments, bank community development activities and other aspects of bank operations.

## 3.3.5 The US Treasury

The Treasury department is the executive agency responsible for promoting economic prosperity and ensuring the financial security of the US. It is responsible for a wide range of activities, such as advising the President on economic and financial issues, encouraging sustainable economic growth, and fostering improved governance in financial institutions. It operates and maintains systems that are critical to the nation's financial infrastructure, such as the production of coin and currency, the disbursement of payments to the American public, revenue collection, and the borrowing of funds necessary to run the federal government. The department works with other federal agencies, foreign governments and international financial institutions to encourage global economic growth, raise standards of living, and, as far as possible, predict and prevent economic and financial crises. The Treasury also performs a critical and far-reaching role in enhancing national security by implementing economic sanctions against foreign threats to the US, identifying and targeting the financial support networks of national security threats, and improving the safeguards of the financial systems of the US.

## 3.3.6 The Financial Industry Regulatory Authority (FINRA)

The Financial Industry Regulatory Authority (FINRA) is the largest independent regulator for all securities firms doing business in the US. All told, FINRA oversees nearly 4,535 brokerage firms, about 163,000 branch offices and approximately 632,000 registered securities representatives.

FINRA touches virtually every aspect of the securities business – from registering and educating industry participants to examining securities firms; writing rules; enforcing those rules and the federal securities laws; informing and educating the investing public; providing trade reporting and other industry utilities; and administering the largest dispute-resolution forum for investors and registered firms. It also performs market regulation under contract for the National Association of Securities Dealers Automated Quotation (NASDAQ) Stock Market, the American Stock Exchange (AMEX), the International Securities Exchange (ISE) and the Chicago Climate Exchange (CCX).

**The Role of FINRA**

- Safeguards the investing public against fraud and bad practices.
- Enforces industry rules and federal securities laws.
- Registers, tests and educates brokers.
- Works to ensure investors are not misled.
- Keeps an eye on the markets.
- Educates and informs investors.
- Demands fairness.

### 3.3.7 Commodity Futures Trading Commission (CFTC)

The US Commodity Futures Trading Commission (CFTC) is an independent agency of the US government that regulates the derivatives markets. The mission of the CFTC is to protect market participants and the public from fraud, manipulation, abusive practices and systemic risk related to derivatives – both futures and swaps – and to foster transparent, open, competitive and financially sound markets. In carrying out this mission, and in promoting market integrity, the CFTC polices the derivatives markets for various abuses and works to ensure the protection of customer funds. Further, the agency seeks to lower the risk of the futures and swaps markets to the economy and the public.

To fulfil these roles, the CFTC oversees designated contract markets, swap execution facilities, derivatives clearing organisations, swap data repositories, swap dealers, futures commission merchants, commodity pool operators and other intermediaries.

The CFTC has implemented the majority of the requirements of the Dodd-Frank Act in respect of swaps, although at times they have been accused of going too far in terms of its extra territorial reach in respect of its rules and guidance in implementing the Act.

## 3.4 Financial Services in Asia

### 3.4.1 China

- **The main bodies responsible for regulating financial services in China are:**
  - The China Securities Regulatory Commission (CSRC).
  - The China Banking Regulatory Commission (CBRC).
  - The China Insurance Regulatory Commission (CIRC).
  - The People's Bank of China (PBOC).

- **What does each of these bodies regulate?**
  The CSRC has ultimate responsibility for regulation in relation to the stock markets in Shanghai and Shenzhen, the futures exchange in Shanghai and the commodities exchanges in Zhengzhou and Dalian, with the local exchanges retaining certain frontline regulatory functions under CSRC supervision.

  Since 2003, banking regulation has primarily been carried out by the **CBRC**. It has broad supervisory and disciplinary functions in relation to banking activities in mainland China: among other things, it licenses banking institutions, sets their authorised business scope and formulates and enforces regulations governing their operation.

  The **CIRC** regulates the mainland Chinese insurance market. In addition to setting regulations, it oversees the establishment and operation of insurance companies and their subsidiaries and monitors the standard of insurance agents' and insurance companies' senior management.

  The functions of the **PBOC** include controlling monetary policy and regulating financial institutions in the capacity of a central bank. In addition to its role in relation to monetary policy, the PBOC retains responsibility for the inter-bank lending, bonds and FX markets, and is the lead agency for anti-money laundering (AML) activities.

## 3.4.2 Hong Kong

- **The main bodies responsible for regulating financial services in Hong Kong are:**
    - Securities and Futures Commission (SFC).
    - Stock Exchange of Hong Kong (SEHK).
    - Hong Kong Futures Exchange (HKFE).
    - Hong Kong Monetary Authority (HKMA).
    - Office of the Commissioner of Insurance (OCI).

- **What does each of these bodies regulate?**
The **SFC** is responsible for regulating the securities and futures market. It is responsible for issuing licences to all corporations and individuals wishing to engage or engaging in a wide range of activities, namely dealing in securities and futures contracts and leveraged FX trading, advising on securities, futures contracts and corporate finance, providing automated trading services, securities margin financing and asset management.

The SFC also oversees the Hong Kong Exchanges and Clearing (HKEx), which is the holding company of the SEHK and the HKFE. The **SEHK** is the front-line regulator of stock exchange participants and companies listed on the main board and growth enterprise market (GEM) of the Stock Exchange.

The **HKFE** is primarily responsible for regulating futures exchange participants. The SFC is also responsible for the discipline and sanctioning of sponsors and compliance advisers. The SFC also regulates all persons participating in securities and futures trading, by investigating and taking action in respect of market misconduct and other breaches of securities and futures law.

The **HKMA** regulates the banking industry and generally performs the obligations of a central bank.

The **OCI** supervises a self-regulation system governing the insurance industry, with a view to protecting the interests of policyholders. Insurance intermediaries such as agents and brokers are required to be registered with various self-regulatory bodies that ensure their proper conduct. The OCI is responsible for granting authorisation to insurers to carry on insurance businesses and examining their financial statements and returns.

## 3.4.3 Japan

- **The main bodies responsible for regulating financial services in Japan are:**
    - Financial Services Agency (FSA), which includes planning, supervisory and inspection functions.
    - Securities and Exchange Surveillance Committee (SESC), which is part of the FSA and works closely with its inspection function.
    - Self-regulatory organisations (SROs), such as the various Japanese securities exchanges and the Japan Securities Dealers' Association (JSDA).

The FSA and SESC are under the direction of the Commissioner of the FSA, who reports to the Minister for Financial Services.

_The Financial Services Industry_

### 3.4.4 Singapore

- **The main bodies responsible for regulating financial services in Singapore are:**
  - Monetary Authority of Singapore (MAS).
  - Singapore Exchange (SGX) Securities Trading.
  - Securities Industry Council (SIC).

- **What does each of these bodies regulate?**
  The **MAS** is Singapore's central bank. It also regulates the securities, banking and insurance sectors.

  The **SGX** is Asia Pacific's first demutualised and integrated securities and derivatives exchange. Its **members** include trading derivatives and trading securities organisations. The SGX operates the securities and derivatives exchange and the respective clearing houses and securities depository. The SGX performs all steps in the value chain of businesses – order routing, trading, matching, clearing, settlement and depository functions.

  The **SIC** is an advisory body that assists the Minister of Finance on all matters relating to the securities industry. The SIC remains a non-statutory body consisting of representatives from the MAS, private and public sectors or such persons as the Minister may appoint.

## 4. Government and Central Banks' Roles in Financial Markets

### Learning Objective

1.1 Understand the factors that influence the UK financial services industry:

1.1.4 The role of government and central banks in financial markets: interest rate setting process; money market operations; fiscal and quantitative easing; other interventions

## 4.1 The Interest Rate Setting Process

Setting UK interest rates was once the Chancellor's responsibility. The system was subject to abuse. Chancellors periodically overruled the advice of Treasury experts, especially when an election approached.

For this reason, following Labour's May 1997 election victory, one of the Chancellor's first actions was to depoliticise the rate-setting process. Responsibilities for setting interest rates were assigned to the BOE MPC (see Section 1.3). The MPC has operated in an extremely able and transparent manner during recent years. It announces each decision to change rates or keep them unchanged precisely at 12 noon on the day each meeting ends. Gone are the days when sudden and unexpected rate announcements would spook investors.

As already explained in Section 1.3, the organisation attempts to fully explain its views to the public. MPC members frequently give speeches outlining their views. Meeting minutes, including the voting record of each voting member, are made available soon after each meeting. Post-meeting press conferences are the norm, not the exception.

The MPC is made up of nine members – the governor, the two deputy governors, the Bank's chief economist, the executive director for markets and four external members appointed directly by the Chancellor. The appointment of external members is designed to ensure that the MPC benefits from thinking and expertise, in addition to that gained inside the BOE. Members serve fixed terms, after which they may be replaced or reappointed. Compared to other government rate-setting agencies in Washington and Brussels, the MPC is a model of openness.

Each MPC member has expertise in the field of economics and monetary policy. Members do not represent individual groups or areas. They are independent. Each MPC member of the Committee has a vote to set interest rates at the level they believe is consistent with meeting the inflation target. The MPC's decision is made on the basis of one person, one vote. It is not based on a consensus of opinion. It reflects the votes of each individual MPC member.

A representative from the Treasury also sits with the committee at its meetings. The Treasury representative can discuss policy issues but is not allowed to vote. The purpose is to ensure that the MPC is fully briefed on fiscal policy developments and other aspects of the government's economic policies, and that the Chancellor is kept fully informed about monetary policy.

## 4.2 Money Market Operations

The BOE's framework for its operations in the sterling money markets is designed to implement the MPC's interest-rate decisions while meeting the liquidity needs, and so contributing to the stability of the banking system as a whole.

The BOE is the sole issuer of sterling central bank money, the final, risk-free settlement asset in the UK. This enables the bank to implement monetary policy and makes the framework for the Bank's monetary operations central to liquidity management in the banking system as a whole and by individual banks and building societies. The Bank's market operations have two objectives, stemming from its monetary policy and financial stability responsibilities as the UK's central bank.

The objectives are to:

- implement monetary policy by maintaining overnight market interest rates in line with the bank rate, so that there is a flat risk-free money market yield curve to the next MPC decision date, and very little day-to-day or intra-day volatility in market interest rates at maturities up to that horizon;
- reduce the cost of disruption to the liquidity and payment services supplied by commercial banks. The Bank does this by balancing the provision of liquidity insurance against the costs of creating incentives for banks to take greater risks, and subject to the need to avoid taking risk onto its balance sheet.

The framework has four main elements, outlined below.

### 4.2.1 Reserves-Averaging Scheme

Eligible UK banks and building societies undertake to hold target balances (reserves) at the bank on average over maintenance periods running from one MPC decision date until the next. If an average balance is within a range around the target, the balance is remunerated at base rate.

### 4.2.2 Operational Standing Facilities

Operational standing deposit and (collateralised) lending facilities are available to eligible UK banks and building societies. They may be used on demand. In normal circumstances, the lending/deposit rates are 25 basis points (bps) higher than base rate and 25bps below base rate respectively.

The purpose of the operational standing facilities is to stabilise expectations that overnight market interest rates will be in line with base rate; and, to that end, to give banks a means to manage unexpected frictional payment shocks that could otherwise take their reserve accounts either below zero or to a level where they would otherwise be unremunerated. The bank will seek to satisfy itself that use of the facility is consistent with these purposes.

### 4.2.3 Discount Window Facility (DWF)

This is a facility to provide liquidity insurance to the banking system. Eligible banks and building societies may borrow gilts, for up to 30 days, against a wide range of collateral, in return for a fee, which will vary with the collateral used and the total size of borrowings.

The purpose of the DWF is to provide liquidity insurance to the banking system.

### 4.2.4 Open Market Operations (OMOs)

Open Market Operations (OMOs) are used to provide to the banking system the amount of central bank money needed to enable reserve-scheme members, in aggregate, to achieve their reserves targets. OMOs comprise short-term repos at base rate, long-term repos at market rates determined in variable-rate tenders and outright purchases of high-quality bonds.

The Bank uses OMOs to provide sufficient central bank money to the market to enable reserve-scheme members in aggregate to meet their targets.

## 4.3 Fiscal Easing and Other Interventions

Quantitative easing (QE) is a way of pouring money into a cash-starved banking system. The banks get cash in exchange for government bonds, helping them to build up their reserves. The hope is that they lend some of it to families and businesses.

The US was the first country in the current recession to turn to quantitative easing. With interest rates across the Atlantic slashed to between 0% and 0.25%, the Federal Reserve, is buying billions of dollars' worth of assets, including mortgage-backed assets, to try to unblock markets.

Quantitative easing was used by Japan when it faced deflation – a period of falling prices – from 2001 until 2006. Driving up the price of bonds reduces their yield, and in effect the interest rate. As interest rates across the economy are set in relation to gilt yields, quantitative easing acts as an extra lever pushing down borrowing costs.

But there is a longer-term threat: by plunging into the debt markets the government risks inflating a bubble in bonds, which will burst in a few years' time, once the economy begins to bounce back, driving up interest rates and making the government's massive debt burden extremely costly to service.

In March 2009, the BOE injected £75 billion through quantitative easing, increasing that amount to £200 billion by the end of 2009.

In October 2011 it announced a further £75 billion of quantitative easing, expanding its programme in February 2012 by £50 billion – taking the total size of the programme to £325 billion.

## 4.4 Money Supply and its Effects

**Money supply** is used to describe the total amount of money circulating in an economy – and, as with many concepts in economics, there are different ways of measuring it. For example, economists often talk about:

- **Narrow money** – a term used to describe the total sum of all financial assets (including cash) which meet a pretty narrow definition of money; for example, they must be very liquid and available to finance current spending needs. A deposit which is fixed for a long period does not, therefore, meet this definition.
- **Broad money** – in contrast, this term is used to describe the total sum of a wider range of assets – including some which are not as liquid as those falling within the definition of narrow money. It may include, for example, money held in savings accounts which are not instant access accounts.

When governments attempt to affect the economy, one of their tools is the money supply. This is measured by reference to the monetary aggregates – of which there are four, all published by the BOE. The most important of the four are known as M0 and M4:

- **M0** is the measure of notes and coin in circulation outside the BOE, plus operational deposits at the BOE. (This is, therefore, quite a narrow definition of money.)
- **M4** is the measure of notes and coin in circulation with the public, plus sterling deposits held with UK banks and building societies by the rest of the private sector. (This is thus a broader definition.)

### 4.4.1 How Money Supply Affects Inflation, Deflation and Disinflation

**Inflation** is the term used to measure the general rise in prices in an economy. The BOE is charged with taking steps to keep inflation within a certain range. Interest rates are the main, and most promptly effective, tool it has at its disposal for doing this; but the money supply is also a factor. In this section we will look at why this is so.

The Financial Services Industry

If money is regarded as being held mainly for transactional (spending) purposes, an excess of money will mean that more money is chasing the same amount of assets, and therefore pushing their prices up. Conversely, if there is less money in supply, there is less to be spent – so asset prices will fall correspondingly.

**Deflation** is the term used to describe a general fall in the level of prices, and **disinflation** is the term for a reduction in the rate of inflation (ie, a slowing of price growth – as opposed to a fall in prices). Using the quantity theory of money, price growth can, in theory, be slowed (disinflation) or even reversed (deflation) through changes to the money supply.

### 4.4.2 How Money Supply Affects Interest Rates

Money supply is also important to interest rates.

We can think of interest rates as being the price of money – that is, if a bank lends us money it is the price we are willing to pay that bank for the use of its cash (and the price the bank is willing to accept for having to forgo the opportunity to use the money for other, potentially more lucrative activities). Conversely, if we place our cash on deposit with a bank, the interest we earn on it is what the bank is willing to pay us.

Monetary economic theory states that interest rates are largely determined by the demand and supply of loanable funds. If the money supply increases, and there is no increase in the demand for money (eg, for investment purposes), this increases the amount of loanable funds available (eg, for savings). As there is more money available for savings, this acts to depress interest rates.

### 4.4.3 The Relationship between Money Supply, Inflation and Employment

The monetarist explanation of inflation operates through the Fisher equation.

$$MV = PT$$

M = Money supply
V = Velocity of circulation
P = Price level
T = Transactions or output

There is a direct relationship between the growth of the money supply and inflation, as monetarists assume that V and T are fixed. Individuals spend their excess money balances directly on goods and services. This has a direct impact on inflation by raising aggregate demand. The more inelastic aggregate supply in the economy, the greater the impact on inflation.

An increase in demand for goods and services may cause a rise in imports. Though this leakage from the domestic economy reduces the money supply, it also increases the supply of pounds on the FX market, thus applying downward pressure on the exchange rate. This may cause **imported inflation**.

23

If excess money balances are spent on goods and services, the increase in the demand for labour will cause a rise in money wages and unit labour costs. This may cause **cost-push inflation**. This inflation is bad news as it means that real national income will fall and prices will rise.

Inflation can be bad for businesses, because their costs will rise if the amount they have to pay for goods goes up. Their sales may fall, as consumers will not want to buy as much when the prices have gone up. Exports will fall as UK prices rise in comparison to other countries' prices. Inflation can also cause a disruption of business planning; uncertainty about the future makes planning difficult, and this may reduce the level of investment. Budgeting becomes a problem as businesses become unsure about what will happen to their costs. This may have a knock-on effect on employment. However, it is possible that some businesses will benefit from inflation as consumers carry on buying their goods or services at the higher price. This will lead to an increase in revenue.

# 5. Economic, Financial and Stock Market Cycles

### Learning Objective

1.1 Understand the factors that influence the UK financial services industry:

1.1.5 The main stages of economic, financial and stock market cycles, including: national income; global influences and long-term growth trends

## 5.1 National Income (NI)

In order to make goods and services they create, firms use labour provided by households. They have to pay those households for the labour (work) they provide – thereby providing households with income.

Households pay firms for the goods and services they need and consume – therefore the income of firms form the sales revenue received from goods and services purchased and consumed by households.

This creates a circular flow of income and expenditure: income and output are different sides of the same coin.

Three key measures of economic activity are:

- national income (NI);
- gross national product (GNP);
- gross domestic product (GDP).

## 5.1.1   National Income (NI)

UK national income is defined as *'the sum of all incomes of residents in the UK which arise as a result of economic activity, from the production of goods and services. Such incomes, which include rent, employment income and profit, are known as factor incomes because they are earned by the so-called factors of production: land, labour and capital'* (Office for National Statistics).

Measuring NI is useful for the following purposes:

- measuring the standard of living in a country (national income per head);
- comparing the wealth of different countries;
- measuring the change in national wealth and the standard of living;
- ascertaining long-term trends;
- assisting central government in its economic planning.

## 5.1.2   Gross Domestic Product (GDP)

National income is largely derived from economic activity within the country itself. Domestic economic activity is referred to as total domestic income or domestic product. It is measured gross. The term gross domestic product (GDP) refers (in the UK) to the total value of income/production from economic activity within the UK.

## 5.1.3   Gross National Product (GNP)

As we noted at the start of Section 5.1, NI assumes that the circular flow of income in the economy is closed. However, in reality, of course some of the UK's NI arises from overseas investments and some is generated within the UK by people who are non-residents.

The difference between these items is net property income from abroad. The sum of gross domestic product, plus net property income from abroad, is the GNP. We can, therefore, show the relationship between GDP, GNP and national income like this:

|  | **GDP** |
| --- | --- |
| **Plus** | Net property income from abroad |
| **Equals** | GNP |
| **Minus** | Capital consumption |
| **Equals** | NI (net) |

## 5.1.4 Injections and Withdrawals

As a measure for NI, we can use a method that measures total expenditure in the economy.

We add a number of injections to, and withdrawals from, the circular flow. These arise from:

- **savings by consumers** – withdrawal from the cycle, money is no longer circulating if it is being saved;
- **investment flows into firms** – injection, money that firms can use in their economic activity;
- **imports** – withdrawal, as money goes overseas to pay for goods and services bought from abroad;
- **exports** – injection, overseas buyers make payments into the UK to pay for goods and services;
- **government spending** – injection, the government adds to the revenues of firms providing it with goods and services; and
- **taxation** – withdrawal, reducing the income households have available to spend on goods and services.

You should be able to see that we are moving away from – or at least building on – the simplified, closed-economy model that we started this section with.

## 5.1.5 Summary

The gross domestic product is made up of:

$$C + I + G + (X - M)$$

This measure gives us one way of looking at the level of national economic activity. It also shows us that if a government wants to influence levels of activity, it may be able to do so by influencing one or more of the components of the formula above. For example:

- It could try to increase consumer expenditure – that is, spending by households, or C above.
- It could take steps to increase private investment in firms (I).
- It could increase its own spending (G).
- It could try to improve the balance of payments to change (X − M).

From the above you should be able to see that it is possible to measure the amount of economic activity, or output, in a national economy. This is done by **aggregating** (adding together) all the incomes generated, to give a total figure for NI. The bigger the national income in a country, the more income its individual inhabitants are earning on average. A rising level of income means more spending on the output of firms, and more spending means more output of goods and services. Providing that such increases are not simply due to the effects of inflation, the resulting increases in income should lead to a rise in the standard of living.

Rising NI (economic growth) is an economic policy objective of most, if not all, governments. However, it is better if this growth is stable and steady, rather than uncontrolled and erratic. Most UK NI is derived from economic activity within the UK. The measure of economic activity within the UK is referred to as total domestic income or domestic product. It is measured gross, ie, before deducting an amount for capital consumption or depreciation of fixed assets, to give the GDP, referring to the total value of income/production from economic activity within the UK.

But this growth isn't always steady – in fact sometimes there is no growth at all; there is a contraction instead. The patterns of growth and contraction in the economy are known as **economic cycles**. The economic cycle is, therefore, made up of phases of growth in the economy, followed by slow-down, and then a fall in national income (a recession). After a recession, a return to growth will at some point begin again – to be followed eventually by more slowing and, in time, another recession.

The business cycle in a typical developed economy now seems to last for around eight to ten years. **The usual definition of a recession is two or more successive quarters of falling GDP.**

## 5.2 Global Influences

Just as events in other countries affect the UK economy, so they also affect the UK stock market. Rates of growth in the rest of the world are especially important for economies (like the UK's) that have a large foreign trade sector. If trading partners have slow growth, the amount of exports a country can sell to them will grow only slowly. This limits the country's own opportunities for investment and growth.

Different national economies may be at different stages of the business cycle at any one time. However, with increasing globalisation of trade and investment, there is a tendency for their economic cycles to become increasingly correlated (tied in with one another). In particular, the large size and economic wealth of the economy of the US exerts a significant influence on the economies of other countries, particularly its major trading partners such as the UK.

The importance of the US in the world economy means that investment markets, such as equity and bond markets, often react most closely to what is happening in the economy and markets of the US. If there is an economic recovery in the US, it is anticipated that this recovery will soon affect other economies, as US consumers and companies will demand more goods and services available on world markets. The stimulus to other countries will have knock-on effects in those countries as companies' earnings are boosted and employment rises.

As well as monitoring the growth of individual economies, we can measure growth and output for larger regions – and, indeed, for the world as a whole. The International Monetary Fund (IMF) publishes a report called the World Economic Outlook twice a year.

## 5.3 Long-Term Growth Trends

Governments and international organisations try to look forward and not only influence the short-term economic outlook, but also to learn from analysing longer-term trends, and influence these as well.

Even quite small changes in growth, year-on-year, can have a considerable cumulative effect over a longer period. The UK government, for example, has a stated aim of increasing long-term growth (known as the trend growth rate) through strategies aimed at increasing employment opportunities and productivity, by promoting economic stability and by way of its wider economic policies.

## 5.3.1 Market Behaviour

The economy as a whole has a great influence on the financial markets.

- In a recession and at the start of a recovery, inflation and interest rates are typically low or falling. Low interest rates mean that the coupons on yields on fixed-interest securities will look relatively attractive, so investors will be prepared to pay higher prices for such securities.
- Conversely, the higher interest rates generally seen in a boom period will result in lower prices for fixed-income securities. That is, investors will not be willing to pay a high price to secure the fixed coupon attached to the security.

The prices of equities (company shares) also tend to reflect market sentiment about prospects for the economy and so are influenced by the stages of the economic cycle. The main share price indices, such as the FTSE 100 Index in the UK and the S&P 500 Index in the US, serve as **barometers** for the market.

Share prices can be sharply influenced by changes in sentiment, and these can happen quickly – for example, because of news that a particular economic indicator has been announced as being significantly different from what was expected. If there is a new expectation of an economic recovery, for example, share prices may rise in anticipation. People will expect that the recovery will mean better prospects for companies, higher profits, and therefore increasing share prices and dividends. They will therefore be prepared to pay more for those shares – and the expected rise in prices becomes self-fulfilling.

A situation of persistently rising share prices is often called a **bull market**. If expectations about economic recovery are dented – for example, because there are reports of rising unemployment or bankruptcies – then share prices may drop back again. If an economy is booming, higher interest rates or concerns that it might be coming to an end can reverse the general direction of share prices. A persistent downward trend in equities prices is often called a **bear market**.

In the long run, share prices benefit from a steadily growing economy, with rising output, in which corporate earnings can grow.

The Financial Services Industry

# 6. Global Trends and Their Impacts

## Learning Objective

1.1 Understand the factors that influence the UK financial services industry:

1.1.6 The impact of global trends: globalisation of business, finance and markets; advances in technology; regulatory challenges

## 6.1 International Markets

The financial markets in the UK are regarded by many as the main world markets for dealing in a variety of assets – from stocks, shares and bonds, to currencies, derivatives and commodities. But these UK-based markets face stiff competition from other financial centres, which try to compete for international business by introducing innovative financial instruments, ensuring speedier or more secure settlement, or making dealing cheaper and quicker.

In addition to these longer-term considerations, financial markets in the UK are affected on a daily basis by what is going on overseas. For example:

- The price of assets dealt in on UK markets is affected by events on foreign markets. If events in the US mean that its stock market falls sharply, then other world markets invariably suffer as a result. (As the old adage has it, if the US stock market sneezes, the whole world catches a cold.) A good example of this was seen in the immediate aftermath of the 9/11 terrorist attacks – shares in the US plummeted and were quickly followed down by shares on other markets, to such an extent that most markets were suspended until orderly trading could be restored.
- Many multinational companies have their shares traded on more than one stock market. Events affecting the shares in one place will affect the prices at which they are quoted on others, through arbitrage. Arbitrage is activity which aims to take advantage of the different prices at which an asset might be traded on different markets; it has the effect of bringing those prices back into balance.
- Many companies quoted on the LSE have operations around the world – so economic events in other countries affect their value and profitability.
- Events affecting other countries' currencies can have a significant effect on UK markets, through the economy and interest rates.

Because of these and similar factors, the wealth of UK people and businesses, which is tied up in shares or other investments, can be affected by what is happening in the international markets.

## 6.2 Globalisation of Business and Finance

In terms of business and finance, the term globalisation tends to be used in several ways:

- It is often used to describe the increasingly interrelated and interconnected nature of business and financial systems. Businesses which were once essentially local now increasingly cross borders: banks offer services to people and businesses in many different countries, and businesses find their raw materials, and sell to customers, much further afield than used to be the case.

29

- It is also used to describe the way in which various things (products, processes and, in some cases, lifestyles) are becoming more similar around the world – as people and businesses become more mobile, taking their ways of doing things with them, and as international standards are established to make it easier for international trade and activity to take place.

You can probably think of some examples pretty easily: McDonald's is a good example of a retail business that provides a pretty similar consumer experience wherever you are in the world. In the arena of finance, HSBC (which provides banking, investment and a host of other services) has some 5,000 offices in 79 countries and describes itself as *'the World's local bank'* – perhaps in an attempt to show that, while it may be truly global, it also makes an effort to reflect local business practices wherever it operates. A customer of HSBC, or any other global banking organisation, could probably move from one country to another without having to change the banking group with which they deal.

The pace at which trade and finance becomes globalised, and the rate of flow of goods, services and money around the world increases as a consequence, has also been helped by the efforts of governments and many multinational organisations such as the World Trade Organisation (WTO) and the Organisation for Economic Co-operation and Development (OECD).

- The WTO deals with the rules of trade between different nations and among its aims are the liberalisation of trade laws between countries. It provides a forum in which governments can negotiate the basis on which their countries will trade with one another.
- The OECD describes itself as *'an international organisation helping governments tackle the economic, social and governance challenges of a globalised economy'*. Among other things, it aims to help contribute to world trade, and to support sustainable economic world growth.

Another international forum working on liberalising trade, this time within a specific block of countries, is the EU (see Section 6.4).

Globalisation is seen as good by some (for example, if it enables poorer countries to participate in international trade) and as bad by others (for example, if it results in the loss of national identities and an increasingly homogeneous world – or if it results in the rise of huge multinationals, which are so big that they are seen as being beyond the control of governments and regulators). Whatever your view, it is an increasing fact of life.

## 6.3 Impacts of Technology

Technology has had a huge impact on the way businesses interact, and on how profitable they are. A number of issues arise from this, in the context of global dynamics.

- Some businesses – including financial services firms – have found that they can outsource or offshore certain activities (typically call centres and computer programming) to countries where appropriately skilled labour is cheaper, such as India.
- For some types of businesses – including in financial services – the internet has been a key factor in this development: it is easy for buyers and sellers to find one another, and electronic communications – coupled with increasing clarity on the law regarding electronically concluded agreements – has speeded up the pace at which they can do business across borders.

The Financial Services Industry

If one country has access to new technologies which have not yet been adopted, or cannot be afforded, in another, the first country can benefit from a significant economic advantage.

# 6.4    Regulatory Challenges

The recent financial crisis has led to an unparalleled period of regulatory innovation and change impacting the financial services sector. Change on the scale of the US Dodd-Frank legislation and the EU programme of regulatory reform brings with it a unique opportunity to build a regulatory framework that achieves significant gains in levels of protection for customers and levels of financial stability for the global economy.

However, undertaking reform on such a significant scale also risks making changes that are broader in scope than may be necessary or which are focused purely on domestic concerns or issues whilst ignoring the impacts on wider, international financial markets. This can lead to regulation that is inappropriately extra-territorial in effect, and to elements of regulation that diverge significantly between major financial centres. This danger is particularly pronounced in an industry that is as global and interconnected in nature as financial services.

Various trade associations, both in Europe and the US, have highlighted six types of concerns with the current approach being taken by the US and the EU regarding regulatory change. The concerns are:

- duplicative requirements;
- incompatible or conflicting requirements;
- distortion of competition/reduction of customer choice;
- unintended impact on clients/counterparties who are not directly subject to regulation;
- lack of progress for mutual recognition or comparability;
- regulatory uncertainty and disproportionate compliance burden.

## 6.4.1    Duplicative Requirements

Regulators in the US and EU have been calling for consistency in implementing G20 and other reforms to avoid regulatory arbitrage. Introducing identical or similar requirements in different jurisdictions could lead to some entities becoming subject to multiple overlapping regulatory regimes. This could have the effect of:

- introducing unnecessarily duplicative requirements, and distorting competition between market participants by the uneven application of duplicative regimes;
- encouraging participants to make venue choices based on avoidance of administrative complexity, potentially reducing the focus upon execution quality and fragmenting international markets;
- increasing the compliance burden or costs of compliance for regulated entities without achieving any additional benefits by way of customer protection or market stability (eg, where such entities are required to comply with requirements in several different jurisdictions, firms will need to build systems to ensure compliance with the various requirements). There can also be cases where additional obligations can be imposed on non-regulated entities.

## 6.4.2 Incompatible or Conflicting Requirements

In the past, regulators have commented that duplicative regulation is not a particular concern, as firms subject to multiple regimes should comply on a **highest common factor** basis. However, it may not always be possible for a regulated entity (or another entity subject to the relevant regulation) to comply with the requirements it may be subject to in every jurisdiction.

## 6.4.3 Distortion of Competition/Reduction of Customer Choice

If regulation is applied extra-territorially, it may have the effect of distorting competition in particular markets. For example, not all firms operating in a particular jurisdiction may be subject to the same degree of regulation. If local entities are not subject to, eg, capital or margin requirements, but firms operating cross-border are, then local entities will have a competitive advantage.

Regulation may also have the effect of restricting the ability of regulated entities to carry out cross-border business with entities in other jurisdictions (as service providers, clients or counterparties).

## 6.4.4 Unintended Impact on Clients/Counterparties who are not Directly Subject to Regulation

Some regulatory obligations imposed on regulated entities may also have an impact on clients or counterparties who are not directly subject to the relevant obligations. For example, if a financial counterparty in the EU is required to clear a trade, its counterparty (unless it is a counterparty that is exempt from European Markets Infrastructure Regulation (EMIR) or from the EMIR clearing requirement) will not have a choice about whether the trade is cleared or not. Similarly, while the EMIR text may be read to imply that margin requirements could – on occasion – be imposed on only one counterparty to a trade, this will have an impact on the other counterparty, regardless of whether it is also subject to margin requirements. This may result in increased costs or reduced choice for clients.

## 6.4.5 Lack of Progress for Mutual Recognition or Comparability

Some provisions of the proposed EU legislation contain requirements for mutual recognition and in some cases for treaties to be negotiated between states (eg, EMIR/trade repository recognition). In principle, mutual recognition is a valuable arrangement as a means to make regulation more efficient and to avoid having multiple sets of regulation applicable to a single legal entity. However, without a defined process for attaining such recognition, negotiating treaties may take a long time, or may never happen. Proposals do not seem to be being built into legislation in recognition of this and to address the problem.

## 6.4.6 Regulatory Uncertainty and Disproportionate Compliance Burden

This seems to be an issue both in the EU, where legislation has been proposed giving regulators broad powers to impose temporary emergency restrictions, and in the US, where cross-border aspects of Dodd-Frank implementing regulation have been delayed. As we saw with the emergency short-selling bans/reporting regimes imposed in 2008–09, this sort of power can lead to uncertainty for the firms required to comply. They are required to monitor the situation in all countries where they trade, and may be required to set up systems on short notice to comply (or to report/monitor their systems manually if the ban/reporting requirement is only temporary). This can make firms reluctant to trade in particular markets, to the detriment of their clients.

If local regimes have different territorial scope, it can make monitoring and compliance far harder (eg, a firm will not just have to monitor the markets in which it is trading, but may also have to monitor local regulation in other jurisdictions where a particular security is listed, or where a particular entity is established). If the extra-territorial scope of emergency powers is unclear (eg, EU short-selling regulation emergency powers), it may be almost impossible for firms to predict which jurisdictions they should be monitoring.

The trade associations attempted to outline practical solutions as noted below:

- **Global impact assessment** – it is essential that domestic and international regulators build into their impact assessment of proposed regulatory measures an analysis of the overall impact that relevant measures will have on markets globally.
- **Mutual recognition and exemptive relief** – common regulatory standards should be measured against equality of outcomes and effects, and not against the agreement of identical legal text. Recognising that complete and precise commonality of detail is likely to be elusive, mutual recognition – or exemptive relief for certain activities – will usefully extend the effect of broadly comparable standards.
- **Targeted rules convergence** – the G20 process can assist rules convergence as well as mutual recognition. It should address the need for common regulatory standards to be developed. The Financial Stability Board (FSB) is well placed to take a leadership role in providing guidance as to where it is critical to have consistent implementation and where the detail of that implementation is less important for systemic risk mitigation purposes.

# Summary of this Chapter

You should have an understanding and knowledge of the following after reading this chapter:

- The role of government and its policy on taxation, public borrowing and public spending.
- The role of financial investment in the economy – primary and secondary markets (their purpose, who uses them and why).
- The balance of payments – what they are and why they are so important.
- The role and structure of financial services in the UK, Europe, US and Asia – processes and purpose.
- The role of government and central banks:
  - interest rate setting;
  - supply of money, and its effects;
  - fiscal easing.
- The factors that influence the financial services industry in the UK:
  - national income;
  - GDP;
  - global trends – globalisation;
  - EU.

# End of Chapter Questions

Think of an answer for each question and refer to the appropriate section for confirmation.

1.   What is the role of government in the economy?
     *Answer reference: Section 1*

2.   Who sets monetary policy in the UK?
     *Answer reference: Section 1.3*

3.   What is the role of financial investment in the economy?
     *Answer reference: Sections 2.1, 2.2*

4.   What are the main objectives of the ECB?
     *Answer reference: Section 3.2.3*

5.   What are the roles of regulators in Europe and the US?
     *Answer reference: Sections 3.2, 3.3*

6.   What is the role of the Bank of England?
     *Answer reference: Sections 4.1, 4.2*

7.   What are GDP and GNP? Why are they so important?
     *Answer reference: Sections 5.1.2, 5.1.3*

8.   What is the impact of globalisation on financial services firms?
     *Answer reference: Sections 6.1, 6.2*

# Chapter Two
# UK Financial Services and Consumer Relationships

1. Financial Risks and Needs of Consumers　39
2. How the Financial Risks and Needs of UK Consumers are Met　45
3. Professional Conduct and Ethical Practice　59

**This syllabus area will provide approximately 3 of the 80 examination questions**

UK Financial Services and Consumer Relationships

In this chapter you will gain an understanding of:

- The main financial needs, priorities and risks of UK consumers.
- Budgeting and managing finances, lifestyle changes and their impact on finances and provisions for dependants before and after death.
- Financial planning and financial advice.
- How professional conduct and ethical practice affect the perception of consumers.

# 1. Financial Risks and Needs of Consumers

## Learning Objective

2.1 Understand the main financial risks, needs and priorities of UK consumers:

2.1.1 Balancing, budgeting and managing finances; debt acquisition and accumulation

2.1.2 Lifestyle changes and their impact on finances; funding and safeguarding major investments, including: housing; incapacity, unemployment and unplanned difficulty in earning income; income provision during retirement and old age; taxation

2.1.3 Provision for dependants before and after death

## 1.1 Balancing, Budgeting and Managing Finances

One of the key elements of a financial plan is to help the client understand how his financial position is advancing (or deteriorating) over time, and how his income and outgoings balance against one another. The adviser should be able to help him understand his budget by preparing a schedule of income and outgoings. This should include the following elements.

### 1.1.1 Current Income and Outgoings

Income may include such things as:

- earned income from employed and self-employed jobs;
- unearned income on investments and deposits;
- rents on investment property;
- financial support from others, eg, a former spouse or partner, or an existing trust;
- state benefits.

Outgoings may include:

- rent or mortgage payments;
- bills for food, heating and electricity;
- rates/council tax;
- taxes – including National Insurance contributions (NICs);
- TV licence;

39

- maintenance being paid to a former spouse or in respect of a child;
- credit card and loan outgoings;
- regular insurance premiums;
- contributions to regular savings plans and pensions;
- sums budgeted for holidays, Christmas, other major life events.

If outgoings are greater than income, or if there is little difference between the two, then changes must be made to redress the balance. There is no point in consumers undertaking specific financial commitments if they cannot afford or do not need them.

## 1.1.2 Debt Acquisition and Accumulation

At some stage in our lives we will need to borrow money from a financial institution, normally a bank. Even wealthy clients may require access to borrowings from time to time.

In order to fund a sizeable purchase, such as a home or a second property, the loan may be secured on the asset being bought by way of a mortgage. In some cases, if the loan is to be repaid from income and the borrower has little track record, additional security – perhaps by way of a guarantee from a family member – may also be required.

Smaller loans for the purchase of specific things such as a holiday or a car are not normally required to be secured by the bank.

In addition, consumers who are also business people may seek funding to buy into or establish their business – for example, to fund the initial purchase of share or partnership capital and, at a later stage, to fund expansion, take over another business or move into new markets. This may be by way of a loan provided by the client, who may therefore need to borrow this money, perhaps secured on the family home or some other asset. They also may need an advance if the business finds itself in difficulty and needs emergency funding.

## 1.2 Lifestyle Changes and their Impact on Finances

The financial life cycle is a concept that is used for the purpose of considering what people's financial needs typically are at various stages in their lives. Although not everyone's life follows this pattern, many people's do – so it can be a useful tool for predicting what products and services will be in most demand as the population's demographic (in terms of age) changes.

Particular products and services can be target-marketed at people who occupy specific stages in the cycle. For example, the following stages can be identified:

- **Childhood** – characterised by dependence for most needs on adult carers. Financial needs are usually few, though a child may have a need for a savings account, and perhaps a cashpoint card.
- **Single young adulthood** – usually at this stage the person is either in further education or in their first job. Income may still be relatively low, but the individual may also have few financial commitments as yet and a reasonable amount of disposable income. The thought of saving for the future may not be a high priority.

- **Young couple, no children** – at this stage there may be two incomes coming into the household and, with no children, no major financial commitments. However, if the couple are attempting to get on the property ladder, saving for a deposit may be a priority. If they have already bought, then the right mortgage may be important.
- **Parents with dependent children** – usually a couple, but lone parents are becoming increasingly common. At this stage, disposable income is likely to fall: in addition the parent(s) may have less time for leisure activities. Saving for a larger property or for school fees may be a priority.
- **Empty-nesters** – this is the term used for parents whose children have left home and are independent. Such people may suddenly find that they have more disposable income than they have had for a long time – in addition their careers may be well advanced, so their incomes are reasonably high, and if they are fortunate they may also have paid off a large proportion of their mortgages and be living in a property which has increased in value. However, for many this stage has not been so easy – their property may have fallen in value, and because of the difficulty of getting on the property ladder their adult children may still be living at home.
- **Retired** – an increasing proportion of the population. Retirees who have been in employment or otherwise managed to save for much of their lives may have accumulated a reasonable amount of capital; in addition, if they are homeowners, they may have capital locked up in the value of their homes. Their financial needs may centre on ensuring that this capital generates enough income for them to live on; on provision of long-term care when their health is not so good; and perhaps on how they may best leave any surplus assets to their intended beneficiaries on death.

This traditional pattern is, however, changing – for a variety of reasons:

- **Empty-nesters** may find that instead of caring for their children, they are now caring for their elderly parents – which places an additional financial and time burden on them. This pattern is likely to continue, and indeed increase, as the population ages.
- **The increasing longevity of people** means that the issue of paying for care into old age is gaining in importance – especially if the adult children of the elderly population are unwilling or unable to shoulder this burden.
- **Affordability issues** – brought about by the fact that wage inflation has not kept pace with house price inflation – mean that many people, who would, in earlier decades, have been on the housing ladder, are now renting or – increasingly – remaining in the family home until well into adulthood. This means that would-be empty-nesters may, in some cases, have both their own parents and their adult children living with them.

## 1.2.1 Incapacity, Unemployment and Unplanned Difficulty in Earning Income

A welfare state is a concept of government where the state plays a key role in the protection and promotion of the economic and social wellbeing of its citizens. It is based on the principles of equality of opportunity, equitable distribution of wealth, and public responsibility for those unable to avail themselves of the minimal provisions for a good life. The general term may cover a variety of forms of economic and social organisation.

There are two main interpretations of the idea of a welfare state:

1. A model in which the state assumes primary responsibility for the welfare of its citizens. This responsibility in theory ought to be comprehensive, because all aspects of welfare are considered and universally applied to citizens as a right.
2. The creation of a social safety net of minimum standards of varying forms of welfare.

There is some confusion between a **welfare state** and a **welfare society**, and debate about how each term should be defined. In many countries, especially in the US, some degree of welfare is provided not actually by the state, but directly to welfare recipients from a combination of independent volunteers, corporations (both non-profit charitable corporations and for-profit corporations), and government services. This phenomenon has been termed a welfare society, and the term welfare system has been used to describe the range of welfare state and welfare society mixes that are found. The welfare state involves a direct transfer of funds from the public sector to welfare recipients, but, indirectly, the private sector is often contributing those funds via redistributionist taxation; the welfare state has therefore been referred to as a type of **mixed economy**.

## 1.2.2 Planning for Retirement

Planning for retirement is an important element of the process – even for the youngest clients. As people live longer, and (even with rising retirement ages) face the prospect of a longer non-working old age, it is important that they consider the ways in which they can fund their needs as they get older. Pensions and associated products are the main retirement planning products.

### Occupational Pension Schemes → *Provided by Employer*

Occupational pensions are pensions provided by an employer to its employees. They are either salary-related (also known as **defined benefit**), or money purchase (**defined contribution**).

- **Salary-related schemes** pay a pension based on two things: the length of time the employee has been employed, and his salary. Sometimes the salary used as a reference point is his salary on retirement (a **final salary scheme**); other schemes use the employee's average salary over his time with the company. The scheme's assets are looked after by trustees, who should ensure that the employer pays into a scheme regularly.
- **Money purchase schemes** are not directly based on the employee's salary or years of employment (though this will affect how much is paid in). Instead, an individual pension pot is built up for each employee, through contributions made by the employer and the employee – which the employee uses at retirement to convert into an income, usually by buying an annuity.

The value of the employee's salary on retirement will therefore depend on:

- how much has been paid into the scheme over the employee's working life;
- how well it has performed in investment terms;
- what charges have been deducted; and
- what conditions are in the market for converting it to an income at the time when the employee retires.

## Personal Pensions

Personal pensions are offered by commercial financial services providers, such as life companies. All personal pensions are money purchase schemes; they may be set up by a client who is arranging his pension privately – a popular option for the self-employed, or those who move between jobs regularly. Some employers also offer access to them and in this case they are not classified as occupational schemes. Personal pensions, self-invested personal pensions (SIPPs), group personal pensions (GPPs) and retirement annuity contracts are all forms of personal pension; see Section 2.7 for more on SIPPs and GPPs.

Again, the pension that the client will receive on retirement will depend on:

- how much has been paid into the scheme over the individual's working life;
- how well the scheme has performed in investment terms;
- what charges have been deducted; and
- what conditions are in the market for converting it to an income at the point where the employee retires.

**Stakeholder** schemes are a form of personal pension which meet certain requirements, eg, in terms of low charges and accessible minimum contributions; they are designed to make pensions more affordable for those on lower incomes, but have also been popular with other sectors of the population on account of their apparent value for money. Like ordinary personal pensions, they are offered by commercial organisations such as life companies.

People who converted their pension to an annuity after 6 April 2006 have more flexibility and choice than was previously the case – so advisers may find that some of their clients have deferred conversion, to take advantage of this. For example:

- Those in occupational money purchase schemes can shop around on the open market for the best annuity option for them to convert to. This may let them get considerably better value than was previously the case.
- New annuity options are available – for example, **annuity protection lump sum death benefit** is a new option which means that, if the client dies before he reaches 75, his annuity does not die with him. Instead, an amount – calculated as the initial pension fund used to buy the annuity, less the income already paid from it – is paid into his estate. The payment will, however, be taxed.
- In addition to the existing alternative of **income drawdown** (also known as **unsecured pension**, an option which allows pensioners to defer converting their pension pot into an annuity for a period prior to age 75, perhaps until conditions are more favourable, by drawing on the capital of their pension fund), they can now also opt for a **short-term annuity**. This option lets them use part of their pension fund to buy a fixed-term annuity, which may be for up to five years. In the meantime the remainder of the fund stays invested in the markets. When the short-term annuity comes to an end, and depending on his view of conditions in the market at the time, the pensioner has the option to:
  - buy another short-term annuity;
  - buy a lifetime annuity;
  - move to drawdown prior to age 75.

Following the March 2014 Budget, it is no longer required to take out an annuity on retirement. Rather, pension holders are able to draw down their pension.

Further details are expected, but the approach taken by the government is that individuals should be able to control their pension rather than be forced to take out an annuity, which they see as poor value and pay low interest rates.

Some changes came into effect immediately and further changes are due to be introduced in April 2015 following consultation.

## 1.2.3 Taxation

Individuals are liable to tax on their income, and this is accounted for to Her Majesty's Revenue & Customs (HMRC) annually. Income tax is accounted for by reference to income earned in each **tax year**. The tax year runs from 6 April in one year to 5 April in the following year. Income for individuals includes earnings from employment or self-employment and income from investments. It also includes some government benefits.

For people who are employed, the figure that they show as earned income should include their salary or wages, and any bonuses, commission, fees, and benefits in kind. This covers items such as the use of a company car, subsidised loans and the cost of private medical insurance. Earnings for work carried out on an employed basis, in the UK, are subject to the pay as you earn (PAYE) system. Under this system the employer deducts the employee's personal income tax before paying the net amount to that employee, and pays it over to HMRC. Based on the employee's earnings, HMRC issues a tax code for each employee and the employer uses this to calculate how much tax it should deduct each month.

**Tax Rates**

Tax is not charged at a single flat rate. There are different rates for different levels of income. In addition, in some cases there are different rates of tax charged for different types of income, ie, earned income and investment income.

Examples of 2014–15 tax allowances include:

| | |
|---|---|
| Personal allowance | £10,000 |
| Personal allowance – born between 6 April 1938 and 5 April 1948 (aged 66 to 78) | £10,500 |
| Married couples' allowance for individuals born before 6 April 1935 and aged 75+ | £8,165 |

| | | |
|---|---|---|
| Starting rate for savings | 10% | (£0 to £2,880) |
| Basic rate tax | 20% | (£0 to £31,865) |
| Higher rate tax | 40% | (£31,866 to £150,000) |
| Additional rate tax | 45% | (over £150,000) |

## Inheritance Tax (IHT) and Chargeable Transfers

Inheritance tax (IHT) is often thought of as a tax which is levied when someone dies; but this is something of a misnomer, as IHT can, in fact, apply when assets are transferred in a variety of ways – for example, by gifts. If this were not the case, people would avoid it simply by giving away their assets to their children before they died.

IHT is, in fact, primarily a tax on wealth. Usually this means wealth that is left to someone else on its owner's death, but it also applies to gifts within seven years of death and to certain lifetime transfers of wealth.

To summarise, IHT is a tax on gifts or transfers of value. There are two main chargeable occasions:

- gifts made during the lifetime of the donor (lifetime transfers);
- gifts or transfers on death, for example, when property is left to someone in a will (the death estate).

## 1.3 Provision for Dependants before and after Death

Estate planning is the job of planning what will happen to a client's assets on his death. It may include significant elements of tax planning, so as to minimise the effects of tax on what is passed on to the client's legatees (the people he leaves money to). Refer to Section 2.4 of this chapter for further details.

# 2. How the Financial Risks and Needs of UK Consumers are Met

## Learning Objective

2.2.1 Understand how the main financial risks, needs and priorities of UK consumers are typically met: financial planning and financial advice; state benefits; credit finance and management; mortgages; insurance and financial protection; retirement and pension funding; estate and tax planning; and savings and investment

## 2.1 Financial Advice

The relationship between consumer and financial adviser is very important to the success of the planning process. We could think about this relationship from three different perspectives – the legal, the personal, and the skills which an adviser needs to foster such a relationship.

*IFA Adviser = Agent of Customer*

- **Legal** – in some cases, a financial adviser will be an independent financial adviser (IFA), or part of an IFA firm. Here, his relationship with the customer is that of agent – the adviser acts as the agent of the customer in any transactions he arranges on his behalf, and is responsible for providing him with advice, based on a selection of suitable options. In other cases, however, the adviser may be an employee of a single product provider (or of a provider offering its own and a small range of other providers' products) or he may be **tied** or **multi-tied** to one or more providers. In this case he acts as the agent of the provider(s) and not of the client. These differing legal relationships must be disclosed to the customer, and carry different legal responsibilities.
- **Personal** – in order to provide appropriate advice, financial advisers need a good deal of detailed background information about their clients. This includes not only their current financial situation, but also their plans, hopes and aspirations – and sometimes some personal and sensitive information about their families. A client will only disclose this sort of information openly and frankly if he trusts his adviser's integrity, confidentiality and capabilities.
- **Skills** – clearly, an adviser needs special skills to foster a successful relationship with his client. These include:
  - **Personal** – the adviser needs to create a trusting and open relationship with his client. He may need to be sensitive in questioning the client on personal matters, and conciliatory in persuading him to provide background details which he may not initially wish to divulge (eg, for AML purposes).
  - **Organisational** – the busy adviser needs to be able to juggle a full diary of initial contacts and follow-up and repeat meetings. He therefore needs to be well organised and disciplined in managing his diary and activities, and thorough in completing paperwork promptly.
  - **Technical competence** – he needs to have the necessary technical knowledge and skills if he is to gain his client's confidence and provide a competent service.
  - **Integrity** – the client must have absolute confidence in his adviser's integrity; he trusts him with a great deal of sensitive financial information, which must not be improperly disclosed or otherwise abused.

## 2.1.1 Information-Gathering

In order to be able to provide appropriate advice, the adviser needs a clear picture of his client's current and hoped-for financial situation. To achieve this, information has to be gathered from the client – and, to ensure that this is done in an organised and structured way, a standardised form is used.

The actual collection of information may be done face-to-face, or at a distance (by telephone or over the internet): this will depend on the adviser's method of delivering services – face-to-face contact is still popular for many, especially those dealing with the very wealthy or those who value a high level of personal service.

The document used is often called a **fact find** or something similar. It will be a fairly lengthy document, which should collect not only the client's basic details, but also his financial background and information, to build a picture of his plans and aspirations. Typically, the document will include the following:

- Basic information (such as name and address).
- Current financial situation (level of savings, investments, mortgage).
- Current income and outgoings (financial commitments such as loans, mortgage, bills).

## UK Financial Services and Consumer Relationships

- Expected income and outgoings (potential future issues such as school fees, bonuses to be paid by employee).
- Aspirations and goals (retire early, move home).

Financial advisers are under strict obligations to ensure that they have given their client suitable advice in light of his stated needs. (The rules on this are contained in the FCA's Handbook of regulatory rules – the particular part of the Handbook is called the **Conduct of Business Sourcebook (COBS)**.)

Financial advisers should be able to demonstrate that they have done this, through the paperwork they complete. This should show how the adviser assessed the client's situation and needs, and why he selected and recommended the solutions he did. In certain circumstances the adviser's firm must send a suitability report to the client.

One initiative has focused advisers' and product providers' attention more closely on the issue of suitability. This is the FCA's **Treating Customers Fairly** (TCF) initiative. In many ways, the TCF initiative should be nothing new to those in the financial services industry – organisations already have to operate in accordance with a set of principles that include the requirement to act with integrity, consider the information needs of their customers, and other similarly fair approaches to doing business. TCF forces providers to demonstrate that they are behaving fairly in all areas of their activities – from the way in which they communicate with their customers, to the quality of their advice.

TCF will therefore be an important issue in the ongoing assessment of the suitability of advice, and advisers must undertake a thorough assessment of the client's circumstances, taking into account his attitude to risk and ability to afford any premiums. It is also more important than ever that the consequences of any recommended plan of action are clearly and properly explained to the customer, in language which he is likely to be able to understand, including the costs and risks involved.

### 2.1.2   Monitoring and Review

Financial planning is not a one-off process. In part, this is because of the possibility of change. A client's plans can change because:

- the environment changes around him – for example:
  - the tax regime changes (and remember, at the least, tax allowances are generally reviewed every year);
  - he loses his job; or
  - the stock market performs better, or worse, than he had anticipated; or
- the client himself changes, in terms of his circumstances, needs, wants and aspirations. For example, when he marries or divorces, inherits a sum of money or has a child, not only will his needs change – his attitudes to his finance may also alter and he may, for example, become more or less risk-averse.

It is also important that people review their plans so as to monitor how well they are sticking to them. Without regular progress checks, it is impossible to know whether the financial goals that have been set with the financial adviser are likely to be achieved; and quite small changes in financial behaviour can together have a big cumulative effect on someone's finances.

So a periodic review can be very helpful in ensuring that the client stays on track. By repeating the planning exercise (say) a year later, both adviser and client can see whether he is making progress towards his goal, or whether he is drifting off-target and needs to use a little financial discipline.

The adviser should agree early on whether ongoing monitoring and review is going to fall within his remit – in many cases, this will be so. If so, the adviser should advise the customer of how frequently he can expect to see an update of the plan and any new recommendations. Periodic reviews to clients should include the up-to-date value of the customer's investments.

Regulations laid down by the FCA also set out the nature, and usually the content, of information that financial advisers must provide to their clients. These obligations extend not only to the advice provided – including why they are suitable, and what the benefits, disadvantages, risks and costs are – but also to his own regulated status, how he works and on what basis he is paid.

## 2.2 Insurance and Financial Protection

The insurance industry provides a range of protection tools and solutions which may meet the varied needs of a client:

- **Accident, sickness and unemployment policies** are insurance policies which pay out regular amounts if people cannot work, usually through accident, sickness or unemployment for a limited time.
- **Home and contents policies** will pay out in the case of damage to or destruction of the family home, or damage to or loss of its contents. This may be either on an **as new** basis, or taking account of the wear and tear that the property has suffered. Most policies only offer the **new for old** basis now. It is common for the two policies to be combined, but they can also be bought separately. Home insurance is almost invariably required by mortgage lenders, in order to protect their security.
- **Income protection insurance (IPI)** used to be called permanent health insurance and provides an income while the insuree is invalided out of work, until he:
   - recovers and returns to work; or
   - reaches retirement age; or
   - dies.
- **Critical illness insurance (CII)** pays out a lump sum on diagnosis of certain serious conditions – what used to be known as **dread diseases**, including cancer and certain heart conditions. The lump sum can be used as the client wishes – eg, for medical treatment, to adapt a home to his condition, or embark on a round-the-world cruise.
- **Medical insurance** pays out against certain medical bills.
- **Life assurance products** are designed to pay a lump sum out if a named individual dies. They come in various types:
   - **Term assurance** stays in force for a set period only, and pays out a sum on the death of the **life assured**. This sum may be the same throughout the term of the policy (**level term assurance**), or it may rise over the period – perhaps in line with inflation, to preserve its buying power (**increasing term assurance**); or the sum payable may fall throughout the term (**decreasing term assurance**). This latter option is often used in tandem with a repayment mortgage, so that the sum assured decreases in line with the outstanding loan.
   - **Family income benefit** stays in force for a set period only, and can pay out regular annual amounts upon diagnosis of a critical illness/dread disease or upon death.
   - **Whole of life (WOL) assurance policies** stay in force for the whole of the insured's life, as long as premiums are continually paid and no claim is made.

## 2.3 Savings and Investment

There are a number of ways that consumers can save and invest their money:

- **Direct investments** include securities such as bonds and shares. They are usually best suited to clients with substantial sums to invest. Some investment managers will not consider putting their clients into direct investments unless they have at least £500,000 – and sometimes much more – to invest. Direct investments may also include National Savings and Investments (NS&I) products, which are regarded as very safe. They are suited to smaller investors and offer certain, if uninspiring, returns. There is a wide range available, offering both capital growth and income, so NS&I products may be well suited to the smaller, more conservative investor who cannot accommodate any risk of loss.
- **Indirect investments** include vehicles such as unit trusts, open-ended investment companies (OEICs) and investment trust companies. Through such schemes, investors acquire a diversified exposure to a range of underlying investments – ranging from bonds and shares, to property, currencies and derivatives. The level of risk associated with investing in these underlying investments is reduced, because of the risk-spreading effect of diversification; nonetheless, they can still carry an appreciable risk. This will depend on a combination of what the vehicle invests in, and how it combines these investments.
- **Derivatives** include such instruments as options, futures and contracts for differences (CFDs). They can be used in a variety of ways – both to reduce or manage risk within an investment portfolio, and to increase risk (by speculating on the direction of the market). In the latter case, it is quite possible for an investor to lose considerably more than his original investment capital. This is not always the case. For example, if you have sold a call option (and so you have given someone else the right to buy from you at the exercise price) your maximum loss is the difference between the market price and the exercise price at the time of exercise. If you have bought a call option, your maximum loss is the option premium. Consequently derivatives should be regarded as specialist investments that should be used only by experienced clients, and only if the risks of using them are fully understood and accepted.
- **Specialist investments** such as property, timber, antiques and fine wines are also an area for experienced and wealthy clients, although those with particular expertise can do very well from them. Again, they should only form a part of a client's portfolio if the particular risks of investing in them – especially any limits on their liquidity – are well understood and accepted; and even in this case they should probably not form a significant proportion of the overall portfolio.

## 2.4 Estate and Tax Planning

Estate planning is the job of planning what will happen to the assets accumulated on death. It may include significant elements of tax planning in order to minimise the effects of tax on what is passed on to the legatees (the people the money is left to). Depending on the wealth, and the complexity of the arrangements, this will include planning with the use of:

- a will (essential in every case);
- a lasting power of attorney (LPOA);
- trusts;
- life products, eg, life assurance;
- in some cases, other estate-planning vehicles or strategies.

It is important that any financial planning is done with an eye to (legitimately) minimising the tax burden. That said, *'the tax tail should not wag the investment dog'*; there is no point in a tax-efficient strategy which fails to achieve the savings, investment and other needs of the consumer. Recently the government has questioned the ethics of legitimate tax planning.

## 2.5 State Benefits

The benefits system provides practical help and financial support if you are unemployed and looking for work. It also provides you with additional income when your earnings are low, if you are bringing up children, are retired, care for someone, are ill or have a disability.

The Department for Work and Pensions (DWP) manages most benefits through Jobcentre Plus offices. Benefits and entitlements for pensioners are dealt with through a network of pension centres that provide a face-to-face service for those who need additional help and support.

The following is an overview of state benefits available to UK residents.

### Income Support

Income support is available for people on a low income who are not required to be available for work. How much money they have coming in and any capital or savings they have will affect whether or not they receive it and, if so, how much they can get.

If they have more than £16,000 in savings (capital or property), they cannot get income support.

They must be over 16 years of age. They cannot work more than 16 hours per week and, if they have a partner, their partner cannot work more than 24 hours per week.

### Jobseeker's Allowance

Jobseeker's allowance is paid if they are available for work and actively seeking work. To get it they must be under 65 (men), or under 60 (women) and either not working, or working on average fewer than 16 hours per week.

### Child Benefit

Child benefit is a benefit for people raising children. It is paid for each child and is not affected by the income or savings they have. They can claim child benefit if they have a child under 16, or a child under 20 who is studying full-time up to A-Level, NVQ Level 3 or equivalent, or if their child is under 18 and registered with the Careers Service or Connexion for work or work-based training for young people.

Child benefit is paid at £20.50 per week for the first/only child, and then £13.55 per week for any subsequent children.

In the 2012 budget, the Chancellor announced an amended plan effectively to withdraw child benefit from families with one parent who earns more than £50,000. Legislation introducing a new charge on a taxpayer came into effect on 7 January 2013.

The income charge will apply at a rate of 1% of the full child benefit award for each £100 of income between £50,000 and £60,000. The charge on taxpayers with income in excess of £60,000 will be equal to the amount of child benefit paid.

## Council Tax Benefit

Council tax benefit is paid by the local council to help with paying the council tax. They do not have to be on any other benefits. It doesn't matter if they already get a discount on their council tax. Even if they work full time they may be able to claim. They can claim if they are on a low income and liable for council tax. If they have capital (savings or property) of more than £16,000 they cannot claim.

## Housing Benefit

Housing benefit is paid by their local council to help towards paying rent, which they may pay to their local authority, housing association or a private landlord. They do not have to be claiming any other benefits to make a claim, but should have a low income. Even if they work full-time they may be able to claim. If they have capital (savings or property) of more than £16,000 they cannot claim. Housing benefit has now been capped at £400 per week by the government.

## Disability Living Allowance

This can be claimed if they need help to look after themselves. It doesn't affect income support or jobseeker's allowance claims. Different rates apply depending on the extent to which their disability affects them. A claim is not affected by income or savings. Disability living allowance can be claimed by anyone aged at least three years with severe difficulty in walking or anyone aged at least five years who needs help getting around. It cannot be claimed by anyone aged 65 years or over. For a successful claim they must have needed help for three months and be likely to need it for another six months. They may not be able to claim if they are in hospital or residential care.

## Employment and Support Allowance (Incapacity Benefit)

This benefit is relevant when they are unable to claim statutory sick pay (SSP). They can only claim it if they were under the state pension age when they became sick. There are various types of benefit:

- To claim the basic rate of incapacity benefit they must have paid national insurance (NI) for the relevant qualifying period and have been incapable of working due to sickness or disability for four days in a row (including weekends and bank holidays). They can also claim if they have been off work for 28 weeks and are under 20 years old, or 25 if they have been in education or training. They must also have fallen sick after turning 16 years old, or 20 if they were in education.
- **Short-term incapacity benefit** is paid at a lower rate if they have been off work for four days or more and are no longer entitled to SSP. Short-term incapacity benefit is paid at a higher rate if they have been off due to sickness for more than 28 weeks but fewer than 52 weeks.
- **Long-term incapacity benefit** is paid if they have been off work for more than 52 weeks.

## Carer's Allowance

This allowance is paid to the carer if they spend at least 35 hours a week caring for someone. The carer may also be entitled to the following:

- attendance allowance;
- disability living allowance;
- industrial injuries disablement benefit constant attendance allowance;
- war pensions constant attendance allowance.

To claim, they must be over 16 years of age but under 65.

They may not be able to claim if they earn over a certain amount, and they cannot claim if they are in full-time education. It is important to be aware that receiving the allowance may have an effect on any other benefits they claim, and on benefits claimed by the person they care for.

## State Retirement Pension

A state retirement pension is currently payable to women aged 60 and over and men aged 65 and over. For the tax year 2014–15, the single person's allowance is currently £113.10 a week (a rise of £2.95) and the married couple's is £180.90 (an increase of £4.75) – although both partners may be entitled to a single person's pension if they have both worked throughout their lives and have made sufficient NI payments individually.

The age at which the state pension will be payable is changing. Women's state pension age will increase to 65 by 2018. From December 2018 the state pension age for both men and women will increase to reach 66 by April 2020. There are plans to increase the age to 67 and then 68 after that.

To qualify they need to have paid enough NICs throughout their working life. To give them a rough idea they need to have earned at least the same amount as the basic pension for most of their working life.

## Working Tax Credit

This is a tax credit for people who are in paid work. They may be eligible if you are a single person, or you are a married couple living together, or a man and woman living together as if they were married, and are in paid work (including working as a self-employed person) for the required number of hours.

The amount they receive will depend on their annual income, and they must be 16 or over to be able to apply for tax credits.

## Child Tax Credit

This is for families with at least one child. It is made up of the following elements:

- A family element that is payable to any family responsible for a child. It is paid at a higher rate to families with at least one child under the age of one. This is known as the baby element.
- A child element for each child they are responsible for. This is paid at a higher rate if the child has a disability and at an enhanced rate for a child with a severe disability. This is known as the disabled child element.

UK Financial Services and Consumer Relationships

If you also qualify for the childcare element of working tax credit, this will always be paid alongside payments of child tax credit, direct to the person who is mainly responsible for caring for the child or children. It does not have to be paid to the person who receives working tax credit. It will be paid weekly or four-weekly, depending on how often you have chosen to receive payments of child tax credit.

## 2.6 Credit Finance and Management

Credit is any sort of arrangement by which they obtain money, goods or services and agree to repay at a later date. Before a company lends money, they will put in place certain safeguards to make sure that they will repay it.

Safeguards can take different forms depending on the type of credit. For example, the lender may have the right to possess and sell off some property to pay back the debt if the borrower defaults on credit. Other safeguards include guarantees given by a third party, and the last resort is to take the borrower to court to get the money back.

### 2.6.1 Why Do We Borrow?

Borrowing is a considerable responsibility, and should only be taken on with caution. However, at times, borrowing can be very useful. For example, using credit can be a useful way of:

- helping to spread out the cost of big purchases (eg, holidays, furniture for the house);
- making purchases that could not otherwise be afforded (eg, buying a house or a car);
- helping people through cashflow irregularities or through difficult times (eg, losing their job).

### 2.6.2 Credit Cards

A credit card can be a very convenient method of payment and can especially be useful in times of emergencies.

Credit cards are normally used to pay for:

- an item upfront and pay off the balance in several smaller instalments;
- expensive items, especially in emergencies.

There are various considerations when analysing the cost of a credit card. The most obvious item is usually the Annual Percentage Rate (APR), as it is the most advertised. However, the true cost of credit includes not only the APR but also late fees, over-limit fees and annual fees. It is important to consider all of these items before applying for a credit card.

### 2.6.3 Loans

Like other forms of borrowing, a loan helps pay for something when for some reason the money is not available.

There are two types of loans: secured and unsecured. The type applied for often depends on the sum required and why it is needed.

53

## Secured Borrowing

Secured borrowing is when the lender has a legal charge over the borrower's home or other assets they own, so that if he defaults on repayments, the lender can possess that property and sell it to get their money back. A mortgage is a common form of secured borrowing. See Section 2.6.4.

## Consolidated Loans

A consolidated loan is a type of secured loan. It allows the conversion of one or a number of unsecured loans – eg, credit card debts, overdrafts or bank loans – into one loan which is secured, usually against a property. Careful thought should be given before taking one out.

Consolidated loans can be helpful to some people, because they may allow them to make a lower repayment every month than they did previously on their unsecured debts.

However, although the repayments may be lower per month, they will probably have to be made over a longer period of time. This means that the borrower will almost certainly end up paying more on a consolidated loan than on unsecured debts.

Also, given that a consolidated loan is usually secured against a property, the borrower risks losing their home if they do not keep up with repayments. In contrast, if repayments on unsecured debts are not kept up, the penalties are potentially less severe.

## Unsecured Borrowing

This is when no security is taken by the lender. The bank or finance company offers a loan if it is confident the borrower will be able to repay it.

For example, a bank may be prepared to offer a loan for a holiday because it is confident that the borrower has a good credit record and normally has surplus income to fund repayments.

Examples of unsecured borrowing include:

- personal loans;
- overdrafts;
- credit cards;
- student loans;
- store cards.

If an individual defaults on an unsecured borrowing the bank may take action to recover the unsecured debt, which might indirectly put the borrower's property (if they have one) at risk of seizure.

### 2.6.4 Mortgages

A mortgage is a loan that is secured on a property, and is also known as a home loan. A mortgage is usually acquired from a lender to buy residential property. However, it is becoming increasingly popular for existing homeowners to switch mortgage lenders without moving home – this is known as remortgaging.

UK Financial Services and Consumer Relationships

**Flexible mortgages** allow the borrower to pay the mortgage off early, or in some cases late. With a flexible mortgage the borrower may also be able to make early payments, take payment holidays and even borrow back some of the home loan.

The majority of borrowers will not require such features, and so are better off with a more standard form of mortgage, such as an **interest-only** or **repayment mortgage**. Within these types there are further options of **fixed rate**, **tracker** and **capped rate** variations, as well as deals with special introductory rates. The options to the borrower are numerous and can be confusing at times, which is where an adviser can help.

In recent years the number of different mortgage deals available has increased, creating a multitude of different repayment options, interest rates and incentive offers. This increased choice of mortgages has caused remortgaging to increase in popularity in recent years. With mortgage lenders offering introductory incentives and interest rate discounts, borrowers are now starting to treat mortgage lenders much more like gas and electricity suppliers – shopping around carefully in order to make massive long-term savings. A mortgage is no longer seen as something that is only taken out when buying a new house; it has become increasingly easy to switch, with many lenders covering the costs and legal fees of doing so, and as such there are real benefits to be had from switching mortgages.

### How do People Choose a Mortgage?

With all these mortgage options available it can be difficult to choose the right deal for a potential borrower's circumstances, unless he is an expert. An online mortgage resource is a good place to start. One can compare the different mortgage lenders and brokers, apply online and find out all the available mortgage options.

Mortgages are now available to those wishing to buy to let, with no deposit wishing to buy a home, with adverse credit history, who already own a home and want to switch lenders and of course to home-movers and first-time buyers.

Since the financial crisis started in 2008, banks and other lenders have withdrawn 100% mortgages or reduced offering them. It is not uncommon for banks and lenders to request a deposit of between 20–30% from first-time buyers.

## 2.7    Retirement and Pensions

UK pension provision falls into six major divisions:

- basic state pension;
- S2P;
- occupational pensions;
- stakeholder pensions;
- group personal pensions and personal or individual pensions;
- personal accounts – automatic enrolment and a minimum employer contribution. There have been new policies concerning these since 2012.

55

## Additional Pension

Three different state schemes have existed to provide extra pension provision above the basic state pension. These are collectively known as additional state pension. They have been available only to employees paying NI and certain exempted groups (not including the self-employed). The three schemes are/were:

- **Graduated Pension or Graduated Retirement Benefit** – ran from 6 April 1961 until 5 April 1975. Qualification was based on payment of a number of fixed NI payments (stamps). Graduated pension typically pays a small amount (a pound or so per week) to those affected.
- **State Earnings-Related Pension Scheme (SERPS)** – ran from 6 April 1978 to 5 April 2002. As the name implies, the level of pension payable was related to the recipient's earnings via their NICs. Qualification was based on **band earnings** above a lower earnings limit (LEL) in each year. Band earnings lie between the LEL and an upper earnings limit (UEL) at which NICs ceased to be payable by the employee, although the UEL now refers to a threshold where reduced NI payments are made, as opposed to payment ceasing. The UEL is also adjusted annually.
- **State Second Pension (S2P)** – was introduced on 6 April 2002. As with SERPS, the level of pension payable is related to the recipient's earnings via their NICs.

Unlike the basic state pension, participation in the additional pension schemes is voluntary. Those who do not wish to participate can contract out. This option was introduced with SERPS in 1978 and is only available to those who have made alternative pension arrangements through personal or occupational schemes. Further changes introduced in 2012 saw S2P change from an **earnings-related** to a **flat-rate** pension, and individuals lose the right to contract out.

## Occupational, Individual, Personal and Stakeholder Pensions

See Section 1.2.2.

## Group Personal Pensions (GPPs)

Group personal pensions (GPPs) are personal pension arrangements, but are linked to an employer. A GPP can be established by an employer as a way of providing all of its employees with access to a pension plan run by a single provider. By grouping all the employees together in this way, it is normally possible for the employer to negotiate favourable terms with the provider, thus reducing the cost of pension provision to the employees. The employer will also normally contribute to the GPP.

## Self-Invested Personal Pensions (SIPPs)

This is the name given to the type of UK government-approved personal pension scheme that allows individuals to make their own investment decisions from the full range of HMRC-approved investments.

SIPPs are a type of personal pension plan. Another subset of this type of pension is the stakeholder pension plan. SIPPs, in common with personal pension schemes, are tax **wrappers**, allowing tax rebates on contributions in exchange for limits on accessibility. The HMRC rules allow for a greater range of investments to be held in SIPPs than in personal pension plans, notably equities and property. Rules for contributions and benefit withdrawal are the same as for other personal pension schemes.

Investors may make choices about what assets are bought, leased or sold, and decide when those assets are acquired or disposed of, subject to the agreement of the SIPP trustees (usually the SIPP provider).

All assets are permitted by HMRC; however, some will be subject to tax charges. The assets not subject to a tax charge include:

- stocks and shares listed on a recognised exchange;
- futures and options traded on a recognised futures exchange;
- authorised UK unit trusts, OEICs and other Undertakings for Collective Investment in Transferable Securities (UCITS) funds;
- unauthorised unit trusts that do not invest in residential property;
- unlisted shares;
- investment trusts subject to FCA regulation;
- unitised insurance funds from EU insurers and individual pension accounts (IPAs);
- deposits and deposit interests;
- commercial property (including hotel rooms);
- ground rents (as long as they do not contain any element of residential property);
- traded endowment policies;
- derivatives products such as CFDs;
- gold bullion, which is specifically allowed for in legislation.

Investments currently permitted by primary legislation but subsequently made subject to heavy tax penalties (and therefore typically not allowed by SIPP providers) include:

- any item of tangible movable property (whose market value does not exceed £6,000) – subject to further conditions on the use of the property;
- other exotic assets like vintage cars, wine, stamps and art;
- residential property.

Unlike conventional personal pensions where the provider as trustee has ownership and control of the assets, in a SIPP the member may have ownership of the assets (via an individual trust) as long as the scheme administrator is a co-trustee to exercise control. In practice, most SIPPs do not work this way and simply have the provider as SIPP trustee. Sippdeal, a direct-to-consumer online investment platform, launched the first online SIPP in October 2000.

The role of the scheme administrator in this situation is to control what is happening and to ensure that the requirements for tax approval continue to be met.

The pensions industry has gravitated towards three industry terms to describe generic SIPP types:

- **Deferred** – this is effectively a personal pension plan in which most or all of the pension assets are generally held in insured pension funds (although some providers will offer direct access to mutual funds). Self-investment or income withdrawal activity is deferred until an indeterminate date, and this gives rise to the name. In some newer schemes of this type, there are over 1,000 fund options, so they are not as restrictive as they once were.
- **Hybrid** – a scheme in which some of the assets must always be held in conventional insured pension funds, with the rest being able to be **self-invested**. This has been a common offering from mainstream personal pension providers, who require insured funds in order to derive their product charges.
- **Pure or full** – schemes offer unrestricted access to many allowable investment asset classes.

Contributions to SIPPs are treated identically to contributions to personal pensions. The SIPP provider claims a tax refund at the standard rate (20%) on behalf of the customer. This is added to the pot some two to six weeks after the contribution is made. Higher-rate taxpayers must claim any additional tax refund through their tax return. Employer contributions are allowable against corporation or income tax.

In the tax year 2014–15, the taxpayer could pay a gross amount equal to their relevant earnings – subject to a maximum of £40,000, this has been reduced from £50,000 in the tax year 2013–14. However, you are permitted to carry forward unused allowance from the previous three tax years (for this purpose the maximum allowance is £50,000 per tax year and you would need to have sufficient earnings in the tax year of payment to support the relevant contribution).

Income from assets within the scheme is untaxed (although it is not possible to reclaim dividend tax). Growth is free from capital gains tax (CGT).

At any time after the SIPP holder reaches early retirement age (55 from April 2010), they may elect to take a pension from some or all of their fund. After taking up to 25% (as of 2010) as a tax-free pension commencement **lump sum**, the remaining money must be moved into **drawdown** (and continue to be invested) or an annuity purchased. Drawdown income is limited (by the provider) to approximately 7% of the drawdown fund value. This is reviewed every five years. Income taken from drawdown or an annuity is taxed as if it were earned income at the member's highest marginal rate.

Rules exist to prevent the pension commencement lump sum being recycled back into the SIPP (and neither drawdown nor annuity payments count as earned income for the purpose of making SIPP contributions).

If the fund value exceeds the lifetime allowance of £1.25 million (reduced in 2013, the previous limit was £1.5 million) at retirement, then the amount above £1.25 million will be taxed at 55% or 25% depending on whether drawn as a lump sum or as income.

SIPPs can borrow up to 50% of the net value of the pension fund to invest in any assets, although in practice SIPP trustees are only likely to permit this for commercial property purchase.

# UK Financial Services and Consumer Relationships

## 3. Professional Conduct and Ethical Practice

### Learning Objective

2.3.1 Understand how professional conduct and ethical practice can directly affect the experience and perception of consumers

## 3.1 The Main Characteristics of the Market

The retail investment market comprises, at a high level, two broad groups of products:

1. **Protection products** – including pure protection products such as critical illness cover (CIC) and general insurance.
2. **Savings and investments** – including collective investment schemes (CISs) and pension products.

The value chain in the retail investment market contains not just the product provider, the adviser/sales person and the purchaser of the product, but also the fund manager, who is employed by the provider (either within the same group or externally) to manage the portfolio of assets underpinning the product. More recently, the **platform provider** has become part of the chain, providing administration services to ensure efficient management of a wide range of retail investment products. Their activities may include product development, marketing, distribution, advice, execution services, administration and compliance.

### 3.1.1 Product Pricing

The price that the consumer pays for investment products can vary considerably depending on the charging structure and the distribution channel through which the products are sold. When consumers purchase a retail investment product, they will incur explicit charges, which commonly include the following:

- **Initial charges** – these reflect the costs of developing and marketing the product, and the administrative costs associated with its purchase. They usually also reflect the initial commission paid by the product provider to the intermediary distributing the product. In addition there may be a one-off charge in the form of an **exit fee** upon redemption of the product.
- **Annual charges** – these ongoing charges reflect the **annual management charges (AMCs)** as well as other expenses. They may also reflect a **trail commission** paid to the distributor. The actual total ongoing costs are commonly measured by the **total expense ratio (TER)**.

However, these charges, which are levied and disclosed at the provider level, do not necessarily capture what consumers actually pay for the product. Additional distribution fees may be levied at the distribution level, adding an extra layer of charges to those levied at the provider level.

59

## 3.1.2 Distribution Channels

Consumers can purchase these products through a number of distribution channels. In general terms, the consumer may purchase through the advised or non-advised routes. In the former, they will receive information and recommendations from a representative of a firm authorised to give such advice. At present financial advisers fall into four distinct categories:

- **IFAs**, who provide advice on products from across the whole market (for particular products) and offer the consumer the possibility of paying for this advice in the form of a fee.
- **Whole-of-market advisers**, who also provide advice on products from across the whole market but do not offer the fee option, although a consumer may still offer to pay the adviser in this way.
- **Multi-tied advisers**, where the adviser will recommend products from a limited range of providers (the panel).
- **Single-tied advisers**, where the adviser will recommend products from one provider only.

However, the implementation of the FCA's new regime for the sale and distribution of retail investments (the Retail Distribution Review (RDR)) has changed the distribution channels from 31 December 2012.

While, previously, distribution via advisers or directly by the provider was the main route for consumers to purchase products, there have been changes over the past few years, in particular with the emergence of **provider platforms** and **discount brokers** (or execution-only brokers) which serve the retail markets.

Provider platforms are services used by intermediaries (and sometimes consumers directly) to view and administer investment portfolios; they include wraps and fund supermarkets. **Fund supermarkets** are online services that sell products directly to consumers. Platforms are remunerated in a number of ways, but the two principal methods are as follows:

- an explicit fee to the consumer, and any product discounts or rebates received are then passed on;
- a share of product charges negotiated with the product provider.

## 3.1.3 Description of the Value Chain

At present, the retail investment value chain involves several agents. These range from the fund manager, responsible for managing the underlying assets in a product portfolio, through the product provider, packaging the portfolio in the most suitable form for a wide variety of investors, via the intermediary, responsible for advising the ultimate purchaser on the suitability of the product to match his particular requirements. The same overall structure applies to both pure savings/investment products as well as those combining an insurance element with investments.

Costs will arise at all stages along the chain, beginning with the **fund manager** who will incur dealing and administration costs for the portfolio on which the retail product is based. It is not straightforward to isolate these particular costs for a specific retail portfolio, because managers responsible for retail products will tend to combine the assets in a range of funds, both retail and wholesale, that they have under management. The costs of this fund management will be passed on to the product provider in the form of management fees.

## UK Financial Services and Consumer Relationships

The **product provider** is responsible for allocating the assets to a particular (retail) fund and for packaging this fund in the most appropriate form. Costs will be incurred in structuring the fund and in its ongoing administration. In addition, the provider will incur costs in supporting the distribution of the product, which it may undertake itself, or through an intermediary such as a financial adviser.

An **adviser's** costs will arise mainly from prospecting for, and negotiating with, potential customers (marketing) and providing the advice that is given before the consumer makes the final purchase. The adviser will need to be familiar with the product markets in (and between) which they are providing advice, and this information needs to be updated regularly. Before the purchase is made, the adviser must comply with regulatory requirements to ensure that the purchaser is provided with adequate and appropriate information in order to make a suitable choice.

It is generally understood that, in recent years, the development of platforms has further reduced the potential administration costs incurred by advisers. These largely online services enable the adviser to screen investments on offer more efficiently, as well as enabling a more holistic approach to be taken to the management of a client portfolio.

## 3.2 Commission Bias – How Unethical Practice can affect Consumers

In markets involving commission payments to an intermediary, there are incentives for the intermediary to recommend either an individual product that offers the highest commission rates, or products from a particular provider offering high commission rates in general. The former may be termed product bias, the latter provider bias.

In the case of retail financial services, there is a perception that both product and provider bias has existed in the past, although actual evidence to support this perception has often been hard to identify.

Asymmetric information exists in the market for financial products, which makes it difficult for consumers to make an efficient choice of product. There is a lack of transparency about product charges, with rebating and discounting of stated charges being commonplace. Once products have been purchased there is limited evidence of switching if performance is not satisfactory.

The market for the distribution of retail investment products is characterised by a number of market failures, all of which directly affect the experience and perception of consumers, in particular:

- Many retail investment products have complex charging structures and it is often not clear how benefits accrue to consumers. Consumers purchase them relatively infrequently, so have little experience to draw on. They tend to find the risks and commitment involved hard to understand and the price of the product hard to determine. Retail investors do not have the same information as the sellers of these products. As a consequence of this failure, plus the low level of financial capability among many consumers, together with a lack of interest and engagement, consumers do not act as a strong force in the financial services industry.
- Consequently, many consumers rely heavily on advisers through whom retail investment products are sold. Product providers often remunerate advisers, and there can be a misalignment of advisers' interests with those of consumers. This, in addition to the above market failure and the importance of these products to consumers, creates the risk that substantial consumer detriment will occur.

61

But such problems are not limited to commission-based sales. For instance, when products and services are sold directly, incentives for staff to achieve target sales levels, or penalties for not doing so, can lead to poor outcomes for consumers if the risks are poorly managed.

Remuneration-driven sales can also lead to inappropriate advice to switch between different products in order to generate income for advisers, often resulting in high levels of early termination of these long-term products. The costs of this low product **persistency** are borne mainly by providers but may ultimately be passed back to consumers.

- The costs of poor-quality advice may not be fully faced (or perceived to be faced) by advisers, as unsuitable sales may be identified only years after the sale, if at all. There are limitations in the way that capital resources requirements and professional indemnity insurance (PII) requirements for firms currently remedy this. Product providers also have responsibilities for treating customers fairly – again, it may be many years before problems become apparent, for instance with the performance of a product relative to what the consumer was led to believe. The result of this can be uncertainty for consumers, and mean potential claims against those who supplied the product or gave advice, many years after the original purchase. By the time these claims come to light, those who gave the advice may no longer be in business, leaving others in the industry to meet the costs of compensation.

- Those providing advice can do so with relatively little training and testing when compared to other professions. So one reason why the problems of consumer understanding set out above may be occurring is because the provider of the services cannot explain the benefits, risks and costs of the services sufficiently clearly. Consumers have low levels of trust in those selling and advising on investment products, not least because of past cases of widespread mis-selling (such as pensions, split capital investment trusts and mortgage endowments).

The implementation of the FCA's regime for the sale and distribution of retail investments (the RDR) was intended to, amongst many things, change the way that advisers are remunerated for their services. The rules, which became effective from 31 December 2012, improve the clarity with which firms describe their services to consumers, including addressing the potential for adviser remuneration to distort consumer outcomes.

### 3.2.1 Improving Clarity for Consumers about Advice Services

The FCA's rules will make it easier for consumers to distinguish between the different forms of advice on offer to them, with all investment firms clearly describing their services as either **independent advice** or **restricted advice**. The rules and guidance will ensure that firms which describe their advice as independent genuinely do make their recommendations based on comprehensive and fair analysis, and provide unbiased, unrestricted advice. Equally, where consumers choose to use a restricted service – such as a firm that can only give advice on its own range of products – this must be made clear.

## 3.2.2 Addressing the Potential for Remuneration Bias (Adviser Charging)

Under the new rules, all firms that give investment advice must set their own charges, in agreement with their clients, and meet new standards regarding how they determine and operate these charges. The commission-based system of adviser remuneration has ended. The rules prohibit product providers from offering amounts of commission to secure sales from adviser firms and, in turn, ban adviser firms from recommending products that automatically pay commission. Consumers can still have their adviser charges deducted from their investments if they wish, but these charges are no longer determined by the product providers that are recommended.

## 3.3 How Professional Conduct and Ethical Practice can Directly Affect the Customer Experience and Perception

In rebuilding trust by consumers in the financial industry after a number of mis-selling scandals and the general financial downturn, it is relevant to consider whose interests are being served by any sales recommendation.

### Case Study

A bank launches a new product of a type where sales had previously been closely controlled. Now it wants the new product sold more widely and is incentivising its staff with a mixture of rewards, together with implicit threats if targets are not met. The compliance department has not yet signed off unequivocally on this less rigid policy.

**Key points**

- The bank incentivises sales staff, using competitions to reward successful performers.
- At the same time, it publishes details of those who have failed to meet their sales targets.
- A wealth management relationship manager is in a quandary as to how much they should compromise their principles to meet their targets.
- The bank appears not to share their concerns about suitability of the investment product.

**What is/would be unethical?**

From the perspective of the firm's policymakers, it is unethical to put more junior staff in the position of being offered incentives, accompanied by implicit threats, if it encourages them to suspend their usual ethical standards.

From a sales perspective, it is unethical to recommend an investment to a client which is more to their benefit than to the customer's.

Appearing to persuade customers to invest in a product which they do not understand, and which may not serve their best interests, is leaving the adviser, and their employer, open to accusations of mis-selling; putting their and their employer's interests ahead of those of their customers and failing to treat them fairly.

The fact that there are additional incentives for making sales only makes matters worse, should the investment not perform as anticipated.

# Summary of this Chapter

You should have an understanding and knowledge of the following after reading this chapter:

- Financial planning and needs of consumers:
    - lifestyle changes;
    - budgeting and managing finances – while working and in retirement;
    - provisions for dependants before and after death.
- Pensions:
    - state pensions;
    - company pensions/personal pensions.
- Financial advice:
    - how needs and requirements of consumers are met;
    - regulation;
    - suitable advice;
    - different types of investments available to consumers;
    - estate planning;
    - state benefits.
- Managing finances – borrowing:
    - different types of facilities available to consumers.
- Professional conduct and ethical practice:
    - provision of financial advice – products and distribution;
    - RDR – impact on financial advice.

UK Financial Services and Consumer Relationships

# End of Chapter Questions

Think of an answer for each question and refer to the appropriate section for confirmation.

1. What are the main lifestyle changes that can impact consumers?
   *Answer reference: Section 1.2*

2. What is the impact of taxation on consumers' investment opportunities?
   *Answer reference: Section 1.2.3*

3. How are the financial needs of consumers met?
   *Answer reference: Section 2*

4. What is the purpose of financial advice?
   *Answer reference: Section 2.1*

5. What are the different ways that consumers can invest their money?
   *Answer reference: Section 2.3*

6. What are the pension provisions open to UK residents?
   *Answer reference: Section 2.7*

7. What are the typical charges that consumers will pay for financial advice?
   *Answer reference: Section 3.1.1*

8. What are the main practices that impact consumer trust of the financial services industry?
   *Answer reference: Section 3.2*

9. Looking at the case study, what considerations or tools allow you to judge whether a course of action is ethical?
   *Answer reference: Section 3.3*

# Chapter Three
# UK Contract and Trust Legislation

1. Legal Concepts Relevant to Financial Advice     69
2. Trusts and Their Purpose     78

**This syllabus area will provide approximately 2 of the 80 examination questions**

*UK Contract and Trust Legislation*

In this chapter you will gain an understanding of:

- Legal concepts relevant to financial advice.
- Power of attorney (POA) – their use and objectives.
- Property ownership.
- Insolvency and bankruptcy.
- The main types of trust.

# 1. Legal Concepts Relevant to Financial Advice

## Learning Objective

3.1 Understand specific legal concepts relevant to financial advice:

3.1.1 Contract, agency and capacity: legal persons – individuals, personal representatives, trustees, companies, limited liability partnerships

## 1.1 Contracts and Capacity

The law of contract is relevant to many aspects of financial advice:

- The financial adviser must establish terms of business with their client, and these terms form the basis of a contract for the provision of services to the client.
- In addition, the client may have a number of contracts with the financial product, or financial services providers, recommended by the financial adviser.
- Many of the other types of arrangement being made, especially later in life, raise issues regarding capacity. It may be important to demonstrate that someone who is elderly, and perhaps rather frail, still has the necessary capacity to make a will, grant authorities such as a POA (see Section 1.4.1) or make gifts. This is especially so if their decisions are likely to be challenged by other members of their family.

For a contract to be valid (and therefore enforceable – ie, legally binding on both parties to it), both parties must have the **capacity to contract**. This is a legal term which means that someone has the power in law to enter into a contract; if they do not have capacity to contract, the contract may be either:

- **Void** – the contract is unenforceable.
- **Voidable** – the contract can continue in force unless and until one of the parties decides that he does not want to be bound by it.

There are a number of ways in which an individual – or a legal person (see Section 1.3) – can lack capacity to contract. For example:

- Someone who is under the age of 18 cannot enter into certain types of contract.
- Someone who is bankrupt has certain restrictions on the contracts they can enter into.
- Someone who is mentally incapable lacks the legal capacity to contract.

69

- Someone who is drunk lacks capacity, and any agreement entered into may be void if the person they were contracting with knew that he was in no condition to understand the implications of what they were agreeing to.
- Companies may lack capacity to do something, if it is not provided for in their **powers**. A company's powers are set out in its constitutional documents – its Memorandum and Articles of Association. Nowadays this is not the problem that it used to be, as companies tend to have widely drafted powers; but problems do still arise from time to time with older companies, or with companies that have had their powers deliberately drafted so as to be restrictive – perhaps in order to reflect the ethical wishes of the company's founder, for example.

Some legal changes have been made in recent years in relation to mental incapacity. They were introduced under the Mental Capacity Act 2004, which came into force on 7 April 2005. For example, it is now possible for someone to be deemed to have capacity for some purposes but not for others – prior to this, they were deemed to be either fully mentally capable, or mentally incapable for all purposes.

Capacity can be an important issue in financial planning:

- There is no point in an adviser recommending an investment product or strategy which the client cannot put into practice (for example, if he recommends borrowing to a company without the powers to borrow).
- A financial adviser asked to give advice to a minor (someone under 18) should be particularly careful. In some cases, it may be that the advice should be provided to an adult person properly authorised to look after the child's affairs (for example, a guardian or trustee).
- If someone lacks mental capacity, it may be that someone else has been properly appointed to look after their affairs and has the capacity to do so on their behalf – we will consider this further in Section 1.4.

If various planning steps are agreed to by someone who is later shown to have lacked the necessary capacity, they may be challenged. If they are found to be invalid, they may be set aside along with any transactions – payments and gifts – that have been made as a consequence. Such challenges can be very time-consuming and expensive, and can result in bad feeling and distress for the client and their family.

## 1.2 Agency

Advisers that are acting as IFAs act as the **agent** of the client in any transactions they arrange for them. In other cases, the adviser may be an employee of a single product provider, or be **tied** or **multi-tied** to one or more providers. In this case they act as the agent of the provider(s) and not of the client.

The law of agency is a well-established body of law, and imposes a range of duties on the agent towards the person for whom they are acting (their **principal**). It is therefore important that clients understand whether the adviser is acting as their agent, or as that of the product provider, whose products are being recommended. For this reason they are required, under the FCA's COBS rules, to disclose their status to the client before the client is committed to proceeding with any of their recommendations.

# 1.3 Legal Persons

## 1.3.1 Natural Persons (Individuals)

The term **natural person** is a legal one which is used to describe individuals. Human beings, like you and me, are known as **natural persons** in legal terminology.

## 1.3.2 Companies and Limited Liability

In contrast, certain bodies only exist because of the way the law works; they are known as **legal persons**. A good example is a company, an entity which can only exist because of the provisions of the Companies Acts.

A company is separate from:

- its owners (usually the shareholders, though there are some special types of companies which are not owned through shares); and
- the people responsible for operating it (the directors).

It can sue and be sued, and can incur liabilities in its own right. If it does so, its owners cannot – except in a very few circumstances – be found liable for its debts; their liability is limited to what they paid for their shares, hence most companies have the term **limited** in their title. There are some special types of company that are unlimited – these are, however, beyond the scope of this text.

## 1.3.3 Partnerships

A partnership is the relationship that exists between two or more parties carrying on a business together with a view to making a profit. A partnership is not a separate legal entity like a company, and, with some kinds of partnership, the partners remain fully liable for the partnership debts.

Partnerships are common in certain types of profession – for example, the law, accountancy, and architecture.

# 1.4 Powers of Attorney and the Grantor's Affairs

### Learning Objective

3.1 Understand specific legal concepts relevant to financial advice:

3.1.2 Powers of attorney and managing the grantor's affairs: wills, intestacy and administration of estates

## 1.4.1 Power of Attorney (POA)

A **POA** is a mechanism which lets the principal or **donor** (giver) give, or delegate, to the **donee** (the recipient) the power to do certain things on his behalf. Typical powers include the power to:

- sign documents on behalf of the donor;
- handle their financial affairs – for example, buying and selling investments, signing cheques and making bank transfers;
- make purchases on his behalf; and
- dispose of their property, including by making **usual** gifts to third parties.

A POA will not allow the donee to make very large or **unusual** gifts, unless the courts specifically approve it. Nor will it empower them, to make non-financial decisions for the donor – for example, about their personal care or medical arrangements.

A POA must be signed as a deed by the donor; or if not signed by them, signed at their direction and in their presence, and in the presence of two witnesses.

The three types of POA which are most common are:

1. a **specific POA** – this only lets the donee act on specific occasions or in respect of specific property; it is therefore the most limited kind;
2. a **general POA** – this gives the donee a general power to act on behalf of the donor – the deed may, however, state certain limitations on this; and
3. a **lasting POA (LPOA)** – this is a specialist form of POA that replaced its forerunner, the enduring power of attorney (EPOA).

A POA may be executed for a number of reasons. For example:

- Someone who expects to be travelling for long periods may execute a POA so that a trusted relative, friend or adviser can handle their financial affairs in their absence.
- Someone in poor health may delegate powers so that someone else can look after matters while they are recuperating.
- Someone may delegate power to handle their financial affairs simply because they do not want to be troubled with managing their own bank accounts and other financial affairs.

Once a POA has been put in place, it can be terminated at any time using a Deed of Revocation of POA. An individual can choose to grant their attorney authority to undertake only specific tasks on their behalf, for example, the renewal of a car insurance premium or managing a specific bank account. A general POA is most often used by individuals who will be away travelling for a period of time or by those whose mobility is affected and wish to appoint someone who can do things on their behalf.

A general POA will become automatically void in the event that an individual loses their mental capabilities. Accordingly, a general POA is often not suitable for managing the affairs of the elderly or mentally ill. For such individuals, an LPOA should be used. This will continue to be valid once a person loses their full mental abilities, provided that it is registered with the Court of Protection.

An LPOA can only be given by someone who has the mental capacity to do so. It will automatically end in the following circumstances:

- the individual or the attorney dies;
- the individual or the attorney becomes bankrupt;
- a marriage or civil partnership between the individual and the attorney is dissolved or annulled;
- the attorney(s) lack the mental capacity to make decisions;
- the power is **disclaimed** (or rejected) by the attorney.

The POA does not end in the above circumstances if there is another attorney left to act or there is a replacement attorney. If more than one was originally nominated, the POA to make decisions for an individual is transferred automatically.

The Court of Protection can end a lasting POA for reasons such as the attorney not carrying out their duties correctly.

If an individual still has the mental capacity they can revoke the LPOA.

The fact that the POA expires on loss of the donor's capacity can create problems, as this may be precisely the point in their life at which they need outside support and assistance. Because of this, a specialist form of POA, the **EPOA**, arose. This was a special type of POA that continued when the donor was certified mentally incapable, and was intended to provide for the future dealings in their affairs when they could no longer undertake them themselves.

EPOAs were replaced by **LPOAs** as a result of specific legal provisions which came into effect in April 2007. However, those EPOAs which are currently in existence will continue in force. In contrast with EPOAs, under an LPOA the attorney can make decisions and take action with regard to the donor's personal welfare matters, not just their property and financial affairs.

**Receivership** gives the receiver (the term for **attorney** in this instance) very similar powers to those they would have had under an LPOA once it has been granted. However, the method of applying for, and obtaining, receivership status, is different. Essentially this is because a body called the Office of the Public Guardian (OPG) becomes involved – to ensure that the person who needs the help is not being taken advantage of.

In terms of managing the individual's affairs, the OPG will request details of the assets and income of the individual who needs help, and will require the receiver to sign a declaration to say that he will act in the individual's interest.

On an ongoing basis, the receiver will manage the individual's income so as to ensure their day-to-day needs are met, his bills (including taxes) are properly paid and his property is maintained. If the receiver needs to use any of the individual's capital, this must be approved by the Court of Protection. The receiver must also liaise with the Court over the individual's investments, and about any sales of their property. The receiver must submit annual accounts to the court of protection, and arrange a **security bond** to safeguard the individual's assets – but the cost of this can be reclaimed from the individual's assets.

### 1.4.2 Trusts and Trustees

Trusts can also be an important tax and estate-planning tool. They are not products per se, but arrangements which allow an individual (the **settlor**) to settle their assets in such a way that certain parties keep legal control of it (the **trustees**) – and look after it for the benefit of certain other people (the **beneficiaries**).

For more on trusts, see Section 2.

### 1.4.3 Wills

Almost everyone should make a will, and review it at various points in their lives – even those who believe that they have relatively little in the way of assets, or that their affairs are simple. Even quite young people may have assets, and will want to have some say as to how they are disposed of if anything happened to them. Making a will is important because:

- When someone dies without having made a will (called dying **intestate**), a series of rules dictate how their property and cash will be divided up. This may not be the way that they would have wanted them to be distributed.
- Unmarried and same-sex partners who have not registered a civil partnership under the Civil Partnership Act 2004, will not automatically inherit from each other unless there is a will – so the death of one partner can mean serious financial problems for the remaining partner.
- People with children usually want to provide for them in the event of their death. It can be very important that the arrangements are set out by way of a will, so that arrangements can be made if either or both parents die.
- In some cases, proper planning in the drafting of wills – and sometimes their use in combination with arrangements such as trusts – can help reduce the amount of IHT paid on eventual death.

Whenever a client's circumstances change, the latest will should be reviewed to ensure it reflects their intentions. For example, a marriage, civil partnership or serious relationship, the breakdown of a marriage or partnership, or the birth of a new child may cause him to want to reconsider his arrangements.

## 1.4.4 Intestacy

When someone dies, their assets are dealt with under the laws of intestacy – rules which state how the assets will be disposed of.

You should also note that there are some minor regional variations (that is, in the duchies of Lancaster and Cornwall) to the *bona vacantia* provisions. The term *bona vacantia* literally means **vacant goods** and is the legal name for ownerless property, which by law passes to the Crown.

## 1.4.5 Personal Representatives and Administration of Estates

The administration of the estate of a deceased person is carried out by one or more personal representatives. These may be either:

- **executors** – if the deceased died testate, the executors will obtain a **grant of probate**; or
- **administrators** – if the deceased died intestate, the administrators will obtain **letters of administration**.

Letters of administration *cum testamento annexo* (with the will annexed) are needed when a will was left but, owing to some small defect in it, probate could not be granted.

# 1.5 Property

### Learning Objective

3.1     Understand specific legal concepts relevant to financial advice:

3.1.3   Real property, personal property and joint ownership

## 1.5.1 Real and Personal Property

Property is, in legal terms, regarded as falling into two categories:

- real property; and
- personal property.

The term **real property** refers to land and buildings, as opposed to other types of property (personal items and financial property). Hence you may come across the term **realty** – often used in the US to mean land and buildings. Both terms can also be used to include some intangible rights – for example, rights attaching to land such as rights of way and of access.

**Personal property**, or **personalty**, on the other hand, means property that is not real property. It therefore includes all movable property (land is clearly immovable) and **chattels** (personal possessions).

### 1.5.2 Joint Ownership

If people own something together – jointly – they do so either:

- as a joint tenancy; or
- as tenants in common.

Under a **joint tenancy**, all the joint owners have an identical interest in the property. On the death of one owner, their interest passes to the remaining surviving owner(s). So, for example, if the asset jointly owned is a bank account and one party dies, the other owns the whole contents of the account.

Under a **tenancy in common**, however, each joint tenant owns a separate share in the property. On the death of one of the joint owners, their share passes to their beneficiaries – whether these are established under their will, or under the laws of intestacy. So in our example above, the surviving joint owner would not necessarily become the owner of all of the bank account proceeds; the deceased might have left his half (or whatever proportion of it he had owned) to someone else; it would simply form a part of his estate and be distributed accordingly.

A decision as to whether an investment should be owned jointly at all, and if so whether by the parties as joint tenants or tenants in common, can be important – both for estate-planning purposes (to ensure that each party's assets go to the people they intend), and also for tax-planning purposes (since it can affect how a disposal or transfer is considered for tax purposes).

## 1.6 Insolvency and Bankruptcy

### Learning Objective

3.1 Understand specific legal concepts relevant to financial advice:

3.1.4 Insolvency, receivership and bankruptcy

The term **bankruptcy** was originally defined under the Bankruptcy Act 1914, now replaced by the Insolvency Act 1986. It is the term used when an individual is insolvent (ie, they cannot pay their debts as they fall due, and will not be able to do so in the near future).

The bankruptcy process is intended to ensure a fair distribution of their assets among the people to whom they owe money. It also allows the bankrupt individual to be freed from their debt burden, so that they can start again – subject to certain constraints lasting for a defined period – with a **clean sheet**.

Generally speaking, anyone with the capacity to contract can be made bankrupt – though there are some exceptions:

- An individual cannot be bankrupted once they are deceased; however, their estate can be **administered in bankruptcy** if they die leaving more debts than assets.

# UK Contract and Trust Legislation

- An infant is unlikely to be bankrupted, because they are largely unable to incur binding debts (remember, we saw in Section 1.1, that minors have limited contractual capacity). It is, however, theoretically possible (for example, over unpaid debts for necessaries, unpaid taxes, or liabilities arising from judgments against the infant).
- Someone who is mentally incapable can be made bankrupt for debts which they incurred while of sound mind. In addition, with the consent of the courts they can be made bankrupt over debts incurred while of unsound mind.
- A spouse can be made bankrupt in connection with their separate property as if they were single.

A bankruptcy order can be made if a person has debts in excess of £750. It can come about in one of the following ways:

- **Debtor's petition** – the debtor may apply voluntarily to the courts for a bankruptcy order. They may do this because, while the process is unpleasant, it gives them the opportunity to put their debt problems behind them and begin again.
- **Creditor's petition** – one or more of the individual's creditors can petition the courts for an enforcement order.

The Insolvency Act 1986 also introduced an alternative procedure to bankruptcy, known as a **voluntary arrangement**. An **individual voluntary arrangement (IVA)** is a scheme available to individuals, and it allows for them to make arrangements with their creditors without becoming bankrupt – subject to certain rules. Similar arrangements, with certain differences of detail, can be made in respect of companies, in which case they are an alternative to winding up.

**Insolvency** is the term used for companies that cannot repay their debts (a company therefore becomes insolvent but not bankrupt). When a company becomes insolvent, there are a variety of procedures established in law which can take place. They include:

- **Liquidation** – if the company is insolvent, this may be a creditor's voluntary liquidation (where the shareholders decide to put the company in liquidation themselves) or compulsory liquidation (where the courts order that the company should be wound up).
- **Informal arrangement** – where the company writes to all its creditors to see if some mutually agreeable timetable for repayments can be found.
- **Company voluntary arrangement (CVA)** – a formal version of the informal agreement described above. The arrangement is sanctioned by the courts and overseen by an authorised insolvency practitioner.
- **Administration** – where the courts grant an order designed to give the company some **breathing space** to try and put its affairs back on a firmer financial footing. This may allow the company to survive as a going concern, or at the least manage to realise a better proportion of the money owed to creditors.

Naturally, financial advisers may hope that bankruptcy and insolvency are not things that they will – in terms of their clients' finances – encounter often, although there are specialist advisers who assist people in precisely these circumstances. However, in reality, even wealthier clients can find themselves in financial straits; for example, following a job loss, business disaster or divorce. In addition, a working knowledge of company insolvency issues can be of help if the client has invested in, or through, a company that gets into financial difficulty.

# 2. Trusts and Their Purpose

**Learning Objective**

3.2.1 Understand in outline the main types of trust and their purpose, creation and administration

3.3.1 Apply knowledge of the creation and administration of trusts

## 2.1 The Purpose of Trusts and Types of Trust

As stated in Section 1.4.2, trusts can also be an important tax- and estate-planning tool.

There are various types of trust, each with their specific uses in different circumstances. A few examples of the types of estate-planning needs they can solve are:

- To ensure that the financial needs of the settlor's family will be provided for after they die. This may be done in such a way as to give the trustees a certain amount of flexibility.
- To minimise the tax burden on the settlor's estate on their death, perhaps by taking a gift out of the settlor's estate now while retaining the ability to decide exactly who will get what at a later stage.
- To make gifts for the benefit of people who may not be old enough, or sensible enough, to handle them at the outset.
- To make a gift of income to one individual, while reserving the capital for the benefit of someone else, after the income beneficiary's death.

Trusts are not separate legal entities in the way that companies are; they are simply legal arrangements, governed – usually – by a trust deed, and also by a well-established body of trust law.

## 2.2 Trust Creation

Trusts can be created by a variety of means including orally, by deed, by will, by statute or in secret. We will now look at the methods most commonly used by settlors.

### 2.2.1 Creation by Deed

This is the most common method of creating a trust. There is no prescribed format but most solicitors and trust corporations will have tried and tested templates that can easily be adapted to suit the settlor's particular requirements.

The deed will specify the:

- trust property;
- names of the trustees;
- names of the beneficiaries;
- name of the protector (if there is one);
- powers of the trustees;
- rights of the beneficiaries.

It must be signed by the settlor and is usually also signed by the trustees to confirm their acceptance. Trusts can also be created over life policies very simply, by filling out the life insurance company's trust form.

## 2.2.2 Creation by Will

A trust can be expressly stated in a will or arise because of a gift to a minor. Even if the will does not include provisions to set up a trust, the executors are effectively holding the entire estate on trust for the beneficiaries until they can fully distribute it.

Clearly, a will trust will not come into operation until after the testator has died. Therefore the trust may not receive any assets until many years after the will is prepared. There is also the possibility that the will may be revoked prior to death, so the trust never comes into operation.

Some wills avoid the need and possible expense of setting up trusts, by providing permission for the parents of any minors to provide a valid receipt for property left to their children.

## 2.2.3 Creation by Statute

There are many trusts created or implied by statute.

The following are two examples of such trusts:

- **Section 33 Administration of Estates Act 1925** – this provides for the creation of a trust for sale on intestacy. This was altered by **Section 5** of the **Trusts of Land and Appointment of Trustees Act 1996**, the effect of which is that personal representatives now have a power, but not a duty, to sell land held within the estate.
- **Section 36 Law of Property Act 1925** – if a legal estate is held by two or more persons as joint tenants, it is held in trust.

## 2.3 Legal Requirements for a Valid Trust

### 2.3.1 The Three Certainties

In order to create a valid express trust, three certainties are required.

1. **Certainty of intention** – words must be used indicating an intention to create a trust. The equitable maxim *'equity looks at the intention not the form'* means that no particular form of words is used but the court will look at the words used in light of all the circumstances. **On trust for** is sufficient in this regard.
2. **Certainty of object** – it must be clear for whom the trust is intended. This could be a simple case of naming the beneficiaries *'to A & B in equal shares absolutely'* or a class of people, for example, *'any of my children who survive me'*.
3. **Certainty of subject matter** – it must be established, with clarity, what property is to be held on the express trust. If the subject matter is not certain, the whole trust fails (although hopefully, if the settlor is still alive, they would be able to clarify the position).

### 2.3.2 Constitution of the Trust

Depending on what type of property is involved, certain formalities need to be satisfied before the property is validly transferred, and the general principle is that *'equity will not perfect an imperfect gift'*. Thus, in the case of land, there needs to be a deed, and in the case of shares, Sections 182–183 of the Companies Act 1985 provide that, in general, a share transfer form must be executed and delivered with the share certificates, followed by entry of the name of the new owner in the company books.

## 2.4 Parties of a Trust

Every trust has a settlor, trustees and beneficiaries. Some trusts also have a **protector**. We will look at each of these participants in turn.

### 2.4.1 Settlor

The settlor is the person who sets up the trust by transferring money or other property to trustees to hold upon the terms of the trust they are seeking to establish. The terms of the trust will be laid out in a trust deed for gifts during the settlor's lifetime (*inter vivos*) or in the will, for gifts on death.

The placing of property into trust is effectively a gift of the assets, which means that the settlor no longer has any control over them. However, some settlors find this unpalatable and therefore many modern trust deeds include provisions, which reserve certain powers for the settlor. Commonly the settlor will wish to reserve the power to appoint and remove trustees, but they can go further and reserve the power to appoint investment managers or, more unusually, retain the investment powers completely.

On a practical point, settlors need to be careful not to retain too much control, since the courts could set aside the trust as a **sham** in such circumstances. This would mean that the trust is ignored for tax purposes and therefore any potential tax benefits of setting up the trusts are lost. This is far more common with offshore trusts, where it may be possible for the settlor to also be a beneficiary.

### 2.4.2 Trustees

The trustees are the legal owners of the trust property and on appointment the property will be vested in them by the settlor. This process is known as **constituting the trust**.

The original trustees are appointed by the trust deed, sometimes called a **settlement**. The original trustees of will trusts are appointed in the will. If someone dies intestate (without a valid will), the administrators will be the trustees of any trust, set up as a result.

Anyone capable of owning a legal interest in property may be appointed as a trustee, which means that they have to be over 18 and of sound mind (*sui juris*). This also includes corporate entities known as trust corporations, empowered by their memorandum and articles to act as a trustee. Most major banks have subsidiaries who perform this function.

There can be any number of trustees, although most trusts will have between two and five. If the trust contains land, in order to give a valid receipt for the proceeds of sale, there must be at least two trustees (unless one is a trust corporation) and no more than four.

## Duties of Trustees

As we have seen the job of the trustee is to hold the trust property for the benefit of the beneficiaries in accordance with the trust provisions.

The role carries with it the following principal general duties:

- **To comply with the terms of the trust** – the trustee must be familiar with the terms of the trust and comply with the duties and powers contained in the trust instrument.
- **To take control of the trust property** – the trustee must ascertain the assets of the trust and ensure these are vested in the names of the trustees.
- **To act impartially between the beneficiaries** – trustees must act in the best interests of the beneficiaries but, importantly, must also act impartially between all the beneficiaries.
- **Duty to keep accounts** – a trustee must keep clear and accurate accounts of the trust, and provide them to beneficiaries on request.
- **Duty to provide information** – a trustee must produce information and documents on request of the beneficiaries.
- **Duty of care** – in addition to the above general duties, there has always existed an overarching duty of care which covers all the actions of a trustee.
  - ○ **Common law duty of care** – this has been developed from case law over the years, and interestingly (for us) most of the important cases were concerned with investment-related issues.
  - ○ **Statutory duty of care** – the Trustee Act 2000, which came into effect on 1 February 2001, established a new statutory duty of care for trustees. This is found in Part 1, which reads *'Whenever the duty under this subsection applies to a trustee, he must exercise such care and skill as is reasonable in the circumstances, having regard in particular – a. to any special knowledge or experience that he has or holds himself out as having; and b. if he acts as trustee in the course of a business or profession, to any special knowledge or experience that it is reasonable to expect of a person acting in the course of that kind of business or profession.'*

    The statutory duty of care will only apply to the following: exercising the powers of investment; acquisition of land; using agents, nominees or custodians; insurance of trust property. Furthermore, it is possible (under Schedule 1, Section 7 of the Trustee Act 2000) to exclude the statutory duty of care in the trust instrument.

## Powers of Trustees

The trust deed will commonly confer additional powers to the trustees. This could be specific investment powers or, if there is a life policy held in trust, the power to pay premiums, make claims, exercise options and switch funds.

All trustees must act unanimously in the exercise of their powers.

The Trustee Act 1925 also conferred statutory powers on trustees with regard to the power to apply income (Section 31) or capital (Section 32) to beneficiaries.

## Trustee Act 2000

The Trustee Act 2000 conferred new statutory **powers of investment** on trustees.

In addition, this Trustee Act gave trustees a statutory **power to delegate day-to-day duties** to an agent, including the powers of investment. The Act requires the trustees to set out a policy statement stating how the investment management functions should be managed in the best interest of the trust.

The Act also created an express **professional charging clause** for non-charitable trusts, which allows the payment of fees to a trustee appointed in a professional capacity, if there is no charging clause in the deed. The general rule is that trustees cannot benefit from their position, therefore laypersons are not allowed to charge for acting as a trustee, but can claim reasonable out-of-pocket expenses.

The Act also gave the trustees the **power to insure** 100% of the trust property.

### 2.4.3 Beneficiaries

The beneficiaries are the persons or objects for whose benefit the trust is created. Beneficiaries can either be named in the trust instrument (*'my children Jenny and Sarah in equal shares'*) or described by a class (*'all my children in equal shares'*). Clearly the latter approach provides extra flexibility if a settlor is intending to have more children. In certain cases, the trustees may be given the power to exercise discretion as to who benefits from the trust.

There are various types of beneficial interest:

- **Absolute vested interest** – the beneficiary has a full equitable ownership, which cannot be taken away. There are three conditions which must be satisfied for an interest to be vested:
    - the identity of the beneficiary is known; and
    - any conditions are satisfied; and
    - the respective shares are known.
    
    If any of these conditions is not satisfied, the interest is known as a **contingent interest**.
- **Life interest** – a beneficiary (called the life tenant) is entitled to the income on the trust property but not the capital. An immediate right to the income is called an **interest in possession**. If there are successive life interests, the person who is not enjoying the immediate right to the income has an **interest in remainder**.
- **Remaindermen** – these beneficiaries will receive the capital of the trust fund on the death of the life tenant. Until that time their interest is known as an **interest in reversion** (or **reversionary interest**).

### 2.4.4 Protector

Protectors are much more common in offshore trusts than in England and Wales, and their most usual role is to veto the proposals of trustees. Unlike trustees, they do not have trust property vested in their name.

The scope of the protector's powers are set out in the trust instrument, and these can be either reactive or proactive.

- **Reactive** – the protector reacts to the actions of a trustee, for example, to distribute money to a beneficiary.
- **Proactive** – the protector takes the initiative and instigates an action, for example, to remove a trustee.

Clearly, the more power given to the protector, the more cumbersome the administration of the trust could become. However, appointing a protector may give the settlor the desired peace of mind that someone will be able to oversee the activities of the trustees, hence the term often used to describe this role is **settlor's comfort**.

## 2.5    Types of Trust

### 2.5.1    Bare Trust

A bare trust is where the trustee holds the trust property for a single beneficiary who is of full age and mental capacity. The beneficiary who holds the whole of the equitable interest, may, under *Saunders v Vautier (1841)*, call for the legal interest from the trustee which will give them absolute ownership of the property held in trust, and therefore end the trust.

Bare trusts are particularly useful for grandparents who wish to pass on assets to their grandchildren or set aside money for their school fees or university education. The named beneficiary has an **absolute entitlement** to the assets that are placed in trust, but they will be held in the name of the trustee until the child reaches the age of 18.

This could be useful for settling assets which the beneficiary cannot hold directly, for example, stocks and shares (because minors cannot contract to buy and sell them). On reaching age 18, the beneficiary will be able to call on the assets. The trustees will have no discretion over whether to comply with this request.

The income on a bare trust is deemed to be that of the beneficiary, who will be able to use any unused personal allowance to mitigate, or avoid completely, any income tax on the income arising within the trust fund. For parents, this type of trust is not so attractive, since any income over £100 is deemed to be that of the parents, for income tax purposes. For grandparents, however, this rule does not apply.

Any growth of the assets held in trust is outside the estate of the settlor and, provided the settlor survives seven years from the date of creating the trust, there will be no IHT to pay.

The disadvantage of bare trusts is the lack of flexibility – the beneficiary can get their hands on the funds at 18, which may not be desirable (for the settlor!).

## 2.5.2 Interest in Possession Trust

An **interest in possession** is the right to receive an income from the trust fund, or use of the trust assets.

For an interest in possession to exist, there must be an immediate right to the income or enjoyment of the property in the trust (as opposed to the possibility of receiving it at the discretion of the trustees).

Interests in possession are generally established in a will, and are a potentially useful way of providing a safe income for dependents of the settlor, whilst ensuring that some assets are saved in order to be passed on at a later date.

Typically, the settlor will leave assets to be held in trust for their widow(er) to enjoy the income or use of property for the rest of their lifetime, and on their death the assets in the trust will be distributed between the children or grandchildren.

Sometimes **lifetime settlements** are created to provide an interest in possession. An example is putting a property in trust to give the spouse a right to live there for the rest of their life but effectively gifting the property down the generations on their death. However, new legislation enacted in 2006 changed the tax treatment of these trusts, and new interest in possession trusts are now treated in much the same way as discretionary trusts, for IHT purposes. As such, whilst an interest in possession trust may well still be a viable option, some settlors will wish to investigate other possibilities, particularly discretionary trusts (Section 2.5.4), which provide greater flexibility.

## 2.5.3 Power of Appointment (or Flexible) Trusts

Trusts can be fixed interest trusts in as much as once they are set up, the beneficial interests cannot normally be altered. However, it is also possible to set up a trust where the trustees are given a **power of appointment** to appoint or vary beneficiaries or vary the terms of the trust.

The class of potential beneficiaries can be drafted very widely, giving the trustees maximum flexibility. This can cater for any changing family or personal circumstances like marriage breakdowns or bankruptcy. There will be a default beneficiary who has a right to the income (ie, an interest in possession) and possibly capital if the trustees do not make an appointment to any of the other beneficiaries.

These types of trust are commonly used for **life assurance policies** written in trust. This gives the settlor power to change beneficial interest and appoint new trustees during their lifetime.

There are, of course, other advantages in setting up a life policy under a trust. These are:

- The proceeds, subject to certain conditions, are paid outside of the deceased's estate and therefore avoid any potential IHT charge.
- The trust funds can be paid to the trustees without the need for grant of representation (outside probate). This means that the proceeds can be paid by the insurance company within a matter of days after production of the death certificate.

### 2.5.4 Discretionary Trust

Discretionary trusts, along with bare trusts, have become the family trust of choice. In a discretionary trust, no beneficiary has a right to the income. The trustees have the power to accumulate, and distributions will be entirely at their discretion.

The trustees have discretion in two ways:

- They can select which beneficiary or beneficiaries from a **class** of beneficiaries receive payments of either income or capital.
- They can decide the amount of trust income or capital each beneficiary receives.

An example would be *'on trust for such of my children or grandchildren as the trustees shall, from time to time, appoint'*.

The surviving spouse can be included as one of the beneficiaries of the trust. Before the ability to transfer IHT nil-rate bands, this was a popular way of using the nil-rate band on the first death rather than simply transferring all the assets to the spouse absolutely. Although that benefit is now not so attractive, there are still many circumstances when a discretionary trust is desirable.

For example, a discretionary trust could be appropriate if the value of the assets placed in trust is likely to grow at a faster rate than the nil-rate band. It may also be useful to take advantage of current legislation regarding business property relief or agricultural property relief.

However, the main advantage of discretionary trusts is their flexibility. Again, this can cater for changes in circumstances such as the possible future divorce of a child, remarriage of the surviving spouse, or the threat of bankruptcy to any beneficiary. Discretionary trusts are also useful to guard against spendthrift beneficiaries, who will not be able to have access to the capital, and will only benefit from the income if the trustees so decide. Placing funds in a discretionary trust can also mean that potential beneficiaries can continue to receive means-tested benefits, which would otherwise cease. For example, this type of trust could prove very useful for providing for beneficiaries who have learning difficulties.

The settlor can guide the trustees, normally by leaving a **letter of wishes** with the will. Although not binding, this could be a useful steer for the trustees in exercising their discretion during the lifetime of the trust.

### 2.5.5 Accumulation and Maintenance Trust

These were a special type of discretionary trust, which were popular due to their beneficial inheritance tax treatment.

One or more of the beneficiaries had to be legally entitled to the trust capital on a specified age not exceeding 25, and until then the trustees could accumulate income or apply it for the beneficiary's maintenance, education or benefit.

However, following the Finance Act 2006, no new accumulation and maintenance trusts can be set up and any existing trusts had to change to another type of trust in order to avoid the more onerous IHT regime.

## 2.5.6 Charitable Trust

A charitable trust is a type of purpose trust in that it promotes a purpose and does not primarily benefit specific individuals.

Whilst there is no legal definition of a charitable trust, it must be of a charitable nature, for the public benefit and wholly and exclusively charitable. For tax purposes, HMRC states that the definition of a **charitable trust** is a trust established for charitable purposes only.

In *IRC v Pemsel (1891)*, Lord Macnaghten stated that in order to be charitable, a trust must be for one of the following purposes:

- The relief of poverty.
- The advancement of education.
- The advancement of religion.
- Other purposes beneficial to the community.

The Charities Act 2006 replaced the above four categories and introduced 13 new purposes.

1. The prevention or relief of poverty.
2. The advancement of education.
3. The advancement of religion.
4. The advancement of health or the saving of lives.
5. The advancement of citizenship or community development.
6. The advancement of the arts, culture, heritage or science.
7. The advancement of amateur sport.
8. The advancement of human rights, conflict resolution or reconciliation or the promotion of religious or racial harmony or equality and diversity.
9. The advancement of environmental protection or improvement.
10. The relief of those in need, by reason of youth, age, ill-health, disability, financial hardship or other disadvantage.
11. The advancement of animal welfare.
12. The promotion of the efficiency of the armed forces of the Crown; or the efficiency of the police, fire and rescue services or ambulance services.
13. Any other purposes charitable in law.

In fact the above list covers the majority of purposes which were previously considered charitable. The final category meant that everything which was previously considered charitable remained so.

Prospective charities must apply to the Charity Commission to claim charitable status.

### The Benefits of Being a Charitable Trust

Generally speaking, charitable trusts are subject to the same rules as private trusts, but they enjoy a number of advantages over private trusts.

As you would expect, charitable trusts and charities enjoy significant tax advantages, and this is the main motivation for bodies seeking charitable status.

- Investment income is exempt from income tax, providing that it is applied for charitable purposes.
- No CGT is payable on disposals by the trust.
- Stamp duty is not payable by charities, if an asset is bought for charitable purposes.
- No CGT is payable on gifts by individuals to charity (this is an exempt disposal).
- No IHT is payable on outright gifts by individuals to a charity.
- Charities benefit from a mandatory 80% business rate relief for the premises that they occupy. The further 20% is discretionary and may be awarded by the local authority to whom the rates are payable.
- Gifts to charitable trusts may qualify for income tax relief under gift aid or a payroll-giving scheme.

## Summary of this Chapter

You should have an understanding and knowledge of the following after reading this chapter:

- Legal concepts relevant to financial advice:
  - contracts and capacity;
  - legal person – individual, personal representative, trustees, companies, limited liability partnerships.
- POAs:
  - when and how used;
  - legal concepts;
  - wills and intestacy.
- Property – joint ownership.
- Insolvency and bankruptcy.
- Trusts and their purposes:
  - purpose and creation;
  - legal requirements;
  - parties to a trust;
  - types of trust.

# End of Chapter Questions

Think of an answer for each question and refer to the appropriate section for confirmation.

1. What does acting as agent mean?
   *Answer reference: Section 1.2*

2. What is the definition of a legal person?
   *Answer reference: Section 1.3*

3. What are the different types of power of attorney?
   *Answer reference: Section 1.4.1*

4. What is joint tenancy?
   *Answer reference: Section 1.5.2*

5. What procedures exist when a company is insolvent?
   *Answer reference: Section 1.6*

6. What are the methods for setting up a trust?
   *Answer reference: Section 2.2*

7. Who are the parties to a trust?
   *Answer reference: Section 2.4*

8. What are the different types of trust?
   *Answer reference: Section 2.5*

9. What is a charitable trust?
   *Answer reference: Section 2.5.6*

# Chapter Four
# Integrity and Ethics in Professional Practice

| | |
|---|---:|
| **Introduction** | **91** |
| 1. **Professional Ethics** | **92** |
| 2. **Codes of Ethics and Codes of Conduct** | **105** |
| 3. **Professional Integrity** | **109** |

**This syllabus area will provide approximately 8 of the 80 examination questions**

# Introduction

Ethics and integrity – what do these words mean to you? You think you know? Well, of course you do! Who doesn't? Everyone knows. It is about being good or behaving well, isn't it?

Well, perhaps it is rather more than that, as you will begin to see.

We are faced with ethical choices on a regular basis but perhaps do not always realise so; and doing the right thing or acting with integrity is often obvious, but not always so.

In which case, why are there so many reported situations in which seemingly rational people are said to have behaved unethically or acted without integrity?

- Is it because they chose to do so?
- Is it because they consider that there are some situations where ethics apply and others where they do not?
- Is it because they did not think that their behaviour was unethical?
- Is it because they simply were unaware that there was an ethical consideration?
- Or maybe it was just that they thought they could get away with it?

Or could it be that, in actual fact, it is a bit more complicated and involves all of these thoughts and actions and some more besides?

Then there is the question of why an understanding of ethics and integrity has become such an issue. If ethics and integrity are as important as people are now saying, then surely they have always been important? The answer to that is a resounding 'yes'. Ethical behaviour has always been important, and it has been the collective failure of those working in the financial services industry in not keeping this in the forefront of their minds and actions; a major contributory factor in the huge loss of trust suffered by the sector, which it is now finding enormously hard to restore.

So, let's start at the beginning by setting out how we are going to consider ethics and integrity in the context of this chapter.

First, it must be stressed that, despite the possible implications in the title of the chapter, ethics should not be seen as a subset of regulation, but as an important topic in its own right. Ethics existed before regulation; regulation did not invent ethics. Calls by the regulator for greater ethical responsibility should make people think about and discuss at all levels a subject which was largely being ignored.

To aid understanding it might be helpful to regard 'ethics' as the overarching principles of correct behaviour and 'integrity' as the practical application of these principles. In practice, the terms tend to be used interchangeably and are really different aspects of the same thing.

In order to understand the role and context of ethics and integrity we shall consider very briefly the views of some of the leading contributors to the development of ethical thought and behaviour in Western civilisation.

This will lead us to the consideration of how society behaves today and how we behave as individuals. This in turn will enable us to reflect on our own behaviour and consider the thought processes that we use to inform our behaviour, both generally and using examples of specific situations, particularly in the context of the financial services industry.

Although some of the examples are shown in the environment of financial services, the thought processes which one should use will apply in similar situations in other industries or walks of life.

# 1. Professional Ethics

## 1.1 Core Ethical Theories, Principles and Values

**Learning Objective**

4.1.1 Understand core ethical theories, principles and values

### 1.1.1 Early Ideas

The Greek philosophers Socrates, Plato and Aristotle are widely held to be the fathers of modern ethical philosophy, with Aristotle (384–322 BC) being the foremost of these.

Aristotle's ethical philosophy as set out in his work *Nicomachean Ethics* is generally described as **virtue ethics** with a central philosophy that requires that individuals actively do good, rather than just being a good person within themselves. This philosophy includes the idea that the act of doing good leads in turn to the final cause (purpose) behind the action itself.

Aristotle has also been linked to the idea of the **natural law**, which suggests that there exists an innate law or coded behaviour, with which everyone is born. Although this was not a central tenet of his philosophy, the work of the 12th-century Christian philosopher Thomas Aquinas led to the idea of natural law becoming fundamentally embedded into Christian thinking.

### 1.1.2 Later Developments

Although a number of philosophers such as Thomas Hobbes (1588–1679), John Locke (1632–1704) and David Hume (1711–76) are well known for their ethical philosophies, particularly with regard to the relationship between individuals and the state, it is the work of the German philosopher Immanuel Kant (1724–1804) that has continued to have the greatest impact on ethical thinking right up to the present day.

The idea most commonly associated with Kant is the **categorical imperative**, which has been translated as:

'*Act only according to that maxim whereby you can, at the same time, will that it should become a universal law.*'

This is sometimes known as the universalisation test, and you may notice that this bears considerable similarity to what is frequently referred to as the **golden rule**:

'*Do unto others as you would have them do unto you.*'

Although frequently spoken of as being a solely Christian tradition, a similar tenet appears in most other forms of belief, and is so widespread that it may be regarded as a societal rather than a religious norm.

Nevertheless, Kant also elaborates on his argument of the categorical imperative by saying that what really counts is one's intent when doing something, not just doing it out of a sense of duty:

'*When moral worth is at issue, what counts is not actions, which one sees, but those inner principles of actions which one does not see.*'

In other words, act because you want to, not because you have to.

Significant 19th-century figures in the development of ethical thinking include Jeremy Bentham (1748–1832) and John Stuart Mill (1806–73), both of whom were advocates of the **utilitarianism** school of ethical thinking. The overriding principle of utilitarianism is that the most ethical decision is the one which will do the greatest good for the greatest number of people, within reason.

It should not be assumed that philosophy has not continued into the 20th and 21st centuries; a number of recent thinkers such as Lawrence Kohlberg (1927–87) have been very influential in the development of moral philosophy and moral education. Kohlberg concentrated on the development of moral thinking in children, exploring areas which were not considered by previous philosophers or psychologists. Kohlberg was a strong advocate of the moral discussion approach, which research demonstrated led to a measurable increase in the development of moral reasoning.

Accordingly, as society has developed, so has moral and ethical thinking, but, until the advent of mass or universal education within the last 100 years, the majority of teaching or leading of the population in these matters, was carried out by religious organisations; this remains the case in some societies today.

Consequently, most developed and many undeveloped societies have similar basic tenets in their morality, and these have formed the roots of the norms of society and have been the foundation for much fundamental legislation.

# 1.2 Differences between Ethical, Unethical and Unprofessional Practice

### Learning Objective

4.1.2 Understand the differences between ethical values, qualities and behaviours in professional practice contrasted with unethical or unprofessional practice

This might be simply rephrased as *'understand the difference between doing the right thing and the wrong thing'* or between *'acting with integrity'* and *'not acting with integrity'*.

One of the observations sometimes made about ethics is that the benefit of ignoring ethical standards and behaviour far outweighs the benefit of adhering to them, both from an individual and also from a corporate perspective. In other words, an action taken simply because it seems in the best interests of the doer makes obvious sense.

However, what this argument ignores is that, whilst such a policy may seem to make sense and be sustainable for a short period, in our society the likely outcome is that there will be at least social and at worst criminal sanctions. Additionally, the fact is that either of these outcomes is likely to overturn whatever economic justification there appeared to be for the unethical behaviour. In other words, any apparent short-term advantage is likely to be a small fraction of the likely long-term damage.

In the context of financial services, an obvious example is the selling of investment products that carry a high level of commission for the salesman. Although there may be benefits to all three parties to the transaction – the product provider (originator), the intermediary (salesman) and the purchaser (customer) – the structure of the process contains a salient feature (high commission) which has the capability to skew the process in a way not anticipated and not to the benefit of the customer.

Let us consider the various factors:

### Example

An originator has designed an acceptable product and needs a means of differentiating it from its competitors. The originator considers that the best means of doing this is to pay an attractive sales commission for each product sold.

The sales force is remunerated on the basis of performance. The more they sell, the more they earn.

The customer who buys a financial product is buying something whose performance is likely to be determined over a period of time.

It can be argued that there is nothing wrong with such a structure, which simply reflects an established method of doing business around the world and applies to almost any large or even not so large items.

But there are fundamental differences in the financial services industry which particularly may affect the relationship between the salesman and the customer.

Integrity and Ethics in Professional Practice

For example, if you buy a car, you can see it, you can try it out and you will discover very quickly whether it performs in the manner advertised and which you expect. You will also be provided, in the case of a new car, with a warranty from the manufacturer. You can thus make your purchase decision with considerable confidence, despite knowing that the reward system in the motor industry means that the salesman will almost certainly receive a commission as a result of your purchase.

Contrast this with an imaginary financial product:

## Example

You, the customer, wish to make financial provision for the future either by buying a product for a lump sum, or via a stream of payments over a period. You see an advertisement for a financial product which seems attractive: it promises a return of 5% per annum, compared with the 2% per annum which your savings will receive in the bank.

You contact the company, which has a well-known name, although you have had no previous dealings with them. A salesman comes to see you and explains the product in general terms, focusing particularly on the return offered by the product. He explains to you the mechanism by which the company improves the return to you, over and above what you would receive from your bank deposit account. You are not financially aware and do not really understand what he is saying.

You are now entering the area where, particularly in the financial services industry, the greatest opportunity arises for the salesman either to display adherence to ethical values and behaviours, or to ignore them.

The ethical salesman will take you through the structure of the product offered in such a manner that you may be reasonably sure that you understand what it is and from whom you are buying the product. He will explain the factors which determine the rate of return that is offered, and tell you whether that is an actual rate, or an anticipated rate, which is dependent upon certain other things happening, over which the product originator may have no control. He will clearly explain any risks associated with the product as compared with a simple bank deposit account. He will also tell you what he is being paid by way of commission if you buy the product.

In other words he will give you all of the facts that you need to make an informed decision as to whether you wish to invest. He will be **open, honest, transparent** and **fair**. In other words, he will act with integrity, having proper regard to ethical principles.

Conversely, an unethical salesman may seek to convince you with phrases such as *'No one else has asked me about that'* or *'Don't worry, I wouldn't sell a product that I didn't have confidence in'* or *'No, I don't understand it either, but we have rocket scientists to design these things'*. Or he may suggest that *'this is a limited opportunity and you need to decide now if you wish to take advantage of it'*.

He will seek to reassure and convince you with bland words that actually convey nothing, and you will be encouraged to make a decision without sufficient facts. Consider, was he being **open, honest, transparent** and **fair**? Fairly obviously not.

Was he displaying ethical values, qualities and behaviours and acting with integrity?

Again, it is fairly obvious that he was not.

The **RDR banned provider-commission-led sales.**

**The FCA has recently published Final Guidance FG13/01: Risks to customers from financial incentives. This contains reference to a number of examples of mis-selling where the FCA has taken action against firms.**

Readers may also be familiar with the disastrous impact upon banks resulting from poorly designed incentive schemes in their payment protection insurance (PPI) sales programmes. These schemes are likely to result in a total bill for the banks in excess of £10 billion for financial redress to customers who were mis-sold PPI. This has caused a considerable loss of trust in the banking industry which, it is generally accepted, will take considerable time to re-established.

## 1.3 The Impact of Applying an Ethical Approach

### Learning Objective

4.1.3 Understand the impact of the following when applying an ethical approach/acting with integrity within an organisational or team environment: self-interest; the role of the agent; the role of the stakeholders; the role of the group or team

Stephen Green, the former group chairman of HSBC, said *'Part of the responsibility of top management is to ensure that the culture of the organisation reinforces the ethical behaviour that is a prerequisite of our industry. The example set by the people at the top will always have a huge influence on how the rest of the organisation behaves'*.

What we are considering here is the role of the ethical culture, how it is disseminated and the impact of it on those involved. This leads to the fundamental question of *'what is meant by an ethical culture?'*

### 1.3.1 Ethical Culture

Culture can be described but not easily defined. Nor can it be imposed in an organisation by just putting in a programme; it must be accepted and acted upon by those who are employed, and recognised by those who come into contact with the business. At its most basic, corporate culture expresses itself in staff behaviour and the way a business is run. Staff are particularly sensitive to management style. For example, if the prevailing culture is one characterised by greed or arrogance, it is soon reflected in the way staff behave. On the other hand, if it is one of trust, integrity and openness, staff generally will feel confident at work and be proud of their organisation. This is likely to be reflected in dealings with others, whether it be fellow members of staff, other businesses or, most importantly, customers.

Culture is also expressed in attitudes. When faced with a business problem, a manager has to balance the legitimate requirements of attaining business objectives and the ethical requirements of honesty and integrity in the way this is achieved. The culture of an organisation will be affected internally and externally, both by the way the issues are handled and how subsequent policy is implemented.

Integrity and Ethics in Professional Practice

For an ethical culture to be successful, it must have regard to all of those people and organisations who are affected by it, and it also must consider the impact it has upon the motivations and behaviours of those same individuals and groups.

For example, we can identify the principal constituents and their financial relationships in the following table. These are all the people, groups and interests with whom a business has a relationship and who thus will be affected by its fundamental ethical values.

| Stakeholder | Financial Relationship |
| --- | --- |
| Shareholder | Dividends and asset value growth |
| Provider of finance (lender) | Interest and principal repayments |
| Employee | Wages, salary, pensions, bonus, other financial benefits |
| Customer | Payments for goods and services (receipts) |
| Supplier | Payments for goods and services (invoices) |
| Community | Taxes and excise duties, licence fees, charitable donations |

If we look at these groups we can identify a network of interests, some of which have the capacity to work against one another, as well as support one another; but if a sound ethical framework exists there should be an obvious community of interest.

Self-interest is an obvious motivation in any action and, taken to extremes, leads to a situation where one of the parties in any engagement will take advantage of another, to the detriment of that second party, and possibly third parties. The salesman in the example in Section 1.2 clearly allowed his self-interest to predominate at the expense of the customer.

An example of where the party affected is less obvious is common in the world of the jobbing builder and related activities.

## Example

A builder (supplier) offers a customer an apparent incentive: the frequently seen 'discount' for cash payment. But what is his primary motivation? Whilst it **may** be to give the customer a good deal and so to win the business for himself, this is being achieved through the likely under-reporting of his income and thus under-collection of legitimate taxes, both income and VAT. This would, of course, constitute a criminal offence by the builder, to which you would have indirectly contributed.

So what would you do? Would you insist that you would make payment only against a proper invoice knowing that you will also have to pay VAT? Or would you be willing to compromise your ethical standards, using the argument that what you are doing *goes on all the time*. Would this be acting with integrity?

Would you do that on a business contract at work? Does your company policy allow it? Almost certainly not. And in the business context there are numerous, other interests to be taken into account when considering who will be affected and in what way.

This starts with the smallest participant – you as an individual – and can be followed through to affect all of the stakeholders in the business.

Your actions will affect your team, which may be defined as any colleagues with whom you work, up to the whole business itself, depending upon its size.

The business may well have shareholders and, as a result of your actions improving the profitability of the business, a dividend may be paid that otherwise would not have been paid. So your action will have impacted them, apparently positively.

Had you asked them whether they supported your activities? However, knowing what was involved (the firm being a party to under-reporting/collection of VAT), is it likely that the shareholders would have agreed?

And what about the impact upon your external stakeholders – your other suppliers and customers who become aware of the standards your firm has adopted? Are they likely to be reassured?

So what may have started out as a well-intentioned but inadequately thought-out action may have consequences which extend far beyond your immediate area, similar in nature to tugging a loose thread on a sweater and subsequently discovering the garment unravelling!

## 1.4 Positive Effects of Ethical Approaches on Corporate Sustainability

### Learning Objective

4.1.4 Understand the evidence relating to the positive effects of ethical approaches on corporate profitability and sustainability when contrasted with the results of unethical or less ethical practices which lack integrity

Regrettably we are only too familiar with examples of unethical behaviour having a terminal impact on business, with the names of Enron, Tyco, Worldcom and Parmalat springing readily to mind. Or, more recently, the disaster of the BP Deepwater Horizon oil rig in the Gulf of Mexico, where an apparent lack of integrity led to calamity, which reached far beyond those immediately and obviously affected.

Another salutary example is the continuing generally low public regard in which the banking industry is held, largely as a result of what seems to be unethical remuneration practices coupled with perceived responsibility for the financial crisis, often described as **rewards for failure**.

Integrity and Ethics in Professional Practice

One reason for the poor regard that the public has for business people and their lack of integrity is that, until quite recently, business leaders rarely discussed business values and ethics in public or even in private. As a result, there existed a reluctance among employees, as well as among many independent non-executive directors, to challenge management strategy, to question decisions of management or raise concerns, especially in difficult economic conditions, for fear of unpopularity or even reprisal.

The reticence of leaders to speak up about standards in commercial life may be due to a disinclination to stick their head above the parapet, or uncertainty about the business case for insisting on high ethical standards in *'the way we do business'*. If a link could be established between always doing business responsibly and consistently good financial performance, then there would be more obvious reason for directors of companies to speak up about, and insist on, high ethical standards in their organisations. This includes policy and strategy decisions in the boardroom, and integrity throughout their organisations and in their relations with all those with whom they do business and other stakeholders.

Research[1] shows more business leaders now understand that the way they do business is an important aspect of fulfilling their financial obligations to their shareholders, as well as other stakeholders. They are responding to accusations of poor behavioural standards in different ways. For instance, more companies are putting in place corporate responsibility and/or ethics policies. The principal feature of these is a code of ethics/conduct/behaviour to guide their staff.

Some economic sectors, eg, defence and chemicals, have drawn up sector-wide standards, of course, but throughout the financial services industry, particularly in banking, ethics is now a main board item. Companies now increasingly accept that an ethics policy is one of the essential ingredients of good corporate governance.

Modern corporate governance procedures include risk assessments. Until recently these tended to be confined to the financial, legal and safety hazards of the organisation. But growing numbers are recognising reputational issues around lack of integrity as a possible source of future problems. Royal Dutch Shell identifies this among its risk factors in its 2008 annual review:

*An erosion of Shell's business reputation would adversely impact our licence to operate, our brand, our ability to secure new resources and our financial performance.*

At the heart of these types of response is board insistence that the organisation will do its business on the basis of agreed and explicit core values. These normally consist of business values (profitability, efficiency) and ethical values (honesty, integrity, fairness). According to the Cadbury Report[2] in 1992, employees at all levels of an organisation are entitled to guidance on how to resolve ethical dilemmas they may encounter in the course of their day-to-day business life. But can the time and effort put into designing and implementing such guidance, including a code of conduct/ethics/practice, be shown to make a difference? In other words, does doing business ethically, pay?

---

1    Webley, S. and Werner, A., 'Employee Views of Ethics at Work', Institute of Business Ethics, 2009.
2    Report of the Committee on the Financial Aspects of Corporate Governance, 1992.

Past studies have provided a positive answer to this question. In 2002–03 the Institute of Business Ethics (IBE) undertook research showing that, for large UK companies, having an ethics policy (a code) operating for at least five years correlated with above-average financial performance, based on four measures of value. The performance of a control cohort of similar companies without an explicit ethics policy – no code – was used for comparison. This research was published by the IBE in April 2003 under the title 'Does Business Ethics Pay?'[3]

The methodology developed for this project was used in a more recent study by researchers at Cranfield University and the IBE using more up-to-date data. They came to a similar conclusion.[4]

So what makes the difference? A pilot study for the Cranfield/IBE report investigated the distinguishing features, if any, of the operations of companies with explicit ethics policies compared with those with a less robust policy. The business case for paying attention to ethics, while a second-order question, can be argued by using some non-financial indicators.

## 1.4.1 Employee Retention

One non-financial indicator is the retention of high-quality staff. This is recognised as important to a profitable and sustainable organisation. A survey by the Industrial Society (now known as the Work Foundation) of 255 UK professionals in 2000 indicates that there is increasing pressure on companies to become employers of choice as a way to recruit and retain best talent.[5] 82% of people surveyed said they would not work for an organisation in whose values they did not believe. Some 59% said that they chose the company they work for because they believe in what it does and what it stands for. Further, 85% of UK workers agree that knowing that the company they work for is engaged in activities that help to improve society would/does increase their loyalty to their company.

The attraction and retention of high-quality staff would be expected to be reflected in higher productivity and ultimately, profitability. This is well explained in 'Putting the Profit Chain to Work'[6] in which the authors describe the links in the service-profit chain. They argue that profit and growth are stimulated by customer loyalty; loyalty is a direct result of customer satisfaction; satisfaction is largely influenced by the value of services provided to customers; value is created by satisfied, loyal and productive employees; and employee satisfaction, in turn, results from high quality support services and policies that enable employees to deliver results to customers.

---

3  Webley, S. and More, E., 'Does Business Ethics Pay? Ethics and Financial Performance', Institute of Business Ethics, 2003.
4  Ugoji, K., Dando, N. and Moir, L., 'Does Business Ethics Pay? Revisited: The Value of Ethics Training', Institute of Business Ethics, 2007.
5  Draper, S., 'Corporate Nirvana: is the Future Socially Responsible?', Industrial Society (renamed Work Foundation), London, 2000.
6  Heskett, James L., Jones, Thomas O., Loveman, Gary W., Sasser, W. Earl, Jr., and Schlesinger, Leonard A., 'Putting the Profit Chain to Work', HBR, July/August 2008.

Integrity and Ethics in Professional Practice

## 1.4.2 Customer Retention

A second non-financial indicator is customer retention; it too is recognised as a significant factor in the long-term viability of a company. A research paper in 2002[7] showed that corporate ethical character makes a difference in the way that customers (and other stakeholders) identify with the company (brand awareness). The author argues that this connection is an emotional one when it comes to stakeholders and is not all about business measurables.

Besides retaining good staff and customers, how providers of finance and insurance rate an organisation is a major factor in determining the cost of each. What ratings agencies have developed, with varying degrees of success, are measures of risk – the lower the risk, the lower the capital cost. One study, using S&P and Barclays Bank data, has indicated that companies with an explicit ethics policy generally have a higher rating than those without one. This in turn generates a significantly lower cost of capital.[8]

What is apparent from these research projects, and others in the US, is that the leadership of consistently well-managed companies accepts that having a corporate responsibility/ethics policy is an important part of their corporate governance agenda. It is also noteworthy that companies with ethics policies and codes are consistently recorded as more admired by their peer group compared with those that are not explicit about ethics.[9] In other words, maintaining a high standard of ethical behaviour is seen by them to be a critical element of a company's culture, reputation and success.

It can, of course, be argued that leaders of businesses that pay more than lip service to maintaining ethical standards do not need any assurance that their approach to the way they do business will also enhance their profitability: they know it to be true. Indeed, having an ethics policy can be said to be one hallmark of a well-managed organisation. But others need convincing.

## 1.5 Creating Awareness, Assessing Dilemmas and Implementing Decisions

### Learning Objective

4.1.5    Apply processes to: create ethical awareness; assess ethical dilemmas; implement ethical decisions

Few of us deliberately set out to act unethically, and many firms and individuals maintain the highest ethical standards, without feeling the need for a plethora of formal policies and procedures documenting conformity with accepted ethical standards.

Nevertheless, it is apparent that it cannot be assumed that ethical awareness will be absorbed through osmosis. Accordingly, if we are to achieve the highest standards of ethical behaviour in our industry, and industry more generally, it is sensible to consider how we can create a sense of ethical awareness.

---

7    Chun, R., 'An Alternative Approach to Appraising Corporate Social Performance: Stakeholder Emotion', Manchester Business School. Submitted to the Academy of Management Conference, Denver, Colorado, 2002.

8    Webley, S. and Hamilton, K., 'How Does Business Ethics Pay?' in Appendix 3 of 'Does Business Ethics Pay? Revisited', 2007, op.cit.

9    Op.cit. Footnote 1.

Very few people set out to act unethically, and yet frequent examples of unethical behaviour can be found in all walks of life. Clearly, therefore, the creation of an environment of ethical awareness is important.

If we accept that ethics is about both thinking and doing the right thing, then we can seek first of all to instil the type of thinking which causes us to reflect upon what we are considering doing, or what we may be asked to do, before we carry it out.

Obviously there are many things that we do as a matter of routine and which are part of our normal day-to-day work. They may be governed by our firms' operations manuals or other forms of laid-down procedure, such as custom and practice, although the latter can be a dangerous precedent upon which to rely.

But the question then arises as to how you might respond if you were asked to amend a documented procedure or established practice. What would you think and what would you do? Does your firm have an environment where such reflection is encouraged, is it one of *'we require all staff to maintain high standards based upon our core beliefs of customer service'*, or alternatively one where no opportunity should be lost to seize a competitive advantage, almost regardless of what this may involve?

There is a widespread perception that business standards are somehow different from and less exacting than those which we apply in our private lives, and this may govern people's behaviour at work. So the first thing to understand is that there is not one set of rules of ethical behaviour to apply when you are at home and a second, rather less demanding, set to apply when you get to work. If something is wrong, it is wrong.

Accepting that to be the case, there may be situations, particularly at work, where we are faced with a decision where it is not immediately obvious whether what we are being asked to do is actually right.

A simple checklist will help to decide; is it: **open, honest, transparent, fair?**

- **Open** – is everyone whom your action or decision involves, **fully aware** of it, or will they be made aware of it?
- **Honest** – does it **comply** with applicable law or regulation?
- **Transparent** – is it **clear** to all parties involved what is happening /will happen?
- **Fair** – is the transaction or decision **fair** to everyone involved in it or affected by it?

A simple and often quoted test is whether you would be happy to have your name appear in the media in connection with the transaction or decision.

Although not central to this chapter, the impact of the UK Bribery Act 2010 on corporate and individual behaviour is relevant in the context of assessing dilemmas. The Act caused a lot of uncertainty about what, for the purposes of the Act, was or was not acceptable, particularly regarding corporate hospitality, where there was a very wide range of what was considered to be acceptable.

An important facet of a defence against a charge of bribery, particularly where the act in question is not an obvious **bribe** (and corporate hospitality may fit within that definition), is that the organisation in question has in place **adequate procedures** to seek to prevent bribery by its employees and agents.

The result of this is that many organisations and individuals have entered into an ongoing and broader dialogue about behaviours within their organisations, leading to the subject of ethics and integrity becoming much more central and thus something in which everyone must be involved. This has led to a much wider application of the test of openness, honesty, transparency and fairness, when considering behaviours and, it may be hoped, a greater application of these both in a conscious and subconscious manner.

## Example

### Background

You are the new Administration Manager of a London-based bank incorporated three years ago, and you have responsibility for all back office matters.

Senior front office staff have been travelling extensively for the bank to promote its business, and a junior member of the administration team looks after all business travel arrangements and flight booking. She has taken over only recently from a more senior administrator who recently left the department to join another firm.

The amount of overseas business travel is running at a high level, incurring significant expense and your managing director (MD) asks you to consider ways of curtailing these costs.

One of your team mentions to you that the bank has accumulated a substantial number of air miles, as it is the bank's policy to accrue air miles generated by business travel in its name, rather than permit staff to collect them personally. No attempt seems to have been made to use these air miles to defray the cost of business trips and there are no policies or rules covering the air miles scheme, leading you to conclude that there exists some general uncertainty about these arrangements.

### The Situation

On investigating the air miles total, which proves to be very substantial, you notice that, while no business flights have ever been booked, surprisingly there appear to be a number of flights booked in the personal names of both the former administrator who has left the bank and her successor who is now responsible for the scheme administration.

Analysis of the records indicates that these flights were for holiday purposes, judging by the destinations, the fact that the air miles were also used for hotel bookings and that on at least one occasion a non-member of staff also travelled. It transpires that the non-member of staff was the former administrator's boyfriend.

You interview your junior administrator, who appears somewhat naïve and who says that her predecessor told her that the former head of administration had said that it was OK to use the air miles in this way. You also contact the former administrator, who confirms what you have already heard, namely that your predecessor had said that it was acceptable for her to use the air miles as a perk. When you express surprise at the fact that her boyfriend also had his travel and accommodation paid for by the bank, she replies that the bank did not pay for anything; she and her boyfriend had paid all of the airport taxes, *'which were a lot of money'*, and they only used the air miles. She repeats that her former boss knew about this and permitted it.

On checking, you find that there is nothing in writing to confirm what you have been told and there is absolutely nothing in the bank's procedures to cover this situation.

Accordingly, you decide to contact your predecessor who has now retired and ask him whether he did in fact give permission for these two administration staff, or indeed anyone else, to use the bank's air miles for private travel and accommodation.

He says that he really cannot remember specific situations and is generally vague about the whole matter, leaving you feeling somewhat uncomfortable about the situation you are now faced with.

To complicate matters further, the team member who first informed you of the bank's air miles account complains to you that it is unfair that only those staff directly responsible for administering the air miles scheme can benefit from it. He considers that everyone in the back office should be able to benefit.

What would you do?

## The Issues

- There are no bank procedures to control the scheme. **How open, honest, transparent or fair is this?**
- Two staff who have been responsible for administering the air miles scheme have personally benefited from it. **How open, honest, transparent or fair is this?**
- It is unclear whether the former head of administration actually gave permission to any of his staff to use the air miles for personal travel. **How open, honest, transparent or fair is this?**
- It is unacceptable that only the staff responsible for administering the scheme benefit personally from the air miles without specific permission being given each time and within the context of formal scheme rules and independent controls. **How open, honest, transparent or fair is this?**
- You have received a complaint from another staff member about the apparent unfairness of the distribution of bank air miles.

Judging current practice against the tests of **openness, honesty, transparency and fairness**, it is easy to see that, at each stage, what is happening fails some or all of the tests. Consequently, it becomes much simpler to take the right action and put in place procedures which meet all of the tests, although they will not tell you whether to make the air miles available to everyone, or no-one!

What is equally clear is that if the participants in this practice had asked themselves the same questions, they should have felt uncomfortable about what they were doing.

# 2. Codes of Ethics and Codes of Conduct

## 2.1 The Relationship between Ethical Principles, the Development of Regulatory Standards and Professional Codes of Conduct

**Learning Objective**

4.2.1 Understand the relationship between ethical principles, the development of regulatory standards and professional codes of conduct

For any industry in which trust is a central feature, the need to have demonstrable standards of practice and the means to enforce them is a key requirement. Hence the proliferation of professional bodies in the fields of health and wealth, areas in which consumers are more sensitive to performance and have higher expectations than in many other fields.

Although the terms **code of ethics** and **code of conduct** are often used synonymously, using the term ethics to describe the nature of a code whose purpose is to establish standards of behaviour does, undoubtedly, convey to those required to conform with it, and those benefiting from it, that it involves commitment to and conformity with standards of personal morality, rather than simply complying with rules and guidance relating to professional dealings.

Such instructions may be contained more appropriately within a document described as a code of conduct or, where it is considered that more specific guidance of standards of professional practice are beneficial, such standards might be set out in an appropriately entitled document, or in **regulatory standards**.

Within financial services we have a structure where detailed and prescriptive regulation is imposed by the PRA and the FCA.

Nevertheless, professional bodies operating in the field of financial services developed codes of conduct for their members, and the chart below indicates the areas of responsibility that these cover.

| Body | Society | Client | Employer | Professional Association | Profession | Colleagues/ Employer | Self | Others |
|---|---|---|---|---|---|---|---|---|
| A | ✓ | ✓ | ✓ | ✓ | ✓ | ✓ | ✓ | ✓ |
| B |  | ✓ | ✓ |  | ✓ | ✓ | ✓ | ✓ |
| C |  | ✓ |  | ✓ | ✓ |  | ✓ | ✓ |
| D | ✓ | ✓ | ✓ | ✓ | ✓ | ✓ | ✓ | ✓ |
| E |  | ✓ | ✓ | ✓ | ✓ | ✓ | ✓ | ✓ |
| F | ✓ | ✓ |  | ✓ | ✓ | ✓ | ✓ |  |
| G | ✓ | ✓ |  | ✓ | ✓ |  | ✓ | ✓ |
| H |  | ✓ | ✓ | ✓ | ✓ |  | ✓ | ✓ |
| I | ✓ | ✓ |  |  | ✓ |  |  | ✓ |

It is apparent from this chart that there are only two areas, 'responsibility to the client' and 'responsibility to the profession', which all the sampled codes of professional bodies have in common. This falls short of the aim of regulatory standards, which by their very nature must apply to everyone.

Consequently, whilst regulatory standards may draw on professional codes of conduct, they will not simply mirror them. However, the overarching connection between all three of these areas is an explicit requirement for the highest standards of personal and professional ethics.

## 2.2 Decisions and Outcomes Relating to Rule-Based Compliance, Ethical Behaviour and Decision-Making

### Learning Objective

4.2.2 Understand how decisions and outcomes for the industry, firms, advisers and consumers may be limited by reliance on rule-based compliance, and how ethical behaviour and decision-making can enhance these outcomes

One of the paradoxical outcomes of the financial crisis is that rule-based compliance has been strengthened as it is judged that reliance upon principles-based decision-making is deemed to have failed.

However, while this may be a natural reaction, the strengthening of regulation, far from being an indication of the failure or weakness of an ethically based approach, should in fact be seen as a clarion call for the strengthening of ethical standards.

In March 2010, Hector Sants, then chief executive of the FSA, expressed the opinion that *'if we really do wish to learn lessons from the past, we need to change not just the regulatory rules and supervisory approach, but also the culture and attitudes of both society as a whole, and the management of major financial firms'*.

This represents a major challenge and one in which you have chosen to become involved. So we should be considering how our ethical behaviour can be used to enhance the rather rigid structures of the legislative framework and produce enhanced outcomes for all stakeholders.

At this point it is worth considering the principal features of what we can describe as the **ethics** versus **compliance** approach:

| Ethics | Compliance |
| --- | --- |
| Prevention | Detection |
| Principles-based | Law/rules-based |
| Values-driven | Fear-driven |
| Implicit | Explicit |
| Spirit of the law | Letter of the law |
| Discretionary | Mandatory |

Once again it is back to the choice of doing things because you **ought** to, because it is the right thing to do (ethics) rather than because you **have** to (regulatory).

### Example

A fairly basic example occurs when driving. As a driver approaches a pedestrian crossing with pedestrians waiting to cross, the driver ought to stop to allow the pedestrians to cross, but the driver does have a choice and may choose not to stop. In other words you **ought** to, but do not **have** to. Your action is governed by the choice that you make.

However, once the pedestrian is on the crossing, the dynamic changes and you no longer have a choice. The Highway Code requires that you **have** to stop, as the pedestrian now has priority. Your action is governed by the rules.

At a considerably higher level, when the US SEC announced its intention to prosecute a major US investment bank for a number of its actions in relation to the sale of securities supported by sub-prime mortgages, initial comment in the financial media suggested that it was not at all clear that the actions taken by the bank in what were highly complex transactions, were actually illegal.

Nevertheless, whether the activities were legal or not, tremendous damage was done, not only to the bank in question, but to the whole industry in terms of significantly reduced share price, professional reputation and public perception, which has still not recovered.

Although the legal situation in the UK is not quite the same, the reputation of the industry is equally poor in the eyes of the general public, the fundamental reason for which may be described as an absence of integrity. This may be illustrated at grass roots level by the continuing high profile of the PII saga, at the shareholder level, by the increasing number and size of shareholder votes over banks' executive remuneration policies and, at the legal level, by continuing parliamentary debates about legislating to cap bankers' bonuses.

## 2.3 Applying Codes to Professional Practice

### Learning Objective

4.2.3 Apply the Chartered Institute for Securities & Investment's Code of Ethics to professional practice

The change in the UK regulatory structure has meant changes to the approach taken by the new regulators (the FCA and the PRA).

These principles are covered in Chapter 5. However, it is worth noting that the key verb in both sets of principles is the word **must**, a command verb, indicating that the subject has no discretion in what decision they make, because the principle determines the correct course of action.

Events since 2007 caused regulators to revise their belief in the adequacy of the approach that combines regulation with principles, since it is felt that this resulted in an overly black and white approach, ie, if an action is not specifically prevented by the regulations or principles then it is acceptable to follow that course of action. Such an approach is popular in a number of countries, but is now felt to fall short of what is required in order to produce properly balanced decisions and policies.

### 2.3.1 The Chartered Institute for Securities & Investment (CISI) Code of Conduct

**Principles**

1. To act honestly and fairly at all times when dealing with clients, customers and counterparties and to be a good steward of their interests, taking into account the nature of the business relationship with each of them, the nature of the service to be provided to them and the individual mandates given by them.
2. To act with integrity in fulfilling the responsibilities of your appointment and to seek to avoid any acts, omissions or business practices which damage the reputation of your organisation or the financial services industry.
3. To observe applicable law, regulations and professional conduct standards when carrying out financial service activities, and to interpret and apply them to the best of your ability according to principles rooted in trust, honesty and integrity.
4. To observe the standards of market integrity, good practice and conduct required or expected of participants in markets when engaging in any form of market dealings.
5. To be alert to and manage fairly and effectively and to the best of your ability, any relevant conflict of interest.

# Integrity and Ethics in Professional Practice

6. To attain and actively manage a level of professional competence appropriate to your responsibilities, to commit to continuing learning to ensure the currency of your knowledge, skills and expertise and to promote the development of others.

7. To decline to act in any matter about which you are not competent unless you have access to such advice and assistance as will enable you to carry out the work in a professional manner.

8. To strive to uphold the highest personal and professional standards.

Accompanying the CISI Code of Conduct is a statement regarding its application, stating that where you are uncertain about what you should do, you are recommended to seek advice.

You will find that, in situations where you are uncertain of the most appropriate course of action, consideration of the action against the code of conduct, together with the basic open, honest, transparent, fair test, will go a long way to making your decision for you. It is suggested that you apply this in all the examples in this workbook.

# 3. Professional Integrity

## 3.1 Key Principles of Professional Integrity

### Learning Objective

4.3 Understand key principles of professional integrity:

4.3.1 Openness, honesty, transparency and fairness

4.3.2 Relationship between personal, corporate and societal values

4.3.3 Commitment to professional ideals and principles extending beyond professional norms

Let us consider this very important area through the example of the following real-life scenario.

## Example

You are the managing director of a major company. It is six weeks before the year end. Two days ago, one of your sales teams made it onto the shortlist for an important and profitable tender from a major existing client. Success will mean that you will meet key annual targets.

Your team has been asked to make a presentation, along with a number of other short-listed competitors, and while sitting in the waiting area they discover, by accident, a presentation pack left behind, they believe, by their key competitor. As they are reading it, the boardroom door opens and they are ushered in to make their presentation. They keep the pack and take it back to their office.

Later that day they are told they have made it to the final two and are asked to return in three days with their final offer. They review the competitor's document regularly in finalising their tender.

At the start of the third day, by chance, you find out what has happened.

What are you going to do?

Option 1   Congratulate the team for being so observant in this competitive environment.

Option 2   Go deaf – you didn't hear what you had been told.

Option 3   Something – you inform the client that you have in error obtained a competitor's presentation and revert to your original offer.

Option 4   Everything – you apologise to the client and your competitor, withdraw from the bid, and take disciplinary action against your team members.

Before making your decision, consider what has happened and then, using the key measures of **openness, honesty, transparency** and **fairness**, decide what you should do.

There is a widely held view that in business all is fair in winning an important contract, providing that what you do is not obviously illegal.

In this case, your competitor has left behind, by mistake, some important confidential information. A member of your team finds it. It is only human nature to take a look and most people would probably skim through it, in the manner that they read a magazine in a doctor's waiting room.

You are then called into your meeting. What do you do at this point?

- Do you hand the pack to the client, saying that another team appears to have forgotten it?
- Do you leave it where you found it?
- Do you put it in your briefcase?

Essentially, you have a choice between taking it or leaving it.

Which action would meet all of the open, honest, transparent and fair tests?

Clearly you should leave the presentation where you found it.

Integrity and Ethics in Professional Practice

But say that in your haste, as an automatic reaction, you have put it in your bag. You get back to the office and you still have it in your bag. What will you do?

- Shred it without looking at it any further.
- Shred it without looking at it any further and tell the owners what you have done.
- Think that, having got the presentation, you might as well read it.
- Tell your boss and give it to him without reading it.
- Share the information with your team, so that you can construct a winning bid.

Which action(s) meet(s) all of the open, honest, transparent and fair tests?

The choices at this stage are whether or not you make use of the information, or how best you resolve the problem that you are now in possession of something that does not belong to you.

Do you believe that it would be right to make use of the information, because this is a competitive business and if you win the bid you will meet your sales target? If so, before taking any action, consider the following:

- How do you think that your competitor would react if they were in your position?
- How do you think that the client would react if they knew how you had constructed a winning bid?
- How would you react if you knew that a competitor was using your confidential information against you?

At a personal level, is this any different from leaving your briefcase containing personal information in an office when you go for a job interview and one of the other applicants then using information that they had gleaned about you, to enhance their own CV?

Would you be happy with that? How might the prospective employer react? Are they likely to congratulate the other candidate on being observant, or might they question their standards of honesty?

The fact is that this scenario should not present those involved with an insuperable dilemma.

- In the first place they should not have removed the presentation.
- Having done so, they should not then have read it.
- Having read it, they should not have taken advantage of the knowledge gained.
- They should not have concealed the fact that they had made use of the information gained.

Overall, therefore, the team's behaviour was not open, honest, transparent, or fair.

So, in the terms of your original choices what might be an appropriate response?

**Option 1** Congratulate the team for being so observant in this competitive environment. *Clearly this is a bad response.*

**Option 2** Go deaf – you didn't hear what you had been told. *You cannot pretend that you are unaware, and from a broader perspective this is almost worse than simply doing the wrong thing, because you know that it is wrong but are not prepared to do anything about it.*

**Option 3** Something – you inform the client that you have in error obtained a competitor's presentation and revert to your original offer. *You have taken positive action in so far as you have told the client what has happened and have not taken action to improve your position. So this is quite a good answer but it does not resolve all of the issues.*

**Option 4** Everything – you apologise to the client and your competitor, withdraw from the bid, and take disciplinary action against your team members. *This is the most appropriate response in the circumstances as not only have you taken decisive action, but you have also taken steps to remind your own staff, as well as those with whom your firm comes into contact, what the standards are to which you operate and what you are prepared to do to ensure that they are maintained. It is also the most difficult course to take and may well be a step beyond what your peers or competitors would do. But it does represent a public declaration of your firm's standards and your intention to maintain them.*

## 3.2 Behaviours that Reflect Professional Integrity

### Learning Objective

4.4 Apply behaviours that reflect professional integrity:

4.4.1 Commitment and capacity to work to accepted professional values

4.4.2 Ability to relate professional values to personally held values

4.4.3 Ability to give a coherent account of beliefs and actions

4.4.4 Strength of purpose and ability to act on the values

We shall continue to use the example of confidential information when considering these elements, but will add some more detail.

### Example

You have recently moved to Greenbank as a manager in the corporate finance department, a prestigious position which impresses all your friends.

On joining the firm, you are sent on an induction course to learn about the structure of the firm and its values, including the seriousness with which it takes adherence to its ethical standards.

Your first assignment is hectic and you are engaged with two other colleagues, one senior and one junior to you, in making a pitch for a valuable piece of business with an established client.

While you are sitting in the client's reception area before giving your presentation, you discover on the floor, half under the chair in which you are sitting, the presentation pack left behind by accident, you assume, by your key competitor, Bluebank.

You mention it to your boss, who tells you to give it to him, and he starts to leaf through it. Suddenly the door to the boardroom opens and you are invited in to give your presentation. Your boss chucks the Bluebank presentation on to the table and you go in to the meeting.

Integrity and Ethics in Professional Practice

The meeting seems to go well and later that day you hear that you have been invited back in two days' time to make your best and final offer.

The next morning the team gathers to prepare for the final bid and you are surprised to see on your boss's desk the Bluebank presentation, which you saw him leave on the table.

He grins and says *'It's a good thing that Mark (your junior) was alert, otherwise we might have left this behind.'*

You express concern at the ethical implications of using proprietary information belonging to a competitor, particularly since this was a topic specifically covered in your induction, which stressed the importance of acting with integrity in all situations.

Your boss brushes aside your concerns, saying that what you were told on the induction programme is just PR and the reality is that it's a dog-eat-dog world. If you want to meet the almost impossible targets that you have been set, you must take advantage of every opportunity that you are given. And this presentation is manna from heaven.

This presents you with an enormous dilemma.

Your induction stressed the importance of the firm's ethical values.

You are now faced with an obvious breach of these values, which support your own personal beliefs that you should conduct yourself in business as you would in your private dealings.

But you are new to the bank and the department (and still on probation). Your boss tells you that no one takes much more than superficial notice of the firm's ethical standards, at least not when money is at stake. It would be career suicide to go against your boss.

Nevertheless, you pluck up courage to argue with the boss, saying that you believe in the importance of all staff adhering to the firm's code, not just because the firm has recently been fined by the regulator, but also because you know from your previous job that the market perception of Greenbank is that they are only too happy to bend rules.

Your boss, looking angry, is just about to respond, when the office door opens and the MD enters. He says that he has just received a phone call from his opposite number at Bluebank, where there is great concern that they have lost a numbered copy of their presentation. They believe that it was left in the client's reception area, but they have been told by the client that it is no longer there. They know that Greenbank followed them and have asked whether we have the presentation.

Your boss replies that you did find it on the floor and he did look at it for about ten seconds and left it on the table when he went into the boardroom. But he will check with the rest of the team to see that it wasn't scooped up in their papers and will come back to him immediately. The managing director thanks him and leaves the office.

Your boss looks at you challengingly and says *'As you were saying?'*

What are you going to do now, and what might be your reasons?

Doing the right thing should be obvious and has just been made a bit easier.

But we might usefully examine the position of each of the three team members.

- **Your boss** appears to be happy to use the proprietary information, as he argued against you and he endorsed Mark's action in bringing the competitor's presentation back to your office. Up to that point, he has shown complete disregard for the firm's ethical stance. However, he now has the opportunity to put that right and advise the MD that the presentation has been found amongst Greenbank's papers and return it to Bluebank.
- **You** have acted properly throughout and sought to protect your personal and professional standards and those of the firm.
- **Mark, the trainee,** has so far not acted with integrity because he took a deliberate action in picking up Bluebank's presentation and bringing it back to your office. His future ethical development may be affected by what happens next, but he seems already to have been tainted by the attitude displayed by your boss.

However, there are two possible further strands for consideration. Suppose that your boss tells the MD that your team does not have the presentation.

1. **Are you prepared to go to the MD and report the true situation?** If so, what might be the cost to you and your career? What is likely to be the impact on your boss and on Mark, the junior team member?
2. **Or are you going to keep quiet?**

The right answer must be that, regardless of the personal consequences, you cannot keep quiet if you know that the presentation has been retained by the team but the MD has been told that you do not have it. Any other course of action represents a complete denial of your own personal standards and those of the firm.

An additional consideration in this scenario is how the MD reacts when told that Greenbank does, in fact, have the Bluebank presentation.

He has a number of options, which are similar to those discussed in the earlier section example.

1. The worst option must be for him to tell Bluebank that you do not have the presentation because, like your boss, he sees a competitive advantage for Greenbank.
2. Or, the MD may choose simply to say to Bluebank that yes, you have found the presentation, which had been scooped up with Greenbank's papers. Greenbank will shred it or immediately send it back, as Bluebank wishes. This is a straightforward response, but may leave the lingering suspicion in Bluebank's mind that Greenbank will have read the presentation and used it to their advantage. So is it enough? That depends on how seriously Greenbank considers the need to appear above suspicion and to act with the highest standards of integrity.
3. The third option is that the MD decides that he wishes Greenbank to be entirely above suspicion and so not only does he return the presentation, but he withdraws Greenbank from the tender, advising both the client and Bluebank of his reasons for so doing. This is the most appropriate course of action in the circumstances, if Greenbank is serious about preserving or enhancing its reputation for integrity, whatever the actual circumstances of Bluebank presentation's having ended up at Greenbank.

As before, the third course of action provides a tangible example of Greenbank's commitment to the highest standards of professional integrity.

**NB, a firm's corporate culture and attitude to ethics is set by the behaviour of the board and the executive. The more senior the member of management who is seen to bend the rules, the more likely it is that junior staff will follow the example set.**

# 3.3 Professional Integrity and Ethics within Financial Services

### Learning Objective

4.5.1 Understand the meaning of professional integrity and ethics within financial services and how this is typically demonstrated in the: operation of financial markets and institutions; personal conduct of finance professionals; duties of fiduciaries and agents in financial relationships

*'Professionals within the securities and investment industry owe important duties to their clients, the market, the industry and society at large. Where these duties are set out in law, or in regulation, the professional must always comply with the requirements in an open and transparent manner.*

*Membership of the Chartered Institute for Securities & Investment requires members to meet the standards set out within the Institute's Principles. These Principles impose an obligation on members to act in a way beyond mere compliance.'*

These words from the introduction to the CISI Code of Conduct, and the Principles themselves, which incorporate the Code of Conduct for financial advisers, set out clearly the expectations upon members of the industry *'to act in a way beyond mere compliance'*. In other words, we must understand the obligation upon us to act with integrity in all aspects of our work and our professional relationships.

Accordingly, it is appropriate at this stage to revisit the Code of Conduct and to remind ourselves of the stakeholders in each of the individual principles.

| | **The Principles** | **Stakeholder** |
|---|---|---|
| 1. | To act honestly and fairly at all times when dealing with clients, customers and counterparties and to be a good steward of their interests, taking into account the nature of the business relationship with each of them, the nature of the service to be provided to them and the individual mandates given by them. | Client |
| 2. | To act with integrity in fulfilling the responsibilities of your appointment and to seek to avoid any acts, omissions or business practices which damage the reputation of your organisation or the financial services industry. | Firm/industry |
| 3. | To observe applicable law, regulations and professional conduct standards when carrying out financial service activities, and to interpret and apply them to the best of your ability according to principles rooted in trust, honesty and integrity. | Regulator |
| 4. | To observe the standards of market integrity, good practice and conduct required or expected of participants in markets when engaging in any form of market dealings. | Market participant |
| 5. | To be alert to and manage fairly and effectively and to the best of your ability any relevant conflict of interest. | Client |
| 6. | To attain and actively manage a level of professional competence appropriate to your responsibilities, to commit to continuing learning to ensure the currency of your knowledge, skills and expertise and to promote the development of others. | Client Colleagues Self |
| 7. | To decline to act in any matter about which you are not competent unless you have access to such advice and assistance as will enable you to carry out the work in a professional manner. | Client Self |
| 8. | To strive to uphold the highest personal and professional standards. | Industry Self |

Perhaps the most obvious avowal of the application of ethical standards at both an individual and corporate level was the Latin motto of the old LSE, *'**dictum meum pactum'** (My word is my bond)*, which in its English form is now the motto of the CISI and its members.

What these short words are intended to say is: you can trust me/us. There is no qualification, there is no small print, there is no attempt to provide wriggle-room. Because the LSE consisted of individuals who were a mixture of employees and partners in their firms, this motto became, by extension, the motto of the stockbroking profession and was regarded as synonymous with the City.

Similar sentiments were expressed recently by a former senior industry practitioner reminding members of the City of the order of priorities of the firm at which he started and of which he became a partner.

- Client first.
- Firm second.
- Self third.

The purpose of these short words, and the much more encompassing words of the codes of conduct, are intended to provide direction to members of the professional bodies and, via the FCA/PRA APER, to other members of the financial services industry, as to what their behavioural requirements are in dealing in all areas and with all stakeholders involved in the activity of financial services.

At the corporate and institutional level this means operating in accordance with the rules of market conduct, dealing fairly (honestly) with other market participants and not seeking to take unfair advantage of either. That does not mean that you cannot be competitive, but that rules and standards of behaviour are required to enable markets to function smoothly, on top of the actual regulations which provide direction for the technical elements of market operation. This is specifically referred to in Principle 4 of the Code, together with support from Principles 2 and 8.

At the individual client relationship level, Principles 1, 5, 6 and 7 remind us of our ethical responsibilities towards our clients, in addition to complying with the regulatory framework and our legal responsibilities. But, as we have been discussing throughout this chapter, if you are guided by ethical principles, compliance with regulation is much easier!

At the conclusion of this chapter, let us consider the words of Guy Jubb, Investment Director and head of Corporate Governance at Standard Life, when speaking at the CISI annual ethics debate in 2009.

*'It's personal; we as individuals are the City. We must take our responsibility for restoring trust and there can be no abdication of responsibility to third parties; we must conduct our affairs as good stewards; we must sort out right from wrong and behave accordingly... members must live out being good stewards in the interests of their clients.'*

## Summary of this Chapter

Consider what you have just read and think how you could apply what you have learnt to:

- a situation at home or in your private life;
- a situation at work;
- a situation reported in the media.

You should now be able to think about what has influenced you to make the choice that you did.

Now consider the situation at work and review your choice against the CISI Code of Conduct. Although you may be complying with FCA/PRA regulation, might you breach any of the CISI Principles?

Now consider the situation reported in the media and review how it stands up against the criteria of **open, honest, transparent, fair**.

If it is lacking in any of these, consider what might have been done to ensure that it met these criteria.

You may find it helpful to undertake this with a colleague or friend so that you can discuss your thoughts.

# End of Chapter Questions

Think of an answer for each question and refer to the appropriate section for confirmation.

1.  What is the distinction between 'integrity' and 'ethics'?
    *Answer reference: Introduction*

2.  How is an ethical culture established most effectively?
    *Answer reference: Section 1.3*

3.  Name a non-financial indicator that ethical approaches to corporate profitability have a positive effect.
    *Answer reference: Section 1.4*

4.  Name two key words describing ethical behaviour.
    *Answer reference: Section 1.5*

5.  What are some of the areas of responsibility that codes of conduct of financial services professional bodies cover?
    *Answer reference: Section 2.1*

6.  List three descriptors of each of ethics versus compliance.
    *Answer reference: Section 2.2*

7.  How many Principles does the CISI Code of Conduct contain?
    *Answer reference: Section 2.3*

8.  What are the key principles of professional integrity?
    *Answer reference: Section 3.1*

9.  What was the purpose of the motto of the London Stock Exchange?
    *Answer reference: Section 3.3*

# Chapter Five
# The Regulatory Infrastructure of the UK Financial Services

| | |
|---|---|
| 1. The Regulatory Infrastructure | 121 |
| 2. The FCA and The PRA Statutory Objectives | 129 |
| 3. The Scope of Authorisation and Regulation of the FCA and the PRA | 135 |
| 4. Relevant European Regulation | 141 |

**This syllabus area will provide approximately 6 of the 80 examination questions**

The Regulatory Infrastructure of the UK Financial Services

In this chapter you will gain an understanding of:

- The structure of financial regulation in the UK.
- Which body is responsible for financial regulation.
- The structure, purpose and statutory objectives of the FCA and the PRA.
- FCA regulation of financial markets and exchanges.
- Relevant European regulation:
    - MiFID, UCITS, the Prospectus Directive and the Capital Requirements Directive (CRD).

# 1. The Regulatory Infrastructure

## Learning Objective

5.1 Understand the wider structure of UK financial regulation including the responsibilities of the main regulating bodies and the relationship between them:

5.1.1 Market regulators: the Financial Conduct Authority (FCA) and the Prudential Regulation Authority (PRA)

5.1.2 Other regulators: the UK Competition Commission; the Information Commissioner; and the Pensions Regulator

5.1.3 The relationships and co-ordination between the following: the Financial Conduct Authority (FCA); the Prudential Regulation Authority (PRA); Her Majesty's Revenue & Customs (HMRC); the Financial Ombudsman Scheme (FOS); the Financial Services Compensation Scheme (FSCS); the Financial Policy Committee (FPC); the Upper Tribunal (Tax and Chancery); the Bank of England (BOE); HM Treasury (HMT)

# 1.1 The Financial Services and Markets Act (FSMA) 2000

The Financial Services and Markets Act (FSMA) 2000 introduced a new structure for the regulation of the financial services industry in the UK, which came into effect from midnight on 30 November 2001. It established a new regulatory regime, replacing a number of **self-regulatory organisations** with a single statutory regulator, the FSA.

## 1.1.1 The New Regulatory Structure in the UK

The government published a consultation document entitled *A New Approach to Financial Regulation: Judgement, Focus and Stability* in July 2010. The paper outlined and consulted on their proposed overhaul of the UK financial regulatory system by disbanding the FSA and establishing a new system of more specialised and focused regulators:

- A macro-prudential regulator, the **Financial Policy Committee (FPC)**, established within the BOE.
- A prudential regulator, the **Prudential Regulation Authority (PRA)**, established as a part of the BOE.
- A conduct of business regulator, the (**Financial Conduct Authority (FCA)**), focusing on wholesale and retail markets and delivering better levels of protection to consumers.

While most respondents welcomed the proposed framework for financial regulation, most also supported the specific emphasis on promoting financial stability and the enhanced focus on macro-prudential as well as micro-prudential regulation.

In February 2011 HM Treasury published a further consultation document entitled *A New Approach to Financial Regulation: Building A Stronger System.* This announced the following:

- The **FPC** – established in the BOE, with responsibility for macro-prudential regulation, or regulation of stability and resilience of the financial system as a whole.
- The **PRA** – established (as an operationally independent part of the BOE) for regulation of deposit takers (ie, banks), insurers and systemically important investment firms.
- The **FCA** – responsible for conduct issues across the entire spectrum of financial services; it would also be responsible for market supervision as well as the prudential supervision of firms not supervised by the PRA.

HM Treasury has overall responsibility for the UK's financial system, the institutional structure of financial regulation and the legislation that governs it, both domestic and international.

To ensure that the new regulatory structure would be in place as at 1 April 2013, the FSA moved to a **twin peaks** model – this meant that banks, building societies, insurers and major investment firms had two groups of supervisors: one focusing on prudential and one focusing on conduct. All other firms (ie, those not dual-regulated) would be solely supervised by the conduct supervisors.

The FCA and the PRA now run their own risk mitigation programmes and firms have two separate sets of mitigating actions to address: Advanced Risk-Responsive Operating frameWork (ARROW) has not been retained by either the FCA or the PRA.

## 1.2 The Prudential Regulation Authority (PRA)

Operating as part of the Bank of England, the PRA is a focused prudential regulator, with responsibility for the prudential supervision of deposit-takers, insurers and major investment firms.

The PRA's role is to contribute to the promotion of the stability of the UK financial system through the micro-prudential regulation of the types of firms set out above. It has an overall objective to promote the safety and soundness of regulated firms, and meets this objective primarily by seeking to minimise any adverse effects of firm failure on the UK financial system and by ensuring that firms carry on their business in a way that avoids adverse effects on the system.

For insurance supervision, the PRA has two complementary objectives – to secure an appropriate degree of protection for policyholders and, as needed, to minimise the adverse impact that the failure of an insurer or the way it carries out its business could have on the stability of the system.

The PRA supervises around 1,000 deposit-takers, some 330 banks, 50 building societies and 600 credit unions, as well as a number of investment banks that have the potential to present significant risk to the stability of the financial system.

## The Regulatory Infrastructure of the UK Financial Services

# 1.3 The Financial Conduct Authority (FCA)

The FCA is a proactive force for enabling the right outcomes for consumers and market participants.

The FCA has a single strategic objective, to ensure that the relevant markets are functioning well. It also has three operational objectives, which are to:

- secure an appropriate degree of protection for consumers;
- protect and enhance the integrity of the financial system;
- promote effective competition in the interests of consumers.

Underlining the operational objectives are the following three broad outcomes:

- Consumers get financial services and products that meet their needs from firms they can trust.
- Firms compete effectively with the interests of their customers and the integrity of the market at the heart of how they run their business.
- Markets and financial systems are sound, stable and resilient with transparent pricing information.

The FCA kept the previous regulator's (the FSA) policy of credible deterrence, pursuing enforcement cases to punish wrongdoing. Its market regulation will continue to promote integrity and carry on the fight against insider dealing, in which the previous regulator secured 20 criminal convictions since 2009.

The FCA's approach to and style of supervision is different to that of the previous regulator (the FSA). The FCA carries out in-depth structured supervision work with those firms with the potential to cause the greatest risks to their objectives. This means fewer supervisors allocated to specific firms – but allows the FCA greater flexibility to carry out more reviews on products and issues across a particular sector or market thematic reviews. This new approach is underpinned by judgement-based supervisions.

The FCA's integrity objective includes within it the *soundness, stability and resilience* of the UK financial system. With regards to resilience, the FCA expects firms to operate high standards in their risk management, having procedures in place to ensure continuity of critical services. Firms are required to comply with standards for resilience and recovery set in this area.

To ensure that the relevant markets work well, the FCA has increased its focus on delivering good market conduct. The FCA's key priorities in delivering good market conduct are:

- a renewed focus on wholesale conduct – in particular inherent conflicts of interest;
- trust in the integrity of markets;
- preventing market abuse.

The National Audit Officer (NAO) is the statutory auditor of the FCA, with the power to carry out value-for-money reviews. HMT can also carry out economy, efficiency and effectiveness reviews.

## 1.4 HM Treasury (HMT)

The FCA is accountable to the HMT through a variety of mechanisms.

1. HMT has the power to appoint or dismiss the FCA's board and chairman.
2. The FCA must carry out an investigation and report to HMT if there has been a significant regulatory failure.
3. HMT has the power to commission reviews and inquiries into aspects of the FCA's operations. Reviews will be conducted by someone whom HMT feels is independent of the FCA, and are restricted to considering the economy, efficiency and effectiveness with which the FCA has used its resources in discharging its functions. Such inquiries may relate to specific, exceptional events occurring within the FCA range of regulatory responsibilities.

## 1.5 The Bank of England (BOE)

At one time, the Bank of England (BOE) was a key regulator of the banking industry in the UK, supervising the commercial banks. However, in 1998, its regulatory role was withdrawn, and these functions were transferred to become a part of the FSA's responsibilities.

At the same time, the BOE was given an important role, under the Bank of England Act 1998, in effecting economic policy, by being given the ability to set interest rate levels through its MPC. A key interest rate, known as **base rate**, is reviewed monthly by the MPC and, if necessary, altered to keep inflation within the range determined by the government. For more details see Chapter 1, Section 1.3.

Following the financial crisis and the government decision to split the FSA up into a prudential and conduct regulator, the PRA is a part of the BOE. It is the prudential regulator for deposit-takers, insurance companies and certain large investment firms.

The Office of Fair Trading (OFT) also has a role in mergers, to review information and where necessary commission further investigation if it feels the merger will lead to a substantial lessening of competition.

## 1.6 The UK Competition Commission (CC)

It is the role of the competition authorities to decide whether a takeover should be blocked. Most takeovers in the UK are subject to the UK merger control regime under the Enterprise Act 2002.

The Competition Commission (CC) is a public body originally established under the Competition Act 1998. It replaced the Monopolies and Mergers Commission. The chair and members of the CC are appointed by the Secretary of State for Business, Innovation and Skills (formerly known as the Secretary of State for Business, Enterprise and Regulatory Reform).

The CC's role is to investigate and report on matters referred to it relating to mergers, monopolies, anti-competitive practices, the regulation of utilities and the performance of public sector bodies. The CC has the final say in respect of cases which are referred to it for further investigation.

The CC's investigation may last up to 24 weeks and, at the end of this time, it determines whether the bid is cleared or prohibited, or whether steps may be taken to maintain competitiveness. Any appeal may be made to the Competition Appeals Tribunal, an independent body.

## 1.7 The Information Commissioner (ICO)

The Information Commissioner (ICO) is the UK's independent authority set up to uphold information rights in the public interest, promoting openness by public bodies and data privacy for individuals. It rules on eligible complaints, gives guidance to individuals and organisations, and takes appropriate action when the law is broken.

The ICO enforces and oversees the Data Protection Act (see Chapter 8, Section 6), the Freedom of Information Act, the Environmental Information Regulations, and the Privacy and Electronic Communications Regulations.

## 1.8 The Pensions Regulator

The Pensions Regulator is the UK regulator of work-based pension schemes. It works with trustees, employers, pension specialists and business advisers to protect members' benefits and encourage high standards in the running of pension schemes.

## 1.9 The Financial Ombudsman Service (FOS)

Among other matters, the FSMA required that the regulator (FSA) to establish an **ombudsman scheme** for dealing with disputes between consumers and financial services firms. The FSA established the FOS, which is designed to provide quick resolution of disputes between **eligible complainants** and their product/service providers with a minimum of formality, by an independent person.

The chairman and other directors of the FOS are appointed by the FCA, but the terms of their appointment must be such as to secure their independence from the FCA. The FCA requires an annual report on the scheme.

The FCA dictates who is eligible to use the FOS (the eligible complainant) and also requires financial services firms to set up and maintain complaints-handling and -resolution procedures themselves. The hope is that most disputes will be resolved between the firm and the customer, and that the customer will not need to resort to the FOS. If an eligible complaint does reach the FOS, the FOS is able to make judgements to compensate customers that are binding on the firm. Consumers do not have to accept any decision the FOS makes and they can choose to go to court instead. But if they do accept the FOS decision, it is binding on them (and the firm).

The FOS comprises three jurisdictions. These are compulsory, voluntary and consumer credit jurisdictions.

Its **compulsory jurisdiction** extends to complaints from eligible complainants against FCA-authorised firms in relation to their regulated activities (and any ancillary activities) which the firm is unable to resolve to the satisfaction of the complainant within the timescales.

Its **voluntary jurisdiction (VJ)** covers complaints which are not within the compulsory jurisdiction. Currently, the following can be considered under VJ:

- lending on mortgages by non-FCA-authorised firms;
- other specified lending activity;

- providing payments on plastic cards (excluding store cards);
- accepting deposits and providing general insurance when the service was provided from elsewhere within the European Economic Area (EEA) but was directed at the UK customer.

Its **consumer credit jurisdiction** covers certain complaints against licences (and businesses which were licensees at the time of the events complained about).

It is important to appreciate that firms can choose to utilise the VJ, but must accept the compulsory jurisdiction, if it applies, for eligible complainants. Those firms choosing to use the VJ are known as **VJ participants**. The FCA stated that certain complaints which do not fall within the compulsory jurisdiction can be considered under the VJ.

The FOS can require a firm to pay over money as a result of a complaint. This monetary award against the firm will be an amount which the FOS considers to be fair compensation; however, the sum cannot exceed £150,000. If the decision is taken to make a monetary award, the FOS can award compensation for financial loss, pain and suffering, damage to reputation and distress or inconvenience. If the FOS finds in a complainant's favour, it can also award an amount that covers some, or all, of the costs which were reasonably incurred by the complainant in respect of the complaint.

The Financial Services Act 2012 set out two new ways for FOS to bring issues to the attention of the FCA. It is required to provide the FCA with information about the level and nature of the complaints it receives when it thinks this information would or might help the FCA achieve its objectives. It can also refer matters to the FCA if one or more firms are regularly failing to meet requirements and consumers have suffered, or are likely to suffer, as a result.

## 1.10 The Financial Services Compensation Scheme (FSCS)

Similarly, the FSMA required that the then regulator (the FSA) establish a body, known as the Financial Services Compensation Scheme (FSCS), to provide a safety net for customers of financial services firms which become unable to repay them.

If an authorised financial services firm (for example, a bank) becomes insolvent, or appears likely to cease trading and fall insolvent, the customers of that firm (for example, the people with money deposited at the bank) can make a claim under the FSCS for compensation for any loss. As with the FOS, the FCA appoints the chairman and other board directors, with the terms of their appointment being designed to secure their independence from the FCA. The FSCS is required to make an annual report to the FCA.

The amount of compensation is dependent upon the amount of loss and the type of business to which it relates.

There are limits to the amount of compensation which the FSCS will pay to eligible claimants:

- For protected deposits – 100% of the first £85,000 per person.
- For protected investment business – 100% of the first £50,000 per person.

The FSA amended the FSCS rules to increase the limit for deposits up to £85,000 on 1 January 2011. The limit of £85,000 is for each customer, so joint accounts will be guaranteed up to £170,000. The previous limit was £50,000 per person.

The FCA is considering whether accounts with different banks that are owned by the same parent company should be covered. Currently, customers are covered only for one account under each banking licence, so if they have accounts with banks that are owned by the same parent company then they will only have a total of £85,000 guaranteed.

An example of this confusion is that the Halifax and the Bank of Scotland only have one banking licence, meaning a customer is only covered once up to £85,000, whereas NatWest and the RBS have separate banking licences, meaning cover applies to both savings accounts held separately with NatWest and the RBS up to the full amount of £170,000.

The changes to the compensation payable for **protected investment business** came into effect on 1 January 2010. This means that the compensation limit for investments, and home finance advice is now £50,000 (the previous limit for protected investment business was 100% for the first £30,000 and then 90% of the next £20,000 – so the maximum compensation payable was £48,000). In October 2008, the ECOFIN agreed that all EU member states should increase their deposit guarantee limit to a minimum of €50,000. The FCA's current limit of £50,000 exceeds this level; however, fluctuations in exchange rates could cause the limit to breach the requirements.

Funding of the FSCS is being reviewed as part of the move to the new regulatory structure.

## 1.11 The Upper Tribunal (Tax and Chancery)

The Tax and Chancery Chamber of the Upper Tribunal took over the role of the Financial Services and Markets Tribunal (FSMT) on 6 April 2010.

The current role of the Upper Tribunal is almost identical to that of the FSMT and the procedure has been left relatively unchanged.

The Upper Tribunal is a Superior Court of Record. The Tax and Chancery Chamber has UK-wide jurisdiction in tax cases and references against decisions of the FCA; for charity cases its jurisdiction extends to England and Wales. In references against decisions of the Pensions Regulator it has jurisdiction in England, Wales and Scotland. The chamber also has the power of judicial review in certain instances.

The Upper Tribunal is an agency of the Ministry of Justice.

See Chapter 6, Section 2.3.

### 1.11.1 Financial Services Cases

References can be made by the firm or the individual to whom the FCA or Pensions Regulator notice is directed. The decision notices may cover a wide range of regulatory and disciplinary matters.

In references against decisions of the FCA, decision notices that are referable may cover:

- **Authorisation and permission** – secondary legislation under Section 22 of the FSMA specifies **regulated activities**, the carrying out of which require authorisation by either the FCA or the PRA. People may apply to either the FCA or the PRA to carry on particular regulated activities, to approve a person acquiring or increasing control over an authorised person and to authorise a unit trust scheme. The FCA and/or the PRA gives permission to firms and has the power to vary or revoke it at a later stage. The list of referable decisions is not a complete one.
- **Penalties for market abuse** – the FCA may impose penalties for market abuse. The FCA is required to produce a Code which helps to determine whether particular behaviour amounts to market abuse. Its decisions on market abuse by people (whether authorised or unauthorised) are referable to the Upper Tribunal. In addition, a legal assistance scheme has been established for market abuse cases brought by individuals before the Upper Tribunal. There are separate regulations made by the Lord Chancellor under Section 134(1) of the FSMA setting out details of the scheme.
- **Disciplinary measures** – the FCA may issue public statements about and/or impose penalties on authorised people who have failed to comply with requirements imposed by or under the FSMA.
- **Official listing** – certain decisions by the FCA in its role as competent authority are referable to the Upper Tribunal; for example, refusing to admit securities to the official list and suspending official listing of securities if necessary. The FCA is empowered to censure or impose penalties on issuers who breach listing rules.
- **Other powers** – the FCA and/or the PRA will make decisions on the approval and discipline of employees and people who carry out certain functions on behalf of authorised people. They may prohibit certain people, including professionals, from carrying out particular functions.

## 1.12 The Financial Policy Committee (FPC)

The Financial Policy Committee (FPC) is an official committee of the BOE. It focuses on the macro-economic and financial issues that may threaten the stability of the financial system and economic objectives including growth and employment.

It is charged with identifying, monitoring and taking action to reduce systemic risks with a view to protecting and enhancing the resilience of the UK financial system.

The FPC makes recommendations and gives directions to the PRA on specific actions that should be taken in order to achieve its objectives. The PRA is responsible for implementing FPC recommendations on a **comply** or **explain** basis, and for complying with the FPC's directions in relation to the use of macro-prudential tools, specified by HMT legislation. The PRA reports to the FPC on its delivery of these recommendations and directions.

The PRA provides firm-specific information to the FPC, to assist its macro-prudential supervision. The FPC's assessment of systemic risks influences the PRA's judgements in pursuit of its own judgement.

# 2. The FCA and PRA Statutory Objectives

## Learning Objective

5.2 Financial Conduct Authority (FCA) and Prudential Regulation Authority (PRA) Regulatory Principles, Statutory Objectives, Structure, Powers and Activities

5.2.1 Understand the strategic and operational objectives, structure, powers and activities of the Financial Conduct Authority (FCA)

5.2.2 Understand the strategic and operational objectives, structure, powers and activities of the Prudential Regulation Authority (PRA)

5.2.3 Understand the eight regulatory principles

5.3 Understand the scope of authorisation and regulation of the FCA and the PRA under the FSMA (as amended):

5.3.2 Principles, rules, guidance and rule-making powers: regulation and enforcement relating to financial crime and market abuse; supervision, investigations and enforcement

## 2.1 The FCA and PRA Statutory Objectives, Structure, Powers, and Activities

### 2.1.1 FCA Strategic and Operational Objectives, Statutory Objectives Structure, Powers and Activities

As noted above in Section 1.3 the FCA is a proactive force for enabling the right outcomes for consumers and market participants.

As well as its stated objectives (see Section 1.3), the FCA:

- focuses on the conduct regulation of all firms, covering the range of their dealings with retail customers, through to their activities in wholesale markets. It regulates about 27,000 firms in total, including those prudentially supervised by the PRA;
- is responsible for the prudential supervision of all firms not prudentially supervised by the PRA (approximately 24,500);
- supervises trading infrastructure including the investment exchanges and over-the-counter (OTC) markets and monitor firms' compliance with the market abuse regime;
- has criminal powers to investigate and prosecute insider dealing;
- took on the FSA's responsibilities as the United Kingdom Listing Authority (UKLA); and
- be responsible for overseeing the FOS, the Money Advice Service (MAS) and (jointly with the PRA) the FSCS.

The Financial Services Act 2012 gave the FCA new powers to help it achieve its outcomes. One of the important new powers is the ability to ban financial products that pose unacceptable risks to consumers – including publishing details of misleading financial promotions and letting people know when the FCA is proposing to take disciplinary action against a firm.

ARROW has been replaced by the **Firm Systematic Framework (FSF)**. This is designed to assess a firm's conduct risk and aims to answer the question: *'are the interest of customers and market integrity at the heart of how the firm is run?'*.

The FSF will use a common framework across all sectors, which is targeted to the type of firm. The common features involve:

- **Business model and strategy analysis** – giving a view on how sustainable the business is in respect of conduct, and where the future risks might lie (linking with the business model threshold condition check carried out at authorisation).
- **Assessment of how the firm embeds fair treatment of customers and ensures market integrity.** The assessment has four modules:
    - **governance and culture** – assessing the effectiveness of a firm's process for identifying, managing and reducing conduct risks;
    - **product design** – determining the processes a firm has in relation to determining whether products meet customers' needs;
    - **sales or transaction processes** – assessing firms' systems and controls;
    - **post-sales/services and transaction handling** – determining how effective firms' processes are to ensure customers are treated fairly after the point of sale, service or transaction, and including complaints handling.
- **Deciding what actions are required by the firm** – addressing issues highlighted by the FCA.
- **Communication to the firm** – setting out the assessment and actions required.

## Changes from the Previous Regulator

| ARROW | Firm Systematic Framework |
|---|---|
| Point-in-time assessment | Form of continuous assessment for C1 and C2 firms |
| Primarily issues-based, ie, discovery work on issues considered to be higher risk | Assessment of key drivers of conduct risk, with work targeted by business model and strategy analysis (BMSA) |
| Assessment results in letter and risk mitigation programme that frequently has many actions | Assessment results in letter and risk mitigation programme focused on a few key areas to be addressed |
| Extensive follow-up work by supervisors | Follow-up work done by firm with greater use of Section 166 Powers |

The FCA has increased the focus on the conduct at the top of firms. Firms' senior management set the culture of their organisations so the FCA is looking to ensure that what is decided and agreed by senior management turns out to be good outcomes for consumers. The six retail consumer outcomes that were set out in the TCF initiative remain core to how they expect firms to treat their customers.

The FCA created a new department called the **Policy, Risk and Research Division** to act as the radar of the organisation. It combines research into what is happening in the market and to consumers with better analysis of the type of risks and where they appear.

The Regulatory Infrastructure of the UK Financial Services

In summary the new divisions:

- identify and assess risks to consumers, firms and markets – both emerging and current;
- create a common view of the risks in financial markets to inform the FCA's authorisation, supervision and enforcement decisions;
- use the knowledge of these risks to make evidence-based policy that changes behaviour.

By bringing together the information gathering, analysis, research and policy making into one place – the FCA's intention is that it will be in a position to make timely and effective interventions where it identifies risks.

## 2.1.2 PRA Strategic and Operational Objectives, Structure, Powers and Activities

As noted above in Section 1.2 the PRA is a focused prudential regulator, with responsibility for the prudential supervision of deposit-takers, insurers and major investment firms.

The PRA achieves this by:

- seeking to ensure that any firms that fail do so in a way that avoids significant disruption to the supply of critical financial services;
- emphasising resolution planning to permit **orderly** failure;
- co-operating closely with the FPC and the FCA to ensure macro- and micro-prudential regulation is aligned across the markets; and
- working with the FCA and others to ensure the UK authorities have a strong voice in international – particularly European – policy-making.

The PRA's approach to supervision relies significantly on judgement. The PRA supervises firms to judge whether they are safe and sound, and whether they meet, and are likely to continue to meet, the threshold conditions. It is forward looking and assesses firms not just against current risks, but also against those that could rise in the future.

The PRA focuses on those issues and those firms that pose the greatest risk to the stability of the UK financial system. The frequency and intensity of the supervision experienced by firms has thus increased in line with the risks that they pose. The PRA focuses on material issues when engaging with firms.

As the PRA's approach relies significantly on judgement, it relies on experienced staff and detailed analysis.

The PRA has developed a new risk framework; ARROW will no longer be used. The framework will capture three key elements:

- The potential impact that a firm could have on financial stability in the UK, both by the way it carries on its business and in the event of failure.
- How the external context in which a firm operates and the business risks it faces (together, its risk context) might affect the viability of the firm.

- Mitigating factors including: a firm's management and governance and its risk management and controls (operational mitigation); its financial strength, specifically capital and liquidity (financial mitigation) and its resolvability (structural mitigation).

### Enforcement Powers

The PRA's preference is to use its powers to secure ex ante remedial action, given its approach of intervening early to address emerging risks. However, the PRA has the authority to impose financial penalties and publish censures for cases where sanctions are inappropriate. It also uses its powers where directions or restrictions imposed by the PRA are ignored by the firm.

*[handwritten annotation: Forecast, not actual results.]*

The PRA's intention in deploying disciplinary powers include: reinforcing the PRA's objective and priorities; changing and promoting high standards of regulatory behaviour; the need to send a clear signal to a firm (and to the regulated community) about the circumstances in which the PRA considers a firm's behaviour to be unacceptable; and deterring future misconduct.

### Structure

The PRA's approach is advanced primarily by its front-line supervisors. Their judgements are grounded in analysis, supervisory experience and a strong understanding of the sectors they supervise, gained through direct exposure with the senior management of firms. The supervisors are supported by risk specialists.

The structure of the PRA is:

The CEO is supported by three business areas (banking; insurance and policy):

- **Banking**:
    - domestic UK banks;
    - international UK banks;
    - investment banks and overseas banks;
    - risk specialists.

- **Insurance**:
    - general insurance;
    - life insurance.

- **Policy**:
    - banking policy;
    - insurance policy.

## 2.1.3 Rules, Guidance and Rule-Making Powers, Regulation and Enforcement relating to Financial Crime and Market Abuse; Supervision, Investigations and Enforcement

The FCA is primarily responsible for undertaking investigations and enforcement action in relation to financial crime. It will take forward the good work that the previous regulator (the FSA) started since the financial crisis.

The Regulatory Infrastructure of the UK Financial Services

New powers provided by the Financial Services Act 2012 are that it can publicly announce that it has begun disciplinary action against a firm or an individual. The FCA is able to publish details of a **warning notice** proposing disciplinary action, to signal the start of formal enforcement proceedings. However, the FCA has to consult the recipient of the warning notice before publishing.

The FCA stated (*Journey to the FCA*, published October 2012) that it will build on the progress already made by the then regulator (the FSA) and that it is committed to bringing more enforcement cases and pressing for tougher penalties for infringements of rules; pursuing more cases against individuals and holding members of senior management accountable for their actions; pursuing criminal prosecutions, including insider dealing and market manipulation in appropriate cases; and continuing to prioritise getting compensation for consumers.

Refer to Section 2 of Chapter 6 for further and more in-depth details about the FCA's approach to enforcement – including the disciplinary and enforcement powers available to the FCA and how they are used.

## 2.2 The Eight Regulatory Principles

The following principles are laid out in the Financial Services Act 2012 and apply to both the PRA and the FCA:

a. both regulators need to use their resources in the most efficient and economic way;
b. the principle that a burden or restriction which is imposed on a person, or on the carrying on of an activity, should be proportionate to the benefits, considered in general terms, which are expected to result from the imposition of that burden or restriction;
c. the desirability of sustainable growth in the economy of the UK in the medium- and long-term;
d. consumers should take responsibility for their decisions;
e. the responsibilities of the senior management of persons subject to the requirements imposed by or under this Act, including those affecting consumers, in relation to compliance with those requirements;
f. the desirability, where appropriate, of each regulator exercising its functions in a way that recognises differences in the nature of, and objectives of, businesses carried on by different persons subject to requirements imposed by or under this Act;
g. the desirability, in appropriate cases, of each regulator publishing information relating to persons on whom requirements are imposed by or under this Act, or requiring such persons to publish information, as a means of contributing to the advancement by each regulator of its objectives;
h. the principle that the regulators should exercise their functions as transparently as possible.

## 2.3 The FCA's Principles for Businesses

The FCA Handbook includes 11 key Principles for Businesses, which authorised firms must observe. The principles apply with respect to the carrying on of regulated activities, activities that constitute dealing in investments as principal, ancillary activities in relation to designated investment business, home finance activity, insurance mediation activity and the accepting of deposits, as well as the communication and approval of financial promotions.

If a firm breaches any of the principles that apply to it, it will be liable to disciplinary sanctions. However, the onus is on the FCA to show that the firm has been at fault.

The FCA is also pursuing **Treating Customers Fairly (TCF)** to encourage firms to adopt a more ethical **frame of mind** within the industry, leading to more ethical behaviour at every stage of a firm's relationship with its customers.

The 11 Principles for Businesses are:

1. **Integrity** – a firm must conduct its business with integrity.
2. **Skill, care and diligence** – a firm must conduct its business with due skill, care and diligence.
3. **Management and control** – a firm must take reasonable care to organise and control its affairs responsibly and effectively, with adequate risk-management systems.
4. **Financial prudence** – a firm must maintain adequate financial resources.
5. **Market conduct** – a firm must observe proper standards of market conduct.
6. **Customers' interests** – a firm must pay due regard to the interests of its customers and treat them fairly. (It is worth noting that the FCA defines the term **customers** differently from **clients**, the term **client** covering a variety of parties doing business with the firm, including those counterparties which are market professionals. The term **customer** applies, very broadly, to those **clients** who are not market professionals and who may, therefore, need protection.)
7. **Communication with clients** – a firm must pay due regard to the information needs of its clients and communicate information to them in a way which is clear, fair and not misleading.
8. **Conflicts of interest** – a firm must manage conflicts of interest fairly, both between itself and its customers, and between customers and other clients.
9. **Customers: relationships of trust** – a firm must take reasonable care to ensure the suitability of its advice and discretionary decisions for any customer who is entitled to rely upon its judgement.
10. **Clients' assets** – a firm must arrange adequate protection for clients' assets when it is responsible for them.
11. **Relations with regulators** – a firm must deal with its regulators in an open and co-operative way and must disclose to the FCA appropriately anything relating to the firm of which the FCA would reasonably expect notice.

## 2.3.1 Fair Treatment

It should be apparent from a reading of the above that a general theme of overriding **fair play** runs through the principles; this is coupled with a recognition that there is often an information imbalance between the firm and its customers (since the firm is usually more expert in its products and services than its customers).

Refer to Chapter 7 for more details on the Principles for Businesses, fair treatment and the FCA's **TCF** initiative.

# 3. The Scope of Authorisation and Regulation of the FCA and the PRA

## 3.1 Regulation of Financial Markets and Exchanges

**Learning Objective**

5.3 Understand the scope of authorisation and regulation of the FCA and the PRA under the FSMA (as amended):

5.3.1 Regulation of UK financial markets and exchanges; recognition of overseas exchanges, investment exchanges and clearing houses; UK listing of financial instruments; authorisation of firms, individuals and collective investment schemes

### 3.1.1 Recognised Investment Exchanges (RIEs) and Recognised Overseas Investment Exchanges (ROIEs)

Since a large proportion of trades in financial instruments are carried out via established exchanges, such as the LSE, the FCA has been given the responsibility of recognising and supervising them (under FSMA).

Any body corporate or unincorporated association may apply to the FCA for an order declaring it to be a **recognised investment exchange (RIE)**. The FCA will seek to establish whether the applicant is **fit and proper** to operate as an exchange, including whether it has sufficient financial resources to properly carry out its activities.

The applicant must be willing and able to share information with the FCA, and to promote and maintain high standards of integrity and fair dealing, including laying down rules for activities on the exchange. It must record, monitor and enforce compliance with these rules.

Once recognised, these exchanges are subject to supervision and oversight by the FCA. Being granted recognised status relieves the organisation of the requirement to be an authorised person to conduct financial services business.

RIEs can be UK- or overseas-based; in the latter case, they are often referred to as **recognised overseas investment exchanges (ROIEs)**.

There are currently seven RIEs based in the UK, offering membership and access to their market to UK firms:

1. **The London Stock Exchange (LSE)** – this is the largest formal market for securities in the UK. It facilitates deals in shares, bonds and some derivatives (for example, those that take the form of covered warrants).
2. **LIFFE Administration & Management** – this is the largest derivatives exchange in the UK, trading a wide range of instruments, including equity futures and options and some commodity products. LIFFE originally stood for the London International Financial Futures and Options Exchange.

3. **ICE Futures Europe** (formerly known as the International Petroleum Exchange (IPE)) – this exchange is owned by a company listed on the New York Stock Exchange (NYSE), called InterContinentalExchange – hence ICE. It deals in futures for energy products, such as crude oil and gas, and also in such new instruments as carbon emission allowances.
4. **The London Metal Exchange (LME)** – this exchange provides trading in a variety of futures and options on base metals and some plastics.
5. **ICAP Securities & Derivatives Exchange (ISDX)** – an equity listings venue for small- and medium-sized enterprises.
6. **BATS Trading Ltd** – a pan-European MTF for equities operating under the brand name of BATS Chi-X Europe. BATS Chi-X Europe was formed through the combination of two MTFs in 2011 (BATS Europe and Chi-X Europe) and is a wholly owned subsidiary of BATS Global Markets Inc., an operator of stock and options markets in the US and Europe. BATS Chi-X Europe supports competition and drives innovation in the European equities markets. It offers trading in more than 1,800 of the most liquid equities across 25 indices and 15 major European markets, as well as ETFs, ETCs and international depositary receipts. BATS Chi-X Europe is a subsidiary of BATS Global Markets Inc., a leading operator of stock and options markets in the US and Europe.
7. **CME Europe Ltd** – a derivatives exchange which received authorisation in March 2014.

**ROIEs**, in contrast, are based outside the UK, but carry on regulated activities within the UK (for example, by offering electronic trading facilities to members in this country) and, to this extent, are regulated and supervised by the FCA. They do not have physical UK operations (except some support representation), so they are necessarily electronic marketplaces. They include the NASDAQ, established in the US, and the **Australian Securities Exchange (ASX)**. At the time of writing there are nine ROIEs.

## 3.1.2 Designated Investment Exchanges (DIEs)

Designated investment exchanges (DIEs) are, like ROIEs, overseas-based, but unlike ROIEs they do not offer membership and access to participants based in the UK. Instead, the designated status indicates that the exchange is regulated and supervised to standards that the FCA believes meet certain criteria, in terms of protection for investors dealing on it. At the time of writing there are 30 DIEs, ranging from the **NYSE** to the **Minneapolis Grain Exchange**.

## 3.1.3 Recognised Clearing Houses (RCHs)

Clearing houses are recognised by and regulated by the Bank of England. Clearing houses facilitate the clearing and, sometimes, also the settlement of trades.

There are currently five recognised clearing houses in the UK:

1. **LCH.Clearnet** – this acts as central counterparty for trades executed on Euronext.LIFFE, the LME and ICE Futures, and for certain trades executed on the LSE. LCH stands for London Clearing House.
2. **Euroclear UK & Ireland (formerly CRESTCo)** – this firm is owned and operated by Euroclear, and offers the facility – via the CREST system – to settle trades in dematerialised form. It is mainly known for UK and Irish equity clearing, and also provides clearing and settlement for a variety of other equities, bonds and funds.

The Regulatory Infrastructure of the UK Financial Services

3. **European Central Counterparty (EuroCCP)** – a wholly owned subsidiary of the Depository Trust & Clearing Corporation (DTCC). It was created to provide clearing and settlement services mainly for Turquoise, a new pan-European trading platform, backed by nine investment banks.
4. **ICE Clear Europe** – a recently formed subsidiary of the ICE Group of companies that operates global electronic marketplaces for trading futures, options and OTC energy and chemical contracts. It acts as a clearing house and central counterparty (CCP) specifically for contracts executed on, or through, ICE Futures. See Section 3.1.1 for more details on ICE Futures.
5. **CME Clearing Europe** – provides OTC clearing for international customers. CME stands for Chicago Mercantile Exchange.

As with an RIE, recognition as an RCH means that the clearing house does not need to become an **authorised person** in order to conduct financial services business in the UK.

## 3.1.4   Multilateral Trading Facilities (MTFs)

In Section 4.1 we will look in more depth at the impact of the Markets in Financial Instruments Directive (MiFID), a European Directive which brought into force a raft of new rules, implemented by changes to the law and to the FCA Handbook on 1 November 2007. For now, it is enough for you to be aware that under MiFID a new activity became regulated – that of operating a multilateral trading facility (MTF).

An MTF is described by the FCA as being any system that *'brings together multiple parties (eg, retail investors or other investment firms) that are interested in buying and selling financial instruments and enables them to do so. These systems can be operated by an investment firm or a market operator. Instruments may include shares, bonds and derivatives. This is done within the MTF operators' system'*. Examples include firms such as Brokertec (ICAP), MarketAxess, Tradeweb and Creditex.

In fact, while operating MTFs was not a regulated activity prior to November 2007, most, if not all, of those that were previously operating within the UK were already caught under the earlier regime of regulated activities; in particular – albeit in a slightly different capacity – those firms operating what were then known as alternative trading systems (ATSs). The regulated activity they carried out was that of **arranging deals in investments** – we will look at this in Chapter 6, Section 2. This activity is carried out by some investment firms/banks and it includes operating an organised marketplace/trading facility in financial instruments.

## 3.1.5   The UK Listing Authority (UKLA)

The FCA, acting as the competent authority for listing, is referred to as the UKLA, and maintains the Official List.

The FCA is governed by Part 4A of FSMA in terms of what its duties are in relation to acting as the competent authority. Before a company can be listed and allowed on to the Official List, it must meet certain conditions. The UKLA is responsible for determining which companies are eligible to join the Official List, as well as writing and enforcing the Listing Rules that apply to all listed companies.

## Listing Rules

The LSE is a listed company whose object is to run a marketplace in securities. It should be noted that it has no monopoly powers over the running of the marketplace, and other operators may compete against it.

The FCA regulates the LSE and has granted it the status of RIE. The LSE operates two levels of entry into the market, namely the Official List and the Alternative Investment Market (AIM).

As noted above, the UKLA determines which companies are eligible to join the Official List, and writes and enforces the listing rules that apply to these companies. In contrast, the LSE determines which companies are eligible to join the AIM, and writes and enforces the AIM rules that apply to these companies.

The LSE's rules govern trading in the shares of listed and AIM companies by shareholders and intermediaries.

Listing rules comprise general rules for listed companies, including the provisions for listing, overarching listing principles and continuing obligations. The format follows the FCA/PRA Handbook structure, with rules and guidance shown in a single text.

### 3.1.6 Authorisation of Firms

The scope of the FCA's and the PRA's authority is set out in the Financial Services Act 2012.

Some financial services, such as occupational pension schemes, are not regulated by either the FCA and/or the PRA. In addition, some businesses that may appear to be offering financial services, such as buy-to-let property clubs or compensation claim handlers, fall outside its scope.

Only Parliament currently has the authority to add to either the FCA's or the PRA's remit.

The FSMA is concerned with the regulation of financial services and markets in the UK. Under Section 19 of the FSMA, any person who carries on a regulated activity in the UK must be either authorised by the FCA/PRA or exempt (eg, an appointed representative or some other exemption). Breach of Section 19 may be a criminal offence and punishable on indictment by a maximum term of two years' imprisonment and/or a fine.

Firms need to establish whether their proposed business requires them to apply for authorisation to carry on regulated activities. For most smaller firms, this will typically include intermediaries selling investments and/or home finance activities and/or general insurance.

For each regulated activity, firms must also identify with which investment type their activities will be concerned.

The activities and specified investments are detailed in the FSMA 2000 (Regulated Activities, Order (RAO) 2001, which is secondary legislation under FSMA. This is explained in greater detail in Chapter 7.

# 3.1.7 Collective Investment Schemes (CISs)

The FCA not only authorises investment firms undertaking activities as contained in the RAO, it also approves and regulates collective investment schemes (CISs).

## Unit Trusts

Applications for authorisation of a UK unit trust need to be made by the **manager** and **trustee**, who need to:

a. be authorised persons under the Financial Services Act 2012 with a Part 4A permission to act as manager and trustee respectively;

b. be independent of each other;

c. submit a joint application giving details of themselves and the scheme;

d. provide:
   i. a copy of the trust deed;
   ii. a copy of the prospectus and simplified prospectus;
   iii. a solicitor's certificate stating that the trust deed complies with the rules made under Section 247 of the Act (trust scheme rules); and
   iv. a business plan.

The name of the scheme must not be undesirable or misleading and its purpose must be reasonably capable of being successfully carried into effect. The FCA's Collective Investment Schemes sourcebook COLL 6.9 provides guidance on what the FCA considers undesirable or misleading names. Application forms are available free of charge from the FCA's website. An application fee is payable.

Under Section 244 of the Act (Determination of Applications), the FCA has up to six months in which to consider a completed application following its receipt, and must inform the manager and trustee of its decision within that timescale. In practice, the FCA aims to process a completed application relating to an UCITS scheme within six weeks.

If the FCA is satisfied with the application, an authorisation order is issued for the scheme.

If the FCA proposes to refuse an application, it must give a warning notice, which will contain the reasons for the refusal. If, having given the warning notice, it decides to refuse the application, a decision notice will be sent and the applicant may refer the matter to the Tax and Chancery Chamber of the Upper Tribunal.

## Open-Ended Investment Companies (OEICs)

The FCA requires an application for authorisation to be made by the **authorised corporate director (ACD)** and **depositary**, who must:

a. be authorised persons under the Act with the appropriate Part 4A permission;

b. be independent of each other;

c. submit a joint application giving details of themselves, and of any other person proposed as a director of the investment company with variable capital (ICVC);

d. provide:
   i. a copy of the proposed ICVC's instrument of incorporation;

ii. a copy of the prospectus and simplified prospectus;
iii. a solicitor's certificate to the effect that the instrument of incorporation complies with Schedule 2 to the OEIC Regulations and with COLL; and
iv. a business plan.

The name of the ICVC must not be undesirable or misleading and must not be the same as that of an existing company. Regulation 19 includes a list of words and expressions that are prohibited from inclusion within the name of an ICVC.

As with unit trusts, the FCA has up to six months to determine a completed application, but aims to process an application within six weeks for UCITS schemes. If the FCA is satisfied with the application, an authorisation order is issued. The ICVC becomes incorporated when the authorisation order is issued.

## 3.2 Financial Capability

### Learning Objective

5.3 Understand the scope of authorisation and regulation of the FCA and the PRA under FSMA 2000 (as amended):

5.3.3 National strategy for financial capability and consumer support

The FSA passed responsibility for financial capability issues to the Money Advice Service (MAS). In partnership with the government, the financial services industry, employers' organisations, consumer organisations and the not-for-profit sector, the MAS is working to improve the financial capability of people in the UK.

Financial capability means:

- being able to manage money;
- keeping track of finances;
- planning ahead;
- making informed decisions about financial products; and
- staying up-to-date about financial matters.

The MAS leads this strategy. It brings together interested parties from industry, consumer bodies, voluntary organisations, government and the media – all aiming to find ways to improve the nation's knowledge and understanding of personal finance.

One of the original four objectives that Parliament set the then regulator (the FSA) was to promote public understanding of the financial system, and one of its strategic aims was to ensure that customers achieve a fair deal. As part of its work to deliver against these, in autumn 2003, it brought together a partnership of key people and organisations in government, the financial services industry, employers, trades unions, and the educational and voluntary sectors. Together they have established a road map for delivering a step change in the financial capability of the UK population. The responsibility has now been handed over in this area to the MAS.

The Regulatory Infrastructure of the UK Financial Services

**Why is the MAS doing it?**

People are, more than ever before, being asked to take responsibility for managing their finances. They can find this daunting and confusing, particularly if they are struggling to manage debt or meet other commitments.

The number and complexity of choices to be made has increased dramatically over the last 25 years.

Meanwhile, the comforting arm of the state or employers is being steadily withdrawn. Individuals are being required to take on more responsibility for their financial decisions. Yet many are not equipped with the skills or knowledge to do so, and some groups are particularly vulnerable.

# 4. Relevant European Regulation

## Learning Objective

5.5.1   Understand the relevant European Union (EU) directives and regulations and their impact on the UK financial services industry in respect of: MiFID – passporting within the European Economic Area (EEA) and home versus host state regulation; UCITS – selling collective investment schemes cross border; Prospective Directive – selling securities cross border; Capital Requirements Directive – firms undertaking investment business; AIFMD – regulation of AIFMD and the promotion of AIF within the EU; EMIR – requirements placed on EEA established counterparties

As a member of the EU, the UK plays a part in the attempt to create a single market across Europe for financial services. Primarily, this is achieved by the European Parliament issuing directives to the member states, and their implementation into national legislation.

## 4.1   MiFID – Passporting within the EEA

The Investment Services Directive (ISD) was issued in 1993. Broadly, it specified that if a firm had been authorised in one member state to provide investment services, this single authorisation enabled the firm to provide those investment services in other member states without requiring any further authorisation. This principle was, and still is, known as the **passport**.

The state providing authorisation is where the firm originates and is commonly referred to as the **home state**. States outside the home state where the firm offers investment services are known as **host states**.

The ISD was repealed and replaced by another EU directive, MiFID. MiFID provisions came into force in the UK from 1 November 2007. One of the key aims of MiFID was to provide investor protection rules across the EEA. Investor protection is ensured, **inter alia**, via the obligation to obtain the best possible result for the client, information disclosure requirements, client-specific rules on suitability and appropriateness and rules on inducements. As a general principle, MiFID places significant importance on the fiduciary duties of firms.

141

That is why MiFID established a general obligation for firms to act in the client's best interests. MiFID has been designed to support two key policy goals of the EU. These are:

- extending the scope of the passport to include a wider range of services; and
- removing a major hurdle to cross-border business by the application of home state rules.

Previously, under the ISD, firms were only able to passport a limited range of investment services into other host states. MiFID widens the range of passportable activities – for example, it now includes:

- investment advice (which under ISD was only permitted if it was an **ancillary service** to some other core service being provided – for example, dealing in investments); *Not the main business activity*
- some underwriting activities;
- operating an MTF (see Section 3.1.4);
- investment activities relating to commodity derivatives, credit derivatives and CFDs, since MiFID has extended the scope of the passport to cover these instruments for the first time;
- investment research, if it is an ancillary service to some other core service.

## 4.1.1 Activities that can be Passported under MiFID

The following activities can be passported:

| MiFID activity | Broadly equivalent to UK-regulated activity |
|---|---|
| Receipt and transmission of orders in relation to one or more financial instruments | Arranging deals in investments |
| Execution of orders on behalf of clients | Dealing as agent |
| Dealing on own account | Dealing as principal |
| Portfolio management | Managing investments |
| Investment advice | Advising on investments |
| Underwriting of financial instruments and/or placing of financial instruments on a firm commitment basis | Dealing as principal<br>Dealing as agent |
| Placing of financial instruments without a firm commitment basis | Dealing as agent<br>Arranging deals in investments |
| Operation of MTFs | Operating an MTF (formerly known as an ATS) |

## 4.1.2 Ancillary Activities

The services in the following table cannot be passported in their own right – they can only be passported if they are being provided in conjunction with a core investment service from the previous table.

| MiFID ancillary activity | UK-regulated activity |
| --- | --- |
| Safekeeping and administration of financial instruments for the account of clients, including custodianship. Also related services such as the management of cash and collateral | Safeguarding and administering investments<br>Sending dematerialised instructions<br>Agreeing to carry on regulated activities |
| Lending to investors to allow them to effect a transaction in one or more financial instruments when the lender is involved in the transaction | N/A |
| Advice to undertakings on capital structure, industrial strategy and related matters; also, advice/services relating to mergers and the purchase of undertakings | Dealing as principal<br>Dealing as agent<br>Arranging deals in investments<br>Advising on investments<br>Agreeing to carry on regulated activities |
| Foreign exchange services (but only if these are connected with the provision of investment services) | Dealing as principal<br>Dealing as agent<br>Arranging deals in investments<br>Advising on investments<br>Agreeing to carry on regulated activities |
| Investment research and financial analysis, or other forms of general recommendation in relation to transactions in financial instruments | Advising on investments<br>Agreeing to carry on regulated activities |
| Services in relation to underwriting | Arranging deals in investments<br>Advising on investments<br>Agreeing to carry on regulated activities |
| Investment services and activities, and ancillary services, related to the underlying assets of certain derivatives when these are connected to the provision of investment or ancillary services | Dealing as principal<br>Dealing as agent<br>Arranging deals in investments<br>Operating an MTF<br>Managing investments<br>Advising on investments<br>Agreeing to carry on regulated activities |

### 4.1.3 Financial Instruments Covered by MiFID

MiFID applies only to activities in relation to a specified list of financial instruments. These are:

- transferable securities;
- money market instruments;
- units in collective investment undertakings;
- derivatives relating to securities, currencies, interest rates or yields, or other derivatives which may be settled physically or in cash;
- commodity derivatives that are traded on a regulated market and/or an MTF even if they are physically settled;
- OTC commodity derivatives with a cash-settled option other than on default or other termination event;
- other OTC commodity derivatives which are physically settled, which are not for commercial purposes, and which are similar to other derivatives in certain criteria;
- credit derivatives;
- financial contracts for differences; and
- derivatives relating to climatic variables, freight rates, emission allowances or inflation rates or other statistics and certain other derivatives.

Financial instruments not covered by MiFID include:

- bank accounts;
- FX (unless it relates to the provision of an investment activity or service, for example, buying/selling an option on FX).

## 4.2 MiFID – Home versus Host State Regulation

Not all firms authorised by the FCA/PRA are directly subject to the requirements of MiFID: whether they are or not depends on the nature of their activities. Very broadly, all those firms that were subject to the ISD formed the core of the MiFID population – but as we saw in Section 4.1, MiFID broadens the scope of activities caught within its scope, so many new firms which were not previously ISD firms became MiFID firms on 1 November 2007.

Broadly, the range of UK firms which are classified as MiFID firms is as follows:

- investment banks;
- portfolio managers;
- stockbrokers and broker dealers;
- many futures and options firms;
- firms operating an MTF;
- venture capital firms that meet certain criteria;
- energy market participants, oil market participants and commodity firms if they meet certain criteria;
- corporate finance firms if they meet certain criteria;
- certain advisers;
- credit institutions which carry on MiFID business; and
- exchanges, UCITS investment firms and some professional firms.

Non-MiFID firms are sometimes referred to as **out-of-scope** firms, or as carrying an **out-of-scope business**. They include insurance undertakings, employee schemes, people administering their own assets, and any firms which do not provide investment services and/or perform investment activities.

As mentioned in Section 4.1, the concept of passporting under MiFID relies on the concept of home state and host state regulators. In essence, the home state is where the firm carrying on activities is established; the host state is the state in which it is providing services as a **guest**.

One of the problems under the ISD was that passporting did not work as smoothly as had been hoped. It was not a simple matter of a firm advising the host state that it was appropriately authorised in its home state, and then starting to do business in the host state. In most cases, under ISD, although only one licence was needed (home state), the host state rules were applied to business passported into that country, creating huge difficulties for firms trying to do cross-border business in several countries, since instead of relying on their own home rules being sufficient, they had to try and comply with the (often quite different) rulebooks of all those different states into which they were selling. Imagine, for example, the complexity of trying to arrange brochures or a website compliant with the rules of all the EU states.

MiFID tackles this hurdle to a **single market** in the following ways:

- It allows firms to carry on cross-border business from their home state, solely on the basis of their home country conduct of business rules.
- It harmonises these home country rules so that they are all sufficiently similar, meaning that an investor is, in theory, just as well protected under the rules of one EU member state as they are under the rules of another. There are common standards of investor protection.
- Host state conduct of business rules apply where a passported MiFID branch of a firm conducts business with host state residents.
- Home state rules apply where the services of the passported MiFID branch in the previous bullet point are provided from the host state to residents in another EEA member state.

For this reason, EU member states have been encouraged to stick to the MiFID terminology as closely as possible.

## 4.3    The European Commission (EC) Review of MiFID

The European Commission (EC) is reviewing MiFID, as was agreed at the time that MiFID was formally adopted and approved by the European Parliament and the Council.

MiFID is a central pillar of European regulation of financial markets. It provides for more competition, economies of scale, a greater variety of participants in the market, and thus better and cheaper services for investors. In turn, this leads to more integrated, more liquid and better-functioning financial markets. Rules for investor protection are also included in MiFID.

However, since MiFID came into force, financial markets have changed substantially. New factors (for example, new types of trading venues) and products have come on to the scene and technological developments, such as high-frequency trading (HFT), have altered the landscape dramatically. All these have revealed shortcomings in MiFID. This is why MiFID is being reviewed by the EC.

The MiFID II proposals contain two separate pieces of European legislation:

- A revised directive, which will be an amendment and restatement of MiFID. This will cover a number of areas, including market structure, the scope of exemptions from financial regulation, organisational and conduct of business requirements for investment firms and trading venues, powers of national authorities, sanctions, and rules for third-country (non-EEA) firms operating through a branch.
- A new regulation (MiFIR) which sets out requirements for trade transparency, the mandatory trading of derivatives on organised venues and the provision of services by third-country firms without a branch. It will also confer a number of new powers on European regulators.

Unlike a directive, a regulation is directly applicable in the law of member states and does not require national implementing legislation.

The key proposals and impacts are:

- **Scope**
    - The scope of MiFID will be extended to more firms, such as certain commodity firms, data providers and third-country firms.
    - Additional instruments will be brought into the scope of MiFID, such as structured deposits and emissions allowances.

- **Electronic trading**
    - Derivatives, which are sufficiently liquid and eligible for clearing, will need to be traded on eligible platforms.
    - A new category of trading venue, called organised trading facilities (OTFs), will be introduced.
    - Requirements will be imposed on operators of OTFs and the operation of OTFs will be introduced as a separate permission.

- **Transparency and transaction reporting**
    - Transparency requirements will be extended to additional instruments, such as bonds and derivatives.
    - Trade reports will need to be published through approved publication arrangement (APA) firms, which will also be subject to authorisation and certain organisational requirements.
    - Transaction reports will need to capture additional information.

- **Third-country firms**
    - An equivalence decision will need to be made by the EC in respect of third countries before firms from these jurisdictions can request to provide services.
    - As a minimum, third-country firms seeking to access the retail market will be required to establish branches.

- **Investor protection**
    - Receipt of monetary inducements by certain firms, such as portfolio managers and firms giving independent investment advice, will be banned.
    - Advice must meet certain criteria in order to be classified as **independent** and additional information will need to be provided to clients.
    - The definition of non-complex instruments will be updated to remove **structured UCITS**, which will prevent these funds from being sold without an assessment of their appropriateness for the client.

The Regulatory Infrastructure of the UK Financial Services

- **Product intervention**
  - National regulators will have powers to permanently ban products, in co-ordination with ESMA, and ESMA will also be able to ban products temporarily.
  - Position limits for products, such as commodity derivatives, will be introduced. This will include powers for regulators to require existing positions to be reduced.

There is some overlap with existing UK regulatory requirements and planned regulatory changes, such as the RDR, which could lead to implementation challenges for firms. For example, the MiFID II proposals set out that in order to qualify as **independent**, advice should be based on a *'sufficiently large number of financial instruments available on the market'*. However, this is different to the definition adopted as part of the RDR. In addition, the proposed scope of MiFID II extends to include structured deposits but the confirmed scope of the RDR does not. Under the RDR changes, advisers giving restricted advice (as well as independent advisers) are unable to receive commission. These differences will need to be addressed by the relevant bodies prior to implementation.

A political agreement has been reached for the Regulation and Directive, however the exact dates for implementation of MiFID II and MiFIR will not be known until the final text is formally adopted by the Parliament and the Council and also published in the EU Official Journal – once published it enters on to force after 20 days.

At the time of writing it is expected that the Regulation and Directive will be published in the official journal in June 2014. This means that member states would be required to transpose into national law in 2016 – the precise dates should be known once they are published.

## 4.4 UCITS (Undertakings for Collective Investments in Transferable Securities) – Selling Cross-Border Collective Investment Schemes

The family of UCITS directives is aimed at securing a common set of regulatory standards for open-ended funds (commonly known as OEICs) and unit trusts in the UK and Société d'Investissement à Capital Variable (SICAVs) in part of Europe) across the EU – again, with the aim of removing barriers to cross-border trade.

Put simply, if a collective fund is set up in accordance with the UCITS rules, it should be able to be sold across the EU, subject only to local tax and marketing laws. So, a UCITS scheme can gain a single authorisation from its home state regulator, and need not apply for further authorisation in other member states before being sold to the public there.

Therefore the UCITS Directive should be seen as a directive on a product rather than on a service.

The original UCITS Directive was approved in 1985 and adopted by the UK in 1989. It aimed to provide common standards of investor protection for publicly promoted CISs across the EU. However, only a relatively limited range of scheme types could qualify as UCITS and therefore be freely marketed throughout the EU. The requirements which needed to be satisfied included:

- the scheme had to be solely invested in **transferable securities**;
- no more than 10% of the fund could be in the shares or bonds of a single issuer;

147

- no more than 5% of the assets of the scheme were allowed to be invested in other CISs;
- the scheme was only able to hold money in bank deposits as **ancillary liquid assets** and not as a major part of the investment strategy of the scheme;
- the scheme was only able to invest in, or utilise, financial derivatives for efficient portfolio management or hedging purposes.

As a result of these requirements, some UK CISs were described as **UCITS-compliant**, while others were not. For example, UK-authorised money market schemes (funds investing in bank deposits and the like) and funds of funds could not be UCITS schemes.

Demand for a wider variety of funds marketable throughout the EU rendered these investment restrictions somewhat out of date. As a result, two new UCITS directives were introduced:

- one affecting the operators of funds (the Management Directive); and
- one broadening the range of underlying investments and strategies that could qualify as UCITS (the Products Directive).

Collectively these are known as **UCITS III**.

The **Management Directive** deals mainly with the management companies operating UCITS funds – for example, the degree to which they can delegate activities, their capitalisation, internal administration and accounting requirements.

It widens the previous investment powers of UCITS schemes, to enable them to invest in money market instruments, other CISs, deposits and financial derivatives. It also allows certain UCITS to use strategies designed to replicate the performance of stock market indices (index tracker funds).

The **Products Directive** allows the following:

- Investment in money market instruments such as Treasury bills and certificates of deposit (CDs). This enables **money market funds** to be UCITS-compliant for the first time, as long as no more than 10% of the fund is invested in instruments from any single issuer.
- Up to 100% of a fund to be invested in other UCITS schemes, or up to 30% in a non-UCITS retail scheme which is a regulated scheme. This gives the ability for funds of funds (FOFs) to be UCITS-compliant.
- Investment in bank deposits, providing that no more than 20% of the scheme's assets are held with the same institution.
- Investment in financial derivatives (for example, warrants) as part of the scheme's investment policy, rather than just for efficient portfolio management. There are conditions that look through the derivatives, requiring that the underlying instruments must be capable of being held directly by the scheme.
- Index tracker funds which are intended to replicate the performance of an index are, under UCITS III, permitted to invest up to 20% of their value in a single issue; this can be raised to a maximum of 35% where justified by exceptional market conditions.

The changes allowed under UCITS III permitted funds to hold a much wider range of asset types than previously. However, the constantly evolving nature of products and markets has led to uncertainty about whether certain types of securities and derivative contracts meet the directive standards. Member states' regulators have interpreted the requirements in differing ways, so that UCITS schemes in some states are allowed to undertake transactions forbidden to UCITS authorised in other member states. Therefore, the Commission mandated the Committee of European Securities Regulators (CESR), now replaced by ESMA, to review the situation. The Commission issued a directive in March 2007, entitled *Eligible Assets* – which provides new detailed definitions for certain terms used in the original UCITS directive.

The **Eligible Assets Directive (EAD)** was required to be implemented into national legislation by 23 March 2008 and its provisions applied to all UCITS schemes by 23 July 2008. The UK met this deadline.

Since the aim of the EAD was to ensure that regulators and regulated firms apply a consistent interpretation of the directive, the UK implemented its provisions in the form of rules. The key developments arising from the EAD are:

- It expands on the directive's general definition of a transferable security, a term which applies to a wide range of shares, bonds and other negotiable securities. It sets out a list of criteria which must be eligible, including provisions on liquidity, availability of reliable valuations and appropriate information and the need for their risks to be adequately captured by the authorised fund manager's risk-management process.
- It clarifies that a transferable security may be backed by, or linked to the performance of, any other asset. This is providing that the security itself meets all the criteria applicable to transferable securities generally.
- Closed-ended funds become transferable securities, rather than collective investment undertakings, providing that they fulfil the general requirements for transferable securities and also are subject to the same corporate governance arrangements as companies.
- Credit derivatives are considered as eligible assets for a UCITS fund, providing that they comply with the criteria applicable to OTC derivatives, that they do not result in the delivery of non-permissible assets for UCITS, and that their specific risks are adequately captured by the UCITS risk-management process.
- Derivatives on a single commodity still remain prohibited.
- Financial indices, whether or not composed of eligible assets, can be considered as eligible assets providing that they are sufficiently diversified and that they represent an adequate benchmark for the market to which they refer and that they are published in an appropriate manner.

## 4.4.1 UCITS Directive Amendments (UCITS IV)

The EC's amendments to the UCITS Directive, titled UCITS IV, were approved by the European Parliament in January 2009.

- **Notification procedure** – the previous process of cross-border fund notification took a minimum of two months, although it was not uncommon for some member states to ask for more information and so delay the registration process. The Commission proposed to clarify member state supervisory responsibilities and ensure that a duly authorised UCITS has the right to access the market of another member state. Notification will be a simple electronic regulator-to-regulator communication, which effectively means that a UCITS has a right to access the market of another member state without delay.

- **Fund mergers** – the average fund size in Europe is much lower than in the US, while fund charges are higher. The ability of a UCITS to merge and pool assets should bring economies of scale and specialisation.
- **Asset pooling (master/feeder structure)** – master/feeder structures will enable fund managers to pool similar funds into a master fund while still preserving the different funds' labels (as opposed to merging the funds). The structure should benefit investors with economies of scale when pooling assets of the feeder/master funds, centralising the core investment management activity and preserving greater tax-efficiency for the end investor.
- **Simplified prospectus** – the previous simplified prospectus was too long and complex. The new proposal replaced this with a short and easily readable key investor information report.
- **Management company passport** – this was the most controversial of the Commission's proposals. This allows the activities performed by the management company to be undertaken in a member state other than where the funds are domiciled/registered. This allows fund managers, and outsourced fund administrators who perform the activities of the management company, to centralise the administration of fund ranges in one location within the EEA.

### 4.4.2  UCITS Directive Amendments (UCITS V)

UCITS V focuses on rules covering depositaries, remuneration and sanctions – aiming to align UCITS with the Alternative Investment Fund Mangers' Directive (AIFMD).

It is expected that the Level 1 text will be agreed Q3–4 2013.

## 4.5  Prospectus Directive – Selling Securities Cross-Border

The Prospectus Directive is another example of a Directive aimed at creating common standards across the EU, this time with the aim of simplifying the issue of a prospectus throughout the EEA.

It was implemented in the UK in July 2005. Before the Prospectus Directive came into force, a prospectus for the offer of securities could only get recognition in another state if it:

- had been approved by the relevant home state competent authority;
- contained certain information; and
- met any additional requirements imposed by the host state; this last element could include a requirement that the prospectus be translated into the host state's language.

The Prospectus Directive sets out common standards in terms of the information that must be provided about the issuer and the securities being issued or admitted for listing. It can be thought of as a **single passport for issuers**. It means that, once a prospectus has been approved by a home state listing authority, it must be accepted for the purpose of listing or public offers throughout the EU. The purpose of the Prospective Directive is therefore to make it easier and cheaper for companies (issuers) to raise capital in Europe.

## 4.6 AIFMD – Alternative Investment Fund Managers' Directive

In April 2009 the EC published a draft proposal for a Directive on alternative investment fund managers (AIFMs). The Commission claims that the AIFMD is a response to the fundamental risks in these sectors thrown up by the global financial crisis (such as the use of leverage and the governance of portfolio companies). However, industry members fear the directive as drafted could severely damage the industry's competitiveness.

The Directive is following the ordinary legislative process in the EU. Before the directive became law, it had to be agreed by both the European Parliament and the EU Council. The European Parliament and the Council agreed the text of the Directive on 26 October 2010. It was approved by the European Parliament in its plenary session on 11 November 2010.

The AIFMD effectively introduces a regulatory framework for managers of any collective investment undertaking, other than those covered by the UCITS Directive, if the manager is domiciled in the EU, or if the fund is domiciled or marketed within the EU. The Commission estimates that roughly 30% of hedge fund managers, managing almost 90% of the assets of EU-domiciled hedge funds, will be caught by the directive, and that the directive will also apply to almost half the managers of other non-UCITS funds.

While public and media focus has been primarily on hedge and private equity funds, the directive's drafting means that it also extends to managers of other types of funds, such as commodity, real estate and infrastructure funds, long-only non-UCITS funds, closed-end funds (such as investment trusts in the UK), non-UCITS retail scheme (NURS) funds in the UK, and qualified investor schemes (QISs).

The Commission argues that it would be *ineffective and short-sighted* to limit new regulation to hedge and private equity funds alone, as any particular definitions might not capture those at whom the legislation is aimed; and in the Commission's view many of the underlying risks which the directive attempts to tackle are present in other types of alternative investment funds (AIFs).

The Directive imposes a number of requirements on AIFMs that fall within its scope, including authorisation, capital requirements, conduct of business and organisational requirements (including the appointment of service providers; an independent valuator and depository for each AIF), and specific initial and ongoing disclosure to investors and regulators. These basic authorisation and organisational requirements will apply to all AIFMs, but will be varied dependent on the type of AIF. On top of these common requirements sits another layer of bespoke provisions for those AIFMs employing high degrees of leverage or acquiring controlling stakes in companies.

The Directive creates a scheme under which EU fund managers are authorised in their member states in accordance with EU standards and are then permitted to market their AIFs to professional investors across the EU in reliance on a passport. The directive also makes provision for non-EU funds to be marketed in the EU. This was one of the main disagreements and stumbling blocks on negotiation of the directive between the European Council and the European Parliament.

The AIFMD includes requirements for AIFMs and AIFs on the following:

- authorisation;
- capital requirements;

- limits on AIFM activities (including leverage);
- conduct of business and organisational requirements (including valuation and delegation);
- disclosure requirements – general and major shareholdings and control;
- marketing;
- remuneration;
- depository requirements.

## 4.7 Capital Requirements Directive (CRD IV) – Firms Undertaking Investment Business

The Capital Requirements Directive (CRD) requires firms to satisfy certain financial requirements. In particular, firms need to have financial resources in excess of their regulatory financial resource requirements. These requirements aim to minimise the risk of a firm's collapsing by being unable to pay its debts and are generally referred to as prudential rules.

The aim of the CRD is to ensure the financial soundness of credit institutions (essentially banks and building societies, but also investment firms). The CRD stipulates how much of their own financial resources such firms must have in order to cover their risks and protect their depositors.

The CRD amends two significant existing directives – the Banking Consolidation Directive (BCD) and the Capital Adequacy Directive (CAD) – for the prudential regulation of credit institutions and investment firms across the EU. It is a major piece of legislation that introduces a modern prudential framework, relating capital levels more closely to risks.

The CRD implements in the EU the revised Basel Framework, which is based on three pillars:

- **Pillar 1** – minimum capital requirements for credit, market and operational risks.
- **Pillar 2** – supervisory review – establishing a constructive dialogue between a firm and the regulator on the risks, the risk-management and capital requirements of the firm.
- **Pillar 3** – market discipline – robust requirements on public disclosure intended to give the market a stronger role in ensuring that firms hold an appropriate level of capital.

## 4.8 EMIR (European Markets Infrastructure Regulation)

EMIR is a regulation on over-the-counter (OTC) derivatives, central counterparties and trade repositories, which entered into force on 16 August 2012.

EMIR improves the transparency of, and introduces requirements to reduce the risks associated with the OTC derivatives market. Along with elements in CRD IV and MiFID II they represent the EU's commitment to the G20 agreement on the reform of OTC derivatives.

EMIR provides rules around reporting of certain derivative contracts to a trade repository, risk mitigation – reconciling contracts with the counterparty and also centrally clearing all derivative contracts. The rules apply to all EEA-incorporated and established entities, catching for the first time in direct regulation corporate companies.

# The Regulatory Infrastructure of the UK Financial Services

From 15 September 2013 measures for risk management of OTC derivatives were implemented. All EEA counterparties are required to undertake a portfolio reconciliation of their outstanding derivative contracts – the frequency ranges from daily, monthly or quarterly for financial counterparties (regulated firms) to quarterly or annually for non-financial counterparties (corporates). In addition, firms must agree on the process for dispute resolution where they disagree on trade details. They must review and consider a process known as 'trade compression'.

From 12 February 2014 all EEA entities were required to start reporting derivative contract (both OTC and exchange-traded) details to a trade repository. The difference being that both counterparties must report, unless one entity is a third country entity (non-EEA). The trade repositories report the trade details to ESMA.

Another piece of EMIR, which has yet to enter into force, is for OTC derivative contracts to be centrally cleared. No central counterparties have been approved and the mandatory instruments that are required to be cleared have not been determined – this is due anytime from September 2014 onwards.

Margin requirements for non-centrally cleared trades will be phased in between 1 December 2015 and 1 December 2019.

## Summary of this Chapter

You should have an understanding and knowledge of the following after reading this chapter:

- The UK financial regulatory structure:
    - main regulatory bodies and the relationship between them;
    - including the HMT, BOE and the FCA/PRA and the FPC;
    - FSMA 2000 – purpose and scope;
    - the purpose of FOS and FSCS, and their limitations.
- The FCA and PRA strategic and operational objectives, structure, powers and activities.
- Regulation of financial markets and exchanges.
- Financial capability.
- European regulation:
    - MiFID:
        - home/host state;
        - passport;
    - UCITS;
    - AIFMD;
    - CRD IV;
    - Prospectus Directive;
    - EMIR.

# End of Chapter Questions

Think of an answer for each question and refer to the appropriate section for confirmation.

1.  What powers does the Financial Services Act 2012 give the FCA and the PRA to regulate the financial services industry?
    *Answer reference: Sections 1.2, 1.3*

2.  Who are the FCA and the PRA accountable to?
    *Answer reference: Sections 1.2, 1.3*

3.  What is the ICO responsible for?
    *Answer reference: Section 1.7*

4.  What is the relationship between the FCA and the FOS?
    *Answer reference: Section 1.9*

5.  What are the FCA and PRA strategic and operational objectives?
    *Answer reference: Sections 2.1.1, 2.1.2*

6.  What are the Principles for Businesses?
    *Answer reference: Section 2.3*

7.  What is the difference between an RIE and a DIE?
    *Answer reference: Sections 3.1.1, 3.1.2*

8.  What is an MTF?
    *Answer reference: Section 3.1.4*

9.  Who is responsible for approving companies seeking to list on a regulated market and be admitted to the Official List?
    *Answer reference: Section 3.1.5*

10. What is the FCA's strategy for financial capability?
    *Answer reference: Section 3.2*

11. What is passporting?
    *Answer reference: Section 4.1*

12. What responsibilities are imposed by MiFID on home state and host state regulators?
    *Answer reference: Section 4.2*

13. What is the purpose of the CRD?
    *Answer reference: Section 4.7*

14. What are the FCA's expectations in relation to integrity and ethics and individual behaviour?
    *Answer reference: Whole Chapter*

# Chapter Six
# FCA and PRA Supervisory Objectives, Principles and Processes

| | |
|---|---|
| 1. The FCA and PRA Supervisory Approach | 159 |
| 2. Performance of Regulated Activities | 166 |
| 3. The FCA Handbook | 180 |
| 4. Prudential and Liquidity Standards | 182 |
| 5. The Remuneration Code | 190 |
| 6. Promotion of Fair and Ethical Outcomes and Why this is not Always Achieved | 194 |

**This syllabus area will provide approximately 7 of the 80 examination questions**

In this chapter you will gain an understanding of:

- The supervisory approach adopted by the FCA and the PRA.
- Effective corporate governance.
- The regulatory enforcement process.
- The structure of the FCA and the PRA handbook.
- Prudential and liquidity standards.
- The remuneration code.

# 1. The FCA and PRA Supervisory Approach

As noted in Chapter 5, the FCA and the PRA have different supervisory approaches. However this can be explained based on the different statutory objectives that they must comply with.

The FCA has been created to work with firms to ensure that they put consumers at the heart of their business. Underlining this are three outcomes:

1. Consumers get financial services and products that meet their needs from firms they can trust.
2. Firms compete effectively with the interests of their consumers and the integrity of the market at the heart of how they run their business.
3. Markets and financial systems are sound, stable and resilient with transparent pricing information.

The PRA has a statutory objective to promote the safety and soundness of firms. It is required to pursue this primarily by seeking to avoid adverse effects on financial stability and in particular seeking to minimise adverse effects resulting from disruption to the continuity of financial services that can be caused by the way firms run their business or upon their failure.

It is worth noting that the PRA and the FCA do not operate a no-fail regime.

## 1.1 The Risk-Based Approach

### Learning Objective

6.1.1 Understand the merits and limitations of the FCA's conduct risk, outcomes and principles-based approaches to regulation

6.2.1 Understand the sources of information on the FCA's and the PRA's supervisory approach, including the annual risk outlook document, speeches and newsletters

The FCA supervision model is based on three pillars:

1. **Firm Systematic Framework (FSF)** – preventative work through structured conduct assessment of firms.

2. **Event-driven work** – dealing more quickly and decisively with problems that are emerging or have happened, and securing customer redress or other remedial work where necessary – covering issues that occur outside the firm assessment cycle, utilising data better and improving monitoring and intelligence.
3. **Issues and products** – through fast, intensive campaigns on sectors of the market or products within a sector that are putting or may put consumers at risk.

This approach is driven by what the FCA calls sector risk assessment – looking at what currently is and which may cause poor outcomes for consumers and market participants. The risk assessment will use data analysis, market intelligence and input from the firm assessment process, as well as working closely with the FCA's new policy, risk and research area.

The FCA's new approach to supervision is built on ten principles, which form the basis of their interaction with firms of all categories:

1. **Ensuring fair outcomes for consumers and markets.** This is the dual consideration that runs through all their work; how they will assess issues according to their impact on both consumers and market integrity.
2. Being **forward-looking and pre-emptive**, identifying potential risks and taking action before they have a serious impact.
3. Being **focused on the big issues and causes of problems**. Where they will concentrate their resources on issues that have a significant impact on their objectives.
4. Taking **a judgement-based approach**, with the emphasis on achieving the right outcomes.
5. **Ensuring firms act in the right spirit**, which means the FCA will consider the impact of their actions on consumers and markets rather than just complying with the letter of the law.
6. Examining **business models and culture**, and the impact they have on consumers and market outcomes. The FCA is interested in how a firm makes its money, as this can drive many potential risks.
7. **An emphasis on individual accountability**, ensuring senior management understand that they are personally responsible for their actions – and that the FCA will hold them to account when things go wrong.
8. Being **robust when things go wrong**, making sure that problems are fixed, consumers are protected and compensated, and poor behaviour is rectified along with its root causes.
9. **Communicating openly** with industry, firms and consumers to gain a deeper understanding of the issues they face.
10. **Having a joined-up approach**, making sure firms get consistent messages from the FCA, the FCA will engage with the PRA to ensure effective independent supervision of dual-regulated firms, and work with other regulatory and advisory bodies including the Financial Ombudsman Service, Financial Services Compensation Scheme (FSCS), Money Advice Service (MAS) and international regulators.

The FCA has assigned firms to one of four categories for conduct supervision: **C1**, **C2**, **C3** and **C4**. These broadly reflect a firm's size and retail customer numbers or wholesale presence, and the corresponding level of risk the firm potentially poses to FCAs objectives. Each category is subject to a different level of supervision, allowing the FCA to use its resources as efficiently as possible and concentrate on the areas that pose the greatest risks to their objectives.

FCA and PRA Supervisory Objectives, Principles and Processes

There are also **four prudential supervision categories**. These are independent of the conduct categories: a firm or group can fit into any of the prudential categories regardless of what conduct category they are in.

- **C1** – firms with the largest number of retail customers, and wholesale firms with the most significant market presence. They have a named supervisor and a high level of firm-specific supervision. This currently covers 11 major groups.
- **C2** – firms with large retail customer numbers and wholesale firms with a significant market presence. They have a named supervisor and a high level of firm-specific supervision. This currently covers around 120 groups.
- **C3** – retail and wholesale firms with a medium-sized customer base. They are supervised with a sector-based approach, with less frequent firm-specific engagement. This currently covers around 400 firms and groups.
- **C4** – retail and wholesale firms with a small number of customers. They are supervised with a sector-based approach, with less frequent firm-specific engagement. This currently covers around 25,000 firms.

## 1.1.1 Supervising What Matters

The FCA's aim is to protect consumers and ensure market integrity by examining the areas that have an impact on them. The FCA wants to know how a firm runs its business rather than how they control risks.

The FCA will examine the following areas to see how firms put the integrity of the market and the fair treatment of consumers at the heart of how they run their business:

- **Business model and strategy** – firms should be commercially successful, but not at the expense of customers.
- **Culture** – greater emphasis on understanding the culture within firms.
- **Front line business processes** – firms' business processes, from product development to complaints handling, should be designed to give customers what they need and meet their expectations.
- **Systems and controls** – the FCA expects firms to have effective, independent controls – usually in the compliance, risk and internal audit functions – that provide challenge to business units and assurance to senior management and the board.
- **Governance** – senior management and the board play a key role in determining its business model, strategies and business practices, and ensuring appropriate systems and controls are in place.

## 1.1.2 The Three-Pillar Supervision Model

Supervision work is based around three pillars of activity.

- **Pillar 1 – proactive group supervision** – assessment that firms have the interests of customers and the integrity of the market at the heart of their business.
- **Pillar 2 – event-driven, reactive supervision** – FCA will respond to significant risks to consumers or markets.
- **Pillar 3 – issues and products supervision** – sector analysis and potential drivers of poor outcomes for consumers and markets.

161

## 1.1.3 Summary of Conduct Supervision Activity

### C1 Firms and Groups

- **Business model and strategy analysis every two years**, reviewed at the halfway stage.
- **Regular meetings** between FCA supervisors, senior management, board members, key control functions and external auditors.
- **Regular reviews of management information.**
- **Annual strategy meeting** between FCA senior management and firms CEO and executives.
- **One or two 'deep dive' assessments** during each annual assessment cycle.
- Annual **firm evaluation**.
- **Regular baseline monitoring** of regulatory returns.
- **Routine and other activities** such as transfers, acquisitions and permission changes.
- **Participation in thematic reviews and market studies.**

### C2 Firms and Groups

- **Annual peer group business model and strategy analysis.**
- **Regular meetings** between FCA supervisors, senior management and board members.
- **Regular reviews of management information.**
- **Annual strategy meeting** between FCA senior management firms executives.
- **One or two 'deep dive' assessments** during each two-year assessment cycle.
- **Firm evaluation every two years.**
- **Regular baseline monitoring** of regulatory returns.
- **Routine and other activities such as transfers.**
- **Participation in thematic reviews and market studies.**

### C3 Firms

- **Annual peer group business model and strategy analysis.**
- Routine interaction with the FCA via the **Firm Contact Centre**.
- Other interaction via trade body events and roundtable discussions.
- **Regular baseline monitoring** of regulatory returns.
- **Occasional routine tasks.**
- **Participation in thematic reviews and market studies.**
- **Periodic assessment** at least once every four years.

### C4 Firms

- The supervisory regime for many C4 firms is similar to the previous regime under the FSA in terms of the intensity and type of supervision. However, the FCA is now also looking at the culture and practices of firms to ensure that they consider consumers and market integrity in everything they do.
- Ongoing supervision by **sectoral analysis and thematic reviews**.
- **Regular baseline monitoring** of regulatory returns.
- **Occasional routine tasks.**
- **Four-yearly assessment** via a phone or face-to-face interview, an online assessment, or a combination of these.

## 1.2 Prudential Supervision

Although the Prudential Regulation Authority (PRA) has prudential responsibility for deposit-takers, insurers and significant investment firms, the FCA is the prudential supervisor for a wide range of firms across the financial services industry, such as asset managers, independent financial advisers, and mortgage and insurance brokers.

The FCA's approach aims to minimise the harm to consumers, wholesale market participants and market stability when firms experience financial stress or fail in a disorderly manner.

### Prudential Categories

Firms that are prudentially regulated by the FCA fall into four prudential categories: **P1, P2, P3** and **P4**. These categories reflect the impact that the disorderly failure of a firm could have on markets and consumers.

- **P1 firms and groups** could cause significant, lasting damage to the marketplace, consumers and client assets, due to their size and market impact.
- **P2 firms** whose failure would have less impact than P1 firms, but would nevertheless damage markets or consumers and client assets.
- **P3 firms** whose failure, even if disorderly, is unlikely to have a significant market impact. They have the lowest intensity of prudential supervision.
- **P4 firms** are those with special circumstances – for example, firms in administration – for which bespoke arrangements may be necessary.

Like the conduct categories, the prudential categories determine the intensity of their prudential supervision for each firm.

Through prudential activities the FCA seeks to ensure that:

- firms maintain adequate financial resources in line with legal requirements;
- the FCA has an early warning of financial issues that could drive behaviours that endanger a firm's compliance with conduct, financial crime, client assets and other core regulatory standards;
- any wind-down of a firm could happen with little or no damage to markets and consumers.

### Prudential Risk Analysis for P1 and P2 Firms

For **P1 and P2 firms**, comprehensive capital and liquidity analysis and assessment of a firm's risk management capability.

### Financial Resources Requirements (FRR)

The FCA Handbook specifies minimum FRR for all firms. Firms must maintain sufficient resources to meet their financial obligations at all times, and must be able to show how they have determined what is sufficient. This is the starting point for any prudential supervisory review.

The specific scope and nature of FRR varies by firm type and permissions:

- **P1 firms have a capital and (if applicable) liquidity assessment every two years.**
- **P2 firms have a capital and (if applicable) liquidity assessment every three to four years** – examining firms own assessments of requirements.

## 1.3 Effective Corporate Governance

### Learning Objective

6.8.1 Understand how the FCA's and PRA's approaches to supervision support corporate governance and business risk management

Although poor governance was only one of many factors that contributed to the financial crisis, it was an important one, along with failures on capital and liquidity plus some failures of the regulatory system.

The previous regulator (the FSA) acknowledged that if it was to meet its regulatory responsibilities and reduce the likelihood of another such crisis, just as it is taking action on capital and liquidity and improving regulation, it was also needed to address issues around governance and the culture within firms.

In its business plan for 2010 the FSA CEO stated that there had been a revolution in the intensity of their supervisory approach, which included its approach to governance and risk in firms. The financial crisis had highlighted and exposed significant shortcomings in the governance and risk management across numerous firms, for example where boards:

- did not sufficiently challenge the executive;
- did not understand their business models sufficiently;
- needed a better understanding of higher-risk activities and products; and
- did not receive appropriate management information to be able to carry out their important oversight role.

Improving regulation and the outcomes for firms and consumers is not just about moving the regulatory telescope – the FCA needs to change its focus and look at behaviour and culture in firms more closely, particularly ensuring that good culture and behaviour:

- in firms are being driven by senior management; and
- are being reinforced by effective corporate governance and the role of the boards.

The regulator recognised that its regulatory approach before the crisis underestimated the importance of governance, and is now committed to putting that right.

The FCA is carrying forward the work started by the FSA, a point noted in its 2013 business plan.

The FCA's focus and approach is on effective governance within firms. It considers that good governance enables a firm's board and executive to work together to deliver a firm's agreed strategy. In particular, it is about managing the risks the firm faces. Good governance enables the board to share a clear understanding of the firm's risk appetite and to establish a robust control framework to manage that risk effectively across the business, with effective oversight and challenge along the way.

The FCA focuses on supervising governance in action – which it states as meaning evaluating the outcomes of the processes and structures firms have put in place and greater scrutiny of individuals before they are in positions of influence, and once they are in place.

The FCA is aware that it will not remove all risks from the system, but it is looking for firms to be well run, recognise the risks they face and put in place appropriate strategies, systems and controls.

This is why, alongside the development of its supervision of firms, it has also been working to strengthen the way it approves and supervises individuals performing **significant influence functions** (SIFs) under the approved persons regime (see Chapter 7, Section 4.2).

The FCA has carried forward the previous regulator's work on introducing a number of new, more specific controlled functions within the approved persons regime. Within controlled functions, the SIFs capture those individuals who, in the regulator's opinion, exercise a significant influence on a firm.

The SIFs cover many important roles under one broad heading, so currently one individual can carry out a number of roles under just one controlled function. Some of these underlying roles are essential to effective governance.

For example, a person approved as a director could move within a firm, from being, for example, the marketing director to being the credit risk officer or chief financial officer, without further approval by the FCA/PRA. In future the FCA and the PRA will be able to identify and assess the competence and capability of individuals performing these key roles. These will be roles such as:

- chairman;
- senior independent director;
- chairman of the risk, audit, and remuneration committees; and
- finance, risk and internal audit functions.

However, as well as proposing new SIF roles, the FCA and the PRA have carried forward the FSA's work on raising the standards for people performing these roles, and increased their scrutiny of these individuals once they are in place, as part of their more intensive supervision.

The FCA and PRA's approval of individuals, based on their fitness and propriety (see Chapter 7, Section 1.4), has always been part of their statutory responsibilities. See Chapter 7 for more details on the approach of the FCA and the PRA.

# 2. Performance of Regulated Activities

**Learning Objective**

6.3 Understand the FCA's main disciplinary and enforcement powers and how they are used:

6.3.1 Decision Procedure and Penalties Manual (DEPP)

6.3.2 Perimeter Guidance Manual: Authorisation and Regulated Activities (PERG 2)

6.3.3 Unauthorised investment business; enforceability of agreements, penalties and defences

6.3.4 Powers to require information and carry out investigations (FSMA 2000 s.165 & 167/8 as amended)

6.3.5 Powers of intervention (products and financial promotions)

Within the block of the FCA Handbook called **Regulatory Processes** (dealing with how the FCA carries on its regulatory activities) there are two sections:

1. The **Supervision (SUP)** manual sets out the relationship between the FCA and persons that are already authorised.
2. The **Decision Procedure and Penalties (DEPP)** manual deals with the FCA's procedures for taking various disciplinary actions.

In the regulatory guides block of the FCA Handbook, the **Perimeter Guidance (PERG)** manual gives guidance about the circumstances in which authorisation is required, or where exempt person status is available, including guidance on the activities which are regulated under the Act and the exclusions which are available. In addition, the FCA's **Enforcement Guide (EG)**, which is in the same block, sets out the FCA's approach to how it exercises the main enforcement powers it has, both under FSMA and under the Unfair Contract Terms regulations. It does this mainly through the activities of its enforcement division.

## 2.1 The Regulatory Decisions Committee (RDC)

In the interests of fairness, the FSMA requires that when the FCA makes decisions about the issue of warning and decision notices, it follows procedures that are *'designed to secure, among other things, that the decision which gives rise to the obligation to give any such notice is taken by a person not directly involved in establishing the evidence on which that decision is based'*.

Thus, rather than allowing the FCA's enforcement team to make the decisions which are implemented in the statutory notices outlined above, these decisions are made by a relatively independent committee: the Regulatory Decisions Committee (RDC).

The RDC is a committee of the FCA's board, and is accountable to that board; however, it is independent to the extent that it is outside the FCA's management structure. Only the chairman is an FCA employee; the rest of the members represent the public interest and are either current or retired practitioners with financial services knowledge and experience, or non-practitioners.

The RDC meets either in its entirety, or as a panel – depending on the issue under review. In either case, the chairman or deputy must be present. The RDC also has its own legal function. It is not advised on cases by the same legal team that advises the FCA's enforcement team, who will have originally brought the case to the RDC.

The RDC has responsibility for statutory decisions, such as to:

- specify a narrower description of a regulated activity than that applied for in a Part 4A permission, or limit Part 4A permission in a way which will make a fundamental change;
- refuse an application for Part 4A permission, or cancel an existing Part 4A permission;
- refuse an application for approved person status, or withdraw an existing approval;
- make a prohibition order in relation to a person that will prohibit them from gaining approved person status, or refuse to vary such an order;
- exercise the FCA's powers to impose a financial penalty, make a public statement on the misconduct of an approved person, issue a public censure against an authorised person, or make a restitution order against a person.

If a statutory notice decision is not made by the RDC it will be made under the **executive procedures** of the FCA. These executive procedures enable the FCA to use statutory powers when individual guidance or voluntary agreement is felt to be inappropriate. A typical example of when these executive procedures might be used is if the FCA has particular concerns and, therefore, requires a firm to submit reports, such as those on trading results, customer complaints, or reports detailing the firm's management accounts.

## 2.1.1 Notices

FSMA gives the FCA the power to issue a variety of notices to authorised firms and/or approved persons, collectively referred to as **statutory notices**. These are:

- **Warning notices** give the recipient details about the action the FCA proposes to take and why it proposes to do so. They also give the recipient the right to make representations as to why the FCA should not take this action. New powers provided in the Financial Services Act 2012 permit the FCA to announce publicly that it has begun disciplinary action against a firm or individual. It can be able to publish details of a **warning notice** proposing disciplinary action, to signal the start of formal enforcement proceedings. However, the FCA will have to consult with the recipient of the warning notice before publishing the details.
- **Decision notices** give details of the action that the FCA has decided to take, leaving room for appeal by the recipient.
- **Supervisory notices** give the recipient details regarding the action the FCA has taken, or proposes to take. A typical supervisory notice might limit a firm's Part 4A permission with immediate effect (and hence it would seem reasonable for the FCA to alert the public to the fact that the firm is no longer permitted to carry on certain activities).

In addition, the FCA can issue the following notices, but they are not referred to as 'statutory notices'. These are:

- **Further decision notices** may follow the issue of a decision notice, when the FCA has agreed with the recipient to take a different action from that proposed in the original decision notice. The FCA can issue a further decision notice only with the consent of the recipient.

- **Notices of discontinuance** let the recipient know that if the FCA has previously sent it a warning notice and/or a decision notice, it has decided not to proceed with the relevant action.
- **Final notices** set out the terms of the final action which the FCA has decided to take and the date that it is effective from. They are also – unlike warning and decision notices – published by the FCA, on its website. The FCA would need to get approval from the recipient if they wish to publish a warning notice.

## 2.2 The Regulatory Enforcement Processes

Regulatory enforcement measures are one of the ways the FCA can address instances of non-compliance with its requirements by firms or individuals. There are three possible forms of formal disciplinary sanction:

- public statements of misconduct (relating to approved persons, ie, individuals);
- public censures (relating to authorised persons, ie, firms); and
- financial penalties (fines).

The imposition of regulatory enforcement measures (such as fines and public statements/censures) assists the FCA in meeting its statutory objectives.

In addition to these formal measures, the FCA can take a lower-key approach if it feels this is more appropriate. It could, for example:

- issue a private warning; or
- take supervisory action, such as:
    - varying or cancelling the firm's Part 4A permissions or removing its authorisation;
    - withdrawing an individual's approved person status;
    - prohibiting an individual from performing a particular role in relation to a regulated activity.

These measures might be used if the FCA considers it necessary to take protective or remedial action (rather than disciplinary action), or when a firm's ability to continue to meet its threshold conditions, or an individual approved person's fitness and propriety, are called into question.

When the FCA is considering formal discipline against an authorised firm and/or an approved person, it is required by FSMA to issue one or more notices (these are the statutory notices we looked at in Section 2.1.1). As we saw, these notices fall into two categories: warnings and decisions.

Warnings are not in themselves disciplinary events, since for an action to be regarded as disciplinary action a decision must have been made – and a warning is just that, no more and no less. Indeed, the decision notices themselves may not be absolutely final. They may be:

- discontinued by the issue of a **notice of discontinuance**;
- varied with agreement in a **further decision notice**; or
- simply confirmed in a **final decision notice**.

FCA and PRA Supervisory Objectives, Principles and Processes

## 2.2.1 Criteria for Disciplinary Action

In determining whether to take regulatory enforcement measures, the FCA will consider the full circumstances which may be relevant to the case. These include, but are not limited to, the following:

- The nature and seriousness of the suspected breach:
  - Was it deliberate or reckless?
  - Does it reveal serious or systemic weakness of the management systems or internal controls of the firm?
  - How much loss, or risk of loss, was there to consumers and other market users?
- The conduct of the firm after the breach:
  - How quickly, effectively and completely was the breach brought to the attention of the FCA?
  - Has the firm taken remedial steps since the breach was identified? For example, by identifying and compensating consumers who suffered loss, taking disciplinary action against the staff involved, addressing systemic failures and taking action to avoid recurrence of the breach in the future.
- The previous regulatory record of the firm or approved person:
  - Has the FCA (or a previous regulator) taken any previous disciplinary action?

## 2.2.2 The Measures

1. **Private warnings** – these are issued by the FCA when it has concerns regarding the behaviour of the firm or approved person, but decides it is not appropriate to bring formal disciplinary action. It might include cases of potential (but unproven) market abuse, or cases when the FCA considered making a prohibition order but decided not to do so.

   In such circumstances, the FCA believes it is helpful to let the recipient know that they came close to disciplinary action, and the private warning serves this purpose. The circumstances giving rise to a private warning might include a minor matter (in nature or degree), or when the firm or approved person has taken full and immediate remedial action. The benefit of a private warning is that it avoids the reputational damage that would follow from more public sanctions, such as a fine or public censure.

   The private warning will state that the FCA has had cause for concern but, at present, does not intend to take formal disciplinary action. It will also state that the private warning will form part of the FCA's compliance history and will require the recipient to acknowledge receipt and invite a response.

2. **Variation of permission** – the Part 4A permission granted to the firm by the FCA can be varied on the FCA's own initiative. The FCA's powers to vary and cancel a person's Part 4A permission are exercisable in the same circumstances. However, the statutory procedure for the exercise of each power is different, and this may determine how the FCA acts in a given case.

   When it considers how it should deal with a concern about a firm, the FCA will have regard to its statutory objectives and the range of regulatory tools that are available to it. It will also have regard to the:

   a. responsibilities of a firm's management to deal with concerns about the firm or about the way its business is being or has been run;
   b. principle that a restriction imposed on a firm should be proportionate to the objectives the FCA is seeking to achieve.

169

Examples of circumstances in which the FCA will consider varying a firm's Part 4A permission because it has serious concerns about a firm, or about the way its business is being or has been conducted, include when:

a. in relation to the grounds for exercising the power under section 45(1)(a) of the Act, the firm appears to be failing, or appears likely to fail, to satisfy the threshold conditions relating to one or more, or all, of its regulated activities, because for instance:
    • the firm's material and financial resources appear inadequate for the scale or type of regulated activity it is carrying on; for example, if it has failed to maintain professional indemnity insurance or if it is unable to meet its liabilities as they have fallen due; or
    • the firm appears not to be a fit and proper person to carry on a regulated activity because:
        ○ it has not conducted its business in compliance with high standards which may include putting itself at risk of being used for the purposes of financial crime or being otherwise involved in such crime;
        ○ it has not been managed competently and prudently and has not exercised due skill, care and diligence in carrying on one or more, or all, of its regulated activities;
        ○ it has breached requirements imposed on it by or under the Act (including the principles and the rules), for example, in respect of its disclosure or notification requirements, and the breaches are material in number or in individual seriousness;
b. in relation to the grounds for exercising the power under section 45(1)(c), it appears that the interests of consumers are at risk because the firm appears to have breached any of Principles 6 to 10 of the FCA's Principles (see PRIN 2.1.1R) to such an extent that it is desirable that limitations, restrictions or prohibitions are placed on the firm's regulated activity.

3. **Withdrawal of a firm's authorisation** – the FCA will consider cancelling a firm's Part 4A permission in two major circumstances:

    • if the FCA has very serious concerns about a firm, or the way its business is conducted; or
    • if a firm's regulated activities have come to an end, but it has not applied for cancellation of its Part 4A permission.

The grounds on which the FCA may exercise its power to cancel an authorised person's permission under Section 45 of the Act are the same as the grounds for variation. They are set out in section 45(1) and described in EG 8.1. Examples of the types of circumstances in which the FCA may cancel a firm's Part 4A permission include:

• non-compliance with an FOS award against the firm;
• material non-disclosure in an application for authorisation or approval, or material non-notification after authorisation or approval has been granted. The information which is the subject of the non-disclosure or non-notification may also be grounds for cancellation;
• failure to have or maintain adequate financial resources, or a failure to comply with regulatory capital requirements;
• non-submission of, or provision of false information in, regulatory returns, or repeated failure to submit such returns in a timely fashion;
• non-payment of FCA fees or repeated failure to pay FCA fees except under threat of enforcement action;
• failure to provide the FCA with valid contact details or failure to maintain the details provided, such that the FCA is unable to communicate with the firm;
• repeated failures to comply with rules or requirements;
• a failure to co-operate with the FCA which is of sufficient seriousness that the FCA ceases to be satisfied that the firm is fit and proper; for example, failing without reasonable excuse to:

## FCA and PRA Supervisory Objectives, Principles and Processes

- ◦ comply with the material terms of a formal agreement made with the FCA to conclude or avoid disciplinary or other enforcement action; or
- ◦ provide material information or take remedial action reasonably required by the FCA.

Section 45(2A) of the Act sets out further grounds on which the FCA may cancel the permission of authorised persons which are investment firms. Depending on the circumstances, the FCA may need to consider whether it should first use its own-initiative powers to vary a firm's Part IV permission before going on to cancel it. Among other circumstances, the FCA may use this power if it considers it needs to take immediate action against a firm because of the urgency and seriousness of the situation.

4. **Withdrawal of approval** – as well as having the power to withdraw authorisation of the firm, the FCA has the power to withdraw the approval of particular individuals which allows them to fulfil controlled functions. The FCA is required first to issue a warning notice to the approved person and the firm, followed by a decision notice. The FCA's decision can be referred to the Tax and Chancery Chamber of the Upper Tribunal (Upper Tribunal) (see Section 2.3).

The FCA recognises that withdrawing approval will often have a substantial impact on those concerned. When considering withdrawing approval it will take into account the cumulative effect of all relevant matters, including:

- The competence and capability of the individual (embracing qualifications and training). Do they have the necessary skills to carry out the controlled function they are performing?
- The honesty, integrity and reputation of the individual. Are they open and honest in dealings with consumers, market participants and regulators? Are they complying with their legal and professional obligations?
- The financial soundness of the individual. Have they been subject to judgement debts or awards which have not been satisfied within a reasonable period?
- Whether they failed to comply with the Statements of Principle, or was knowingly involved in a contravention of the requirements placed on the firm.
- The relevance, materiality and length of time since the occurrence of any matters indicating that the approved person is not fit and proper.
- The degree of risk the approved person poses to consumers and to the confidence consumers have in the financial system.
- The previous disciplinary record and compliance history of the approved person.
- The particular controlled function and nature of the activities undertaken by the approved person.

The FCA will publicise the final decision notice in relation to the withdrawal of approval, unless this would prejudice the interests of consumers.

5. **Prohibition of individuals** – under Section 56 of the FSMA, the FCA has the right to make a prohibition order against an individual. This order can prohibit the individual from carrying out particular functions, or from being employed by any authorised firm if the FCA considers it necessary for the achievement of its four statutory objectives. The prohibition order may relate just to a single specified regulated activity, or to all regulated activities. It may also relate to the individual's ability to work for a particular class of firms, or to all firms.

Prohibition orders are generally used by the FCA in cases which it sees as more serious than those that would merit mere withdrawal of approval, ie, there may be a greater lack of fitness and propriety. The FCA will consider all the factors listed above which could otherwise have resulted in a withdrawal of approval. It will also consider factors such as whether the individual has been convicted of, or dismissed or suspended from employment for, the abuse of drugs or other substances, or has convictions for serious assault. The FCA might feel it appropriate to issue a prohibition order against someone who continues to fulfil a controlled function after approval has been withdrawn.

As with withdrawal of approval, the FCA is required first to issue a warning notice to the approved person and the firm, followed by a decision notice. The FCA decision can be referred to the Tax and Chancery Chamber of the Upper Tribunal (Upper Tribunal) (see Section 2.3). It will generally publicise the final decision notice in relation to the prohibition of an individual.

6. **Public censure and statement of misconduct** – the FCA is empowered under FSMA to issue a **public censure** on firms it considers to have contravened a requirement imposed on it by, or under, the Act. For approved persons, the FCA may issue a public statement of misconduct when a person has failed to comply with the Statements of Principle, or has been knowingly involved in a firm's contravention of a requirement imposed on it by, or under, the Act.

As with other disciplinary actions, the steps required of the FCA are to:

- issue a warning notice (including the terms of the statement or censure the FCA is proposing to issue);
- follow this by a decision notice;
- subsequently provide the right to go to Upper Tribunal (see Section 2.3).

7. **Financial penalties** – as an alternative to public censures/statements of misconduct, the FCA is able to impose financial penalties on firms contravening requirements imposed on it by, or under, FSMA, and on approved persons failing to comply with the Statements of Principle, or having been knowingly involved in a firm's contravention of requirements.

The FCA provides guidance as to the criteria used to determine whether to issue public censures/statements (and no fine), rather than impose a financial penalty. It includes the following factors:

- If the firm or person avoided a loss or made a profit from their breach, a financial penalty will be more appropriate to prevent the guilty party from benefiting from its/his actions.
- If the breach or misconduct is more serious in nature or degree, a financial penalty is likely to be imposed.
- Admission of guilt, full and immediate co-operation and taking steps to ensure that consumers are fully compensated may lessen the likelihood of financial penalty.
- A poor disciplinary record or compliance history may increase the likelihood of a financial penalty, as a deterrent for the future.
- Whether FCA guidance has been followed by the firm.

As is usual for disciplinary matters, there will be a warning notice, decision notice and final decision notice, and ordinarily the final decision will be made public by the FCA's issuing a press release. However, in circumstances where it would be unfair on the person, or prejudicial to the interests of consumers, the FCA may choose not to issue a press release.

## 2.2.3 Defences

Under Section 22 of FSMA (Regulated Activities), for an activity to be a regulated activity it must be carried on **by way of business**.

The activity of accepting deposits will not be regarded as carried on by way of business by a person if they do not hold themselves out as accepting deposits on a day-to-day basis and if the deposits they accept are accepted only on particular occasions. In determining whether deposits are accepted only on particular occasions, the frequency of the occasions and any distinguishing characteristics must be taken into account.

- A person managing assets on a discretionary basis while acting as trustee of an occupational pension scheme may in certain circumstances be regarded as acting by way of business even if he would not, in the ordinary meaning of the phrase, be regarded as doing so.
- A person who carries on an insurance mediation activity will not be regarded as doing so by way of business unless he takes up or pursues that activity for remuneration.

Whether or not an activity is carried on by way of business is ultimately a question of judgement that takes account of several factors (none of which is likely to be conclusive). These include the degree of continuity, the existence of a commercial element, the scale of the activity and the proportion which the activity bears to other activities carried on by the same person but which are not regulated. The nature of the particular regulated activity that is carried on will also be relevant to the factual analysis.

Section 19 of the Act (the general prohibition) provides that the requirement to be authorised under the Act only applies in relation to activities that are carried on **in the UK**. In many cases, it will be quite straightforward to identify where an activity is carried on. But when there is a cross-border element, for example, because a client is outside the UK or because some other element of the activity happens outside the UK, the question may arise as to where the activity is carried on.

# 2.3 The Upper Tribunal

As has been noted in Chapter 5, Section 1.12, any person who receives a decision notice (including a supervisory notice) has the right to refer the FCA's decision to the Upper Tribunal. The individual or firm has 28 days in which to do so, and during this period FCA cannot take the action it has proposed; it must give the person or firm the full 28 days to decide whether to refer the decision.

The Upper Tribunal is independent of the FCA and is appointed by the government's Ministry of Justice (formerly the Department of Constitutional Affairs).

The Upper Tribunal will involve a full rehearing of the case and will determine on the basis of all available evidence whether the FCA's decision was appropriate. The rehearing may include evidence that was not available to the FCA at the time; the Tribunal's decision is binding on the FCA. While the Upper Tribunal has generally not overturned many of the regulator's decisions to date (indeed it would be worrying if it had!), it has been known to do so – an important factor in demonstrating that it is independent in its decision-making and prepared to challenge the FCA where it sees fit.

It is possible for a firm or individual to appeal a decision of the Upper Tribunal itself (but only on a point of law: for this, permission is needed either from the Upper Tribunal itself or from the Court of Appeal).

## 2.4 The Cost of Non-Compliance 2011–13 (Analysis of Fines)

The previous regulator's (the FSA) approach to enforcement and the severity of its warnings changed following the financial crisis of 2008–09. Early in 2009 the FSA chief executive warned that *'people should be very frightened of the FSA'* and made a firm commitment to correct any view to the contrary. It would look to take enforcement action against individuals – whereas it had previously only taken actions against firms. Back in 2008 the FSA's director of enforcement and financial crime set out enforcement as a strategic tool at the forefront of the drive to achieve credible deterrence through delivering results that make people sit up and pay attention. The FCA is continuing with the work that the previous regulator (the FSA) started.

The new rules establish a consistent and more transparent framework for the calculation of financial penalties; have increased enforcement fines dramatically increase in size. It can be concluded from the approach to enforcement, and from fines handed out in 2011, 2012 and to date in 2013, that enforcement action is now very much central to the regulator's strategic vision, and that higher penalties are an inevitable part of that process.

The regulator's approach to financial enforcement penalties supports its ongoing commitment to the principle of credible deterrence and the improvement of standards within firms in relation to market misconduct and their dealings with customers. The imposition of harder-hitting financial penalties that better reflect the scale of a firm's wrongdoing will become a feature of enforcement activity in the future. However, the FCA has sought to reassure firms that it is not an enforcement-driven regulator.

There is now a structured five-step penalty-setting framework, based on the three principles of disgorgement, discipline and deterrence. The total amount payable is intended to achieve disgorgement of any benefit and to penalise according to the severity of the breach. The framework is:

- Removing any profits made from the misconduct.
- Setting a figure to reflect the seriousness of the breach.
- Considering any aggravating and mitigating factors.
- Achieving the appropriate deterrent effect.
- Applying any settlement discount.

More recently the regulator's shift from being a principles-based regulator to an outcomes-focused regulator has given firms a clear warning that the regulator is no longer looking at failures in **tick-box** compliance with individual rules; rather, it is looking at what firms and individuals did and the real impact of these outcomes.

It can be seen that during 2011, 2012 and the first half of 2013 that the regulator has taken a serious view of, and imposed some heavy fines on firms, who neglected to rectify control failings.

Firms need to understand and realise that the regulator has changed its focus: now firms can be facing a significant penalty and demand for remedial action for a weak control framework, even without evidence of actual consumer detriment – as was the case for a number of fines. In most cases the fines levied on major organisations will not pose a problem to the firms paying them. Rather, the reputational damage is far more important, as this could lead to corporate and institutional clients taking their business to other firms.

FCA and PRA Supervisory Objectives, Principles and Processes

What the examples of fines below highlight is the change in the regulator's stance towards firms who breach their rules. Candidates should be aware of the consequences for non-compliance and the importance of why firms should ensure that they have robust and adequate systems and controls for the business activities that they undertake, plus senior management who take responsibility for ensuring the firm complies with the regulatory rules and requirements.

## 2.4.1 Summary of Fines and how they Interact with the Rules and Requirements

In the last few years there has been an increasing number of decisions against individuals, including two fines against compliance officers. The regulator also outlined its focus on senior management. A number of its final notices made reference to the actions of senior management both in establishing (or neglecting) the correct regulatory culture, processes and controls within their firms.

It is safe to assume that the FCA will hold to account approved persons whose conduct is culpable.

### Summary of Key Fines Levied

*[This information is meant to provide a background to the regulator's record of enforcement activity. However, candidates will not be examined on it.]*

#### Suitability of Advice

A UK bank was fined £7.7 million, and ordered to pay approximately £17 million in compensation, for failures in relation to the sale of two funds by its advisers. For a period of around two years the bank sold the two funds to 12,331 customers, pulling in £692 million of sales. However, there were a number of serious failings in the way the funds were sold. In particular: suitability reviews carried out on customers; failing to train sales staff adequately and explain the risks associated with the funds; failing to ensure that product brochures and other documents given to customers clearly explained the risks involved and could not mislead customers; and failing to have adequate procedures for monitoring sales processes and responding promptly when issues were identified.

Another UK bank was handed the largest-ever retail fine of £10.5 million because of inappropriate investment advice provided by one of its subsidiaries. For a five-year period the firm advised 2,485 customers to invest in asset-backed investment products, typically investment bonds, to fund long-term care costs for elderly customers. These products were sold to individuals entering, or already in, long-term care and in many cases these elderly customers were reliant on their investments to pay for their care. The advice and sales were unsuitable because in most cases the individual's life expectancy was below the recommended five-year investment period.

The private banking arm of an investment bank was fined £5.95 million for systems and controls failings in relation to sales of structured capital-at-risk products. However, the regulator identified serious failings in the systems and controls in respect of those sales. These included inadequate systems and controls in relation to assessing customers' attitudes to risk: failing to take reasonable care to evidence the suitability of these products for customers properly and failing to monitor staff effectively to ensure that they took reasonable care when giving advice.

As you can see, there are consistent themes – the biggest contributing factor to the issues was the lack of appropriate systems and controls and senior management oversight.

**Market Abuse**

The head of European credit sales at an investment bank was fined £210,000 for improper market conduct in disclosing client confidential information ahead of a significant bond issue in November 2009. During a call with a fund manager the individual signalled the following information: a specific company was potentially about to bring a big bond issue to market; the issue was intended to be announced the next day; the potential rating of the issue; that the company would redeem outstanding bonds; and the issue was mergers and acquisitions (M&A) related.

A former MD in corporate broking at an investment bank was fined £350,000 for engaging in market abuse by improperly disclosing inside information ahead of a significant equity fundraising by a publicly listed company in June 2009. While the regulator accepted that the actions were not deliberate, this was a serious case of market abuse which undermined the integrity of the market and damaged market confidence.

**Complaints Handling**

Three large fines were handed out following a review of complaint handling by UK banks.

A fine of £3.5 million for mishandling of complaints, many from older customers with little or no experience of investment products was given.

There was a fine of £2,170,000 on two insurance companies that are part of a UK bank. During the collation of files requested, a large number were altered improperly before they were submitted because the firms had failed to act with due skill, care and diligence. The majority of the alterations were minor in nature and none resulted in detriment to customers.

Two UK banks were fined £2.8 million for multiple failings in the way they handled customers' complaints, responding inadequately to more than half the complaints reviewed. The investigation found that there was an unacceptably high risk that customers were not treated fairly, due to a number of failings within the banks' approach to routine complaint handling, including delays in responding to customers and poor quality investigations into complaints.

A UK retail bank was fined £4,315,000 for failings in its systems and controls that resulted in up to 140,000 customers receiving delayed payment protection insurance redress.

Again, there are similar issues and failings in all the above examples.

**Money Laundering (ML)**

A foreign, privately owned bank was fined £525,000 and its former money laundering reporting officer (MLRO) £17,500 for failure to take reasonable care to establish and maintain adequate AML systems and controls. The failings at the bank lasted almost three years and exposed the firm to an unacceptable risk of money laundering (ML).

A bank '*was fined £7.6 million for failures in its anti-money laundering policies and procedures over corporate customers connected to politically exposed persons (PEPs).*' This is the first case that the regulator (both the FCA and its predecessor, the FSA) has brought in relation to money laundering that is focused on commercial banking.

## FCA and PRA Supervisory Objectives, Principles and Processes

### Client Money

A firm was fined £494,900 for providing misleading information in relation to client money breaches. The firm was not compliant with Client Asset Sourcebook (CASS) requirements and this only became apparent after the regulator, as part of a CASS visit to the firm, discovered the breaches.

The investment banking arm of a UK retail bank was fined £1.12 million for failing to protect and segregate, on an intra-day basis, client money held in sterling money market deposits. For over eight years, between December 2001 and December 2009, the firm failed to segregate client money maturing from its sterling money market deposits on an intra-day basis. Such client monies were segregated overnight, but matured into a proprietary bank account and were mixed on a daily basis with the firm's own funds, typically for between five and seven hours within each trading day.

A firm specialising in financial planning and portfolio management was fined £26,600 and its compliance officer £11,550 for failings in relation to the protection of client money. The firm and the compliance officer had insufficient knowledge and oversight of compliance with the CASS rules, which led to serious regulatory breaches.

### London Interbank Offered Rate (LIBOR)

A number of UK and European banks have received heavy fines from the FCA, the US authorities and their local regulators for serious failings around their LIBOR submissions. Traders and submitters treated LIBOR submissions as a potential way to make money – with no regard for the integrity of the market. The false submissions were noted as occurring globally for the banks concerned.

### Miscellaneous

An investment management firm was fined £3.5 million for failing to manage a conflict of interest between two of its clients. This is the largest fine ever imposed in a conflict of interest case. In addition to the fine issued by the UK regulator, the SEC also fined the firm in the US.

An insurance broker was fined £6.895 million for failings in its anti-bribery and corruption systems and controls. These failings created an unacceptable risk that payments made by the firm to overseas third parties could be used for corrupt purposes.

An individual was fined £3 million and banned from performing any role in regulated financial services for not being fit and proper. This is the largest fine for an individual in a non-market abuse case. The individual was the CEO of a hedge fund management company based in London. The regulator considered that the individual and the firm failed to satisfy the threshold conditions, because it failed to ensure that its business was conducted soundly and prudently and in compliance with proper standards.

Two firms were fined (£205,128 and £49,000) for failing to provide timely transaction reports to the regulator in respect of all the reportable transactions they carried out.

The regulator published a decision notice to ban and fine a former non-executive director £154,800 for failing to disclose conflicts of interest.

*An investment firm was fined £25,000 after two of its appointed representatives mis-sold insurance. The regulator identified that the firm did not have appropriate oversight of its appointed representatives.*

*[Source of information: FSA website – FSA library/communication documents/press releases 2011 and to 31 March 2013 and FCA website from 1 April to 28 February 2014]*

## 2.5 Information required by the FCA

Under Section 165 of FSMA, the FCA is given wide-ranging powers to require information. These powers extend to authorised persons, persons connected with authorised persons, RIEs and RCHs (see Chapter 5, Section 3).

Essentially, the FCA is able to give written notice to an authorised person requiring information and/or documents to be provided within a reasonable period. Indeed, FCA staff (such as supervisors) are able to require documents and/or information without delay. This requirement applies only to information and documents reasonably required in connection with the exercise by the FCA of functions conferred on it by or under this Act.

Section 167 of the FSMA gives the FCA further information-gathering powers:

- It requires authorised firms (and certain persons connected with such firms) to appoint **one or more competent persons** to provide the FCA with a report on any matter about which the FCA has required or could require the provision of information under Section 165. The nature of that/those competent person(s) will depend on the issue being investigated – they are often solicitors or accountants.
- The purpose of the appointment by the FCA of competent persons to carry out general investigations is to identify the nature, conduct or state of business of an authorised person or an appointed representative, a particular aspect of that business, or the ownership or control of an authorised person (firm).

Section 168 of the FSMA permits the FCA to appoint persons to carry out investigations in particular cases, such as:

- if a person may be guilty of an offence under Section 177/191 (offences) or 398(2) (misleading the FCA);
- if an offence has been committed under Section 24(1) (false claim to be authorised or exempt); or misleading statement and practices;
- if there may have been a breach of the general prohibition of regulated activities, market abuse may have taken place or there may have been a contravention of Section 21 or 238 of the Act (Restrictions on Financial Promotions).

In addition, the FCA may undertake the appointment of a person to carry out investigations in particular cases when it appears to it that someone:

- may be carrying out authorised activities when they are not authorised to do so (Section 20 of FSMA);
- may be guilty of an offence under prescribed ML regulations;
- contravened a rule made by the FCA;

# FCA and PRA Supervisory Objectives, Principles and Processes

- may not be a **fit and proper** person to perform functions in relation to a regulated activity carried on by an authorised or exempt person;
- may have performed or agreed to perform a function in breach of a prohibition order;
- or if:
  - an authorised or exempt person may have failed to comply with a prohibition order (Section 56(6));
  - a person for whom the FCA has given approval under Section 59 (approval for particular arrangements) may not be a **fit and proper** person to perform the function to which that approval relates or a person may be guilty of misconduct for the purposes of Section 66 (disciplinary powers).

## 2.6 Powers of Intervention

### 2.6.1 Temporary Product Intervention

The FCA stated in *Journey to the FCA*, published October 2012, that it will intervene earlier than the previous regulator in order to ensure an appropriate degree of consumer protection.

The Financial Services Act 2012 provided the FCA with temporary rules – for up to a period of 12 months, to prohibit or ban any product that it considers is, or will cause consumer protection problems.

As noted in Chapter 5, the FCA's style of supervision means that it will intervene earlier in a product's lifespan and seek to address root causes or problems for consumers.

Previous experience has taught the regulator that products designed for specific markets/consumers are routinely sold outside them. Therefore, the FCA will intervene directly by making product intervention rules to prevent harm to consumers – for example, by restricting the use of specified product features or the promotion of particular product types to some or all consumers.

The key to the FCA using the new powers will be consumer protection.

The FCA has stated the instances when it feels that it will/could use the temporary product intervention rules. They are:

- Products being sold outside their target market or being inappropriately targeted.
- Products that would be acceptable but for the inclusion or exclusion of particular features.
- Products where there is a significant incentive for inappropriate or indiscriminate targeting of consumers.
- Markets where competitive pressure alone will not address concerns about a product, eg, where competition focuses on irrelevant features or exploits systemic consumer weaknesses such that market-based solutions will not address the problem.
- Products which may bring about significant detriment as result of being inappropriately targeted.
- In some particularly serious cases, a product may be considered inherently flawed – for example, a product that has such disadvantageous features that the majority of consumers, or specified types of consumer, are unlikely to benefit.

179

The FCA is subject to the wider EU legislative framework, and this has implications for firms which practice cross-border business. When a product provider is domiciled overseas, FCA rules do not apply to the development of potentially harmful products by such firms. However, where products from overseas providers are sold by intermediaries based in the UK, they will be subject to regulatory action by the FCA.

### 2.6.2 Financial Promotions

One of the new powers provided by the Financial Services Act to the FCA is to ban misleading financial promotions. This means that the FCA can remove financial promotions immediately from the market, or prevent them being used in the first place, without having to go through the enforcement process.

The use of this new power will be determined by the specific promotion and not used against a firm as a whole. It can be used on its own or before the FCA takes enforcement action against a firm. It will work separately from existing disciplinary powers – which the FCA can/will use when firms fail to comply with the rules and their overall systems and approach are poor.

The FCA will give a direction to an authorised firm to remove its own financial promotion or one it approves on behalf of an unauthorised firm, setting out its reasons for banning it. The next step is for firms to make representations to the FCA if they think that it is making the wrong decision. Finally the FCA will decide whether to confirm, amend or revoke its direction. If it is confirmed, it will publish it – along with a copy of the promotion and the reasons behind its decision.

## 3. The FCA Handbook

### Learning Objective

6.4.1 Understand the six types of provisions used by the FCA/PRA in its Handbook and the status of the approved industry guidance

The FCA's Handbook sets out the rules and guidance for authorised firms and also rules on the way the FCA itself operates in matters such as enforcement and disciplinary action. These rules are subject to regular amendment and change. The FCA, therefore, publishes changes to the Handbook, and to the instruments which will effect these changes, on its website, and provides details of these changes to subscribers of its hard copy services.

The Handbook consists of sourcebooks and manuals, which contain six different types of provisions, each type being indicated by a single letter. The six different types of provisions are:

- **R.** **Rules** are binding on authorised persons (firms) and, if a firm contravenes a rule, it may be subject to discipline. The FCA's Principles for Businesses are given the status of rules.
- **D.** **Directions and requirements** dictate, for example, the form of content of applications for authorisation. They are binding on those to whom they are addressed.
- **P.** The **Statements of Principle for Approved Persons**, binding on approved persons.

# FCA and PRA Supervisory Objectives, Principles and Processes

**C.** Paragraphs which describe behaviour that does not amount to market abuse. The letter 'C' is used because these types of behaviour are **conclusively not market abuse**.

**E.** An **evidential provision** is a rule but is not binding in its own right. It will always relate to another binding rule. Compliance with an evidential provision is indicative (but not conclusive) evidence that the binding rule has been complied with or contravened, as appropriate.

**G.** **Guidance**, which might be used by the FCA to explain the implications of other provisions, to indicate possible means of compliance, or to recommend a particular course of action. Guidance is not binding, nor does it have **evidential** effect. As a result, a firm cannot be disciplined for a failure to follow guidance.

## 3.1  FCA-Confirmed Industry Guidance

The FSA developed a framework for industry to gain recognition on the guidance that it produces. Industry guidance is defined as: '*information created, developed and freely issued by a person or body, other than the FSA, which is intended to provide guidance from the body concerned to the industry about the provisions of the Handbook*'. The FCA is continuing the work and process for industry guidance that the FSA developed.

### 3.1.1  Status of FCA Confirmed Industry Guidance

A firm's defence against the FCA is in essence the same whether it follows FCA guidance or FCA-confirmed industry guidance – FCA rules say '*The FCA will not take action against a person for behaviour that it considers to be in line with guidance, other materials published by the FCA in support of the Handbook or FCA-confirmed industry guidance, which were current at the time of the behaviour in question*' (DEPP 6.2.1(4)G). Similarly, as industry guidance is not mandatory (and is one way, but not the only way, to comply with requirements), the FCA cannot presume that, because firms are not complying with it, they are not meeting FCA requirements.

However, if a breach has been established, industry guidance is potentially relevant to an enforcement case. The ways in which the FCA may seek to use industry guidance in an enforcement context are similar to those in which it uses FCA guidance or supporting materials. As set out in Chapter 2 of the new Enforcement Guide, these include to:

1. help assess whether it could reasonably have been understood or predicted at the time that the conduct in question fell below the standards required by the Principles;
2. explain the regulatory context;
3. inform a view of the overall seriousness of the breaches, eg, it could decide that the breach warranted a higher penalty in circumstances where the FCA had written to chief executives in that sector to reiterate the importance of ensuring that a particular aspect of their business complied with relevant regulatory standards;
4. inform the consideration of a firm's defence that the FCA was judging the firm on the basis of retrospective standards; and
5. be considered as part of expert or supervisory statements in relation to the relevant standards at the time.

The FCA is conscious that the use of industry guidance in this context should not create a second tier of regulation and that guidance providers are not quasi-regulators. It will take the specific status of FCA confirmation into account when making judgements about the relevance of industry guidance in enforcement cases.

There are three conceptual ways that the FCA can recognise guidance, codes or standards developed by industry. These different forms of recognition have different legal effects, and the requirement to follow statutory processes varies. The methods are:

- **safe harbour** – the FCA has to create rules in the Handbook to give industry guidance this effect and follow full statutory processes; this is a more formal level of recognition;
- **sturdy breakwater** – this only impacts the FCA, which is prevented from taking action against firms;
- **implicit recognition** – this has no legal effect on the FCA or anyone else; the FCA will not make any rules because the industry has found a solution to address a market failure.

The FCA will neither monitor firms' use of FCA-confirmed industry guidance, nor will it expect providers to monitor or enforce compliance with the guidance, pressure guidance providers to produce industry guidance or require industry guidance to plug gaps in the regulatory regime.

# 4. Prudential and Liquidity Standards

## 4.1 Prudential Standards

**Learning Objective**

6.5 Understand the purpose and application of the following Prudential Standards relating to financial services:

6.5.1 General Prudential (GENPRU) Sourcebook;

6.5.2 Prudential Sourcebook for banks, building societies and investment firms (BIPRU);

6.5.3 Capital adequacy and liquidity requirements for certain types of firm (IFPRU)

### 4.1.1 Capital Requirements

The **Capital Requirements Directive (CRD)** requires firms to satisfy certain financial requirements. In particular, firms need to have financial resources in excess of their regulatory financial resource requirements. These requirements aim to minimise the risk of a firm's collapsing by being unable to pay its debts and are generally referred to as **prudential** rules.

The aim of the CRD is to ensure the financial soundness of credit institutions (essentially banks and building societies, but also investment firms). The CRD stipulates how much of their own financial resources such firms must have in order to cover their risks and protect their depositors.

The CRD amends two significant existing directives – the Banking Consolidation Directive (BCD) and the Capital Adequacy Directive (CAD) – for the prudential regulation of credit institutions and investment firms across the EU. It is a major piece of legislation that introduces a modern prudential framework, relating capital levels more closely to risks.

The CRD implements the revised Basel Framework in the EU, which is based on three pillars:

- **Pillar 1** – minimum capital requirements for credit, market and operational risks.
- **Pillar 2** – supervisory review – establishing a constructive dialogue between a firm and the regulator on the risks, the risk management and capital requirements of the firm.
- **Pillar 3** – market discipline – robust requirements on public disclosure intended to give the market a stronger role in ensuring that firms hold an appropriate level of capital.

Prudential rules exist for both firms subject to the CRD (CRD firms) and firms not subject to the CRD but still authorised (non-CRD firms).

Within the PRA Handbook there are five Interim Prudential Sourcebooks, each one relating to certain types of firm (ie, banks, building societies, friendly societies, insurers and investment businesses).

The sourcebooks are described as **interim**; there is a transitional period underway as the FCA has introduced its new Prudential Sourcebooks.

## CRD2

As part of the ongoing process of revision that was already under way, and also as a response to the credit market turmoil that emerged mid–2007, the Commission adopted proposals (CRD2) aimed at improving the:

- quality of firms' capital by establishing clear EU-wide criteria for assessing the eligibility of hybrid capital to be counted as part of a firm's overall capital;
- management of large exposures by restricting a firm's lending beyond a certain limit to any one party;
- risk management of securitisation, including a requirement to ensure that a firm does not invest in a securitisation unless the originator retains an economic interest;
- supervision of cross-border banking groups by establishing colleges of supervisors for banking groups that operate in multiple EU countries; and
- operation of the CRD by amending various technical provisions to correct unintended errors and to introduce additional clarity sought by stakeholders since the implementation of the original CRD.

Much of this package takes the EU beyond the content of the internationally agreed BCBS standards, as it is also aimed at achieving greater harmonisation of the single market for financial services. Proposals were also made within the CRD2 package for improving liquidity risk management. The UK did not consult on liquidity risk management as it had already just published its own new liquidity framework for firms.

The rules for CRD2 took effect in the FSA Handbook from 31 December 2010, with transitional provisions.

## CRD3

In 2009 the Commission proposed further changes to the CRD (CRD3) to complement its CRD2 proposals in addressing the lessons of the financial crisis. These changes reflect international developments and build on and mostly follow the agreements reached by the BCBS. They included:

- higher capital requirements for resecuritisations to make sure that firms take proper account of the risks of investing in such complex financial products;
- upgrading disclosure standards for securitisation exposures to increase the market confidence that is necessary to encourage firms to start lending to each other again;
- strengthening capital requirements for the trading book to ensure that a firm's assessment of the risks connected with its trading book better reflects the potential losses from adverse market movements in the kind of stressed conditions that have been experienced recently.

The CRD3 changes also include rules on remuneration policies and practices to tackle perverse pay incentives, by requiring firms to have sound remuneration policies that do not encourage or reward excessive risk-taking. The UK did not consult on this aspect of the CRD as it implemented new rules on remuneration, via its own remuneration code (see Section 5). The FSA published a statement during the third quarter of 2010 (CP 10/19) which assessed the effectiveness of the code so far and provided an update on international implementation and alignment.

The FSA implemented the rules under CRD3, which took effect from 31 December 2011.

## The Interim Prudential Sourcebook for Investment Businesses (IPRU-INV)

The IPRU-INV covers firms which manage investments for others (fund managers) and firms that deal, or arrange deals, in investments (known as securities and futures firms).

## The General Prudential Sourcebook (GENPRU)

The GENPRU contains prudential rules and material applying generally to banking, investments and insurance. It came into force on 1 January 2007 and applies to CRD firms.

## The Prudential Sourcebook for Banks, Building Societies and Investment Firms (BIPRU)

BIPRU came into force on 1 January 2007 and contains prudential rules applying to credit institutions and investment firms. It applies to CRD firms.

## The Prudential Sourcebook for Investment Firms (IFPRU)

IFPRU came into force on 1 January 2014 and contains prudential rules applying to investment firms that are subject to CRD IV.

The Sourcebook is made up of nine chapters:

- application;
- supervisory processes and governance;
- own funds;
- credit risk;

- operational risk;
- market risk;
- liquidity;
- prudential consolidation and large exposures; and
- public disclosure.

## Regulatory Requirements

Two particular rules from the PRA and FCA prudential sourcebooks/handbooks are examinable:

1. Firms are required to have the amount and type of financial resources required by the PRA and the FCA available at all times.
2. If a firm becomes aware that it is in breach of, or expects shortly to be in breach of, the above, then it must notify the PRA (and the FCA for those firms not regulated by the PRA for prudential purposes) immediately.

## 4.1.2    Regulatory Developments

### Basel III

In response to the recent financial crisis, the Basel Committee on Banking Supervision (BCBS) set forth to update its guidelines for capital and banking regulations.

In January 2011 the BCBS issued a proposal to strengthen global capital and liquidity regulations with the goal of promoting a more resilient banking sector. The objective of the BCBS's reform package is to improve the banking sector's ability to absorb shocks arising from financial and economic stress, whatever the source, thus reducing the risk of spillover from the financial sector to the rest of the economy.

Basel III proposes many new capital, leverage and liquidity standards to strengthen the regulation, supervision and risk management of the banking sector. The capital standards and new capital buffers require banks to hold more and higher quality of capital than under current Basel II rules. The new leverage and liquidity ratios introduce a non-risk-based measure to supplement the risk-based minimum capital requirements and measures to ensure that adequate funding is maintained in case of crisis.

On 19 December 2009 the BCBS issued a press release which presented to the public two consultative documents for review and comment:

- Strengthening the resilience of the banking sector.
- International framework for liquidity risk measurement, standards and monitoring.

In Europe, new legislation will be needed to introduce these standards as rules – this is referred to as CRD4.

The implementation process takes time, not all of the provisions in Basel III will be implemented globally until 2019. Further reference is made to this later in this section.

As a result of the financial crisis the EC has reviewed the CRD and has proposed some recommendations for change. The diverse package of changes reflects the strengthening of the European prudential regime in the CRD to address the lessons learned from the credit market turmoil. It therefore also forms part of the follow-up on aspects of the Turner Review publications.

Various packages of changes to the CRD are being proposed quite close together, which the EC is now **numbering** to avoid confusion and for ease of reference.

### 4.1.3 PRA Approach to Prudential Supervision

As with all elements of its approach, the PRA expects firms to take responsibility for ensuring that the capital they have is adequate. But, reflecting the incentives firms have to run their business in a less prudent manner than the public interest would indicate, there is also a clear role for the PRA as prudential regulator to specify a minimum amount of capital for firms to hold. This does not, however, diminish the need for firms themselves to judge the adequacy of their capital position in an appropriately prudent manner, since that is necessary to maintain the confidence of their creditors. Firms should engage honestly and prudently in assessments of capital adequacy, not least because the PRA's limited resource means that it cannot be expected to identify and account for all the risks that firms may face.

Reflecting the importance of combining firm-specific supervision with oversight of the financial system as a whole, there is, in addition, be a macro-prudential objective in respect of capital maintained in aggregate by the banking system. This objective, and elements of macro-prudential assessment more generally, for example top-down stress tests, falls under the purview of the FPC.

The PRA expects firms to take responsibility for maintaining at all times an adequate level of capital, consistent with their safety and soundness and taking into account the risks to which they are exposed. The PRA forms a judgement about how much capital an individual firm needs to maintain, given the risks to which it is exposed and uncertainties about the values of assets and liabilities (except in the case of credit unions, which must abide only by the PRA's minimum prudential standards for these firms). The PRA's judgements informs firms' own assessments. But the PRA expects firms in the first instance to take responsibility for determining the appropriate level of capital they should maintain. Firms should engage honestly and prudently in the process of assessing capital adequacy, and not rely on regulatory minima. And they should not rely on aggressive interpretations of accounting standards, especially in calculating loan loss provisions.

The PRA expects all banks, building societies and designated investment firms to develop a framework for stress testing and capital management that captures the full range of risks to which they are exposed and enables these risks to be stressed against a range of plausible yet severe scenarios. In support of this, the PRA expects all firms to ensure that assets and liabilities are appropriately valued and that provisions are adequate. Firms are expected to take into account the effect of asset encumbrance insofar as it may reduce loss-absorbing capacity in resolution or liquidation. The PRA will review the stresses applied for appropriateness.

Banks, building societies and designated investment firms are expected to develop, as a matter of routine, management actions in response to stress scenarios. The PRA determines the minimum regulatory capital level and a buffer on top of this expressed in terms of the Basel and EU risk-weighted framework for banks, building societies and designated investment firms.

FCA and PRA Supervisory Objectives, Principles and Processes

It will comprise three parts:

- **Pillar 1** – requirements to provide protection against credit, market and operational risk, for which firms follow internationally agreed methods of calculation and calibration.
- **Pillar 2A** – requirements advised by the PRA reflecting:

  i.  estimates of risks either not addressed or only partially addressed by the international standards for Pillar 1 (for example, interest rate risk in the banking book or risks associated with firms' own pension schemes); and
  ii. PRA estimates of the capital needed to compensate for shortcomings in management and governance, or risk management and controls (including valuation and accounting practices).

  The latter is designed to guard against unexpected losses while the deficiencies are addressed and is not a long-term substitute for adequate standards in the underperforming areas.

Pillars 1 and 2A together represent what the PRA regards as the minimum level of regulatory capital a firm should maintain at all times in order to cover adequately the risks to which it is exposed.

- **Pillar 2B** – guidance from the PRA reflecting a forward-looking assessment of the capital required to ensure that firms' minimum level of regulatory capital can be met at all times, even after severe but plausible stresses, when asset valuations may become strained. The PRA's assessment of this **capital planning buffer** (CPB) will take into account the options a firm has to protect its capital position under stress, for example through internal capital generation.

The CPB is intended to be drawn upon in times of stress. The PRA will therefore expect and allow it to be used in stressed circumstances. If a firm's CPB is used, the PRA will expect the firm to indicate how it plans to rebuild it and over what timescale. This framework will be revised in light of forthcoming changes to European directives, particularly to the Capital Requirements Directive (CRD IV), which is likely to set out a number of additional requirements for capital buffers. This will include some buffers agreed via the FSB and covered in Basel III that will reflect a firm's size and systemic importance.

The PRA is carrying out an exercise aimed at amending its prudential handbook/sourcebooks. It is creating a 'rulebook' that will hold all its prudential rules and requirements.

## 4.2    The Liquidity Framework

In December 2008 the previous regulator (the FSA) consulted on a new liquidity regime and produced two further consultation papers in 2009 before publishing its final rules in October 2009. The new liquidity framework became effective from 1 December 2009.

The consultation process set out the regulator's views on the future of liquidity regulation within the UK, including a new quantitative regime for certain firms to anchor the stability of their liquidity positions. The liquidity framework is far-reaching and robust. The new liquidity regime will continue to put the responsibility of adopting a sound approach to liquidity risk management on firms and their senior management.

The new liquidity framework applies to UK-authorised and UK-regulated entities. It was stated, at the time, that many institutions would need to reshape their business model significantly over the next few years as a result of it. The BIPRU Prudential Sourcebook relates to banks, building societies and investment firms. Therefore, this will also include, for example, an incoming EEA firm and a third-country BIPRU firm, such as the UK branch of a foreign bank.

The new requirements do not fully apply to limited-licence firms, and only the **systems and controls** requirements are applicable.

## 4.2.1 Adequacy of Liquidity Resources

The overarching rule (BIPRU 12.2.1) at the heart of the liquidity framework regime stipulates that firms must at all times maintain liquidity resources which are adequate, both as to amount and quality, to ensure that there is no significant risk that their liabilities cannot be met as they fall due.

A firm may not include liquidity resources that can be made available by other members of its group and may not include liquidity resources that may be made available through emergency liquidity assistance from a central bank.

The overall liquidity adequacy rule is expressed to apply to each firm on a solo basis. However, the requirements do recognise that there will be circumstances in which it may be appropriate for a firm or a branch to rely on liquidity support provided by other entities within the group or from elsewhere within the firm.

Lehman Brothers demonstrated that, during a severe liquidity crisis, it is the individual position of the various legal entities within a group that matters most. The PRA (and the FCA) have to be satisfied with the liquidity position of the locally incorporated entity or local branch.

The liquidity policy can be split into four key strands:

- **Systems and controls** – a new systems and controls framework based on the recent work of the BCBS and the EBA, [BIPRU 12.3 and 12.4].
- **Individual liquidity adequacy standards (ILASs)** – a new domestic framework for liquidity management for many of the firms that the PRA and the FCA supervise. This framework is based on firms being able to survive liquidity stresses of varying magnitude and duration [BIPRU 12.5, 12.6 and 12.7].
- **Group-wide and cross-border management of liquidity** – the framework allows firms, through waivers and modifications, to deviate from self-sufficiency if this is appropriate and if it will not result in undue risk to consumers and other stakeholders whom the rules in question are intended to protect [BIPRU 12.8].
- **Regulatory reporting** – the new reporting framework for liquidity, enables the regulator to collect granular, standardised liquidity data at an appropriate frequency, so that it can form firm-specific, sector and market-wide views on liquidity risk exposures.

We will look at these strands in more detail.

FCA and PRA Supervisory Objectives, Principles and Processes

## Individual Liquidity Adequacy Standard (ILAS)

The purpose of the ILAS is to obtain/for firms to provide robust and accurate liquidity information. Firms are required to provide new liquidity mismatch returns, which provide the PRA and the FCA with key contractual liquidity information necessary to undertake detailed and granular analysis of a firm's liquidity positions. As part of the ILAS process, firms are required to complete an ILAA – which must be proportionate to a firm's business model and risk appetite, should take into account all sources of liquidity and must include the firm's assessment and evaluation of its compliance. A key function of the ILAA is to inform a firm's board of the ongoing assessment and quantification of the firm's liquidity risks.

## Regulatory Reporting

The reporting requirements are proportionate to the nature and scale of the firm's activities. Larger firms must report in more detail and more frequently than smaller firms conducting a more restricted range of activities. The report for this latter type of firm is an annual systems and controls questionnaire.

## Systems and Controls Requirements

This requires firms:

- to have in place sound, effective and complete processes, strategies and systems that enable them to identify, measure, monitor and control liquidity risk;
- to ensure that their processes, strategies and systems are comprehensive and proportionate to the nature, scale and complexity of their activities;
- to ensure that a governing body establishes the firm's risk tolerance. The governing body is ultimately responsible for the liquidity risk assumed by the firm and the manner in which this risk is managed;
- to ensure that the governing body undertakes a review (at least annually), confirming that the firm's arrangements remain adequate;
- senior management to review the firm's liquidity position continuously, including its compliance with the overall liquidity adequacy rules, and to report to its governing body on a regular basis, providing adequate information as to that liquidity position;
- to have appropriate contingency funding plans approved by their governing body;
- to conduct regular stress tests so as to identify sources of potential liquidity strain, ensure that current liquidity exposures continue to conform to the liquidity risk tolerance established by that firm's governing body, and identify the effects on the firm's assumptions about pricing.

The PRA and the FCA expect that the extent and frequency of such testing should be proportionate to the size of the firm and to its liquidity risk exposures. A firm's governing body must regularly review the stresses and scenarios tested to ensure that their nature and severity remain appropriate and relevant to that firm.

The objective of the proposed rules is to ensure that firms actively monitor and control liquidity risk exposures and funding needs within and across legal entities, business lines and currencies. Firms can expect to be subject to a more rigorous supervisory review of their governance arrangements, measurement tools, methods and assumptions used in the stress tests, mitigating strategies, business planning assumptions and contingency funding plans.

189

### Group-Wide and Cross-Border Management of Liquidity

Every firm is subject to the overall liquidity adequacy rule, meaning that every firm is required to be self-sufficient in terms of liquidity adequacy and to be able to satisfy this rule, relying on its own liquidity resources.

However, the PRA and the FCA recognise that there may be circumstances in which it will be appropriate for a firm to rely on liquidity resources that can be made available to it by other members of its group, or for a firm to rely on liquidity resources elsewhere in the firm for the purposes of ensuring that its UK branch has adequate liquidity resources in respect of the activities carried on from the branch.

If the PRA and the FCA are satisfied that the statutory tests in Section 148 (Modifications or Waiver of Rules) of the Act are met, they will consider modifying the overall liquidity adequacy rule to permit reliance on liquidity support of this kind.

## 5. The Remuneration Code

### Learning Objective

6.7.1 Apply the principles and rules of the Remuneration Code (SYSC 19A (FCA/PRA) & C)

In *'CP09/10: Reforming remuneration in financial services'* published in March 2009, the regulator (the FSA) proposed a general rule which required firms to establish, implement and maintain remuneration policies, procedures and practices that are consistent with and promote effective risk management. This general rule was supported by eight principles, which were proposed to be added to the handbook as either evidential provisions or guidance. The eight principles related to three areas: governance, the measurement of performance and the composition of remuneration.

The fundamental objective of the remuneration policy is to sustain market confidence and promote financial stability, by removing the incentives for inappropriate risk-taking by firms, and thereby to protect consumers. The need to ensure that remuneration policies and practices are consistent with and promote effective risk management is fundamental.

The remuneration code has been incorporated into the PRA and FCA Handbooks because they want to have clear rules and guidance in place so that firms can incorporate the code into their future planning. It also is believed that the code limits the risk of damage to the UK's competitiveness, especially in the light of the strong G20 endorsement of the Financial Stability Forum Principles on Remuneration and the efforts of the EU and the BCBS to implement these principles within the EU and globally.

In 2010 the regulator issued a further consultation paper (CP10/19) to propose a revised framework for regulating financial services firms' remuneration structures and for an extension of the scope of the code, primarily to implement changes required, as a result of the remuneration provisions in the most recent set of amendments (CRD3).

The proposed revisions to the code, as set out in CP10/19, also took account of other developments, including the provisions relating to remuneration within the Financial Services Act 2010, Sir David Walker's review of corporate governance, and lessons learned from the regulator's implementation of the code so far.

The new framework contained rules, evidential provisions and guidance relating to 12 principles, which continue to cover the three main areas of regulatory scope: governance; performance measurement; and remuneration structures. It also introduced some new rules, for example on: discretionary severance pay; linking remuneration to a firm's capital base; and discretionary pension payments.

The CP also stated the regulator's intention to adopt a proportionate approach to implementation, reflecting the size of the firm and the nature, scope and complexity of its activities. The regulator also proposed a framework for applying proportionality, as well as its intended approach to supervision, setting out its intentions to take a risk-based and proportionate approach.

The fundamental objectives of the remuneration policy remain unchanged. They are to sustain market confidence and promote financial stability, by reducing the incentives for inappropriate risk-taking by firms, and thereby to protect consumers. The need to ensure that remuneration policies and practices are consistent with and promote effective risk management therefore remains fundamental. However, from the regulator's experience to date in day-to-day supervision, the policies and practices of a number of firms continue to exhibit weaknesses which are inconsistent with effective risk management.

The revised code applied from 1 January 2011 to:

- all banks and building societies;
- all CAD investment firms, being investment firms to which the MiFID rules apply; and
- UK branches of firms which would otherwise be caught but whose home state is outside the EEA.

UK branches of firms which would otherwise be caught whose home state is within the EEA do not have to comply with the code, as their home state will have to apply equivalent provisions under CRD 3.

If a firm falls within the code's remit, all its subsidiaries, whether within or outside the UK, and whatever their activities, are caught.

Going forward, the regulator will separate firms into three streams:

- **High impact groups** (broadly, those subject to **close and continuous** supervision) who need to prepare a remuneration policy statement ahead of the end of the financial year, have a specific remuneration meeting with the PRA/FCA and may not be able to pay bonuses without agreement. This year, general considerations will be separated from particular remuneration decisions.
- **Medium high or medium low groups or firms** have to prepare a report which is inspected as part of the risk assessment review.
- **Low impact firms** only need to prepare a report if they are part of a thematic review.

However, there will inevitably be a *de minimis* set of remuneration provisions for all firms (who will have to include some remuneration information in their GABRIEL (GAthering Better Regulatory Information ELectronically) regulatory returns.

The remuneration of all employees within a firm is caught by the code, and remuneration committees need to make sure that the general framework complies with the overall principle on risk.

However, there are particular provisions for more senior employees currently known as **Principle 8 (P8) employees**. Due to some confusion over the scope of the definition, the regulator gave further clarification, as part of the supervisory framework issued to firms in December 2009 and said that all employees with remuneration over £1 million would be caught, but now proposes to use the term **code staff**. It has published a table of key positions, which it believes should be subject to the provisions on code staff (see page 20 of the consultation paper) in addition to staff whose remuneration takes them into the same pay bracket. Those who hold SIF positions (eg, directors, partners and senior managers) are automatically included. Also, its proposals expressly bring secondees within the scope of the code.

It is worth noting that the regulator proposals indicate that code staff whose bonus is less than 33% of their total remuneration and whose annual total remuneration is £500,000 or less are not subject to the provisions regarding deferral of variable remuneration and some other rules, eg, guaranteed bonuses or payment in shares.

Relevant firms must compile a list of code staff ahead of the bonus allocation period and notify staff who are subject to the code's rules, including provisions prohibiting payment of bonuses that do not accord with the code's rules and those providing for recovery of such bonuses. The GABRIEL regulatory returns must confirm that all code staff have been identified and listed.

The Code now applies to all firms that the CRD applies to (ie, all firms that must comply in BIPRU).

## 5.1 The PRA and FCA Remuneration Code

### General Requirement:

Firms must establish, implement and maintain remuneration policies, procedures and practices that are consistent with and promote sound and effective risk management.

### The Principles:

- **Remuneration Principle 1 – Risk Management and Risk Tolerance**
  A firm must ensure that its remuneration policy is consistent with and promotes sound and effective risk management and does not encourage risk-taking that exceeds the level of tolerated risk of the firm.

- **Remuneration Principle 2 – Supporting Business Strategy, Objectives, Values and Long-Term Interests of the Firm**
  A firm must ensure that its remuneration policy is in line with the business strategy, objectives, values and long-term interests of the firm.

- **Remuneration Principle 3 – Avoiding Conflicts of Interest**
  A firm must ensure that its remuneration policy includes measures to avoid conflicts of interest.

# FCA and PRA Supervisory Objectives, Principles and Processes

- **Remuneration Principle 4 – Governance**

  A firm must ensure that its governing body in its supervisory function adopts and periodically reviews the general principles of the remuneration policy and is responsible for its implementation. Firms must ensure that the implementation of the remuneration policy is, at least annually, subject to central and independent internal review for compliance with policies and procedures for remuneration adopted by the governing body in its supervisory function.

  A firm that is significant in terms of its size, internal organisation and the nature, the scope and the complexity of its activities must establish a remuneration committee. The remuneration committee must be constituted in a way that enables it to exercise competent and independent judgement on remuneration policies and practices and the incentives created for managing risk, capital and liquidity. The chairman and the members of the remuneration committee must be members of the governing body who do not perform any executive function in the firm. The remuneration committee must be responsible for the preparation of decisions regarding remuneration, including those which have implications for the risk and risk management of the firm and which are to be taken by the governing body in its supervisory function. When preparing such decisions, the remuneration committee must take into account the long-term interests of shareholders, investors and other stakeholders in the firm.

- **Remuneration Principle 5 – Control Functions**

  A firm must ensure that employees engaged in control functions:
  - are independent from the business units they oversee;
  - have appropriate authority; and
  - are remunerated:
    - adequately to attract qualified and experienced staff; and
    - in accordance with the achievement of the objectives linked to their functions, independent of the performance of the business areas they control.

  A firm's risk management and compliance functions should have appropriate input into setting the remuneration policy for other business areas. The procedures for setting remuneration should allow risk and compliance functions to have significant input into the setting of individual remuneration awards, if those functions have concerns about the behaviour of the individuals concerned or the riskiness of the business undertaken.

- **Remuneration Principle 6 – Remuneration and Capital**

  A firm must ensure that total variable remuneration does not limit the firm's ability to strengthen its capital base.

- **Remuneration Principle 7 – Exceptional Government Intervention**

  A firm that benefits from exceptional government intervention must ensure variable remuneration is strictly limited as a percentage of net revenues when it is inconsistent with the maintenance of a sound capital base and timely exit from government support. It must restructure remuneration in a manner aligned with sound risk management and long-term growth, including, when appropriate, establishing limits to the remuneration of senior personnel; and ensuring that no variable remuneration is paid to its senior personnel unless this is justified.

- **Remuneration Principle 8 – Profit-Based Measurement and Risk Adjustment**
  A firm must ensure that any measurement of performance used to calculate variable remuneration components or pools of variable remuneration components includes adjustments for all types of current and future risks and takes into account the cost and quantity of the capital and the liquidity required; and takes into account the need for consistency with the timing and likelihood of the firm receiving potential future revenues incorporated into current earnings. Firms must ensure that the allocation of variable remuneration components within the firm also takes into account all types of current and future risks.

- **Remuneration Principle 9 – Pension Policy**
  A firm must ensure that its pension policy is in line with its business strategy, objectives, value and long-term interests. When an employee leaves the firm before retirement, any discretionary pension benefits are held by the firm for a period of five years in the form of instruments referred to in SYSC 19A.3.47 (shares or equivalent ownership interests and capital instruments). In the case of an employee reaching retirement, discretionary pension benefits are paid to the employee in the form of instruments referred to in SYSC 19A.3.47 and are subject to a five-year retention period.

- **Remuneration Principle 10 – Personal Investment Strategies**
  A firm must ensure that its employees undertake not to use personal hedging strategies or remuneration- or liability-related contracts of insurance to undermine the risk alignment effects embedded in their remuneration arrangements. A firm must also maintain effective arrangements designed to ensure that employees comply with their undertaking.

- **Remuneration Principle 11 – Avoidance of the Remuneration Code**
  A firm must ensure that variable remuneration is not paid through vehicles or methods that facilitate the avoidance of the remuneration code.

- **Remuneration Principle 12 – Remuneration Structures – Introduction**
  Remuneration Principle 12 consists of a series of rules, evidential provisions and guidance relating to remuneration structures.

# 6. Promotion of Fair and Ethical Outcomes and Why this is not Always Achieved

## Learning Objective

6.6.1 Understand how the FCA's use of outcomes-based regulation, including high-level principles (PRIN), corporate governance, approved persons' responsibilities and treating customers fairly requirements, is intended to promote fair and ethical outcomes and why this may not always be achieved

The FCA's outcomes-based regulation seeks to achieve the desired result for the consumer. However, this requires active participation and support by directors and employees at all levels to achieve effective corporate governance and fulfil the six TCF outcomes for consumers.

An example follows showing the potential for this not always being achieved.

## Case Study

***A new chief executive introduces a strategy which causes you to have serious concerns about the future of the firm. How might you deal with this?***

You work as risk director in a large firm of financial advisers and report directly to the chief executive, as well as being a member of the executive committee, which includes the chief executive, the sales director and the finance director.

After many years, during which your firm has gained a reputation as a solid and reliable, albeit rather staid operator, a new high-profile chief executive with a non-financial background and a reputation as a demanding task-master takes over, and begins to change the focus and culture of the firm. The chief executive now seeks much higher levels of performance and, in an attempt to achieve this, initiates a large increase in the sales force, where the accent is on proven sales success, regardless of the product, rather than financial awareness.

At the same time your firm begins to promote financial products from a wider variety of providers, offering more complex products to existing clients and gaining new clients, attracted by the apparently higher returns. A number of the more experienced advisers are encouraged to leave the firm, for not buying into the new environment and being unable to accept the new sales-driven culture that now prevails.

While you observe these moves as being in the nature of the business environment, you have concerns that the increased risks which will result from this change in the focus of the business are not being fully advised to the board.

Although the initial impact of the changes is almost entirely positive, with significant increases in client numbers and income being generated by the expanded sales force, there are disquieting signs that the improvement is not entirely risk free.

You run a major programme of customer feedback and receive several thousand feedback forms each year, which are analysed monthly. Historically, the forms have shown high levels of customer satisfaction in nearly all categories and your firm performs very well against its peers in industry surveys. Indeed, two years ago, you won an industry award for customer loyalty.

However, the feedback forms are now much less consistently good and the trend over the last six months is downwards in most of the key areas of customer satisfaction. Additionally you have received reports of disquiet from a number of older clients at what they consider to be the high-pressure tactics now being employed. Consequently you prepare a note for discussion at the next executive committee, reporting this disquiet and suggesting that some tempering of the programme might be considered, to enable remedial action to be taken to restore the firm's standing and to ensure that you do not attract the attention of the regulator.

When the executive committee meets, your note is the last agenda item and the chief executive makes it clear that he does not consider it a major issue, saying that the sales figures speak for themselves and he has had no complaints from the finance director about the firm's increased income. The sales director, who was appointed by the chief executive, supports him, saying that, while it is obviously disappointing that client satisfaction has slipped, until it starts to affect financial performance it is not something he is concerned about. In any case the firm's satisfaction rating remains comparable with peer-group firms, and ruffling a few feathers just shows that the sales teams are trying hard.

## The Dilemma

- As risk director you believe that there are serious risks to your firm that other executives, mindful that they owe their position to the chief executive, are unwilling properly to consider.
- You strongly believe that the board should be made aware of these risks and advised of the steps that are being taken to mitigate them.
- You are concerned that the chief executive is focusing exclusively on headline performance, without wanting to consider the risks to the firm in achieving it.

Can this be regarded as effective corporate governance?

# Summary of this Chapter

You should have an understanding and knowledge of the following after reading this chapter:

- PRA and FCA supervisory approach:
  - risk-based – the FCA FSF and the PRA's risk framework;
  - outcomes-focused – what this means, and how it is different from principles-based regulation.
- Effective corporate governance.
- Performance of regulated activities:
  - regulatory processes;
  - regulatory enforcement processes.
- Information required by the FCA – purpose and objectives of Sections 165, 167 & 168.
- FCA Handbook:
  - status of provisions;
  - purpose and status of FCA-confirmed industry guidance.
- Prudential and liquidity standards.
- FCA remuneration code:
  - purpose and who is caught by the code.

# End of Chapter Questions

Think of an answer for each question and refer to the appropriate section for confirmation.

1. What is the PRA and FCA supervisory approach to firms?
   *Answer reference: Section 1*

2. What is the FCA's approach to effective corporate governance within firms?
   *Answer reference: Section 1.3*

3. What is the purpose and function of the RDC?
   *Answer reference: Section 2.1*

4. What are the three forms of formal disciplinary sanctions?
   *Answer reference: Section 2.2*

5. In respect of the measures available to the FCA, what is the difference between a private warning and a prohibition of individuals?
   *Answer reference: Section 2.2.2*

6. What is the purpose and scope of the Upper Tribunal?
   *Answer reference: Section 2.3*

7. What does Section 168 of the FSMA permit the FCA to do?
   *Answer reference: Section 2.5*

8. What is the status of PRA/FCA-confirmed industry guidance?
   *Answer reference: Section 3.1.1*

9. What is the purpose of the CRD?
   *Answer reference: Section 4.1.1*

10. To which types of firms do the new liquidity rules apply?
    *Answer reference: Section 4.2*

11. What is the scope and purpose of the remuneration code?
    *Answer reference: Section 5*

12. Looking at the case study, what considerations or tools allow you to judge whether a course of action is ethical?
    *Answer reference: Section 6*

13. What requirements does the FCA have in relation to integrity and ethics?
    *Answer reference: Whole Chapter*

# Chapter Seven
# FCA and PRA Authorisation of Firms and Individuals

| | |
|---|---:|
| 1. High-Level Standards | 201 |
| 2. Regulated and Prohibited Activities | 216 |
| 3. Authorisation | 225 |
| 4. The Process for Approved Persons | 232 |
| 5. Training and Competence (T&C) | 246 |
| 6. Record-Keeping and Notification | 251 |
| 7. The FCA's and PRA's Changing Approach to Governance | 253 |

This syllabus area will provide approximately 14 of the 80 examination questions

In this chapter you will gain an understanding of:

- The principles for businesses.
- Controlled functions and statements of principle for approved persons.
- Fit and proper test.
- Senior management arrangements systems and controls (SYSC).
- Threshold conditions.
- Regulated and prohibited activities:
  - specified investments;
  - specific activities;
  - general prohibition;
  - exclusions;
  - exemptions.
- Authorisation (PRA and FCA):
  - firms/individuals;
  - exemptions;
  - process for approval.
- The different types of controlled functions.
- Supervision (PRA and FCA).
- Appointed representatives.
- Training and competence.
- Record-keeping and notification.
- FCA and PRA approach to governance.

# 1. High-Level Standards

## 1.1 The FCA's and PRA's Principles for Businesses

### Learning Objective

7.1 Understand the purpose and application of the FCA's and the PRA's high-level standards:

7.1.1 Principles for Businesses (PRIN)

As already outlined in Chapter 5, the FCA Handbook includes 11 key Principles for Businesses, which authorised firms must observe. These principles also apply to the PRA. The principles apply with respect to the carrying on of regulated activities, activities that include dealing in investments as principal, ancillary activities in relation to designated investment business, home finance activity, insurance mediation activity and accepting deposits, as well as the communication and approval of financial promotions.

If a firm breaches any of the principles that apply to it, it will be liable to disciplinary sanctions. However, the onus is on the FCA and the PRA to show that the firm has been at fault.

The FCA also pursues an initiative called **Treating Customers Fairly** (TCF) to encourage firms to adopt a more ethical **frame of mind** within the industry, leading to more ethical behaviour at every stage of a firm's relationship with its customers.

To reiterate, the 11 Principles for Businesses are:

1. Integrity.
2. Skill, care and diligence.
3. Management and control.
4. Financial prudence.
5. Market conduct.
6. Customers' interests.
7. Communication with clients.
8. Conflicts of interest.
9. Customers: relationships of trust.
10. Clients' assets.
11. Relations with regulators.

## 1.2 Controlled Functions and The Statements of Principle for Approved Persons

### Learning Objective

7.1 Understand the purpose and application of the FCA's and PRA's high-level standards:

7.1.4 Statements of Principle and Code of Practice for Approved Persons (APER)

The approach taken by the FCA and PRA to **authorising firms** recognises that a firm is typically a collection of individuals. Some of these individuals are considered to occupy roles which are important to the control or operation of the firm, and to its capacity to meet the requirements of authorisation. These people must be approved by either the FCA or the PRA before they can undertake their roles; hence they are known as **approved persons**.

The roles that the FCA and the PRA have categorised in this way are known as the **controlled functions**; they are broken down into two types:

1. **Significant influence functions (SIFs)** – functions that are governing or managerial. They include the directors of the firm and other key personnel.
2. **Customer functions** – functions involving interaction with the customers of the firm, such as an investment adviser, trader or investment manager.

# FCA and PRA Authorisation of Firms and Individuals

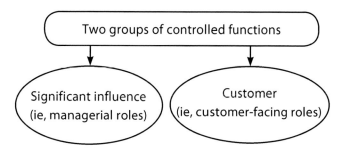

For more detail on controlled functions, see Section 4.2.

In a similar manner to the Principles for Businesses, the FCA and the PRA Handbook details seven **Statements of Principle for Approved Persons** to observe as they carry out their duties. Additionally, the Handbook includes a Code of Practice for Approved Persons (see Sections 1.3 and 1.4).

The first four **statements of principle**, applicable to all functions, state that an approved person must:

1. act with integrity in carrying out his controlled function;
2. act with due skill, care and diligence in carrying out their controlled function;
3. observe proper standards of market conduct in carrying out their controlled function;
4. deal with the FCA/PRA and with other regulators in an open and co-operative way and disclose appropriately any information of which the FCA/PRA would reasonably expect notice.

There are three additional statements of principle, which only apply to those approved to perform SIFs, which state that an approved person must:

5. take reasonable steps to ensure that the business of the firm for which they are responsible in his controlled function is organised so that it can be controlled effectively;
6. exercise due skill, care and diligence in managing the business of the firm for which they are responsible in their controlled function; and
7. take reasonable steps to ensure that the business of the firm for which they are responsible in their controlled function complies with the relevant requirements and standards of the regulatory system.

The following is taken directly from the Code of Practice and shows how it expands on the (relatively broad) principles.

## 1.3 Code of Practice for Approved Persons – Customer Functions/All Approved Persons Functions

The Code of Practice describes conduct which, in the opinion of the PRA and the FCA, does not comply with the Statements of Principle, and also factors that should be taken into account in determining whether or not an approved person's conduct complies with a Statement of Principle.

The Financial Services Act 2012 introduced some changes to the ability of the regulators to issue statements of principle. The Act allows the FCA to issue statements of principle for the conduct expected of persons approved by either regulator, and the PRA to issue statements of principle for:

a. the conduct expected of people it has approved to perform a controlled function; and
b. the conduct expected of people in dual-regulated firms whom the FCA has approved to perform a SIF.

The Act also allows a statement of principle issued by either regulator to relate to conduct expected of approved persons outside of their controlled function, which is a change to the current position in FSMA.

Either regulator will be permitted to take disciplinary action against a person who has failed to comply with a statement of principle. The FCA's version of APER also apply to any person at a single-regulated firm, performing a function which has been designated as a SIF by the FCA as well as to any person at a dual-regulated firm which has been designated as a customer dealing function by the FCA.

The PRA's APER will therefore apply to the performance of any activity which could be a SIF, insofar as it relates to the carrying on of a regulated activity by the firm which originally sought the approval.

## 1.3.1 Code of Practice for Statement of Principle 1

In the opinion of the regulators any of the following is a failure to comply with the requirement for an approved person to **act with integrity in carrying out his controlled function**:

1. Deliberately misleading (or attempting to mislead) a client, the firm (including the firm's auditors or appointed actuary) or the FCA/PRA by either act or omission. This includes deliberately:
    - falsifying documents;
    - misleading a client about the risks of an investment;
    - misleading a client about the charges or surrender penalties of investment products;
    - misleading a client about the likely performance of investment products, by providing inappropriate projections of future investment returns;
    - misleading a client by informing them that products only require a single payment when that is not the case;
    - mismarking the value of investments or trading positions;
    - procuring the unjustified alteration of prices on illiquid or off-exchange contracts;
    - misleading others within the firm about the creditworthiness of a borrower;
    - providing false or inaccurate documentation or information, including details of training, qualifications, past employment record or experience;
    - providing false or inaccurate information to the firm (or to the firm's auditors or appointed actuary);
    - providing false or inaccurate information to the PRA/FCA;
    - destroying or causing the destruction of documents (including false documentation) or tapes or their contents, relevant to misleading (or attempting to mislead) a client, the firm or the PRA/FCA;
    - failing to disclose dealings if disclosure is required by the firm's personal account dealing rules; and
    - misleading others in the firm about the nature of risks being accepted.

2. Deliberately recommending an investment to a customer, or carrying out a discretionary transaction for a customer, if the approved person knows that they are unable to justify its suitability for that customer.
3. Deliberately failing to inform a customer, the firm (or its auditors or appointed actuary) or the PRA/FCA, of the fact that their understanding of a material issue is incorrect. This includes deliberately failing to:
   - disclose the existence of falsified documents;
   - rectify mismarked positions immediately.
4. Deliberately preparing inaccurate or inappropriate records or returns in connection with a controlled function, such as:
   - performance reports for transmission to customers which are inaccurate or inappropriate (for example, by relying on past performance without giving appropriate warnings);
   - inaccurate training records or details of qualifications, past employment record or experience; and
   - inaccurate trading confirmations, contract notes or other records of transactions or holdings of securities for a customer, whether or not the customer is aware of these inaccuracies or has requested such records.
5. Deliberately misusing the assets or confidential information of a client or the firm such as:
   - front running client orders (front running means handling the firm's own orders before those of its client, or before the firm's broker recommendations are released to clients, so as to benefit from price movements that may arise from client-dealing activity);
   - carrying out unjustified trading on client accounts to generate a benefit to the approved person (sometimes known as churning);
   - misappropriating a client's assets, including wrongly transferring cash or securities belonging to clients to personal accounts;
   - using a client's funds for purposes other than those for which they are provided;
   - retaining a client's funds wrongly; and
   - pledging the assets of a client as security or margin in circumstances where the firm is not permitted to do so.
6. Deliberately designing transactions so as to disguise breaches of requirements and standards of the regulatory system.
7. Deliberately failing to disclose the existence of a conflict of interest in connection with dealings with a client.
8. Deliberately not paying due regard to the interest of the customer.
9. Deliberate acts, omissions or business practices that could be reasonably expected to cause consumer detriment.

## 1.3.2   Code of Practice for Statement of Principle 2

In the opinion of the regulator, any of the following is a failure to comply with the requirement for an approved person to **act with due skill, care and diligence in carrying out his controlled function**.

1. Failing to inform a customer or the firm (or the firm's auditors or appointed actuary) of material information in circumstances where he was aware, or ought to have been aware, of such information and the fact that he should provide it. Examples include:
   - failing to explain the risks of an investment to a customer;
   - failing to disclose details of the charges or surrender penalties of investment products;
   - mismarking trading positions;

- providing inaccurate or inadequate information to the firm, its auditors or appointed actuary; and
- failing to disclose dealings if disclosure is required by the firm's personal account-dealing rules.

2. Recommending an investment to a customer, or carrying out a discretionary transaction for a customer, if they do not have reasonable grounds to believe that it is suitable for that customer.
3. Undertaking, recommending or providing advice on transactions without reasonable understanding of the risk exposure of the transaction to the customer. For example, recommending transactions in investments to a customer without a reasonable understanding of the liability of that transaction.
4. Undertaking transactions without a reasonable understanding of the risk exposure of the transaction to the firm. For example, trading on the firm's own account without a reasonable understanding of the liability of that transaction.
5. Failing without good reason to disclose the existence of a conflict of interest in connection with dealings with a client.
6. Failing to provide adequate control over a client's assets, such as failing to segregate a client's assets or failing to process a client's payments in a timely manner.
7. Continuing to perform a controlled function, despite having failed to meet the standards of knowledge and skills as required by the PRA/FCA.

### 1.3.3 Code of Practice for Statement of Principle 3

Statement of Principle 3 requires an approved person to **observe proper standards of market conduct in carrying out his controlled function**. In terms of interpreting what might be regarded as **proper standards of market conduct**, the FCA states that compliance with its Code of Market Conduct will tend to show compliance with Statement of Principle 3.

### 1.3.4 Code of Practice for Statement of Principle 4

Statement of Principle 4 requires an approved person to **deal with the PRA/FCA and other regulators in an open and co-operative way and to disclose appropriately any information of which the PRA/FCA would reasonably expect notice**.

In the opinion of the regulator, the following do not comply with Statement of Principle 4:

- An approved person failing to report promptly in accordance with his firm's internal procedures (or, if none exists, direct to the PRA/FCA) information which it is reasonable to assume is of material significance to the PRA/FCA, whether in response to questions or otherwise.
- An approved person failing without good reason to:
  - inform a regulator of information of which the approved person was aware in response to questions from that regulator;
  - attend an interview or answer questions put by a regulator, despite a request or demand having been made;
  - supply a regulator with appropriate documents or information when requested or required to do so and within the time limits attaching to that request or requirement.

## 1.4 Code of Practice for Approved Persons – Significant Influence Functions (SIFs)

Statements of Principle 5, 6 and 7 (see Section 1.2) relate only to an approved person performing a SIF.

### 1.4.1 Code of Practice for Statement of Principle 5

Statement of Principle 5 requires an approved person performing a SIF to **take reasonable steps to ensure that the business of the firm for which they are responsible in their controlled function is organised so that it can be controlled effectively**.

The regulator expects this to include the following:

1. **Reporting lines** – the organisation of the business and the responsibilities of those within it should be clearly defined, with reporting lines clear to staff. If staff have dual reporting lines there is a greater need to ensure that the responsibility and accountability of each individual line manager is clearly set out and understood.
2. **Authorisation levels and job descriptions** – if members of staff have particular levels of authorisation, these should be clearly set out and communicated to staff. It may be appropriate for each member of staff to have a job description of which he is aware.
3. **Suitability of individuals** – if an individual's performance is unsatisfactory, then the appropriate approved person performing a SIF should review carefully whether that individual should be allowed to continue in that position. The approved person performing the SIF should not let the financial performance of the individual (or group) prevent an appropriate investigation into the compliance with the requirements and standards of the regulatory system.

### 1.4.2 Code of Practice for Statement of Principle 6

Statement of Principle 6 requires an approved person performing a SIF to **exercise due skill, care and diligence in managing the business of the firm for which they are responsible in their controlled function**.

In the opinion of the regulator, the following do not comply with Statement of Principle 6:

1. An approved person failing to take reasonable steps adequately to inform himself about the affairs of the business for which he is responsible.
2. An approved person delegating the authority for dealing with an issue or a part of the business to an individual or individuals (whether in-house or outside contractors) without reasonable grounds for believing that the delegate had the necessary capacity, competence, knowledge, seniority or skill to deal with the issue or to take authority for dealing with that part of the business.
3. An approved person failing to take reasonable steps to maintain an appropriate level of understanding about an issue or part of the business that he has delegated to an individual or individuals (whether in-house or outside contractors).
4. An approved person failing to supervise and monitor adequately the individual or individuals (whether in-house or outside contractors) to whom responsibility for dealing with an issue or authority for dealing with a part of the business has been delegated.

### 1.4.3 Code of Practice for Statement of Principle 7

Statement of Principle 7 requires an approved person performing a SIF to **take reasonable steps to ensure that the business of the firm for which they are responsible in their controlled function complies with the relevant requirements and standards of the regulatory system**.

This can be achieved, in part at least, by establishing a competent and properly staffed compliance department – though that may well not suffice in and of itself.

## 1.5 The Fit and Proper Test

### Learning Objective

7.1 Understand the purpose and application of the FCA's and the PRA's high-level standards:

7.1.5 The Fit and Proper Test for Approved Persons (FIT)

Section 59 of FSMA requires persons fulfilling controlled functions to first be approved by the FCA as **fit and proper**. Approved persons – having been assessed as fit and proper – are also then expected to comply with the APER.

The FCA and the PRA have made significant changes to the way they approach approved persons. Formerly applications for SIFs went through **on the nod**, but now both the PRA and the FCA are interviewing applicants and the process of challenge frequently leads to candidates being withdrawn by firms. They have set up a panel of interviewers, which includes senior industry figures, to lead the process. This has caused firms to pay attention to the process in a way that they never did previously.

An individual may only be permitted to perform a controlled function after they have been granted approved person status by either the PRA and or the FCA. They will grant an application only if it is satisfied that the candidate is a fit and proper person to perform the controlled function stated in the application form. Responsibility lies with the firm making the application to satisfy the PRA and the FCA that the candidate is fit and proper to perform the controlled function applied for.

During the application process, the FCA and/or the PRA may discuss the assessment of the candidate's fitness and propriety with the firm, and may retain notes of such discussions. In making its assessment, the FCA will consider the controlled function to be fulfilled, the activities of the firm and the permission which has been granted to the firm. If any information comes to light that suggests that the individual might not be fit and proper, the FCA will take into account how relevant and important it is.

In assessing the fitness and propriety of a person within the approved persons' regime, the PRA and/or the FCA will look at a number of factors against a set of criteria, of which the most important will be the person's:

- honesty, integrity and reputation;
- competence and capability; and
- financial soundness.

The following criteria are among those which will be considered when assessing an individual's fitness and propriety; note that they do not, however, constitute a definitive list of the matters which may be relevant.

### 1.5.1 Honesty, Integrity and Reputation

The FCA and the PRA will have regard to whether a person has been:

- convicted of a criminal offence; particular consideration will be given to offences of fraud, dishonesty and financial crime;
- the subject of an adverse finding or settlement in a civil case, again with particular consideration given to cases involving financial businesses and fraud;
- the subject of previous investigation or disciplinary proceedings by the FCA or the PRA or another regulatory authority;
- the subject of a justified complaint in relation to regulated activities;
- refused a licence to trade, or had a licence or registration revoked;
- involved in an insolvent business;
- disqualified as a director, or dismissed from a position of trust; or
- able to demonstrate a readiness and willingness to comply with the requirements and standards of the regulatory system.

The FCA or the PRA will treat each application on its merits, considering the seriousness and circumstances of any matters arising, as well as (in some cases) the length of time which has elapsed since the matter arose.

### 1.5.2 Competence and Capability

In assessing an applicant's competence and capability, the PRA and the FCA will have particular regard to whether the person:

- satisfies the relevant requirements laid down in the FCA's Training and Competence (T&C) Sourcebook; and
- has demonstrated the experience and training needed for them to fulfil the controlled function applied for.

They will consider previous convictions or dismissals/suspensions from employment for drugs, alcohol abuse or other abusive acts, only if they relate to the continuing ability of the person to perform the controlled function for which he is to be employed.

### 1.5.3 Financial Soundness

In assessing an applicant's financial soundness, the FCA and the PRA will have particular regard to whether the person has:

- been subject to any judgement to repay a debt or pay another award that remains outstanding, or was not satisfied within a reasonable period;
- filed for bankruptcy, been adjudged bankrupt, had his assets sequestrated or made arrangements with his creditors.

The FCA and the PRA will not normally require a statement of a person's assets and liabilities. The fact that a person may be of limited financial means will not of itself impact his suitability to perform a controlled function.

## 1.6 Senior Management Arrangements

### Learning Objective

7.1 Understand the purpose and application of the FCA's and the PRA's high-level standards:

7.1.2 Systems and Controls (SYSC)

5.4.1 Understand the key internal and external mechanisms within firms that support the regulatory framework: senior and executive management; compliance and risk management; finance function; internal and external auditors and legal advisers; CASS oversight function; regulatory reporting

The FCA and the PRA place certain requirements on financial services firms' directors and senior managers. These requirements are contained in the part of the Handbook called Senior Management Arrangements, Systems and Controls (SYSC).

The five main purposes of these requirements are to:

1. encourage firms' directors and senior managers to take responsibility for their firm's arrangements on matters likely to be of interest to the FCA and the PRA (because they are relevant to the FCA's and the PRA's ability to discharge their regulatory obligations);
2. amplify Principle for Businesses 3, under which a firm must take reasonable care to organise and control its affairs responsibly and effectively, with adequate risk-management systems;
3. encourage firms to vest responsibility for an effective and responsible organisation in specific directors and senior managers, so that everyone knows who is responsible for what activities and so that functions are not, therefore, in danger of **falling between stools** (each director/manager regarding another as being accountable for a given activity or function, for example, so that no one person assumes responsibility for its oversight);
4. create a common platform of organisational systems and controls for firms subject to the CRD and MiFID; and
5. set out high-level organisational systems and control requirements for insurers, as well as for other firms covered by the SYSC requirements.

These requirements have been extended to firms that are not subject to either the CRD or MiFID. These firms are called **non-scope** or **non-common platform** firms. The new requirements are in the form of **guidance** rather than rules. This means that, in most cases, non-common platform firms should read the rules and requirements outlined below replacing the word **must** with **should – accepting the rules as being best practice**.

### 1.6.1 Apportionment of Responsibilities

As part of the above requirements set out in SYSC, the FCA and the PRA require all firms to take reasonable care to maintain a clear and appropriate **apportionment** of significant responsibilities among their directors and senior managers in such a way that:

1. it is clear who has those responsibilities; and
2. the business and affairs of the firm can be adequately monitored and controlled by the directors, relevant senior managers and governing body of the firm.

Firms must make a record of the arrangements they have made to satisfy the FCA and the PRA requirement to apportion responsibilities among directors and senior managers. They must also take reasonable care to keep this record up to date and retain the record for six years from the date on which it was superseded by a more up-to-date record.

### 1.6.2 Systems and Controls (SYSC)

The FCA and the PRA require all firms to take reasonable care to establish and maintain such systems and controls as are appropriate to their business. Clearly, the nature and extent of these appropriate systems and controls will depend on a variety of factors, such as the nature, scale and complexity of the business, geographical diversity, the volume and size of the transactions undertaken and the degree of risk associated with each area of business operations.

### 1.6.3 Governance Arrangements

Firms must have robust governance arrangements, which include clear organisational structure with well defined, transparent and consistent lines of responsibility and effective processes to identify, manage, monitor and report the risks they are or might be exposed to. In addition, they must have adequate internal control mechanisms, including sound administrative and accounting procedures for effective control, and safeguard arrangements for information systems.

These arrangements, processes and mechanisms must be comprehensive and proportionate to the nature, scale and complexity of a firm's activities. Firms must also establish, implement and maintain systems and procedures that are adequate to safeguard the security, integrity and confidentiality of information, taking into account the nature of the information in question.

Firms must also monitor and evaluate on a regular basis the adequacy and effectiveness of their systems, internal control mechanisms and arrangements established, and take appropriate measures to address any deficiencies.

### 1.6.4 Responsibility of Senior Personnel

Senior personnel, including the supervisory function, within a firm are responsible for ensuring that the firm complies with its obligations under the regulatory system. In particular, senior personnel must assess and periodically review the effectiveness of the policies, arrangements and procedures put in place to comply with the firm's obligations under the regulatory system, and take appropriate measures to address any deficiencies.

## 1.6.5 Compliance

The systems and controls mentioned above include taking reasonable care to establish and maintain effective systems and controls for compliance with applicable requirements and standards under the regulatory system and for countering the risk that the firm might be used to further financial crime (including, but not limited to, money laundering).

Firms must maintain a permanent and effective compliance function which operates independently. The compliance function is responsible for monitoring and assessing the adequacy and effectiveness of the measures and procedures put in place by the firm in order to comply with regulatory standards.

The compliance function should advise and assist the persons responsible for carrying out the firm's regulated activities to comply with the firm's regulatory obligations and should have the necessary authority, resources, expertise and access to all information that is relevant for the performance of its role.

A firm must appoint a compliance officer who is responsible for the compliance function of the firm.

## 1.6.6 Internal Audit

Firms must, when appropriate and proportionate in view of the nature, scale and complexity of their business and the nature and range of investment services and activities undertaken, establish and maintain an internal audit function, which is separate and independent from the other functions and activities of the firm.

## 1.6.7 Financial Crime and Anti-Money Laundering (AML)

Firms must ensure that they have adequate and appropriate policies and procedures to enable them to identify, assess, monitor and manage ML risks and that these are comprehensive and proportionate to the nature, scale and complexity of their activities.

Firms must appoint an individual as their MLRO with responsibility for oversight of its compliance with the FCA's rules on systems and controls against ML. The MLRO should have a level of authority and independence within the firm and have access to resources and information sufficient to enable him to carry out that responsibility.

## 1.6.8 Risk Control

Firms must establish, implement and maintain adequate risk-management policies and procedures, including effective procedures for risk assessment, which identify the risks relating to the firm's activities, processes and systems and where appropriate set the level of risk tolerated by the firm.

Firms must also monitor the adequacy and effectiveness of their risk-management policies and procedures, the level of compliance by the firms and their relevant persons with the arrangements, processes and mechanisms adopted, and the adequacy and effectiveness of measures taken to address any deficiencies in those policies, procedures, arrangements, processes and mechanisms.

## 1.6.9 Remuneration

Firms must establish, implement and maintain remuneration policies, procedures and practices that are consistent with and promote effective risk management.

If a firm's remuneration policy is not aligned with effective risk management, it is likely that employees will have incentives to act in ways that might undermine effective risk management. The aim of the remuneration policy is therefore to ensure firms have risk-focused remuneration policies, which are consistent with and promote effective risk management and do not expose them to excessive risk-taking by employees. See Chapter 6, Section 5.

## 1.6.10 Regulatory Reporting

Firms are required to report to both the FCA and the PRA; the most obvious is financial returns. However, firms are required to provide reports to the regulators on a number of additional issues such as:

- annual controllers report;
- annual close links report;
- compliance reports – which include listing of all overseas regulators for each legal entity and organogram showing the authorised entities in the firms group;
- persistency reports;
- annual appointed representatives' reports;
- verification of standing data;
- product sales data reporting;
- integrated regulatory reporting;
- reporting under the payment services regulation;
- client money and asset return;
- reporting under the electronic money regulations;
- prudent valuation reporting;
- remuneration reporting;
- AIFMD reporting.

In addition to the above, firms are required to provide a transaction report to the FCA in respect of any financial instrument that is admitted to trading on an EEA-regulated market or an EEA-prescribed market, as well as in an OTC derivative where the value is derived from (or dependent upon) an equity or debt related financial instrument which is admitted to trading on a regulated market or on an EEA-prescribed market.

## 1.7 Threshold Conditions

### Learning Objective

7.1 Understand the purpose and application of the FCA's and the PRA's high-level standards:

7.1.3 Threshold conditions (COND)

Threshold conditions (TCs) represent **the minimum conditions that a firm is required to satisfy, and continue to satisfy, in order to be given and to retain Part 4A permission**. The PRA/FCA will take into account the context of the size, nature, scale and complexity of the business which the firm carries on, or will carry on, if the relevant application is granted.

The Conditions (COND) Sourcebook gives guidance on the TCs set out in or under Schedule 6 of FSMA. Under Section 41(2) of FSMA, in giving or varying a Part 4A permission or imposing or varying any requirement, the PRA/FCA must ensure that the firm concerned will satisfy, and continue to satisfy, the TCs in relation to all of the regulated activities for which it has or will have permission.

- **Location of offices** – the head office and the place where the firm carries on business must be in the UK.
- **Effective Supervision** – firms must be capable of being effectively supervised by the FCA having regard to the nature, complexity and the way in which firms operate and the regulated activities that they carry on/seek to carry on.
- **Appropriate resources** – must be adequate and appropriate in relation to the business activities carried on/or to be carried on.
- **Suitability** – the firm must satisfy the PRA/FCA that they are a **fit and proper person** having regard to all the circumstances, including:
  a. their connection with any person;
  b. the nature of any regulated activity that they carry on or seek to carry on; and
  c. the need to ensure that their affairs are conducted soundly and prudently.
- **Business Model** – this is a new requirement. Firms must be able to demonstrate the importance that of a firm's ability to put forward an appropriate, viable and sustainable business model, given the nature and scale of business that it intends to carry out.

In addition, the FCA expects firms to be able to demonstrate adequate contingency planning in their business model application. Firms will need to demonstrate that its business model meets the needs of clients and customers, not placing them at undue risk, nor placing at risk the integrity of the wider financial services system – for example, from financial crime. The FCA will also expect firms to provide clear information, with evidence of how it will meet this threshold condition. The FCA has stated that it will recommend refusal at an early stage where it is not satisfied that a firm meets, or will continue to meet, this minimum expected standard.

### 1.7.1 FCA Additional Conditions

When firms first apply for authorisation, or want to vary their permissions, they will be assessed against FCA TCs, meaning that the FCA will be able to set standards that applicants should meet and the FCA can challenge a firm about its business model and strategy.

The FCA will only assess FCA-only regulated firms for conduct and prudential issues; it will assess dual-regulated firms for conduct only – the PRA will assess prudential issues for dual-regulated firms.

The FCA will apply the following principles:

- align the assessments of new applications to the risk they pose to the FCA's statutory objectives; firms will not be authorised whose products and services pose a risk to customers;
- be open with all potential applicants as they go through the authorisations process, making sure that communication occurs early on so that the firm understands what is required of it. Then FCA will look closely at the proposed business model and the viability of the firm over a medium-term horizon;
- processes will be structured to support the operational objectives;
- refuse applications at an earlier stage if it does not think the proposed offering of products or services is in the interests of consumers or, more broadly, if it poses a significant risk to the FCA's objectives;
- share any risks and underlying themes that are identified with supervision colleagues, so they can monitor and assess them on an ongoing basis once a firm or individual is authorised.

## 1.7.2   PRA Additional Conditions

The TCs are the minimum requirements that firms must meet at all times in order to be permitted to carry on the regulated activities in which they engage. Firms will need to meet both the PRA-specific and FCA-specific TCs. The PRA-specific TCs will apply to banks, building societies, credit unions and designated investment firms that are regulated by the PRA for prudential purposes.

No significant amendments were made to the legal status and location of offices conditions.

The effective supervision condition requires firms to be capable of being effectively supervised by the PRA by reference to: business organisation; the nature and complexity of activities undertaken; products offered and close links. In instances giving the PRA responsibility for the suitability condition, the current provision will be amended to require compliance with obligations imposed and information requests made by the regulator. The firm's management will need to demonstrate adequate skills, experience and the ability to act with probity.

The Act bestows responsibility for a new TC on the PRA; namely business to be conducted in a prudent manner. The new TC amends the current adequate resources condition and is broadly the equivalent of the appropriate resources and business model conditions for which the FCA is responsible.

The **business to be conducted in a prudent manner condition** requires firms to hold appropriate financial and non-financial resources. It provides a high-level definition of appropriate resources judged by reference to complexity of activities, firms' liabilities and by reference to effective management and the ability to reduce risks to the firms' safety and soundness. By way of guidance, the Financial Services Act 2012 provides the PRA (and the FCA) with powers to make TC codes, which elaborate on the conditions and how these apply to different classes of firm.

The new TCs and adjoining codes seek to reflect the responsibilities and objectives of the PRA and FCA, as well as providing a clear set of standards for regulated firms. An example of this is the PRA focusing on the capital and liquidity held by the firms it supervises.

### 1.7.3 Summary of Threshold Conditions

The table below provides a quick overview to the TCs that are applicable to firms regulated by the FCA and to dual-regulated firms.

| Condition | FCA firm | Dual-regulated firm ||
|---|---|---|---|
| | | FCA | PRA |
| Legal status | No | No | Yes |
| Location of offices | Yes | No | Yes |
| Prudent conduct | No | No | Yes |
| Effective supervision | Yes | Yes | Yes |
| Appropriate resources | Yes | No | No |
| Appropriate non-financial resources | No | Yes | No |
| Suitability | Yes | Yes | Yes |
| Business model | Yes | Yes | No |

# 2. Regulated and Prohibited Activities

### Learning Objective

7.2 Apply the main concepts, principles and rules relating to regulated and prohibited activities:

7.2.1 Regulated and prohibited activities (Part II/III of FSMA 2000, Regulated Activities Order 2001)

7.2.2 Investments specified in Part III of the Regulated Activities Order

FSMA is subdivided into 30 parts. Part II, **Regulated and Prohibited Activities**, includes the **general prohibition**, which simply states that no person can carry on a regulated activity in the UK, or purport to do so, unless he is either authorised or exempt. It is left to a separate statutory instrument, known as the **Regulated Activities Order (RAO) 2001**, to clarify precisely what these regulated activities are.

For a person to become authorised, that person must first apply to the FCA for permission to perform particular regulated activities; if that person satisfies the FCA's criteria, the FCA will give it/them permission. The term person here means the trading entity or firm, which could be incorporated as a company – or could be an unincorporated entity such as a sole trader or partnership.

Breaches of the regulatory perimeter are investigated by the FCA.

## 2.1 The General Prohibition

The FSMA makes it a criminal offence to carry on regulated activities in breach of the **general prohibition** – in other words, carrying on regulated activities without first being authorised, or being subject to one of the exemptions, is a criminal offence. The offence is punishable by a maximum sentence of two years in prison, and/or an unlimited fine. It may be a defence to show that you have taken all reasonable precautions and exercised all due diligence to avoid committing the offence.

The FSMA gives the FCA the power to make an order (prohibition order) prohibiting an individual from performing a specified function. The prohibition order may relate to a specified regulated activity, any regulated activity falling within a specified description, all regulated activities and authorised persons generally, or any person within a specified class of authorised person.

An authorised person must take reasonable care to ensure that no function, in relation to the carrying on of a regulated activity, is performed by a person who is prohibited from performing that function by a prohibition order.

Any agreement made by a person in contravention of the general prohibition is unenforceable by that person against the other party. This is also the case for agreements made as a result of the activities of someone who was contravening the general prohibition, even if that person is not a party to the agreement. The other party is entitled to recover any money or property transferred under the agreement, and to compensate for any loss suffered.

### Example

Mrs X buys shares in ABC plc. The purchase is made following the recommendation of a firm of brokers, UNA Ltd. Mrs X subsequently discovers that UNA was not authorised under the FSMA.

Mrs X now has two choices: she could simply keep her shares in ABC and take no action against UNA or she could sue UNA for the recovery of her money and damages (handing back her shares in ABC) because UNA has breached the general prohibition.

The relevant staff of UNA have also committed a criminal act, and will be liable to a potential punishment of up to two years in prison, plus an unlimited fine.

In order to understand whether someone is in breach of the FSMA general prohibition it is, of course, necessary to understand what the **regulated activities** themselves are. FSMA provides that these will be defined by reference to two sets of criteria:

1. **a range of investments** (including assets which we might typically think of as investments, such as shares and bonds, but also other assets such as deposits and contracts of insurance); and
2. **a range of activities** which may be carried on in connection with those investments (such as dealing, managing or advising on investments, accepting deposits and effecting contracts of insurance). Not all of the activities can be related to all the investments – some are specific to just one type, eg, effecting a contract of insurance relates only to contracts of insurance.

If a person is performing one (or more) of these specified activities in relation to one (or more) of the specified investments, then that person is performing a regulated activity and requires either authorisation or an exemption. It is the combination of carrying on a specified activity in relation to a specified investment which gives rise to regulated activity.

The investments and activities are detailed in secondary legislation issued under the FSMA – principally the **RAO 2001**, as amended in 2002, 2003, 2006 and 2007.

## 2.2 Specified Investments

The following are defined as specified investments within the RAO:

1. **Deposits** – that is, money paid by one person to another, with or without interest being earned on it, and on terms that it will be repaid when a specified event occurs (eg, when a demand is made). The obvious example is deposits held with banks and building societies. For clarity, the RAO sets out certain exclusions – eg, electronic money (covered separately in point 2), money paid in advance for the provision of goods or services and money paid as a security deposit.
2. **Electronic money** – that is, monetary value (as represented by a claim on the e-money issuer) which is stored on an electronic device, issued on receipt of funds and accepted as a means of payment by third parties. In effect it is an electronic substitute for notes and coins.
3. **Rights under contracts of insurance** – which includes both long-term insurance contracts (eg, life assurance, endowment policies) and general insurance (eg, motor, building insurance). The FCA gives guidance on identifying a contract of insurance (since this is not always as simple as you might think) in the PERG.
4. **Shares** – defined widely as shares or stock in any company (wherever incorporated) or in any unincorporated body formed outside the UK. The RAO definition excludes shares in OEICs, since an OEIC is a CIS and is captured under a separate definition. It also excludes some building society shares, since these can behave like – and are, therefore, captured under – the definition of deposits.
5. **Instruments creating or acknowledging indebtedness** – this includes debentures, debenture stock, loan stock and, as a **mopping-up** clause, specifies also **any other instrument creating or acknowledging debt**. Again, the definition is wide, so the RAO provides for some exclusions – eg, trade bills, cheques and other bills of exchange, and (because they are separately captured) contracts of insurance and government and public securities.
6. **Government and public securities** – eg, gilts and US treasuries and local authority loan stocks. Again, certain instruments are excluded, such as trade bills issued by government bodies, and NS&I deposits and products.
7. **Alternative finance investment bonds/alternative debentures** – a form of Sharia'a-compliant bond or **sukuk**.
8. **Instruments giving entitlements to investments** – essentially, warrants and similar instruments entitling the holder to subscribe for shares, debentures, government and public securities at a set price, and on or between set date(s) in the future.
9. **Certificates representing certain securities** – this item covers certificates and the like which confer rights in (but are not themselves) other instruments such as shares, debentures, gilts and warrants. It includes, for example, American depositary receipts (ADRs), which typically give holders rights over a certain number of a UK company's shares. These ADRs are designed to offer the – typically US-based – investor a more convenient way to invest in UK shares, because they are dealt in, and pay dividends in, US dollars. Also covered here are other depositary receipts, such as global depositary receipts (GDRs).

# FCA and PRA Authorisation of Firms and Individuals

10. **Units in a CIS** – this covers holdings in any CIS, whether it is an authorised scheme or an unregulated scheme. For example, cover units in an authorised unit trust or shares in an OEIC – which you may also see described as an ICVC. This is why OEICs are specifically excluded from the heading of **shares** above. Unregulated schemes can also take other legal forms, such as limited partnerships, and so rights in such partnerships fall within the scope of **units in a CIS**.

11. **Rights under a stakeholder pension scheme** – stakeholder pensions are pension schemes set up under the Welfare Reform and Pensions Act 1999 which have to meet certain criteria and be run in a particular way.

12. **Rights under a personal pension scheme** – these are pensions designed for individuals who do not belong to a company scheme and/or who wish to take control of their own investment decisions for their pension provisions, for example, SIPPs. A wide range of investments may be held within a personal pension scheme.

13. **Options** – options (the right, but not the obligation, to buy or sell a fixed quantity of an underlying asset for a fixed price on or between fixed dates) are only covered if they relate to:
    - securities or contractually based investments (eg, stocks, shares, bonds, or futures on similar instruments);
    - currencies;
    - certain precious metals, including gold and silver;
    - options on futures contracts and other CFDs (see point 15).

14. **Futures** – that is, contracts for the sale/purchase of an asset if delivery and settlement will be made at a future date, at a price agreed when the contract is made. The RAO excludes futures agreed for commercial purposes as opposed to investment/speculative purposes – so a contract to buy cocoa at an agreed price at some future date will not be caught if it is carried out by a chocolate maker to help him secure a certain price for the raw materials needed.

15. **CFDs** – eg, spread bets, **interest rate swaps**. These are contracts where the investor's aim is to secure a profit (or avoid a loss) by making money by reference to fluctuations in the value of an index, or to the price of some other underlying property. The RAO excludes futures and options since these are separately caught.

16. **Lloyd's syndicate capacity and syndicate membership** – this relates to the main activities of Lloyd's members agents and managing agents.

17. **Rights under a funeral plan contract** – ie, certain plans under which the customer pays for benefits which will pay for his (or someone else's) funeral upon their death.

18. **Rights under a regulated mortgage contract*** – ie, mortgage loans secured by first legal mortgages on property, at least 40% of which is to be used for the borrower's, or some related party's, dwelling. This specified investment also includes lifetime mortgages, a type of equity release transaction.

19. **Rights under a home reversion plan*** – home reversion plans are another type of equity release transaction, whereby the customer sells part or all of their home to the plan provider in return for a lump sum or series of payments; their retain the right to stay in their home until they die or moves into residential care.

20. **Rights under a home purchase plan*** – home purchase plans are alternatives to mortgages, which allow people to buy their homes while complying with Islamic principles (financing via an interest-bearing mortgage is not permitted under a strict interpretation of these principles).

21. **Rights under a regulated sale and rent back agreement*** – whereby a person sells all or part of qualifying interest in land/property but remains in occupation of at least 40% of the land/property.

22. **Rights to or interests in other specified investments** – rights in anything that is a specified investment listed, excluding rights in home finance transactions, are themselves a specified investment.
23. **Loans and other forms of credit** – rights under any contract under which one person provides another with credit and contracts for hire of goods – rights under a contract for the bailment or hiring of goods to a person other than a body corporate.
24. **Providing credit reference services** – furnishing persons with information that is relevant to the financial standing of persons other than bodies corporate and is provided to that person for that purpose.
    **Providing credit information services** – taking steps on behalf of a person other than a body corporate in connection with information relevant to that persons financial standing that is or may be held by a regulated person.
    **The setting of benchmarks** – providing information, administration and the determining or publishing benchmark or publishing connected information.

The investments marked * are collectively known as **home finance transactions**.

## 2.3 Specified Activities

This involves classes of activity and categories of investment. An activity is a regulated activity for the purposes of the FSMA if it is an activity of a specified kind which is carried on by way of business and relates to an investment of a specified kind. **Investment** includes any asset, right or interest and **specified** means specified in an order made by the Treasury.

The RAO defines regulated activities by reference first to the range of specified investments; and then to the activities a firm may carry on in relation to those investments. An activity which is listed, but which is carried out in relation to an asset which is not a specified investment, is not a regulated activity.

We also know that if a business is carrying on a regulated activity it must be either authorised or exempt.

The regulated activities themselves are as follows:

1. **Accepting deposits** – mainly the preserve of banks and building societies, but other firms may find themselves caught under this activity.
2. **Issuing e-money** – ie, acting as the issuer of e-money, as it is described above in Section 2.2 (Specified Investments).
3. **Effecting or carrying out contracts of insurance as principal** – this essentially applies to insurers.
4. **Dealing in investments as principal or agent** – this applies only to certain of the specified investments. Dealing is buying, selling, subscribing for or underwriting the investments concerned. When the firm deals as principal (eg, on its own account), it applies only to those investments that are:
    - **securities** – shares, debentures and warrants, or
    - **contractually-based investments** such as options, futures, CFDs, and life policies.

    When the firm deals as agent (ie, on behalf of someone else), it applies to **securities** (as for dealing as principal) and **relevant investments**.
    Relevant investments include contractually based investments (as for dealing as principal) and additionally rights under pure protection and general insurance contracts.

5. **Arranging deals in investments** – this covers:
   - bringing about deals in investments – that is, the involvement of the person is essential to bringing about/concluding the contract, and also
   - **making arrangements with a view to transacting in investments** (which may be quite widely interpreted as any arrangement pursuant to transactions in investments, such as making introductions).

   The arranging activities relate only to specified investments which are:
   - securities (eg, shares, debentures or warrants);
   - relevant investments, (eg, options, futures, CFDs and rights under insurance contracts);
   - underwriting capacity of a Lloyd's syndicate or membership of a Lloyd's syndicate; and
   - rights to or interests in any of the above.

   A typical example might be a broker, making arrangements for its client to enter into a specific insurance contract.

6. **Arranging home finance transactions** – the arranging and making of arrangements in relation to mortgage, home reversion, home purchase plans and regulated sale and rent back agreements are captured in the same way as arranging deals investments.

7. **Operating an MTF –** by an investment firm or a market operator, which brings together multiple third-party buying and selling interests in financial instruments – in the system and in accordance with non-discretionary rules. MTFs can be assimilated to alternative trading exchanges providing additional pools of liquidity to their members (usually banks, major mutual funds and large insurance companies).

8. **Managing investments** – this applies in respect of investments belonging to someone other than the manager, and when the manager exercises discretion over the management of the portfolio. The portfolio must include, or be able to include, securities or contractually based investments. A typical example is a portfolio manager. Non-discretionary management (when the firm does not make the final decision) is not covered under this heading: it is captured under the separately defined regulated activities of dealing in investments and advising on investments.

9. **Assisting in the administration and performance of a contract of insurance** – this is activity carried on by an intermediary after conclusion of a contract of insurance, eg, loss assessors.

10. **Safeguarding and administering investments** – again, this applies in the context of securities (eg, shares, debentures) and contractually based investments (eg, options, futures, CFDs, qualifying insurance contracts). The firm must be holding the assets for someone else, and it must be both safeguarding and administering the assets to be caught under this heading. A typical example is a custodian bank, which might hold title documents to investments, hold dematerialised investments in its name, and administer the collection of interest/dividends or the application of corporate actions.

11. **Sending dematerialised instructions** – this covers firms which operate systems that allow for the electronic transfer of title in certain investments (again, securities and contractually based investments), and those which cause instructions to be sent on those systems. An example of such a system is CREST.

12. **Establishing, operating and winding up a CIS** – this activity captures persons who set up, operate/administer and wind up any type of CIS, whether an authorised scheme or an unregulated scheme. Acting as a trustee of an AUT, or as the depositary or sole director of an OEIC are also separate regulated activities.

13. **Establishing, operating and winding up a pension scheme** – this activity captures those who set up, operate/administer and wind up stakeholder pension schemes and SIPPs. These activities may be carried out by the scheme trustees and/or the scheme administrators.

14. **Providing basic advice on stakeholder products** – this is a special regulated activity, for those who advise only on stakeholder products. Stakeholder products conform to certain criteria for cost and accessibility.
15. **Advising on investments** – this covers giving advice on securities and relevant investments. It does not extend to giving advice about deposits, nor to occupational pensions schemes, nor to generic advice (eg, *'invest in the US, not in Europe'*). Neither does it extend to giving information – facts, which are not tailored to constitute a recommendation – instead of advice.
16. **Advising on home finance transactions** – advising on the merits of entering into, or varying the terms of, a regulated mortgage, a home reversion plan, a home purchase plan and regulated sale and rent back agreements is a regulated activity.
17. **Lloyd's market activities** – in addition to those mentioned above under arranging investments, there are three further Lloyd's-related regulated activities:
    - advising on syndicate participation;
    - managing underwriting capacity as a managing agent;
    - arranging deals in contracts of insurance at Lloyd's.
18. **Entering into a funeral plan contract** – as provider is a regulated activity, the person to whom the pre-payments are made.
19. **Entering into and administering home finance transactions** – this captures the activity of regulated mortgage lenders, home reversion providers, home purchase providers and regulated sale and rent back agreement providers.
20. **Dormant account funds** – the activities of meeting repayment claims and managing dormant account funds, carried on by dormant account fund operators, are regulated activities.
21. **Agreeing to carry on a specified activity** – is itself a regulated activity (and so a firm should not agree to carry on a regulated activity until it is properly authorised, notwithstanding that it may not intend to actually carry out that activity until it has its authorisation).

Advising, dealing and arranging activities, when carried on in connection with a contract of insurance, and the activity of assisting in the administration and performance of a contract of insurance, are collectively known as **insurance mediation activity** and subject to the provisions of the Insurance Mediation Directive.

## 2.4 Exclusions

Activities that fall under these exclusions need not be submitted to the FCA for authorisation.

### 2.4.1 Exclusions from Dealing as Principal – Absence of Holding Out

Dealing in investments as principal is a regulated activity – which (on the face of it) means that persons dealing for themselves in the hope of making profits are required to be authorised or exempt.

However, this regulated activity is restricted to those persons who are holding themselves out as and acting as **professional dealers** (acting as market makers). The result is that a person buying shares solely for himself does not need to be authorised or exempt, unless he is **holding himself out** to be a professional dealer in the investments.

FCA and PRA Authorisation of Firms and Individuals

In other words:

- firms which are professional dealers, such as market makers, and which **hold themselves out** as such, are carrying on a regulated activity; but
- individuals or companies who/which are not in the business of dealing in investments, and who/which invest only for themselves in the hope of making profit, are excluded.

This exclusion relates to both securities (shares and bonds) and contractually based investments (futures, options and CFDs), as long as they are entered into by an unauthorised person.

## 2.4.2 Other Exclusions

There are other exclusions covering situations when dealing as principal is not classified as a regulated activity:

1. A bank providing finance to another person and accepting an instrument acknowledging the debt.
2. A company or other organisation issuing its own shares, warrants or debentures.
3. Using options, futures and CFDs for risk-management purposes, as long as the company's business is mainly unregulated activities and the sole or main purpose of the deals is to limit identifiable risks.
4. Entering into transactions as principal for, or in connection with, the following:
   - the sale of goods or supply of services;
   - the sale of a company;
   - an employee share scheme and overseas persons (see Sections 2.4.5 and 2.4.6);
   - taking place between group companies;
   - while acting as a bare trustee (or, in Scotland, as nominee).

## 2.4.3 Exclusions for Advice in Newspapers

There is a particular exclusion in relation to newspapers and other media from the regulated activity of advising on investments. If a newspaper includes investment advice, and that advice is not the principal purpose of the newspaper, then it is excluded from the regulated activity of advising on investments. The existence of money and city pages or subsections within a newspaper does not make the principal purpose of the paper anything other than the provision of news, so there is no need for authorisation.

If the principal purpose of a publication is the provision of investment advice, with a view to encouraging investors or prospective investors to undertake investment activity, then authorisation is required. This is the case for periodicals that tip certain investments and are often sold on a subscription basis. They are often referred to as tipsheets and include publications like *Warrants Alert* (highlighting those warrants that offer good value to the investor).

## 2.4.4 Trustees, Nominees and Personal Representatives

There is an exclusion from the need for authorisation if the person carrying on the regulated activity is:

- acting as representative of another party;
- not generally holding himself out as carrying on regulated activities; and
- not receiving additional remuneration for providing these investment services.

223

This exclusion can apply to the following types of regulated activity:

- dealing in investments as principal;
- arranging deals in investments;
- managing investments;
- safeguarding and administering investments;
- sending dematerialised instructions;
- advising on investments;
- assisting in the administration and performance of a contract of insurance;
- advising on, entering into, or administering, a home finance transaction.

### 2.4.5 Employee Share Schemes

In order to encourage companies to set up schemes enabling their employees to hold shares in the company they work for, there are exclusions from the need to be authorised to operate such schemes.

The exclusion covers four types of activity:

- dealing in investments as principal;
- dealing in investments as agent;
- arranging deals in investments; and
- safeguarding and administering investments.

### 2.4.6 Overseas Persons

There are a number of exclusions for overseas persons carrying on regulated activities, providing that they do not do so from a permanent place of business in the UK. These exclusions apply only if the business is done through an authorised, or exempt, UK person, or if they are the result of a **legitimate approach**, such as a UK client approaching an overseas person in an unsolicited manner. The exclusions cover mainly the following types of activity:

- dealing in investments as principal;
- dealing in investments as agent;
- arranging deals in investments;
- advising on investments;
- agreeing to carry on the regulated activities of managing investments, arranging deals in investments, and safeguarding and administering investments or sending dematerialised instructions;
- operating an MTF; and
- entering into, or administering, a home finance transaction.

## 2.5 Exemptions

Certain sections of the FSMA, and a statutory instrument called the FSMA Exemption Order 2001, disapply the general prohibition for certain persons when they are carrying on particular regulated activities. In other words, they are exempt from the need to be authorised – even though some of the activities they carry on are, in theory, regulated activities.

See Section 3.2 for more detail.

FCA and PRA Authorisation of Firms and Individuals

# 3. Authorisation

**Learning Objective**

7.3 Apply the main concepts, principles and rules relating to FCA and PRA authorisation:

7.3.1 Related guidance in the Perimeter Guidance Manual (PERG)

7.3.2 Authorised Persons, Exempt Persons (PERG 2) and exclusions (FSMA Exemption Order 2001, SI 2001/1201)

7.3.3 Purpose, provisions, offences and scope of Permission Notices (SUP)

7.3.4 The requirement to act honestly, fairly and professionally (COBS 2.1)

7.3.5 Authorisation: conditions and procedures for firms (COND), and process and criteria for obtaining approval of Controllers including fitness and propriety (FIT (FCA/PRA))

---

Firms wishing to carry on regulated activities in the UK need to be authorised or exempt, unless they are subject to one of the exclusions outlined in Section 2.4. The term **firm** includes individuals, bodies, corporates (companies), branches of companies, partnerships and unincorporated associations.

Authorisation is provided under Part 4A of FSMA (as amended by the Financial Services Act 2012) and is, therefore, referred to as **Part 4A permission**.

Part 4A permission is given by the FCA and/or the PRA, and once, granted, the firm becomes an authorised person. As an authorised person, the firm can carry on regulated activities without breaching the general prohibition and committing a criminal act.

However, permission is not normally granted for all regulated activities. The Part 4A permission specifies which activities the firm can carry on, the investments those activities may relate to, and any further requirements or special conditions (such as a requirement that the firm should report to the FCA/PRA more frequently than is normally the case).

The activities which a firm is given permission to conduct can be limited. For example, it may be permitted to deal as principal, but only for a particular type of client.

## 3.1 Guidance for Authorisation

Under Section 23 of FSMA (Contravention of the general prohibition), a person commits a criminal offence if they carry on activities in breach of the general prohibition in Section 19 of the Act (The general prohibition). Although a person who commits the criminal offence is subject to a maximum of two years' imprisonment and an unlimited fine, it is a defence for a person to show that they took all reasonable precautions and exercised all due diligence to avoid committing the offence.

Another consequence of a breach of the general prohibition is that certain agreements could be unenforceable (see Sections 26 to 29 of FSMA). This applies to agreements entered into by persons who are in breach of the general prohibition. It also applies to any agreement entered into by an authorised person, if the agreement is made as a result of the activities of a person who is in breach of the general prohibition.

Under Section 22 of FSMA, for an activity to be a regulated activity, it must be carried on **by way of business**. Whether or not an activity is carried on by way of business is ultimately a question of judgement that takes account of several factors (none of which is likely to be conclusive). These include the degree of continuity, the existence of a commercial element, the scale of the activity and the proportion which the activity bears to other activities carried on by the same person, but which are not regulated. The nature of the particular regulated activity that is carried on will also be relevant to the factual analysis.

### 3.1.1 Perimeter Guidance Manual (PERG)

The purpose of the Perimeter Guidance Manual (PERG) is to give guidance about the circumstances in which authorisation is required, or exempt person status is available, including guidance on the activities which are regulated under the Act and the exclusions which are available.

PERG guidance is issued under Section 157 of FSMA. It represents the views of the FCA/PRA and does not bind the courts. For example, it will not bind the courts in an action for damages brought by a private person for breach of a rule (see Section 150 of FSMA (actions for damages)), or in relation to the enforceability of a contract where there has been a breach of Sections 19 (the general prohibition) or 21 (restrictions on financial promotion) of FSMA (see Sections 26 to 30 of FSMA (enforceability of agreements)).

Although the guidance does not bind the courts, it may be of persuasive effect for a court considering whether it is just and equitable to allow a contract to be enforced. Anyone reading this guidance should refer to FSMA and to the relevant secondary legislation to find out the precise scope and effect of any particular provision referred to in the guidance, and any reader should consider seeking legal advice if doubt remains. If a person acts in line with the guidance in the circumstances mentioned by it, the FCA/PRA will proceed on the footing that the person has complied with the aspects of the requirement to which the guidance relates.

General guidance on the perimeter is also contained in various FCA/PRA documents (mainly fact sheets and frequently asked questions) that are available at fca.org.uk.

## 3.2 Exemptions

Persons may be exempted from the general prohibition in relation to one or more particular regulated activities. The extent of any exemption may also be limited to specified circumstances (such as if another person who is authorised and has relevant permission has accepted responsibility for the regulated activities in question) or subject to specified conditions (such as a requirement that the activity is not carried on for pecuniary gain).

FSMA provides that appointed representatives, RIEs and RCHs and certain other persons exempt under miscellaneous provisions, are exempt persons. Members of Lloyd's and members of the professions are not **exempt persons** as such, but the general prohibition in Section 19 of the Act only applies to them in certain circumstances.

The distinction is significant in relation to various provisions (such as those in the RAO) that apply only to transactions and other activities that involve exempt persons.

An example of an exemption subject to certain conditions might be a requirement that the activity is not carried on to make a profit.

These exemptions can be split into two groups:

- those described as exempt persons under FSMA, such as RCHs and RIEs; and
- those not described as exempt persons, but who may nonetheless be exempt from the need to apply to the FCA for authorisation – such as a member of a designated professional body (DPB), carrying on the regulated activities in particular circumstances.

This distinction is significant: certain legal provisions apply only to transactions involving exempt persons, and not to non-exempt persons, who are only free from the need to apply for authorisation because of the specific circumstances of their activity.

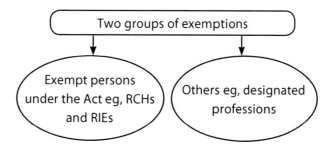

### 3.2.1 Exempt Persons

Those exempt persons who are appointed representatives, or the miscellaneous persons mentioned below, cannot be both exempt in relation to some regulated activities and authorised in relation to others. If a firm is already authorised and wishes to perform additional regulated activities that might otherwise fall under the appointed representatives/miscellaneous persons exemptions, it cannot claim those exemptions; it must extend its authorisation to include all the regulated activities it carries on.

**Appointed Representatives**

The exemption from regulation that appointed representatives enjoy (Section 39 of FSMA – Appointed Representatives Regulations 2001) comes at a price of imposing on the appointing firm the responsibility for vetting and monitoring, which the FCA would normally conduct itself.

The Appointed Representative Regulations 2001 provide that exempt appointed representatives can only carry on the following activities:

- arranging deals in investments;
- advising on investments;
- safeguarding and administering assets;
- dealing in investments as agent in long-term insurance contracts meeting specified conditions;
- advising on and arranging regulated mortgage contracts;
- advising on and arranging regulated home revision and home purchase plans;
- assisting in the administration and performance of a contract of insurance;
- providing basic advice on stakeholder products.

In particular, appointed representatives are not permitted to deal in investments either as agent or principal, or to manage investments.

For more details, see Section 4.4.

## Recognised Investment Exchanges (RIEs) and Recognised Clearing Houses (RCHs)

Substantial amounts of trading in, and issuance of, securities is conducted through formal exchanges such as the LSE. There are often separate clearing systems connected to these formal exchanges that facilitate the settlement of the trades that take place. The firms operating these systems are referred to as **clearing houses**.

FSMA gives the FCA the responsibility of recognising, regulating and supervising exchanges and clearing houses.

Once recognised, the exchanges are referred to as RIEs, and the clearing houses are referred to as RCHs. RIEs and RCHs are exempt persons in that they do not need to seek authorisation from the FCA to carry on regulated activities – they are, instead, **recognised**.

## Miscellaneous Exempt Persons

The Treasury has established certain exemptions from the need to be authorised for particular persons.

Some of these exemptions are restricted in that they only apply in certain circumstances. For example, supranational bodies of which the UK or another EEA member state is a member and central banks of the UK or another EEA member state are exempted from the need to be authorised to carry on any regulated activity, apart from effecting or carrying out contracts of insurance.

In contrast, certain bodies are exempted from the need to be authorised for the sole regulated activity of accepting deposits; these include municipal banks, local authorities and charities.

In the FSMA 2000 (Exemption) Order 2001, the following are the main organisations that are exempt in respect of any regulated activity other than insurance business:

- The Bank of England.
- The central bank of an EEA state other than the UK.
- The European Central Bank (ECB).

- The European Investment Bank (EIB).
- The International Bank for Reconstruction and Development (IBRD).
- The International Monetary Fund (IMF).
- The European Bank for Reconstruction and Development (EBRD).

## 3.2.2 Exemption from the General Prohibition

Certain persons are able to perform limited regulated activities without the need to be authorised or exempt. In effect the general prohibition of FSMA does not apply to them. Such persons include the members of Lloyd's insurance market and certain DPBs.

### Members of Lloyd's

Several activities carried on in connection with business at Lloyd's are regulated activities. These include:

- advising on syndicate participation;
- acting as a managing agent for one or more syndicates; and
- arranging deals in insurance contracts.

However, the FSMA disapplies the general prohibition for members of Lloyd's in relation to contracts of insurance written at Lloyd's. This is further extended to those members that ceased to be underwriting members at any time on or after 24 December 1996; these former members can carry out insurance contracts underwritten at Lloyd's without the need for authorisation.

The reason why the general prohibition does not apply is that the FCA expects the activities at Lloyd's to be suitably supervised and executed by the Society of Lloyd's, and so additional FCA authorisation of members is unnecessary. The FCA does, however, have certain powers to impose rules on the members (or former members) of Lloyd's if it is felt necessary.

### Members of the Professions

There are five professions where individual firms are permitted to carry on particular regulated activities without the need to apply to the FCA. Firms are required to apply to their relevant professional body for permission to conduct these activities. The individual professions are accountants, solicitors, actuaries, chartered surveyors and licensed conveyancers.

The professional bodies that are able to grant permissions are known as designated professional bodies (DPBs) and include the Institute of Chartered Accountants of England and Wales (ICAEW), the Law Society, the Institute of Actuaries and the Royal Institution of Chartered Surveyors (RICS).

The DPB must operate a set of rules with which its members must comply, and the regulated activity must be incidental to the provision of professional services. For example, a firm of accountants providing tax advice might give a client advice as to which investments might best be sold to avoid the accrual of a tax liability.

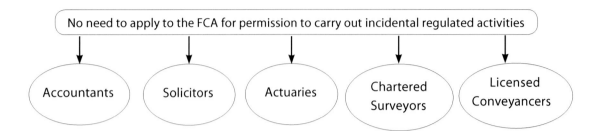

There are other restrictions to the activities carried out by member firms of DPBs. For example, such firms are allowed to receive pecuniary reward only from the client (ie, they should not receive commissions from the providers of products held or bought by the client); and certain regulated activities may not be carried out by the members, namely:

- accepting deposits;
- dealing in investments as principal;
- establishing, operating or winding up CISs or stakeholder pension schemes;
- effecting or carrying out contracts of insurance (including Lloyd's business);
- providing funeral plan contracts;
- issuing electronic money;
- providing basic advice on stakeholder products;
- establishing a pension scheme.

## 3.3 Permission Notices

The FCA and the PRA have the power under Section 45 of FSMA (Variation on the Authority's own initiative) to vary a firm's Part 4A permission. This includes imposing a statutory requirement or limitation on that Part 4A permission.

The circumstances in which the FCA/PRA may vary a firm's Part 4A permission on its own initiative under Section 45 of the Act include where it appears to the FCA/PRA that:

- one or more of the threshold conditions (see Section 1.7) is, or is likely to be, no longer satisfied; or
- it is desirable to vary a firm's permission in order to meet any of the FCA's/PRA's regulatory objectives.

The FCA/PRA may seek to vary a firm's Part 4A permission on its own initiative in certain situations, including the following:

- If the FCA/PRA determines that a firm's management, business or internal controls give rise to material risks that are not fully addressed by its rules, the FCA/PRA may seek to vary the firm's Part 4A permission and impose an additional requirement or limitation on the firm.
- If a firm becomes or is to become involved with new products or selling practices which present risks not adequately addressed by existing requirements, the FCA/PRA may seek to vary the firm's Part 4A permission in respect of those risks.
- If there has been a change in a firm's structure, controllers, activities or strategy which generates material uncertainty or creates unusual or exceptional risks, the FCA/PRA may seek to vary the firm's Part 4A permission.

- If a firm is a member of a financial conglomerate and the FCA/PRA is implementing supplementary supervision under the Financial Groups Directive with respect to that financial conglomerate by imposing obligations on the firm, then the FCA/PRA may seek to vary the firm's Part 4A permission.

The FCA/PRA may seek to impose requirements or limitations which include but are not restricted to:

- requiring a firm to submit regular reports covering, for example, trading results, management accounts, customer complaints and connected party transactions;
- requiring a firm to maintain prudential limits, for example on large exposures, foreign currency exposures or liquidity gaps;
- requiring a firm to submit a business plan (or for an insurer, a scheme of operations);
- limiting the firm's activities;
- requiring a firm to maintain a particular amount or type of financial resources.

The FCA/PRA will seek to give a firm reasonable notice of an intent to vary its permission and to agree with the firm an appropriate timescale. However, if the FCA/PRA considers that a delay may be prejudicial to the interest of consumers, it may need to act immediately using its powers under Section 45 of the FSMA to vary a firm's Part 4A permission with immediate effect.

## 3.4 Acting in the Client's Best Interest

A firm must act honestly, fairly and professionally in accordance with the best interests of its client (the **client's best interests** rule, refer to COBS 2.1.1R).

This rule applies in relation to designated investment business carried on:

- for a retail client; and
- in relation to MiFID or equivalent third-country business, for any other client.

Firms must not, in any communication relating to designated investment business, seek to exclude or restrict, or rely on any exclusion or restriction of, any duty or liability it may have to a client under the regulatory system.

In order to comply with the client's best interests rule, a firm should not, in any communication to a retail client relating to designated investment business, seek to exclude or restrict, or rely on any exclusion or restriction of, any duty or liability it may have to a client other than under the regulatory system, unless it is honest, fair and professional for it to do so.

The general law, including the Unfair Terms Regulations, also limits the scope for a firm to exclude or restrict any duty or liability to a consumer.

## 3.4.1 Fair Treatment

It should be apparent from a reading of the Principles for Businesses (Section 1.1) that a general theme of overriding **fair play** runs through them; this is coupled with a recognition that there is often an information imbalance between the firm and its customers (since the firm is usually more expert in its products and services than its customers).

## 3.5 Threshold Conditions (TCs)

The Conditions (COND) Sourcebook gives guidance on the TCs set out in or under Schedule 6 of the FSMA (TCs). The TCs represent the **minimum conditions which a firm is required to satisfy, and continue to satisfy, in order to be given and to retain Part IV permission**.

See Section 1.7 for full details on the TCs.

## 3.6 Fit and Proper Test for Approved Persons

The purpose of the Fitness Sourcebook is to set out and describe the criteria that the FCA/PRA will consider when assessing the fitness and propriety of a candidate for a controlled function. See Section 1.5.

The criteria are also relevant in assessing the continuing fitness and propriety of approved persons. The criteria that the FCA will consider in relation to an authorised person are described in COND.

Under Article 5(1)(d) of the MiFID Implementing Directive and Articles 31 and 32 of MiFID, the requirement to employ personnel with the knowledge, skills and expertise necessary for the discharge of the responsibilities allocated to them is reserved to the firm's home state (see Chapter 5, Section 4). Therefore, in assessing the fitness and propriety of a person to perform a controlled function solely in relation to the MiFID business of an incoming EEA firm, the FCA/PRA will not have regard to that person's **competence and capability**.

If the controlled function relates to matters outside the scope of MiFID, for example ML responsibilities (see CF11), or to business outside the scope of the MiFID business of an incoming EEA firm, such as insurance mediation activities in relation to life policies, the FCA/PRA will have regard to a candidate's competence and capability as well as their honesty, integrity, reputation and financial soundness.

# 4. The Process for Approved Persons

## 4.1 Authorisation – Approved Persons

**Learning Objective**

7.5 Understand the FCA's and PRA's main regulatory processes and provisions relating to the approval of individuals:

7.5.1 Approval Process

Section 59 of FSMA requires persons fulfilling controlled functions to first be approved by the PRA/FCA as **fit and proper** (see Section 1.5). This is the approved persons regime where, after having been assessed as fit and proper, people are also then expected to comply with the Statements of Principle and Code of Practice for Approved Persons (see Sections 1.2 to 1.4).

FCA and PRA Authorisation of Firms and Individuals

An individual may only be permitted to perform a controlled function after they have been granted approved person status by the PRA/FCA.

## 4.2 Controlled Functions

**Learning Objective**

7.5 Understand the FCA's and PRA's main regulatory processes and provisions relating to the approval of individuals:

7.5.2 Approved Persons

7.5.3 Controlled Functions

The Financial Services Act 2012 amended the powers to regulate approved persons and sets out how the powers may be exercised by the PRA and FCA. The main aspects of change contained in the Act are:

- a split of the current list of controlled functions for firms regulated by both the PRA and FCA (dual-regulated firms), seeking to minimise unnecessary duplication for dual-regulated firms (something required by the Act); and
- an extension of the Statements of Principle in APER to a wider set of activities, and their application to people approved by either regulator – meaning that both regulators will have the ability to discipline certain categories of approved person.

The Act provided for the continuation of the existing approved persons' regime, and for the continuation of the regulators' powers to make rules applying to these persons. It also follows the previous (FSA) legislation in providing that the regulators can bring different roles within their regimes, or **specify** functions, only if they involve either:

a. a function that enables the person concerned to exercise a significant influence over the conduct of a firm's affairs, known as **SIFs**; or

b. a person dealing with the customers of the firm, or with the property of these customers, known as **the customer dealing functions**.

The Act also includes the following detailed provisions on approved persons:

- Both regulators may specify in their rules SIFs for dual-regulated firms, but the FCA must keep its specification of SIFs under review and exercise this power in a way it considers will minimise the likelihood that SIF approvals fall to be given by both the FCA and the PRA to the same person in relation to the same dual-regulated firm.
- The FCA can also specify functions that will involve the person performing them dealing with customers of a regulated firm, or the property of those customers.
- The FCA and PRA must consult each other before specifying SIFs in relation to dual-regulated firms.
- The PRA must obtain the FCA's consent before approving a PRA SIF application submitted by a dual-regulated firm (although the FCA may arrange with the PRA that FCA consent is not needed for certain cases).
- Either regulator may withdraw approval from a person who is carrying on a SIF in connection with a dual-regulated firm, regardless of which regulator gave approval. If withdrawing an approval given by the other regulator, it must consult that other regulator first.

233

- Each regulator can discipline an approved person who has breached a statement of principle that it has issued, irrespective of whether or not it has approved the individual. The FCA may issue statements of principle in relation to any person approved by either regulator; the PRA may issue statements of principle in relation to any person approved by either regulator to perform a SIF for a dual-regulated firm.
- The statements of principle (contained in APER), can relate to conduct expected of persons not just in relation to the controlled functions they perform, but also in relation to other functions they perform where those functions relate to the firm for which they hold their approval carrying on regulated activities.

Individuals carrying out SIFs tend, by the nature of their roles, to occupy relatively senior positions within firms. In many cases, particularly those of the most senior roles, such as the chief executive, this means they will inevitably have responsibilities for both conduct and prudential issues. Therefore the Act takes account of this. The Act made it clear that the PRA and the FCA should not specify the same controlled functions for dual-regulated firms – therefore the existing SIF functions were split between the two regulators as noted below.

However, both regulators can have an interest in the functions specified in the other's rules. The PRA must obtain the FCA's consent before approving an application for a PRA SIF function, and either regulator can discipline or withdraw approval from a SIF of a dual-regulated firm, regardless of which of regulator approved the individual.

The Act requires the FCA to minimise the overlap of SIFs for people in dual-regulated firms (the **minimal duplication** requirement) to reduce the burden on firms. If a firm is seeking approval for a single SIF, whether that is a PRA or an FCA function, it only needs to send in a single application to the relevant regulator. Once the application has been received, the relevant regulator can then involve the other in the process, if and when this is appropriate.

This is relatively straightforward when a single individual is applying to carry out a single controlled function; for example, an application to be appointed only as CF3: chief executive would go to the PRA, while an application to be appointed only as CF1: director would go to the FCA. If a person is applying for two functions – say CF1 and CF3 – within the same firm at the same time, the situation becomes more complex. The procedures for dealing with that will differ depending on which two (or more) functions are involved.

### 4.2.1 The PRA's Approach to Approved Persons and Specifying Controlled Functions

In exercising its power to specify controlled functions, the PRA focuses on the roles that it believes are particularly important in determining whether a firm's business is run in a safe and sound manner and, in the case of insurers, is ensuring appropriate protection of policyholders. However, it is important to note that the powers in the Act described above mean that the PRA can also set out and enforce against standards of conduct for people approved by the FCA to perform a SIF, not just those people approved by the PRA itself.

The PRA has no supervisory interest in any of the functions specified in the FCA's Handbook. In particular the PRA expects all members of a firm's board (or other governing body) to take responsibility, both collectively and individually, for the firm's actions.

The general approach to preparing the PRA and FCA Handbooks at legal cutover (1 April 2013) was to focus on the changes that required to properly implement the requirements set out in the Act. Therefore, the framework of controlled functions and the amendments to APER do not represent the PRA's final view on the approved persons' regime. A more fundamental review of the regime will be undertaken by the PRA, therefore further changes may be considered necessary to ensure that the regime is fully aligned with, and effective in delivering, the PRA's statutory objectives.

## 4.2.2 The FCA's Approach to Approved Persons and Specifying Controlled Functions

For **dual-regulated firms**, the FCA specifies all of the SIF functions that the previous regulator (FSA) did.

For **single-regulated firms** the FCA specifies all existing SIF functions (excluding the actuarial controlled functions CF12: actuarial function, CF12A: with-profits actuary and CF12B: Lloyd's actuary).

The FCA also specifies the existing customer function (CF30), which applies to both dual-regulated and single-regulated firms. The FCA will undertake a review on what longer-term changes are necessary to the approved persons' regime.

There is one particular controlled function that will fall within the FCA's area of responsibility, the mortgage customer function (CF31). The FCA remains committed to the outcomes to achieve the introduction of CF31 (ie, to help to clamp down on mortgage fraud to make all mortgage advisers personally accountable, requiring them to demonstrate they are fit and proper, and to enable the FCA and the industry to track individuals as they move between firms).

The five types of controlled function are:

1. **Governing functions** – these are the persons responsible for directing the affairs of the business. If the business is a company then they will be the directors of that company. If the business is a partnership, then they will be the partners. It is important to remember, however, that the deciding factor is not just whether the person has the title of director – someone who acts as a director, even if they are not formally registered as such (for example a **shadow director**) will also require PRA/FCA approval because of the influence they exert over the firm.
2. **Required functions** – these are specific individual functions which the PRA/FCA expects every firm to have, if it is appropriate to the nature of the business. For example, every firm should have appointed someone to fulfil the compliance oversight function and the ML reporting function. The individual tasked with performing the apportionment and oversight function (CF8) does not need to be an approved person.
3. **Systems and controls functions** – these are the functions which provide the governing body with the information it needs to meet the requirements of Principle 3 of the Principles for Businesses (see Section 1.1).
4. **Significant management function** – this function only occurs in larger firms, if there is a layer of management below the governing body, which has responsibility for a significant business unit, for example, the head of equities, the head of fixed income and the head of settlements. Until recently, several different significant management functions were identified, but now they have been merged into one.

All of the above groups are described by the FCA as **SIFs** as the persons fulfilling these roles exercise a significant influence over the conduct of a firm's affairs.

5. **Customer function** – this function involves giving advice on dealing, arranging deals and managing investments. The individuals have contact with customers in fulfilling their role. Examples of customer functions are an investment adviser, the customer trading function and the investment management function.

Customer functions are not SIFs.

The table below sets out Part 1 of the FCA-controlled functions (FCA-authorised persons and appointed representatives).

| Type | CF | Description of controlled function |
| --- | --- | --- |
| FCA-governing functions* | 1 | Director function |
| | 2 | Non-executive director function |
| | 3 | Chief executive function |
| | 4 | Partner function |
| | 5 | Director of unincorporated association function |
| | 6 | Small friendly society function |
| FCA-required functions* | 8 | Apportionment and oversight function |
| | 10 | Compliance oversight function |
| | 10A | CASS operational oversight function |
| | 11 | Money laundering reporting function |
| | 40 | Benchmark submission function |
| | 50 | Benchmark administration function |
| Systems and control function* | 28 | Systems and controls function |
| Significant management function* | 29 | Significant management function |
| Customer-dealing function | 30 | Customer function |
| | 31 | Mortgage customer function |
| *FCA-significant influence functions | | |

The table below sets out Part 2 of the FCA-controlled functions (PRA-authorised persons).

| Type | CF | Description of FCA controlled function |
|---|---|---|
| FCA-required functions* | 8 | Apportionment and oversight function |
| | 10 | Compliance oversight function |
| | 10A | CASS operational oversight function |
| | 11 | Money laundering reporting function |
| | 40 | Benchmark submission function |
| | 50 | Benchmark administration function |
| Significant management function* | 29 | Significant management function |
| Customer-dealing function | 30 | Customer function |
| *FCA-significant influence functions | | |

The table below sets out the PRA-controlled functions for a PRA-authorised firm.

| Type | CF | Description of PRA controlled function |
|---|---|---|
| PRA-governing functions* | 1 | Director |
| | 2 | Non-executive director function |
| | 3 | Chief executive function |
| | 4 | Partner |
| | 5 | Director of an unincorporated association |
| | 6 | Small friendly society |
| PRA-required functions* | 12 | Actuarial function |
| | 12A | With-profits actuary function |
| | 12B | Lloyd's actuary function |
| Significant management function* | 28 | Systems and controls function |
| *PRA-significant influence functions | | |

So, when a person submits their PRA SIF application, they will be required to declare if they also need approval for one of the FCA functions (see table above). This information is required so that the PRA can assess the person's suitability to perform both roles. As FCA consent is required before the PRA can approve an application, the FCA will also be involved in the assessment process. On approval by the PRA the individual's PRA-controlled function will include the FCA role. Only the PRA-controlled function will be shown on the public register.

**Both the PRA and the FCA will be able to refuse the application.**

To give an example, where someone is appointed to be both a chief executive and a (board level) executive director, they will only need to apply to the PRA for the chief executive function (CF3). They would not also need separate approval for CF1, as they would have under the FSA. However, the PRA's chief executive function will also cover the individual's actions as an executive director.

### 4.2.3 Changes to the Controlled Functions – Non-Executive Director (NED) Function

While the majority of the previous FSA-controlled functions were transferred in their entirety to either the PRA or the FCA, new controlled functions have been created – non-executive director (NED) functions (CF2) for the PRA and the FCA.

The CF2 (PRA) function will cover anyone who falls within the current definition of CF2 and performs one of the following roles:

- chairman;
- senior independent director;
- chair of the audit committee;
- chair of the remuneration committee; or
- chair of the risk committee.

The PRA CF2 function also applies to a member of a committee (including the franchise board) of the Society of Lloyd's to which the Council has delegated authority to perform regulatory functions, in the same way as it applies to other non-executives – ie, they fall within the role if they perform the equivalent of one of the roles set out above. The function also applies to a non-executive in an unregulated parent undertaking or holding company whose decisions or actions are regularly taken into account by the governing body of the firm. (Those performing an executive function at the parent entity will continue to fall within CF1 and will therefore be approved by the FCA.)

### Changes to the Controlled Functions – Chief Executive Function

The previous regulator's approach was that someone who was approved for a governing function, including the chief executive function, did not need separate approval for that part of the customer function (CF30) which relates to bidding in emissions auctions. However under the new structure, the PRA no longer has any power to specify customer functions, and therefore the chief executive function can no longer encompass this element of CF30.

The result is that in future someone holding the chief executive function in a dual-regulated firm who wants to act as a bidder's representative will need to apply to the FCA for separate approval as CF30 – although these cases are deemed likely to be rare.

### The Systems and Controls Function and its relation to the Governing Functions

An individual approved to perform a governing function (other than CF2) did not need additional approval to perform the systems and control function (CF28) under the previous regulator.

FCA and PRA Authorisation of Firms and Individuals

However, this has now changed. Therefore, an individual applying to be approved by the PRA to perform CF28 does not also need to apply to the FCA for approval to perform an FCA governing function. That is to say, if a person wishes to perform both a role that falls within the systems and controls function, and an FCA governing function – for example, someone appointed as finance director – they would need to apply to the PRA for approval to perform the CF28 function. This change is a way of ensuring that the PRA is responsible for granting approval for functions relevant to the safety and soundness of a dual-regulated firms.

### The Interaction between PRA CFs and FCA CFs Section

If they take up both positions at the same time, they would only need approval for CF28 but, the person's FCA role would have to be declared in their PRA application and their suitability to perform their role as a director will be taken into account as part of the assessment of their fitness and propriety for the systems and controls function.

Should a person be approved for CF28 by the PRA and subsequently be appointed to an FCA governing function position, an application to the FCA will be required.

## 4.2.4 Operational Implications

Once an application form has been submitted, the PRA and the FCA, in accordance with the split of controlled functions between the two regulators, assess the competency of the individual for all controlled functions for which approval is sought. Because the PRA must have the FCA's consent before determining an application, both regulators may ask for additional information when considering an application for a PRA-controlled function. Although the PRA and the FCA try to co-ordinate their actions to avoid duplication, both regulators reserve the right to request additional information.

Irrespective of the regulator asking for the information, this will **stop the clock** (there is only one **clock** operating per application) on the statutory time limit for determining the application until the relevant regulator has received the requested information.

As part of the approval process, the PRA and FCA may where necessary interview candidates applying for certain SIFs and the criteria for determining whether or not to conduct an interview will remain unchanged. Again, the general approach is to act in a co-ordinated way where possible and to conduct one interview to help both regulators assess suitability in relation to all the controlled functions for which approval is sought.

However, both regulators reserve the right to conduct separate interviews in certain circumstances where that is deemed the most appropriate approach, whether for operational or other reasons.

Principle 3 of the Principles for Businesses (management and control) requires that firms take reasonable care to organise and control their affairs responsibly and effectively. It is this principle that underpins the approved persons' regime for individuals performing controlled functions. Firms' senior management should ensure that the individuals they have occupying relevant roles are fit and proper for those roles. Indeed, any assessment of the ongoing fitness and propriety of the firm itself incorporates the extent to which it fulfils this obligation, and includes assessing the competence of the staff to ensure they are suitable for their roles.

## 4.2.5 Extending the Scope and Application of Controlled Functions (CF1 and CF2)

The definitions of both CF1 and CF2 were extended to make it clearer that individuals, who have a significant influence on an authorised firm should be approved persons. The role of the extended controlled functions now includes individuals such as directors, NEDs and senior managers employed by a parent undertaking or holding company whose decisions, opinions or actions are regularly taken into account by the governing body of the authorised firm and are therefore likely to have a significant influence on the conduct of an authorised firm.

The reasons for the changes are that the regulator considered that many large, complex firms are not primarily managed within that legal entity. The approved persons' regime did not necessarily reflect the increasing significant influence exerted on an authorised firm by individuals based in the parent undertaking or holding companies to which the authorised firm is accountable.

The regulator provided an example: if a firm relies on a group audit committee to fulfil functions that might otherwise be conducted by the audit committee of the board of the authorised firm, the regulator will seek to register key members of the group audit committee on the basis that their decisions, opinions or actions are regularly taken into account by the board of the authorised firm.

The PRA and the FCA have continued with this approach.

## 4.2.6 Clarification of the Role of a Non-Executive Director (NED)

NEDs are seen as part of the wider board of directors, having a pivotal role to play in the active governance of firms and driving an appropriate culture to meet firms' regulatory responsibilities towards the fair treatment of retail customers.

To help firms manage their retail conduct risks, the PRA and the FCA expect NEDs to consider the following areas and challenge them where appropriate, to ensure that:

- business proposals are aligned with the firm's strategy and are within its stated retail conduct risk appetite;
- the firm's culture is such that it delivers good behaviours and outcomes, both prudentially and for customers;
- the NEDs have the right information to enable them to make robust decisions and if they feel they do not, then they should ask for it;
- they can assist executive colleagues within the firm's governing body in setting and monitoring the firm's strategy;
- they provide an independent perspective to the overall running of the business;
- they scrutinise the approach of executive management and the firm's performance and standards of conduct; and
- they carry out other responsibilities as assigned by the board.

The FSA highlighted a clarification of the existing role as opposed to a changing of the rules. Going forward, the PRA/FCA will look more closely at the roles of a NED, if it believes that they should have intervened when executives are making poor decisions. This is reflective of the move from a principles-based approach to a focus on outcomes.

FCA and PRA Authorisation of Firms and Individuals

Furthermore, NEDs are expected, by way of guidance, to provide an independent perspective, and should constructively challenge and help develop proposals of strategy, and scrutinise the performance and approach of senior managers in meeting agreed goals, objectives and standards of conduct.

The PRA and the FCA have continued with this approach.

## 4.2.7 Extended Definition of Controlled Function (CF29) to include Appropriate Proprietary Traders with the Expectation that this will Capture all Proprietary Traders

Recent events suggest that the risks of proprietary trading in all firms and the current market situation warranted a review of the position of all proprietary traders in relation to the approved persons' regime. This was previously not the case, with the FSA relying on senior management responsibilities and robust systems and controls.

The extension of the approved persons' regime to cover proprietary traders is designed to capture those proprietary traders who are not senior managers but who are likely to exercise a significant influence on their firm through their trading activities – ie, to commit the firm's capital. This includes those currently approved for CF30 (customer function), who also have to be approved for CF29 (significant management).

The PRA and the FCA have continued with this approach.

## 4.2.8 Amended Application of the Approved Persons Regime to UK Branches of Third Country Firms (Firms Outside the EEA) so that all the Controlled Functions may Apply

The CF1 and CF2 functions were extended to cover individuals exercising a significant influence over an authorised firm in the following types of company:

- Regulated and unregulated UK parent undertakings and holding companies.
- Regulated and unregulated third-country parent undertakings.
- EEA-unregulated parent undertakings and holding companies.

Firms not included:

- UK branches with an EEA-unregulated company.
- UK incorporated authorised firms with an EEA-unregulated company.

An individual based in a third country (eg, US, Canada, Australia) who exercises a significant influence on a UK-authorised firm was included in the proposals, but only to the extent of his significant influence on the UK-authorised firm.

As previously noted, the regulator provided an example: if a firm relies on a group audit committee to fulfil functions that might otherwise be conducted by the audit committee of the board of the authorised firm, the FCA sought to register key members of the group audit committee on the basis that their decisions, opinions or actions are regularly taken into account by the board of the authorised firm.

The PRA and the FCA have continued with this approach.

### 4.2.9 Extension of the Rule Obliging Firms to Provide References for Applicants of the Customer Function (CF30) to all Controlled Functions

Previously, firms that employed individuals who had already been approved as a controlled function in another firm, and who wished to register them for CF30 (customer function) status, could request certain information from the previous firm. The onus fell on the previous firm to supply this information.

However, this has been extended to all controlled functions, enabling firms to ask for factually based references (from the previous firm) for those applying for any controlled function.

The obligation to provide this information arises only if that firm is asked to provide the information.

The PRA and the FCA have continued with this approach.

### 4.2.10 Additional Information Pertaining to Approved Persons' Applications

In March 2011, the FSA published a note saying that the implementation of the new SIFs (as noted above in Sections 4.2.1 to 4.2.5) has been deferred until further notice. The FSA remained committed to all of the proposals in its policy statement (PS 10/15: effective corporate governance – SIFs and the Walker Review) and pressed ahead with the other changes designed to promote corporate governance within firms and, in particular, those elements aimed at managing risk. The deferral should not be interpreted as a change of policy; the FCA/PRA they will ensure firms have two notices of the new implementation date.

The PRA and the FCA have continued with this approach.

### 4.2.11 Benchmarking

Following the recent issues with LIBOR, the FCA created two new controlled functions in relation to benchmarking.

A **benchmark submitter (CF40)** who maintains an establishment in the UK must appoint a benchmark manager with responsibility for the oversight of its compliance with this chapter; and ensure that its benchmark manager has a level of authority and access to resources and information sufficient to enable them to carry out that responsibility.

Therefore, an individual is responsible for the firm's submissions.

Firms must appoint a **benchmark administrator manager (CF50)** with responsibility for oversight of its compliance with this section; and ensure that its benchmark administration manager has a level of authority and access to resources and information sufficient to enable them to carry out that responsibility.

# 4.3 Supervision

## 4.3.1 Classification of Regulated Firms

### PRA Approach

The PRA assesses the significance of a firm to the stability of the UK financial system and divides all of the firms it supervises into one of five categories. High risk firms include those firms whose size, interconnectedness, complexity and business type pose a very significant risk, whilst low risk firms have almost no capacity to impact upon the UK financial system.

### FCA Approach

The FCA approach differs from that adopted by the PRA in two key respects:

1. Whilst the FCA is responsible for supervision of the conduct of business of all firms it only has prudential supervisory responsibility for those firms not regulated by the PRA.
2. The FCA conduct supervision approach is to carry out in-depth, structured conduct supervision work with those firms with the potential to cause the greatest risks to the FCA's objectives. Firms are put into one of four categories. High-risk firms will include those firms with very large numbers of retail customers, large client assets or large trading operations whilst those in low risk firms are smaller firms, including almost all intermediaries.

Firms which are supervised by FCA for prudential purposes have a separate prudential categorisation from their categorisation for conduct supervision.

### Consequences for Supervision

The classification of a firm has a direct impact upon the type and intensity of supervision it receives from the PRA and the FCA. Those firms categorised as high-risk will have dedicated (named) lead supervisors and are subject to frequent and intrusive regulatory review of their business at both planning and operational levels.

Those firms categorised as low-risk are not allocated dedicated supervisory staff. Their supervision is based largely around the analysis of standardised returns. Supervisory action is focused on instances where a firm appears to be out of line with its peer group or in response to specific incidents regarding the firm or the market/sector it operates in.

## 4.3.2 PRA Supervision of Firms that pose little Individual Risk to Financial Stability

There are a very large number of firms within this category, made up in practice of small overseas banks (branches or subsidiaries) and credit unions.

At an individual level, these firms have almost no capacity to cause disruption to the UK financial system, through the way they carry on their business. Nevertheless, two considerations motivate a baseline level of supervisory monitoring for them. First, the PRA's general statutory objective is to promote the safety and soundness of all of the firms that it regulates. And second, there is a risk that problems across a whole sector or subsector could generate some disruption to the continuity of financial services, ie, several firms may fail together through a common exposure, with possible wider systemic impact (as occurred in the 1990s' small banks' crisis, for example).

Given that such firms are likely to pose risks to financial stability at an aggregate level only, the PRA supervises them on a portfolio basis.

The PRA also examines individual firms when a risk crystallises (as discovered through, for example, a visit to the firm, or an approach from the firm itself), or in response to authorisation requests from the firm (for example, a request to change its permissions to undertake regulated activities, or to extend the nature or scale of its business).

The PRA still conducts annual assessments of firms, but in large peer groups. In contrast to the higher-impact firms, those in the lowest category contact the PRA through a centralised firm enquiries function and do not have an individual, named supervisor.

## Credit Unions

Credit unions are the major constituent of the lowest-impact category. They are subject to a specific prudential regime, as set out in the Credit Union Sourcebook, including specific minimum capital and liquidity requirements. Credit unions are not subject to the CRD, nor will they be issued with individual guidance for capital and liquidity.

## 4.4 Appointed Representatives

### Learning Objective

7.5 Understand the FCA's and PRA's main regulatory processes and provisions relating to the approval of individuals:

7.5.4 Appointed Representatives

An appointed representative can be either an individual or a company. The appointed representative must be a party to a contract with an authorised person that allows it/him to carry on certain regulated activities – and the authorised person must have accepted responsibility for the conduct of these regulated activities in writing.

The FCA and PRA rules do not apply to appointed representatives because they are not authorised persons; however, any business conducted by the appointed representative, for which the authorised person has accepted responsibility, is treated as having been done so by the authorised person. The authorised person:

# FCA and PRA Authorisation of Firms and Individuals

- itself needs permission to perform the regulated activities undertaken by its authorised representatives; and
- is, potentially, liable for FCA/PRA discipline for the actions of its representatives.

Note that, although appointed representatives do not themselves need to be authorised, the individuals involved may require approval from the FCA/PRA if they are fulfilling CFs at an appointed representative firm.

The exemption from regulation that appointed representatives enjoy (Section 39 of FSMA – Appointed Representatives Regulations 2001) comes at a price of imposing on the appointing firm the responsibility for vetting and monitoring.

The provisions that govern the appointment and monitoring of appointed representatives are in the FCA's Supervision Manual (Chapter 12). The principal provision is as SUP 12.3.2G, which states that *'the firm is responsible, to the same extent as if it had expressly permitted it, for anything that the appointed representative does or omits to do, in carrying on the business for which the firm has accepted responsibility'.* This makes the appointed representative a clone of the firm.

Because appointed representatives are exempt, they can only carry out the following activities, defined under Part III of the Regulated Activities Order, under the Appointed Representatives Regulation 2001:

- arranging deals in investments;
- advising on investments;
- safeguarding and administering assets;
- dealing in investments as agent in long-term insurance contracts meeting specified conditions;
- advising on and arranging regulated mortgage contracts;
- advising on and arranging regulated home revision and home purchase plans;
- assisting in the administration and performance of a contract of insurance;
- providing basic advice on stakeholder products.

In particular, appointed representatives are not permitted to deal in investments either as agent (except as specified above) or principal, or to manage investments.

The descriptions of the following CFs apply to an appointed representative of a firm, except an introducer-appointed representative:

- the governing functions, except for a tied agent of an EEA MiFID investment firm; and
- the customer function other than in relation to acting in the capacity of an investment manager.

Only one of the following governing functions applies, as appropriate, to an individual within that appointed representative, who is required to be an approved person:

a. director function; or
b. chief executive function; or
c. partner function; or
d. director of unincorporated association function.

# 5. Training and Competence (T&C)

## Learning Objective

7.6  Apply the concepts, principles and rules relating to training and competence including appropriate professionalism:

7.6.1  Systems and controls responsibilities in relation to the competence of employees (SYSC 3.2.13; 14; 5.1.1 (FCA/PRA))

7.6.2  The activities and functions to which the T&C regime applies

7.6.3  Measures to demonstrate competence – including those prior to assessment, at assessment, FCA and PRA approval and ongoing through continuing professional development and the need for a statement of professional standing

## 5.1 Overall Requirements

The Principle for Businesses 3 requires that firms take reasonable care to **organise and control their affairs responsibly and effectively**. To comply with this requirement, firms must, clearly, ensure that any employee involved with a regulated activity achieves and maintains the competence needed for this role.

The principles are built on further in the section of the FCA/PRA Handbook dealing with senior management arrangements, systems and controls (SYSC). This incorporates a high-level competence requirement which applies to all UK-authorised firms (including wholesale firms).

This high-level approach is then supplemented – for firms carrying on activities with or for retail customers only and in some limited cases for customers and consumers – by the **Training and Competence** (T&C) Sourcebook. The T&C Sourcebook is more focused on the outcomes achieved by firms through their internal training and competence arrangements.

## 5.2 The Requirements for Retail Firms: Assessing and Maintaining Competence

### 5.2.1 Assessment

The T&C Sourcebook requires that firms do not assess an employee as competent to carry on any of a specified range of activities until that employee has demonstrated the necessary competence to do so and has (if required by the Sourcebook) passed each module of an appropriate examination. This assessment need not take place before they start to carry on the activity.

## 5.2.2 Supervision

Further, firms must not allow an employee to carry on any of those specified activities without appropriate supervision. They are required to ensure that employees are appropriately supervised at all times. The Sourcebook states that the FCA expects that the level and intensity of that supervision will be significantly greater in the period before a firm has assessed its employee as competent, than after. Firms should thus have clear criteria and procedures relating to the specific point at which their employees are assessed by them as being competent, so as to be able to demonstrate when and why a reduced level of supervision was considered appropriate.

At all stages, firms are required to consider the level of relevant experience that an employee has in determining the level of supervision required.

### Supervisors

There are additional requirements in respect of those supervising staff carrying out the activities specified: the firms must ensure that these people have the necessary coaching and assessment skills, as well as the technical knowledge associated with the activity so as to act as a competent supervisor and assessor. In particular, the Sourcebook states that firms should consider whether it is appropriate to require these people to pass an appropriate examination, if the staff that they supervise have not themselves yet been assessed as competent.

If the employee is advising on packaged products to retail customers, however, the firm must ensure that the supervisor has passed an appropriate examination.

## 5.2.3 Qualification Requirements before Starting Activities

The T&C Sourcebook states that firms must not allow their employees to carry on any of a specified activity (other than an overseeing activity) for which there is a qualification requirement without their first having passed the relevant regulatory module of an appropriate qualification. Specifically, firms must not allow their employees to do any of the following without first passing each module of an appropriate qualification:

- certain **advising and dealing** activities;
- acting as a broker fund adviser;
- advising on syndicate participation at Lloyd's; or
- acting as a pension transfer specialist.

### Exemptions from the Requirements

If a firm is satisfied that an employee meets certain conditions, then the requirement to have passed each module of an appropriate qualification only applies if he is carrying on one of the following activities:

- advising retail clients on investments which are packaged products;
- acting as a broker fund adviser;
- advising on syndicate participation at Lloyd's;
- acting as a pension transfer specialist.

The conditions are that the firm must be satisfied that the employee:

- has at least three years' up-to-date relevant experience in the activity, which he gained while employed outside the UK;
- has not previously been required to comply fully with the relevant examination requirements; and
- has passed the relevant module of an appropriate examination.

The customer function does not extend to an individual who is performing the function and is based overseas and, in a 12-month period, spends no more than 30 days in the UK to the extent that they are appropriately supervised by a person approved for this function.

However, the latter two conditions (see the bullet list above) do not apply to someone who is benefiting from the **30-day rule** exemption, unless the employee benefits from the 30-day rule exemption because they are advising retail clients on packaged products or broker funds.

### Selecting an Appropriate Examination

Firms are required to select an appropriate qualification from the list of qualifications maintained by the FCA (TC App 4–1). If they do so, this will tend to demonstrate compliance with the qualification requirements.

## 5.2.4 Training Needs

The T&C Sourcebook states that firms must assess their employees' training needs at the outset, and again at regular intervals (including if their role changes). They should also review the quality and effectiveness of their training.

## 5.2.5 Maintaining Competence

Firms are also required to review their employees' competence regularly – and to take appropriate action, when needed, to ensure that they remain competent for their role. In doing so, they should take account of:

- the individual's technical knowledge and its application;
- their skills and expertise; and
- changes in the market and to products, legislation and regulation.

## 5.2.6 Activities to which the T&C Rules Apply

Designated investment business carried out for a retail client:

- advising;
- dealing;
- managing;
- overseeing on a day-to-day basis.

Regulated mortgage activity and reversion activity carried on for a customer:

- advising;
- designing scripted questions for non-advised sales;
- overseeing non-advised sales on a day-to-day basis.

Non-investment insurance business carried on for a consumer:

- advising.

## 5.2.7  Statements of Professional Standing (SPSs)

Following the RDR, the FCA Handbook now states that individuals wishing to operate as a retail investment adviser must be in possession of a valid SPS from an FCA-accredited body such as the CISI.

SPSs confirm that an adviser has:

- completed a Qualification and Credit Framework (QCF) Level 4 qualification, including any required qualification gap-fill, that appears on the list of approved qualifications in the FCA Handbook;
- completed an annual programme of 35 hours of continuing professional development (CPD) that meets the requirements laid out by the FCA;
- acted in accordance with FCA APER;
- agreed to adhere to a Code of Ethics.

The previous regulator's aim was that it wanted to raise standards of professionalism to inspire consumer confidence and build trust. This complements the package of wider RDR proposals on adviser charging and labelling of services.

There are some exceptions to the qualification requirements for existing advisers, depending on when an individual was first assessed as competent by the FCA.

The FCA says from 2013 advisers must complete a minimum of 35 hours of relevant CPD each year, with at least 21 hours of this being structured learning.

In PS10/18, the FSA published qualifications tables as part of the Handbook, containing the appropriate qualifications that needed to be attained by employees in order to carry out certain activities for retail clients. These activities are set out in Appendix 1.1.1R of the Training and Competence (T&C) sourcebook.

The RDR qualification requirements apply to individuals carrying out one or more of the following regulated activities:

- advising on (but not dealing in) securities (which are not stakeholder pension schemes or broker funds);
- advising on (but not dealing in) derivatives;
- advising on packaged products (which are not broker funds);
- advising on friendly society tax-exempt policies;
- advising on, and dealing in securities (which are not stakeholder pension schemes or broker funds);
- advising on and dealing with or for clients in derivatives.

PS 10/18 confirmed that the deadline for existing advisers to obtain a Level 4 (or higher) qualification was 31 December 2012.

Individuals assessed as competent as at 30 June 2009, had to meet the end-2012 deadline. However, those assessed as competent between 1 July 2009 and 1 January 2011 had a deadline of 1 July 2013 – 30 months after the rule was introduced on 1 January 2011.

Individuals giving advice after 1 January 2011, have a deadline of 30 months after they begin providing advice, although for most activities, individuals may only start the activity once the regulatory module has been attained.

The FCA supervises and enforces the new professional standards, which are set through the FCA Handbook. This implements higher and consistent standards for individual advisers giving investment advice to retail customers. There are requirements about qualifications, CPD and ethics.

This new framework will bring a number of benefits, including:

- a more professional sector that consumers will want to engage with and trust, and new joiners will want to become part of;
- more focus on setting, monitoring and enforcing the standards advisers are required to achieve;
- a greater requirement for advisers to demonstrate both initial and ongoing competence, including ethical behaviour;
- greater accountability for meeting the higher standards arising from the FCA's more intensive approach to regulation;
- a framework for increasing professional standards that is simpler and more likely to deliver the benefits of improved levels of compliance;
- simplicity – new powers will not be required for the FCA as they are already given under the FSMA; and
- greater emphasis on the role of professional bodies.

Advisers will be required to obtain and hold an annual SPS as evidence that they are meeting the standards, which will be issued by an accredited body. The SPS will contain:

- the adviser's name;
- the name and contact details of the accredited body and a named signatory;
- the end date of verification (maximum of 12 months from date of verification);
- confirmation the adviser's qualification(s) have been verified;
- confirmation that the adviser has signed an annual declaration that states that they:
  - have kept their knowledge up-to-date; and
  - adhere to standards of ethical behaviour;
- the adviser's individual reference number as it appears on the FCA Register; and
- a recommendation that the reader should check that the adviser is on the FCA Register, and how to do so.

## 5.3 New Requirements Following Consultation on Competence and Ethics

The FSA previously published proposals to strengthen its requirements on competence for individuals carrying out retail activities, while placing more emphasis on standards of ethical behaviour. This followed a consultation in 2010.

Reflecting the FSA's increased focus on competence, the new requirements introduce a 30-month deadline for individuals to complete all modules of a qualification required for their role. These requirements also removed some transitional provisions which allowed individuals to operate without formal qualifications, due to the arrangements under their previous regulator.

Clarification on how individuals carrying out approved person's roles should demonstrate a good standard of ethical behaviour is also provided. They will be expected to act in the interests of their client, avoiding consumer detriment and taking responsibility for their own level of competence.

The new requirements seek to increase standards of professionalism across the industry, complementing the RDR plans and rules that are already in place for investment advice.

Competence and ethics are key elements of the regulatory regime. The regulator has increased scrutiny of individuals working in the financial services industry over the last few years. Ultimately it is in a firm's commercial interest to recruit, train and retain good-quality individuals, but regulation ensures that standards of competence and ethics are maintained at an appropriate level.

An FCA statutory objective is consumer protection, therefore it wants firms operating robust T&C schemes and individuals demonstrating good standards of ethical behaviour. There are tables of appropriate qualifications based on regulated activities being carried out in the T&C sourcebook (ie, advising on securities, derivatives and packaged products). This means that firms and individuals have an easily accessible and comprehensive source of approved qualifications.

# 6. Record-Keeping and Notification

### Learning Objective

7.4.1 Apply the principles and rules relating to record-keeping and notification for regulatory purposes (SYSC 9.1 (FCA/FRA), PRIN 2.1.1 (11) (FCA/FRA), SUP (FCA/PRA), DISP 1.9)

Principle 11 of the Principles for Businesses refers specifically to a firm's dealings with the regulator and the requirement to notify the FCA/PRA appropriately of anything of which it would reasonably expect notice.

SYSC 9.1 states that a firm must arrange for orderly records to be kept of its business and internal organisation, including all services and transactions undertaken by it, which must be sufficient for the FCA/PRA or any other relevant competent authority under MiFID to monitor the firm's compliance with the requirements under the regulatory system.

In relation to MiFID business, a common platform firm (a firm subject to either MiFID or the CRD) must retain records in a medium that allows the storage of information in a way accessible for future reference by the FCA/PRA or any other relevant competent authority under MiFID, and so that the following conditions are met:

- the FCA or any other relevant competent authority under MiFID must be able to access them readily and to reconstitute each key stage of the processing of each transaction;
- it must be possible for any corrections or other amendments, and the contents of the records prior to such corrections and amendments, to be easily ascertained;
- it must not be possible for the records otherwise to be manipulated or altered.

A firm must retain all records in relation to MiFID business for a period of at least five years. In relation to non-MiFID business, the record-keeping requirement is three years.

The records required should be capable of being reproduced in the English language on paper. If a firm is required to retain a record of a communication that was not made in the English language, it may retain it in that language. However, it should be able to provide a translation on request. If a firm's records relate to business carried on from an establishment in a country or territory outside the UK, an official language of that country or territory may be used instead of the English language.

In relation to the retention of records for non-MiFID business, a firm should have appropriate systems and controls in place with respect to the adequacy of, access to and security of its records, so that the firm may fulfil its regulatory and statutory obligations. With respect to retention periods, the general principle is that records should be retained for as long as is relevant for the purposes for which they are made.

The FCA's Conduct of Business Sourcebook has detailed record-keeping requirements relating to specific activities undertaken by firms, such as:

- **COBS 2.3 (Inducements)** – fee, commission or non-monetary benefit under COBS 2.3.1(2)(b).
- **COBS 3.8 (Client categorisation)** – standard form notice to client and agreements and client categorisation [COBS 3.8.2(i)].
- **COBS 4.11 (Communicating with clients, including financial promotions)** – financial promotion, telemarketing scripts and compliance of financial promotions [COBS 4.11.1 and 4.11.2].
- **COBS 8.1 (Client agreements)** – client agreements [COBS 8.1.4].
- **COBS 9.5 (Suitability, including basic advice)** – suitability [COBS 9.5.1].
- **COBS 10.7 (Appropriateness for non–advised services)** – appropriateness [COBS 10.7.1].
- **COBS 11.5 (Dealing and managing)** – client orders, client orders and decisions to deal in portfolio management, client orders [COBS 11.5.1–11.5.3].
- **COBS 11.6 (Dealing and managing)** – prior and periodic disclosure – use of dealing commission [COBS 11.6.19].
- **COBS 11.7 (Dealing and managing)** – personal account dealing [COBS 11.7.4].
- **COBS 16 (Reporting information to clients)** – confirmation to clients and periodic statements [COBS 16.2.7 and 16.3.11].

DISP 1.9 obliges firms to keep records of any **complaints** received, and the measures taken for their resolution, and retain those records for the following period of time from the date the complaint was received:

- five years if the complaint relates to MiFID business or collective portfolio management services for a UCITS scheme or an EEA UCITS scheme; and
- three years for all other complaints.

# 7. The FCA's and PRA's Changing Approach to Governance

## Learning Objective

7.7.1 Understand how the FCA's and PRA's approach to the authorisation and approval of individuals upholds ethical principles and high standards of professional conduct: consumers; government and regulators; senior management of a regulated firm; employees of a regulated firm

7.8.1 Understand how the FCA's and PRA's approach to the authorisation and approval of individuals supports good corporate governance and business risk management

Poor governance is widely recognised as a factor contributing to the failure of some firms during the financial crisis, and has come under considerable regulatory scrutiny by regulators and governments in the UK and internationally.

The approval of individuals, based on their fitness and propriety, has always been part of their statutory responsibilities, and the core assessment remains unchanged. These are:

- honesty, integrity and reputation;
- competence and capability; and
- financial soundness.

The FCA and the PRA have taken a different approach to that of the FSA. They have decided that they need to make sure that key roles are performed by competent staff – who are up to the job in question.

In broad terms, effective governance enables a firm's board and executive to interact effectively to deliver a firm's agreed strategy – and, in particular, it is about managing the risks the firm faces. Good governance enables the board to share a clear understanding of the firm's risk appetite and to establish a robust control framework to manage that risk effectively across the business, with effective oversight and challenge along the way.

Of course, it is no good just putting structures, controls and processes in place. They must be operated by suitably experienced people, incentivised in the right way, supported by – and themselves supporting – a strong culture. All of this must, of course, work in practice.

During 2008 and 2009 the UK regulator (the FSA) introduced a tougher, more intrusive approach to supervision of firms as part of its supervisory enhancement programme. In particular, the FSA increased its focus on the quality of senior management, and made reforms during 2009 to the approved persons regime and the SIFs.

The FCA sought to increase its focus on the quality of senior management. This was aimed at ensuring that only individuals with the right skill-set and experience took senior management roles, and that their performance is subject to rigorous regulatory scrutiny. Corporate governance has also been a topic of interest in the wider policy arena in the UK; the government commissioned Sir David Walker to carry out a review of UK financial institution corporate governance.

The FCA and the PRA have continued the work that the previous regulator (the FSA) started.

## 7.1 The New Requirements

- **A new framework of classification of controlled functions** – these for the most part represent **tweaks** to the current structure, and do not represent major policy changes or a widening of the regulatory net in real terms.
- **Changes to the approved persons regime, including the scope and definition of some controlled functions** – again these represent minor changes to the current framework.
- **More information on the SIF process** – this contains helpful information for firms and candidates applying for SIFs on the approval processes that the regulator is now employing, with an increased reliance on interviews to assess competence and skills.
- **To provide guidance on expectations in relation to NEDs**, including proposing the intrusive step of considering whether a proposed NED has time to perform its role, and also the concerning step of deleting guidance clarifying NEDs' disciplinary liabilities. This guidance makes it clear that, providing a NED has carried out its role with due care, it will not be held responsible for the failings of the firm or other individuals at the firm. The regulator was concerned that this might undermine its message that it will take action against NEDs who do not perform their role in intervening in poor management decisions.
- **Risk governance guidance and plans for other implementing measures in support of Sir David Walker's recommendations** – the regulator has not addressed remuneration in its consultation paper; rather, it states that this will be dealt with as part of its separate ongoing work on remuneration.

### New Framework of Classification of Significant Influence Functions (SIFs)

Currently, two types of individuals are regulated – those who deal with customers or customers' property, and those who have a significant influence on the conduct of a firm's affairs. Individuals that perform a role which the regulator has specified as either a customer function or a **SIF** are subject to the approved persons regime.

Nine new significant influence controlled functions were proposed and created. These are all roles that the regulator says fall within existing significant influence controlled functions, and so it does not believe that there will be more individuals requiring approval as a result.

The nine new functions (compare with the chart in Section 4.2) are:

- Chairman (CF2a);
- Chairman of risk committee (CF2c);
- Chairman of audit committee (CF2d);
- Chairman of remuneration committee (CF2e);
- Senior independent director (CF2b);
- Parent entity SIF (CF00);
- Finance function (CF13);
- Risk function (CF14);
- Internal audit function (CF15).

The finance, risk and internal audit functions represent a reintroduction of these functions as separate functions. They were merged into one systems and controls function in November 2007, in a drive to simplify the regime.

The parent entity SIF is intended to catch individuals brought within the scope of the CF1 (director) or CF2 (NED) functions by the regime change announced in July 2009. This change is to regulate individuals who are likely to exert significant influence over a regulated firm from a position in the firm's holding company or parent undertaking, except where the parent entity is authorised by the FCA/PRA or an EEA-equivalent authority. The regulator believes that it is useful to identify and assess those individuals separately from the CF1 and CF2 functions.

## Significant Influence Controlled Functions – Other Proposals

The regulator made a couple of small changes to the rule changes that became effective in July 2009, regarding the requirement for individuals exercising a significant influence from within a parent undertaking or holding company of a UK firm to become approved persons. The regulator at that time provided for two groups of firms to be excluded from the rules: limited liability partnerships (LLPs) and non-bodies corporate. These exclusions were deleted, as the regulator does not believe that the corporate status of the parent or holding company of the regulated firm is relevant.

To reflect the growing regulatory interest in retail banking following the introduction of the banking conduct of business regime last year, the regulator extended the significant management function (CF29) to UK branches of incoming EEA firms accepting retail deposits. It acknowledges that this may, in certain circumstances, be potentially stepping on the toes of the home state authority. But the regulator justifies this on the basis that all retail banking is now subject to its jurisdiction in the UK, as it wants to bring retail banking requirements in this respect into line with those applicable to investment business.

### Proposals for Regulation of Non-Executive Directors (NEDs)

The Walker Review recommended a minimum time commitment required of NEDs of FTSE 100 listed banks or insurance companies, and proposed that such time commitments should be included in letters of appointment. In line with these recommendations, the regulator provides guidance that, as part of its **fit and proper** assessment of an individual, it may take the **intrusive** step of considering whether the individual has capacity to meet the time commitment specified in the letter of appointment. The regulator does, however, state that it is for the firm and the individual to demonstrate that the individual will have time, taking into account the demands of the role and the individual's other commitments (including other NED positions held).

### Supervision of Governance

Both the FCA and the PRA target and increase their scrutiny on the quality of governance through the new supervisory approaches. They also increase their focus on NEDs, in particular the senior independent director and the chairs of board committees.

## 7.2 Financial Reporting

On 1 December 2009, the UK Financial Reporting Council (FRC) published a report on the findings of its review of the impact and effectiveness of the Combined Code of Corporate Governance. The code sets out standards of good practice in relation to issues such as board composition and development, remuneration, accountability and audit and relations with shareholders.

As a result of the review the FRC made a number of changes which included new code principles on:

- the roles of the chairman and NEDs;
- the need for the board to have an appropriate mix of skills, experience and independence;
- the commitment levels expected of directors, the board's responsibility for defining the company's risk appetite and tolerance;
- new **comply or explain** provisions including:
    - board evaluation reviews to be externally facilitated at least every three years;
    - the chairman to hold regular development reviews with all directors;
    - companies to report on their business model and overall financial strategy.
- changes to the section of the code dealing with remuneration to emphasise the need for performance-related pay to be aligned with the long-term interest of the company and to the company's risk policies and systems and to enable variable components to be reclaimed in certain circumstances;
- the introduction of a stewardship code for institutional investors;
- the Code to be renamed the UK Corporate Governance Code to make clearer its status as the UK's recognised corporate governance standard.

## Summary of this Chapter

You should have an understanding and knowledge of the following after reading this chapter:

- The principles for businesses.
- Controlled functions and the statements of principle for approved persons.
- Code of practice for approved persons:
  - seven principles.
- The fit and proper test.
- General provisions and fees.
- Senior management arrangements (SYSC):
  - apportionment of responsibilities;
  - systems and controls;
  - governance arrangements;
  - responsibility of senior personnel;
  - compliance/internal audit;
  - financial crime and anti-money laundering;
  - risk control;
  - remuneration;
  - regulatory reporting.
- Threshold conditions.
- Regulated and prohibited activities:
  - general prohibition;
  - specified investments;
  - specified activities;
  - exclusions;
  - exemptions.
- Authorisation:
  - exemptions;
  - appointed representatives;
  - permission notices.
- Fit and proper test for approved persons.
- Approved persons (PRA and FCA):
  - authorisation;
  - controlled functions (PRA and FCA):
    - governing functions, required functions, systems and controls function, significant management function, customer function.
- Supervision (PRA and FCA).
- Appointed representatives.
- Training and competence.
- Record-keeping and notification.
- FCA and PRA's approach to governance.

# End of Chapter Questions

Think of an answer for each question and refer to the appropriate section for confirmation.

1. What is the purpose of the Principles for Businesses?
   *Answer reference: Section 1.1*

2. What is the code of practice for SIFs?
   *Answer reference: Section 1.4*

3. What are the fit and proper test criteria for an individual applying to be an approved person?
   *Answer reference: Section 1.5*

4. What are the main purposes of the SYSC requirements?
   *Answer reference: Section 1.6*

5. What are the threshold conditions?
   *Answer reference: Section 1.7*

6. Name four specified investments.
   *Answer reference: Section 2.2*

7. Name six specified activities.
   *Answer reference: Section 2.3*

8. When is dealing as principal not a regulated activity?
   *Answer reference: Section 2.4.1*

9. When might the FCA/PRA seek to vary a firm's Part 4A permission?
   *Answer reference: Section 3.3*

10. What is the purpose of the fit and proper test?
    *Answer reference: Section 3.6*

11. What is the difference between a governing function and a required function?
    *Answer reference: Section 4.2*

12. What is the purpose of the FCA/PRA's initiative in respect of SIFs?
    *Answer reference: Sections 4.2.5 & 7*

13. What is the purpose of the T&C regime?
    *Answer reference: Section 5.1*

14. What are the authorisation requirements that relate directly to the need to act with integrity and in an ethical manner?
    *Answer reference: Whole chapter*

# Chapter Eight
# The Regulatory Framework Relating to Financial Crime

| | | |
|---|---|---|
| 1. | Market Abuse | 261 |
| 2. | Insider Dealing | 277 |
| 3. | Money Laundering (ML) and Terrorist Financing (TF) | 282 |
| 4. | The Model Code for Directors | 296 |
| 5. | The Disclosure and Transparency Rules | 298 |
| 6. | The Data Protection Act (DPA) | 301 |
| 7. | Whistleblowing | 304 |
| 8. | Financial Crime Prevention | 306 |
| 9. | The Bribery Act 2010 | 308 |

**This syllabus area will provide approximately 18 of the 80 examination questions**

The Regulatory Framework Relating to Financial Crime

In this chapter you will gain an understanding of:

- The Market Abuse Directive (MAD): what it is, how it is defined and enforced against.
- The FCA's code of market conduct:
    - the concept of the regular user;
    - statutory exceptions to market abuse – safe harbours.
- Relationships with other legislation – insider dealing and Section 89–92.
- Misleading statement and practices.
- Insider dealing – legislation (the Criminal Justice Act (CJA)).
    - offences/defences;
    - instruments caught by the act;
    - the FCA's prosecution powers.
- Money laundering (ML) and terrorist financing (TF):
    - Money laundering legislation (Proceeds of Crime (POCA) Act 2002/Money Laundering Regulations 2007);
    - the three stages of ML;
    - the role and purpose of the Joint Money Laundering Steering Group (JMLSG);
    - the role and obligations of the money laundering reporting officer (MLRO);
    - the National Crime Agency – role and purpose;
    - anti-terrorism legislation and guidance.
- The Model Code for Directors.
- Disclosure and transparency.
- The Data Protection Act (DPA) 1998:
    - the role and purpose of the information commissioner.
- Whistleblowing.
- The Bribery Act 2010.
- FCA's approach to financial crime prevention.

# 1.    Market Abuse

## 1.1    The Statutory Offence

**Learning Objective**

8.1     Apply the main concepts, legal requirements and regulations relating to the prevention of market abuse:

8.1.1     Statutory offence of market abuse (Financial Services and Markets Act 2000 s.118 (1–8))

Market abuse is a serious offence that damages investor confidence and the integrity of financial markets.

261

The **Market Abuse Directive (MAD)** was introduced to create a regime to tackle market manipulation in the EU and the proper disclosure of information to the market. It also aimed to update the existing EU insider dealing legislation. It defines and prohibits market abuse and provides for a number of preventative measures, such as prompt disclosure of inside information and management transactions and safeguards of impartiality of investment research.

Market abuse relates to **behaviour** by a person, or a group of persons working together, which occurs in relation to qualifying investments on a prescribed market that satisfies one or more of the following three conditions. The behaviour as it is currently defined is:

- based on information that is not generally available to those using the market and, if it were available, would have an impact on the price; and
- likely to give a false or misleading impression of the supply, demand or value of the investments concerned; and
- likely to distort the market in the investments.

In certain cases, the behaviour is judged on the basis of what a **regular user** of the market would view as a failure to observe the standards of behaviour normally expected in the market.

The Treasury has determined the **qualifying investments** and **prescribed markets** – broadly, they are the investments traded on any of the UK's RIEs, investments where application has been made for trading on such markets and related investments, like derivatives.

The behaviour could amount to market abuse as long as it relates to these investments, regardless of where it takes place. There is some overlap with the insider dealing legislation under the Criminal Justice Act (CJA) 1993, but:

- the CJA provides for a criminal regime, whereas the FSMA market abuse regime provides for civil penalties and, consequently, a lower required standard of proof; and
- the CJA insider dealing regime applies to a more restricted range of investments (the FSMA market abuse regime extends its **insider dealing** provision to other markets, such as commodity and energy).

## 1.2 The FCA's Code of Market Conduct

### Learning Objective

8.1 Apply the main concepts, legal requirements and regulations relating to the prevention of market abuse:

8.1.2 Status of the FCA's Code of Market Conduct [FSMA 2000 s.119(1) – (3)]; the territorial scope of the legislation and regulation [FSMA 2000 s.118]

The FCA is tasked under FSMA Section 119 to prepare and issue a code containing such provisions as it considers will give appropriate guidance to those determining whether or not behaviour amounts to market abuse. This is called the **Code of Market Conduct** and forms part of the FCA's Handbook.

The code may among other things specify:

- descriptions of behaviour that, in the opinion of the authority, amounts to market abuse;
- descriptions of behaviour that, in the opinion of the authority, does not amount to market abuse;
- factors that, in the opinion of the authority, are to be taken into account in determining whether or not behaviour amounts to market abuse.

The code may make different provision in relation to persons, cases or circumstances of different descriptions.

The FCA may at any time alter or replace the code, although this will be undertaken in the normal consultation process.

The code provides guidance on what does and does not amount to market abuse and the factors which are taken into account in the determination of whether market abuse has occurred.

The territorial scope of FSMA Section 118 is such that it only extends to the behaviour of market abuse undertaken in the UK or in relation to qualifying investments traded on any of the UK's RIEs which are either situated in the UK or which are accessible electronically in the UK.

# 1.3    Code of Market Conduct Offences

## Learning Objective

8.1    Apply the main concepts, legal requirements and regulations relating to the prevention of market abuse:

8.1.3    Offences outlined in the Code of Market Conduct [MAR 1.2.2/7, 1.3.1, 1.4.1, 1.5.1, 1.6.1, 1.7.1, 1.8.1, 1.9.1, 1.2.22]

8.1.4    Concepts of effect rather than intention [MAR 1.2.3] and reasonable regular user [MAR 1.2.20/21]

The FCA's **Code of Market Conduct** Sourcebook explains the types of behaviour caught by the market abuse regime. They extend to seven circumstances:

1.  **Insider Dealing**
    When an insider deals in, or attempts to deal in, a qualifying investment or a related investment on the basis of inside information. For market abuse purposes, an insider has inside information:

    - as a result of their membership of the administrative, management or supervisory bodies of the issuer of the investment; or
    - as a result of them holding in the capital of the issuer of the investment; or
    - as a result of having access to the information through his employment, profession or duties; or
    - as a result of criminal activities; or
    - which they have obtained by other means and which he knows, or could reasonably be expected to know, is inside information.

2. **Improper disclosure**
   When an insider discloses inside information to another person other than in the proper course of the exercise of their employment, profession or duties.

3. **Misuse of information**
   When behaviour which is not covered by 1. above (insider dealing) or 2. above (improper disclosure) is based on information that is not generally available to those using the market and that a regular user would regard as relevant and a failure to observe the standard of behaviour reasonably expected.

4. **Manipulating Transactions**
   When the behaviour consists of effecting transactions or orders to trade that are not for legitimate reasons and in conformity with accepted practices on the relevant market, and which:

   - give, or are likely to give, a false or misleading impression as to the supply or demand for, or the price of, the qualifying investment; or
   - secure the price of such investments at an abnormal or artificial level.

5. **Manipulating Devices**
   Behaviour that consists of effecting transactions or orders to trade which employ fictitious devices or any other form of deception or contrivance.

6. **Dissemination**
   When the behaviour consists of the dissemination of information by any means which gives, or is likely to give, a false or misleading impression as to a qualifying investment by a person who knew, or could reasonably be expected to have known, that the information was false or misleading.

7. **Misleading Behaviour and Distortion**
   When behaviour which is not covered by 4. above (manipulating transactions), 5. above (manipulating devices) or 6. above (dissemination):

   - is likely to give a regular user a false or misleading impression as to the supply of, demand for, or price or value of, a qualifying investment; or
   - is regarded by a regular user as behaviour likely to distort the market in such investments.

In both circumstances (misuse of information and misleading behaviour and distortion) the regular user must view the behaviour as a failure to observe the standard of behaviour reasonably expected of a person in their position in relation to the market.

The practical examples mentioned in each of the seven circumstances are drawn from the factsheet, *Why market abuse could cost you money*, published by the FSA in June 2008.

The Regulatory Framework Relating to Financial Crime

## Examples of Market Conduct Offences

### Circumstances 1 and 2 – Improper Disclosure

An employee finds out that her company is about to become the target of a takeover bid. Before the information is made public, she buys shares in her company because she knows a takeover bid may be imminent. She then discloses the information to a friend. This behaviour creates an unfair marketplace because the person who sold the shares to the employee might not have done so if she had known of the potential takeover. The employee's friend also has this information and could profit unfairly from it.

### Circumstance 3 – Misuse of Information

An employee learns that his company may lose a significant contract with its main customer. The employee then sells her shares, based on her assessment that it is reasonably certain the contract will be lost. This behaviour creates an unfair marketplace as the person buying the shares from the employee might not have done so had she been aware of the information about the potential loss of the contract.

### Circumstance 4 – Manipulating Transactions

A person buys a large number of a particular share near the end of the day, aiming to drive the stock price higher to improve the performance of their investment. The market price is pushed to an artificial level and investors receive a false impression of the price of those shares and the value of any portfolio or fund that holds the stock. This could lead to people making the wrong investment decisions.

### Circumstance 5 – Manipulating Devices

A person buys shares and then spreads misleading information with a view to increasing the price. This could give investors a false impression of the price of a share and lead them to make the wrong investment decisions.

### Circumstance 6 – Dissemination

A person uses an internet bulletin board or chat room to post information about the takeover of a company. The person knows the information to be false or misleading. This could artificially raise or reduce the price of a share and lead to people making the wrong investment decisions.

### Circumstance 7 – Distortion and Misleading Behaviour

An empty cargo ship that is used to transport a particular commodity is moved. This could create a false impression of changes in the supply of, or demand for, that commodity or the related futures contract. It could also artificially change the price of that commodity or the futures contract, and lead to people making the wrong investment decisions.

## 1.4 The Regular User

As noted above, for the offences of market abuse (misuse of information) and market abuse (misleading behaviour) and market abuse (distortion), behaviour is measured against the standards of the regular user. Whether or not behaviour amounts to market abuse, as defined in Section 1.1, depends on how a hypothetical reasonable person (the **regular user**), familiar with the market in question, views the behaviour. If a regular user feels that the behaviour falls below the standards expected on the market in question, it is market abuse.

In assessing whether the behaviour falls below the standards expected, the following will be considered:

- The characteristics of the market, investments traded there and the users of that market.
- The rules and regulations of the market in question and any applicable laws (for example, if the behaviour occurred overseas, compliance with the law overseas will be a consideration).
- The prevailing market mechanisms, practices and codes of conduct applicable to the market in question.
- The standards reasonably expected of the person in the light of their level of skill and knowledge (for example, the standards expected of a retail investor may differ from those expected of an institutional investor).
- The need for market users to conduct their affairs in a manner that does not compromise the fair and efficient operation of the market as a whole, or damage the interests of investors.

It is not essential for the person responsible for the behaviour in question to have intended to commit market abuse, although the regular user test may determine that market abuse has not occurred unless the intention of the person was to engage in market abuse.

### 1.4.1 Accepted Market Practices

The FCA will take the following non-exhaustive factors into account when assessing whether to accept a particular market practice:

- The level of transparency of the relevant market practice to the whole market.
- The need to safeguard the operation of market forces and the proper interplay of the forces of supply and demand (taking into account the impact of the relevant market practice against the main market parameters, such as the specific market conditions before carrying out the relevant market practice, the weighted average price of a single session and the daily closing price).
- The degree to which the relevant market practice has an impact on market liquidity and efficiency.
- The degree to which the relevant practice takes into account the trading mechanism of the relevant market and enables market participants to react properly and in a timely manner to the new market situation created by that practice.
- The risk inherent in the relevant practice for the integrity of, directly or indirectly, related markets, whether regulated or not, in the relevant financial instrument within the whole EEA.
- The outcome of any investigation of the relevant market practice by any competent authority or other authority mentioned in Article 12(1) of the MAD, in particular whether the relevant market practice breached rules or regulations designed to prevent market abuse, or codes of conduct, be it on the market in question or on directly or indirectly related markets within the EEA.
- The structural characteristics of the relevant market including whether it is regulated or not, the types of financial instruments traded and the type of market participants, including the extent of retail investors' participation in the relevant market.

## 1.5 The Enforcement Regime

The FSMA gives the FCA the power to impose a penalty, or to make a statement that a person has engaged in market abuse. These powers can be exercised if the FCA is satisfied that a person has engaged in market abuse, or if the person has taken (or refrained from taking) any action which required or encouraged another party to engage in behaviour that would amount to market abuse.

The penalties available to the FCA (ie, they are the sanctions that FSMA empowers the FCA to use) include:

*   withdrawal of approval or authorisation;
*   imposing an unlimited civil fine;
*   making a public statement that a person has engaged in market abuse;
*   applying to the court for an injunction to restrain threatened or continued market abuse, an injunction requiring a person to take steps to remedy market abuse, or a freezing order;
*   applying to the court for a restitution order; and
*   requiring the payment of compensation to victims of the abuse.

However, if there are reasonable grounds for the person to believe that the behaviour in question did not amount to market abuse, or the person took all reasonable precautions and exercised all due diligence to avoid engaging in market abuse, the FCA cannot impose a penalty.

The FCA's Supervision Manual (SUP) states that authorised investment firms and credit institutions, which arrange or execute a transaction with or for a client in a qualifying investment, and which have **reasonable grounds** to suspect that the transaction might constitute market abuse, must promptly notify the FCA. Qualifying investments are those admitted to trading on a prescribed market (SUP 15.10.2).

Strictly, this obligation extends only to executed transactions and not to unexecuted orders – but a firm may bring a suspicious order to trade to the FCA's attention voluntarily. The provisions require that firms decide on a case-by-case basis whether there are reasonable grounds for suspecting that a transaction involves market abuse, taking into account the circumstances. Further, Principle 11 of the Principles for Businesses requires that a firm discloses to the FCA everything of which the FCA would reasonably expect notice, and many firms (or rather their employees) interpret this as giving them grounds to report unexpected transactions as well.

## 1.6 Statutory Exceptions to Market Abuse – Safe Harbours

### Learning Objective

8.1     Apply the main concepts, legal requirements and regulations relating to the prevention of market abuse:

8.1.5     Statutory exceptions (safe harbours) to Market Abuse [MAR 1.10.1–4 (excl. table 1.10.5)]

There are certain **safe harbours** against a charge of market abuse. Safe harbours outline situations when the behaviour in question is categorically not deemed to be market abuse.

### FCA Rules

There are no FCA rules that permit or require a person to behave in a way that amounts to market abuse. There are, however, particular FCA rules that identify behaviour conforming to the rules.

Complying with these will, therefore, mean that you are not be deemed to be engaging in market abuse. They are:

- the rules relating to Chinese walls (covered in more detail in the SYSC Sourcebook); and
- the disclosure rules relating to the timing, dissemination or availability, content and standard of care applicable to the announcement, communication and release of information for listed companies.

## The Takeover Code

During the course of a takeover, both the predator company and its target have to comply with certain rules laid down in the Takeover Code.

There are no rules in the Takeover Code that permit or require a person to behave in a way that amounts to market abuse. Specifically, as long as any announcements, or the release of information, conforms with the timing, dissemination and availability required by the rules of the Takeover Code, is expressly permitted or required by such rules and conforms with the Takeover Code's relevant general principle, it will not amount to market abuse.

## Price Stabilisation and Buy-Backs

Price-support activities carried out in accordance with the price stabilisation rules do not amount to market abuse. (This was also the case with insider dealing.)

# 1.7 Relationship with Other Legislation

### Learning Objective

8.1 Apply the main concepts, legal requirements and regulations relating to the prevention of market abuse:

8.1.6 The distinction between offences under market abuse, insider dealing (CJA) and under Financial Services Act s.89–s.95 – misleading statements and practices

The main types of market abuse, namely:

1. misleading statements and impressions and misuse of information; and
2. behaviour which is likely to give a false or misleading impression of the supply, demand or value of the investments concerned;

are, to an extent, already covered by the legislation relating to insider dealing (CJA) and the legislation relating to misleading statements and impressions in Sections 89–95 of the Financial Services Act 2012.

Due to the recent LIBOR (2012 onwards) scandal, the Act now includes misleading statements in relation to benchmarks.

# The Regulatory Framework Relating to Financial Crime

As noted in Section 1.1, the FSMA market abuse regime is designed to complement the criminal regime for insider dealing and misleading statements and practices.

There will be cases when a possible breach of both the criminal law, as well as the market abuse regime, occurs, and the FCA is then required to assess whether it has sufficient evidence, and whether it is in the public interest, to commence criminal proceedings rather than impose sanctions for market abuse.

The FCA stated that it was its policy not to impose a sanction for market abuse if a person was being prosecuted for insider dealing or misleading statements and impressions.

Similarly, it would not commence criminal proceedings if it had brought, or was seeking to bring, disciplinary proceedings for market abuse.

## 1.8 Ethical Considerations and Consequences to the Market of Market Abuse

### Learning Objective

8.1 Apply the main concepts, legal requirements and regulations relating to the prevention of market abuse:

8.1.7 Ethical considerations and consequences of market abuse in relation to all market participants, clients and the integrity of the market system

One of the overarching objectives of the FCA is to maintain efficient, orderly and clean financial markets. In addition, the FCA seeks to ensure that the UK interest is represented and taken into account in the EU and international regulatory reform. The FCA remains focused on maintaining and developing the UK's listing regime and enforcing the market abuse regime.

The FCA and the regulated community need to work together **in partnership** to achieve clean, efficient financial markets in the UK. The FCA believes that tackling market abuse should not be seen as a job for the regulator alone – it has to be a collaborative effort with the market.

What the FCA sees as tackling market abuse, by both it and firms includes:

- strengthening systems and controls at firms to mitigate market abuse;
- high focus on training and awareness and learning from good practices – identified by the industry or by FCA thematic work;
- reporting wrongdoing;
- each taking tough action when abuse is identified – the FCA aims to take preventative action as a deterrent.

## 1.8.1 What the FCA Expects from Firms

The FCA expects senior management to take responsibility for ensuring that firms identify risks, having due regard to the operation of financial markets as a whole, and for ensuring their firms develop appropriate systems and controls to manage the risks. In particular, there is the need to manage conflicts of interest properly and the need for self-reporting, if senior management suspect that their own staff have engaged in misconduct.

Key to this is the recognition by the FCA of firms' efforts. The FCA's commitment is that, if firms can demonstrate that they have good systems and controls and are complying with them, and an individual within the firm commits market abuse, they will not pursue the firm in an enforcement action, just the individual.

## 1.8.2 Market Cleanliness

The prevalence of insider dealing puts two of the FCA's statutory objectives at risk: firstly, market confidence – maintaining confidence in the financial system; and secondly, the reduction of financial crime – reducing the extent to which it is possible for a business to be used for a purpose connected with financial crime.

A survey undertaken by a specialist financial services consultancy into the trends and potential solutions for market abuse found that those responding to the survey thought that the regulator is not a key driver in this area, beyond providing clarity about the specifics of regulation.

Furthermore, the market views insider dealing as a systemic risk that is largely immune to tougher regulation, and which should be tackled by significant changes in culture, people and technology. A large majority, over two-thirds, of those surveyed were of the opinion that the reasons for market abuse were not simply confined to firm-specific risks, but were actually systemic. Additionally, a similar percentage of those surveyed felt the market as a whole still underestimates both the importance and the impact of market abuse. Why market abuse could cost you money

On the impact of people and culture, there was a high level of support for the engagement of more skilled people in this area, and also a belief that this increase in skilled staff needs to be combined with changes in corporate culture – reversing the trend from an emphasis on short-term results, towards the promotion of a stronger ethical culture.

The Regulatory Framework Relating to Financial Crime

Over the last few years the UK regulator has:

- continued to set standards that firms and other market participants must follow;
- challenged firms to be well governed, and financially sound and to manage their risks effectively;
- monitored compliance with those standards and took action where they found shortcomings; and
- maintained a commitment to being an international leader in financial regulation.

There is a wide range of ongoing issues that affect market confidence, in particular market abuse and insider dealing. The focus of the FCA's approach on enforcement action has shifted to taking a harsher stance. The FCA is strongly committed to continuing to ensure that the momentum that the FSA generated is maintained, with its focus remaining on firms and individuals.

The FCA will also use criminal prosecution where appropriate to reinforce the change in the control regime. In the area of consumer protection, the FCA will continue to use enforcement to achieve significant penalties that will change behaviour and obtain the right outcomes for consumers.

The FCA's new approach to enforcement is clear for market participants who commit or are involved with insider dealing or other market misconduct; it will take tough action and hold them accountable for their behaviour.

Alongside enforcement action, the FCA remains committed to undertaking a programme of thematic work to review anti-market abuse systems and controls in certain key areas, with a view to publishing good practice points and championing industry improvements. The FCA will continue to focus its work in relation to controls to keep information relating to public takeovers confidential, discussions on the controls over pre-soundings and the way in which stock lending is used by firms.

The FCA has had to increase the strength of its intensive supervisory approach. Just as supervision is critical to the delivery of its financial stability objective, it is also an intrinsic element of its efforts to secure market confidence. Building on the foundations that the FSA put in place in 2009, it will continue to:

- emphasise the importance of firms' business models and their management's understanding of the key risks in those models;
- scrutinise the prudential aspects of their models;
- focus attention on firms' risk-management systems;
- monitor firms' compliance with conduct of business standards; and
- take action against market abuse.

The following factors are critical to the success of the FCA in delivering outcomes in firms and markets: FSF, event-driven work, issues and products, and day-to-day surveillance of market risks and developments, including enhancing surveillance of OTC markets to match the regulator's increased focus on identifying and mitigating risk. Reducing market abuse through a credible deterrence agenda is also essential to delivering positive outcomes.

## 1.8.3 Delivering Consumer Protection

Securing the appropriate degree of protection for consumers is critical to restoring and maintaining confidence in the financial services industry. The changing economic environment has had a significant impact on many investment firms, as well as the many different types of consumers.

Many consumers feel their financial situation is less secure, and their needs and expectations have been affected by changes in interest rates and asset prices. Many investment firms are facing decreases in existing revenue streams and profitability pressures, which are leading to significant changes in business models. There are also regulatory changes on the horizon that will influence both firm and consumer behaviour. It is central to the FCA's delivery of consumer protection objective to address these issues, in order to make markets work better for consumers, and to ensure that, when failure does occur, effective redress and enforcement action is taken.

To achieve these goals, the FCA has moved to a more proactive and intensive approach, and the mechanism for achieving this has three key strands:

- seeking to improve the long-term efficiency and fairness of the market;
- intensive supervision of firms to ensure that they are treating their customers fairly – and to equip the FCA to intervene earlier in the development of retail products than the FSA did – interventions of this nature, which necessarily involve the FCA making a judgement on potential detriment, will need to be based on sound business model analysis and integrated firm risk assessment; and
- in the event that failure has occurred, securing the appropriate level of redress and compensation, when justified, and effective credible deterrence, including taking firm action against firms and individuals who have transgressed.

The FCA delivers its new approach, involving early detection and intervention, through intensive supervision. The FCA's consumer protection strategy seeks to achieve three goals:

- making the retail market work better for consumers;
- avoiding the crystallisation of conduct risks that exceed the FCA's risk tolerance; and
- delivering credible deterrence and prompt and effective redress for consumers.

It signals the end of **reactive regulation** where, historically, the FCA waited for clear evidence that a product had been mis-sold and consumers harmed before it took action and relied principally on risk disclosure information at the point of sale to avoid mis-selling occurring.

The new strategy, involving an integrated model of risk analysis and research, will see the FCA making judgements on firms' decisions and actively intervening in product design. The FCA considers that a successful consumer protection strategy must restore consumer confidence in the financial market place – a key element of restoring that confidence is that the consumer can trust the regulator. This strategy will restore trust in the regulator and will benefit everyone, consumers and providers. The FCA has also stated that it must be willing to place itself between consumers and harm. This can only be achieved by taking a proactive stance.

The Regulatory Framework Relating to Financial Crime

## 1.9 Misleading Statement and Impressions

### 1.9.1 The Offences

**Learning Objective**

8.1 Apply the main concepts, legal requirements and regulations relating to the prevention of market abuse:

8.1.8 Understand the purpose, provisions, offences and defences of Financial Services Act 2012 s.89–s.95 – misleading statements and practices

Misleading statements and impressions replaces a previous offence (Section 397 FSMA 2000). A big difference between the old legislation and the new is the inclusion of misleading statements in relation to benchmarks. This has been included in response to the LIBOR scandal.

**Example**

A stockbroker might tell a potential investor that the shares in XYZ plc (a property developer) are very cheap because XYZ has just won a major contract to build a shopping centre in central London.

If the news of the award of the contract to XYZ was false, Section 89–92 could be used to punish the stockbroker for making a false and misleading statement to persuade his client to purchase shares.

This relates not only to false, misleading or deceptive statements, but also to dishonest concealment of any material facts and to reckless statements, promises or forecasts that are materially misleading, false or deceptive. As long as the statement or concealment has the aim of getting another person to enter into, or refrain from entering into, an investment agreement, an offence has been committed.

The section also applies to a person who creates a false or misleading impression of the market for, or the price of, an investment. An offence is committed if this is done in order to induce another person to acquire, dispose of, underwrite, subscribe for or exercise rights in relation to those investments, or to refrain from doing any of these things.

**Example**

A firm of fund managers might let the market know that it is very keen to buy substantial quantities of shares in ABC plc, when actually it holds a smaller quantity of shares in ABC that they plan to sell.

The fund manager's expressions of interest in buying ABC shares might mislead participants in the market to pay more money for the shares in ABC that the fund manager anonymously sells. The fund manager is guilty of misleading the market under Section 89–92.

The purpose of Section 89–92 is to prevent the actions of investors being driven by reckless, misleading, deceptive or false actions of others; the overall aim is, therefore, to protect the integrity of the market.

273

### 1.9.2 Defences

There are three potential defences to a charge under Sections 89–95:

- The first is that the person reasonably believed that his act or conduct would not create an impression that was false or misleading.
- The second relates to actions, statements or forecasts that might be made in conformity with the price stabilisation rules of the FCA. These allow market participants, such as investment banks, to support the price of a new issue of securities for their clients, with the aim of preventing the market from being excessively volatile. The rules themselves require certain disclosures to investors considering investing in the stabilised securities, and restrict the support operation to a particular period.
- The third defence is that the actions, statements or forecasts were made in conformity with the **control of information** rules of the FCA. These rules relate to statements, actions or forecasts being made on the basis of limited information. The remainder of the information may be known to the firm, but it rests behind so-called Chinese walls, and is not known to the relevant individual.

## 1.10 Regulatory Developments

**The EC seeks criminal sanctions for insider dealing and market manipulation to improve deterrence and market integrity.**

In October 2011 the EC published a proposed regulation on insider dealing and market manipulation (ie, market abuse). The proposal aims to update and strengthen the existing framework to ensure market integrity and investor protection provided by the MAD. The objective of the proposed framework will ensure regulation keeps pace with market developments, will strengthen the fight against market abuse across commodity and related derivative markets, reinforce the investigative and sanctioning powers of regulators and reduce administrative burdens on small and medium-sized issuers.

When enacted, the regulation will have **direct effect** in member states without the need for national implementing legislation. The directive on criminal sanctions will require national implementation, which seems to be intended to coincide with the coming into application of the regulation.

The directive aims to set minimum rules on the definition of the most serious market abuse offences, and to impose minimum levels of criminal sanctions to be attached to them. Member states will notably be required to ensure that firms are liable for offences committed for their benefit by persons with leading positions in the firm, and to ensure that firms can be held liable if the lack of supervision or control by such a person enables the commission of a serious market abuse offence.

### Scope of the Commission's Proposals

- The market abuse regime will be extended to cover:
  - financial instruments traded on **MTFs** and **OTFs**, and any **related financial instruments traded OTC** which could impact the covered underlying market;
  - abusive behaviour on **spot commodity markets** impacting on financial instruments, and behaviour in relation to financial instruments impacting the related spot markets;
  - **emission allowances** and other related auctioned products based thereon, for which there will be a modified definition of inside information;

The Regulatory Framework Relating to Financial Crime

- ○ **monitoring** obligations for **MTFs and OTFs**;
- ○ exclusions for **buy-back, stabilisation, monetary and public debt management**, and **climate policy** activities.

## Insider Dealing and Market Manipulation

- Distinct definitions of **inside information** for financial instruments, commodities derivatives, **emission allowances** and information affecting the price of **related spot commodity contracts**.
- A **reasonable investor catch-all** will be added to the definition of inside information, for information that a reasonable investor would regard as relevant in deciding on terms of transactions (such information is not subject to the public disclosure requirements).
- Use of inside information to **cancel or amend pre-existing orders** will be caught.
- **Attempts** to manipulate the market, and attempted insider dealing, will be covered.
- Certain **algorithmic and high frequency trading strategies** including layering, spoofing and quote stuffing will be expressly prohibited as forms of market manipulation.
- Non-exhaustive **lists of indicators of manipulative behaviour**.
- Requirement for **controls** for the prevention and detection of market abuse.

## Disclosure of Inside Information

- Only **price-sensitive inside information** will be required to be publicly disclosed.
- **Non-price-sensitive inside information** may not be used/improperly disclosed (and will therefore need to be controlled).
- **Issuers** will be required to **inform the competent authority of a decision to delay public disclosure** of (price-sensitive) inside information immediately after the information is disclosed.
- Competent authorities will be permitted to allow **delayed disclosure in the interests of financial stability**.
- Modified disclosure requirements for issuers in the small- and medium-sized enterprises (**SME**) **growth markets**.
- **Disclosure** obligations for **emission allowance market participants for inside information regarding emission allowances held for its business**, including installations and aviation activities, owned, controlled or operated by the participant, its parent or affiliate (minimum threshold for emissions/rated thermal input to be set).
- A requirement for managers (persons discharging managerial responsibilities (PDMRs)) within issuers or emission allowance market participants to report transactions in shares, related financial instruments or in emission allowances above a **threshold of €20,000 per annum**; auction platforms, auctioneers and auction monitors in relation to emission allowances or related auctioned products are subject to the same reporting requirement.
- PDMR transactions to be reported expressly include **loans, pledges**, and transactions by **portfolio managers** (discretionary managers included).
- The Commission will be able to prescribe information for **insider lists**.

## European Securities and Markets Authority (ESMA) and Competent Authorities

- ESMA to draft a large number of technical standards, including in respect of appropriate controls to prevent and detect market abuse.
- Requirements for competent authorities to **co-operate** with each other, ESMA and national regulatory authorities for emissions.
- Requirement to **co-ordinate enforcement action** to avoid possible **duplication and overlap** in cross-border cases: ESMA may assume co-ordination role if requested by a competent authority.

- Enhanced **investigation powers** for competent authorities, including to:
  - require access to **spot commodity market traders' systems**;
  - conduct **searches at private premises** and seize documents;
  - obtain **telephone and data traffic records** from telecoms operators.

## Administrative Measures and Sanctions

- Sanctions for market abuse, but also (inter alia) for failure to:
  - have in place **effective controls** to prevent/detect market abuse;
  - **co-operate** in an investigation;
  - **provide documents/information** requested by a competent authority;
  - take reasonable care to ensure objective presentation or disclose conflicts when **producing/disseminating information recommending/suggesting an investment strategy** intended for distribution channels/the public;
  - **maintain insider lists**;
  - **comply with any request(s) to cease** an abusive practice, suspend trading, or publish a corrective statement.
- Minimum rules for administrative **sanctions** for competent authorities, including to:
  - impose **temporary bans**;
  - impose fines of up to **twice profits gained/loss suffered**;
  - impose **fines of up 10% of annual turnover for firms** (relevant annual turnover of ultimate parent);
  - **impose fines of up to €5 million** on individuals.
- **Accepted market practices** to be phased out.
- **Whistleblower protections** to be introduced; national discretion to offer financial incentives for those not already under obligation to report.

## Criminal Sanctions

- **Criminal sanctions** for **intentional** insider dealing and market manipulation, and attempts.
- Criminal sanctions to be **effective, proportionate and dissuasive**.
- **Liability for firms** if offences are committed by **individuals with a leading position** within the firm.
- **Liability for firms** if a **failure of supervision/control** by such individuals made the commission of the offence possible.

Once the regulation comes into application, MAD will be repealed. The intention appears to be that national implementation of the directive should coincide with the coming into application of the regulation, although this obviously cannot be guaranteed. This means that the new regime could (potentially) apply from around mid-2014.

Transitional provisions will allow accepted market practices, existing before the regulation comes into force and notified to ESMA by the relevant competent authorities before the regulation comes into application, to remain in place for a further 12 months thereafter.

# 2. Insider Dealing

## 2.1 Inside Information and the Insider

**Learning Objective**

8.2 Apply the main concepts, legal requirements and regulations relating to the prevention of insider dealing:

8.2.1 Definitions of insider, insider dealing and inside information

To be found guilty of insider dealing, a person must commit one of three specific offences; to do this, he must be an **insider** in possession of **inside information**. The CJA (1993) defines both of these terms, as well as the offences that may be carried out. **Inside information** is information which:

- relates to particular securities or to one or more particular issuers (ie, it is not so wide as to apply to securities or issuers of securities generally). It could, however, include information about the particular market or sector the issuer is active in;
- is specific or precise;
- has not been made public; and
- is price-sensitive (ie, if it were made public, it would be likely to have a significant effect on the price of any securities).

Some of these criteria may seem quite subjective – for example, what is **specific** or **precise**. In practice, the meaning will be determined by the courts when cases come before them. The CJA does give some assistance in interpretation, however: it includes a non-exhaustive list of what **made public** means, from which we can work out when it has not been made public. For example, information becomes **public** when it is:

- published in accordance with the rules of a regulated market to inform investors (for example, a UK-listed company publishing price-sensitive news through the LSE's regulatory news service (RNS)); or
- contained within records open to the public (for example, a new shareholding that is reflected in the company's register of shareholders).

This tells us that it need not be actually published – it just needs to be available to someone who **exercises diligence or expertise** in finding it (ie, you might have to look quite hard for it). It may also be regarded as made public even if it has to be paid for.

Inside information is often referred to as **unpublished price-sensitive information**, and the securities which may be affected by it are referred to as **price-affected securities**.

A person in possession of price-sensitive information is an insider if they know that it is inside information and that it has been knowingly acquired from an **inside source**.

They have obtained it from an inside source if they have got it:

- **because they are an inside source themselves** by being a director, employee or shareholder of an issuer of securities; this need not necessarily be the company whose securities are the subject of the insider dealing; or
- **because they have access to the information by virtue of their employment, office or profession** and, again, this need not necessarily be in relation to the company to which the information relates; an example might be the auditor, legal adviser or corporate finance adviser to a company; or
- **directly or indirectly from a person who obtained it in one of these two ways** for example, a director's husband or wife will have information from an inside source if they see confidential information at home about a takeover bid and then buys shares in the listed company which is the takeover target.

### Example

When a director of, or someone otherwise linked to, a listed company buys or sells shares in that company, there is a possibility that they are committing a criminal act – insider dealing.

This would be the case, for example, if that director or other linked person bought in the knowledge that the company's last six months of trade were better than the market expected (and that information is price-sensitive and had not yet been made public).

The person buying the shares has the benefit of this information because he is an insider to the company. Under the CJA this is a criminal act, punishable by a fine and/or a jail term of seven years.

## 2.2 The Offences

### Learning Objective

8.2 Apply the main concepts, legal requirements and regulations relating to the prevention of insider dealing:

8.2.2 Offences described in the legislation and the instruments covered by the Criminal Justice Act 1993 (CJA s.52 + Schedule 2)

Someone commits the offence of insider dealing if they:

- deal in price-affected securities when in possession of inside information;
- encourage someone else to deal in price-affected securities when in possession of inside information; or
- disclose inside information, other than in the proper performance of their employment, office or profession.

For a deal (ie, an acquisition or a disposal of price-affected securities) to be caught under the insider dealing legislation, it must take place on a regulated market, or through a professional intermediary – otherwise, the legislation does not apply to it.

The Regulatory Framework Relating to Financial Crime

These offences can only be committed by an individual (and, of course, only then by someone holding inside information as an insider); a company cannot commit the offence. However, by arranging for a company to deal, an individual could commit the offence of **encouraging** it to do so.

The offence of encouraging someone to deal need not result in an actual deal for the offence to have been committed (though it may be unlikely that the offence will come to light, if no deal results).

It is unethical to use price-sensitive proprietary information, however it comes into your possession.

### Example – Using Price-Sensitive Information

Your new finance director seems to provide the firm with a vital commercial edge. The firm wins a greater proportion of competitive bids than before he joined.

During the finance director's absence from the office it is revealed that he has possession of valuable proprietary information of a competitor. You also discover that he has shorted the competitor's shares, using CFDs. The finance director admits that he was given the information by his brother, who has since died.

Because this situation will not recur, your first reaction may be that no external action is necessary.

Advising the competitor that you have used their information may result in serious financial and reputational damage.

Saying nothing may seem an attractive option, but will leave you with a possible regulatory investigation plus it should leave you wrestling with your conscience.

## 2.3    The Instruments

Only certain investment instruments are caught under the insider dealing legislation; they are, for the purposes of the CJA, those described as **securities**. (Note, you may find the term **securities** defined differently in different legislation.)

For the purpose of the CJA and insider dealing, securities are:

- shares;
- debt securities (issued by a company or a public sector body);
- warrants;
- depositary receipts;
- options (to acquire or dispose of securities);
- futures (to acquire or dispose of securities); and
- CFDs (based on securities, interest rates or share indices).

This definition of securities does not embrace:

- commodities, and derivatives on commodities such as options and futures on agricultural products, metals or energy products;
- FX, and derivatives on FX, such as forward FX contracts. These are not price-sensitive or affected in the same way as individual securities, because the price of the fund is determined by the prices of the underlying investments held;
- units or shares in open-ended CISs.

## 2.4 The Defences

### Learning Objective

8.2 Apply the main concepts, legal requirements and regulations relating to the prevention of insider dealing:

8.2.3 General defences relating to insider dealing (CJA s.53)

8.2.4 Special defences: market makers acting in good faith, market information and price stabilisation (CJA s.53 and Schedule 1 paras 1–5)

### 2.4.1 General Defences

Broadly, there are four general defences available to the defendant in an insider dealing case:

- **No advantage was expected** – ie, the defendant did not expect the dealing to result in a profit (or the avoidance of a loss) due to information he possessed.
- **The defendant believed the information had been widely disclosed** – and they must have believed this on reasonable grounds.
- **He would have dealt anyway** – regardless of the information (for example, because they were in financial difficulties and would have had to sell their shares to meet their obligations).
- (For the offence of disclosing only): **they did not expect any person to deal because of the disclosure**.

### 2.4.2 Special Defences

There are further defences available to defendants in particular circumstances (**special** defences). These are for market makers, in relation to market information and in relation to price stabilisation activities.

**Market Makers**

As long as a market maker can show that they acted in good faith in the course of their business as a market maker, they will not be deemed guilty of insider dealing. So, a market maker (or their employee) could have unpublished price-sensitive information as an insider and continue to make a market in that security.

## Market Information

An insider is not guilty of **dealing** or **encouraging others to deal** if they can prove that the information they held was **market information**, and it was reasonable for them to act as they did, despite having the information at the time. Market information includes information such as the fact that the sale of a block of securities is under consideration, or the price at which such a transaction is likely to be done.

### Example

A client had been discussing the possibility of purchasing a block of 10,000 shares in XYZ plc with his broker. The client instructs the broker to buy. Clearly, the broker has the unpublished price-sensitive information that the buy order exists before he deals. However, this is market information and is a specific defence against a charge of insider dealing.

The defence would apply equally if it was market information relating to a client's planned disposal of securities.

## Price Stabilisation

The FCA has a set of rules that allow the stabilisation of a security's price after a new issue in order to prevent too much volatility. These are known as the **price stabilisation rules** and as long as these rules are being followed, the participants are not deemed to have undertaken insider dealing. The rules can be found in Chapter 2 of the FCA's Sourcebook **Market Conduct (MAR)**.

# 2.5    The FCA's Prosecution Powers

### Learning Objective

8.2    Apply the main concepts, legal requirements and regulations relating to the prevention of insider dealing:

8.2.5    The FCA's powers to prosecute insider dealing (FSMA s.402 EG 12.7–10)

The FCA has powers under Sections 401 and 402 of the FSMA to prosecute a range of criminal offences in England, Wales and Northern Ireland. The FCA may also prosecute criminal offences for which it is not the statutory prosecutor, but where the offences form part of the same criminality as the offences it is prosecuting under the act.

The FCA's general policy is to pursue through the criminal justice system all those cases where criminal prosecution is appropriate.

In particular, it is able to institute proceedings for an offence, under the CJA, for insider dealing. In addition to the FCA's powers to prosecute, the Secretary of State for Business, Enterprise and Regulatory Reform and the Crown Prosecution Service (CPS) also have the powers to prosecute insider dealing offences in England and Wales.

In addition to the criminal offences discussed above, since July 2005 there have also been civil offences for insider dealing and market manipulation under the market abuse regime.

# 3. Money Laundering (ML) and Terrorist Financing (TF)

### Learning Objective

8.3 Apply the main concepts, legal requirements and regulations to the prevention of money laundering:

8.3.1 The terms money laundering, criminal conduct and criminal property, the application of money laundering to all crimes (Proceeds of Crime Act 2002 s.340) and the power of the Secretary of State to determine what is relevant criminal conduct

## 3.1 Introduction to Money Laundering (ML)

Money laundering (ML) is the process of turning **dirty** money (money derived from criminal activities) into money which appears to be from legitimate origins. Dirty money is difficult to invest or spend, and carries the risk of being used as evidence of the initial crime. Laundered money can more easily be invested and spent without risk of incrimination.

Increasingly, AML provisions are being seen as the front line against drug-dealing, organised crime and the financing of terrorism. Much police activity is directed towards making the disposal of criminal assets more difficult and monitoring the movement of money.

The current rules and regulations in relation to money laundering come from a variety of sources:

- the Proceeds of Crime Act (POCA) 2002;
- the Serious Organised Crime and Police Act (SOCPA) 2005;
- the Money Laundering (ML) Regulations 2007;
- the FCA's Senior Management Arrangements, Systems and Controls (SYSC) Sourcebook; and
- industry guidance in the form of the Joint Money Laundering Steering Group (JMLSG) Guidance.

**The Proceeds of Crime Act (POCA) 2002** is widely drafted. It specifies that ML relates to criminal property – that is, any benefit (money or otherwise) that has arisen from criminal conduct. Property is only criminal property if the alleged offender knows or suspects it is criminal property. The broad requirement is for firms to report suspicions of ML to the authorities. See Section 3.3.1.

## The Regulatory Framework Relating to Financial Crime

**The Serious Organised Crime and Police Act (SOCPA) 2005** amended certain sections of POCA. In particular, one feature of POCA was that **criminal conduct** was deemed to include anything which would have been an offence had it been done in the UK, regardless of where it actually happened. This resulted in the often-cited **Spanish bullfighter** problem – bullfighting is illegal in the UK, but not in Spain, meaning that, arguably, a financial institution should have regarded deposits made by a Spanish bullfighter as the proceeds of crime, even if they represented his legitimate earnings in Spain.

SOCPA addresses this difficulty – in part at least – in that there is a defence for alleged offenders if they can show that they know, or believe on reasonable grounds, that the conduct was not criminal in the country where it happened. However, the Secretary of State has reserved the right to prescribe certain offences as **relevant criminal conduct** that are legal where they occurred, but are illegal in the UK and still need to be reported. For example, the government may specify serious tax evasion or drug cultivation as types of criminal conduct which do need to be reported, despite occurring overseas.

**The Money Laundering (ML) Regulations** are relatively detailed regulations, implemented as the result of EU directives, which deal predominantly with the administrative provisions that firms need to have to combat ML. For example, they deal with firms' requirements for systems and training to prevent ML and their obligations to check the identity of new customers. The most recent version was issued in 2007. See Section 3.3.2.

**The FCA Senior Management Arrangements, Systems and Controls (SYSC) Sourcebook** – this provides rules and guidance on the way AML provisions are implemented in the UK.

**The Joint Money Laundering Steering Group (JMLSG) Guidance** is provided by a combination of UK trade associations including the British Bankers' Association (BBA), the Council of Mortgage Lenders (CML) and the Association of British Insurers (ABI). Guidance is provided to firms on how they should interpret and implement the AML provisions. They are not mandatory but do highlight industry best practice. They are also approved by the Treasury, which means that if a firm can show that it adhered to them, the courts will take this into account as evidence of compliance with the legislation. The preface of the JMLSG Guidance states that *'The FCA Handbook confirms that the FCA will have regard to whether a firm has followed relevant provisions of this guidance when considering whether to take action against a regulated firm (SYSC 3.2, SYSC 5.3, and DEPP 6.2.3); and when considering whether to prosecute a breach of the Money Laundering Regulations (see EG 12.1–2). The guidance therefore provides a sound basis for firms to meet their legislative and regulatory obligations when tailored by firms to their particular business risk profile. Departures from this guidance, and the rationale for so doing, should be documented, and firms will have to stand prepared to justify departures, for example to the FCA.'* See Section 3.4.

## 3.2 The Three Stages of Money Laundering (ML)

### Learning Objective

8.3 Apply the main concepts, legal requirements and regulations to the prevention of money laundering:

8.3.2 The three stages of money laundering

There are three stages to a successful ML operation:

1. **Placement** – introduction of the money into the financial system; typically, this involves placing the criminally derived cash into a bank or building society account, a **bureau de change** or any other type of enterprise which can accept cash, such as, for example, a casino.
2. **Layering** – this involves moving the money around in order to make it difficult for the authorities to link the placed funds with the ultimate beneficiary of the money. This might involve buying and selling foreign currencies, shares or bonds in rapid succession, investing in CISs, insurance-based investment products or moving the money from one country to another.
3. **Integration** – at this final stage, the layering has been successful and the ultimate beneficiary appears to be holding legitimate funds (clean money rather than dirty money). The money is regarded as **integrated** into the legitimate financial system.

Broadly, the AML provisions are aimed at identifying customers and reporting suspicions at the placement and layering stages, and keeping adequate records which should prevent the integration stage being reached.

## 3.3 Proceeds of Crime Act 2002 (POCA) and Money Laundering (ML) Regulations 2007

### Learning Objective

8.3 Apply the main concepts, legal requirements and regulations to the prevention of money laundering:

8.3.3 The key provisions, objectives and interaction between the following legislation and guidance relating to money laundering: Proceeds of Crime Act (POCA) 2002, as amended by the Serious Organised Crime and Police Act (SOCPA) 2005: main offences, tipping off, reporting suspicious transactions, and defences; Money Laundering Regulations 2007 (internal controls), which includes obligations on firms for adequate training of individuals on money laundering

### 3.3.1 The Proceeds of Crime Act 2002 (POCA)

The POCA establishes five **offences**:

1. **Concealing** – it is an offence for a person to conceal or disguise criminal property.

The Regulatory Framework Relating to Financial Crime

2. **Arrangements** – that is, being **concerned in** an arrangement which the person knows, or suspects, facilitates the acquisition, retention, use or control of criminal property for another person. **Being concerned in an arrangement** may be widely interpreted – it could include advising on a transaction, for example.
3. **Acquisition, use and possession** – acquiring, using or having possession of criminal property.

These offences are punishable by a fine and a jail term of up to 14 years.

4. **Failure to disclose** – three conditions need to be satisfied for this offence:
   - The person knows or suspects (or has reasonable grounds to know or suspect) that another person is laundering money.
   - The information giving rise to the knowledge or suspicion came to him during the course of business in a regulated sector (such as the financial services sector).
   - The person does not make the required disclosure as soon as is practicable.

This offence is punishable by a fine and a jail term of up to five years.

5. **Tipping off** – giving another person information, knowing or suspecting that a ML report has been made to the authorities, when that information is likely to prejudice the investigation.

This offence is punishable by a fine and a jail term of up to five years, or two years in relation to the regulated sector. This offence also includes prejudicing an investigation. This applies differently within and outside the regulated sector.

As further detailed in Section 3.5, a person has a **defence** against the first three offences (concealing, arrangements, and acquisition, use and possession) if he makes the required disclosure to the MLRO or, if the person is the MLRO, to the National Crime Agency (NCA).

The offence of failure to disclose suspicions of ML may be committed not only when the person knows or suspects ML but also when there are reasonable grounds to know or suspect ML (even if the person did not know or suspect it). The test as to whether there are reasonable grounds is called the **objective test**: whether a **reasonable person** would have known or been suspicious, even though the offender protests their innocence.

## 3.3.2   The Money Laundering (ML) Regulations 2007

The ML Regulations 2007 place three main requirements on firms:

1. **Administrative** – carry out certain identification procedures, implement certain internal reporting procedures for suspicions and keep records in relation to AML activities.
2. **Training** – adequately train staff in the regulations and how to recognise and deal with suspicious transactions.
3. **Preventative** – ensure the establishment of internal controls appropriate to identify and prevent ML. This is a catch-all requirement.

It is an offence, liable to a jail term and fine, for firms to fail to comply with the ML Regulations, although in deciding if an offence has been committed the court must consider whether the firm followed the relevant guidance at the time.

## 3.3.3 Regulatory Developments – European Commission (EC) Proposals for a 4th Money Laundering (ML) Directive

*(The following will not be tested in the exam, but candidates should be aware of future proposals.)*

The Commission has published its proposals to update the AML and counter-terrorist financing (CTF) framework. In addition to a fourth ML Directive, it published a separate draft regulation for requirements in relation to funds transfers.

The two proposals provide a more targeted and focused risk-based approach.

In summary, the proposals:

- Extend the definition of politically exposed persons (PEPs).
- Lower the exemptions for one-off transactions and expand the perimeter.
- Include new requirements on beneficial ownership information.
- Include tax crimes as predicate offences.
- Reinforce sanctioning powers and requirements to co-ordinate cross-border action.
- Include national and EU wide risk assessments.
- Include new information requirements for fund transfers.

## 3.4 The Joint Money Laundering Steering Group (JMLSG)

### Learning Objective

8.3 Apply the main concepts, legal requirements and regulations to the prevention of money laundering:

8.3.4 The standards expected by the Joint Money Laundering Steering Group guidance notes particularly in relation to: risk-based approach; requirements for directors and senior managers to be responsible for money laundering precautions; need for risk assessment; need for enhanced due diligence in relation to politically exposed persons [JMLSG 5.5.1–5.5.29]; need for high-level policy statement; detailed procedures implementing the firm's risk-based approach [JMLSG 1.20, 1.27, 1.40–1.43, 4.17–4.18]

8.3.5 The money laundering aspects of know your customer (Joint Money Laundering Steering Group's guidance for the financial sector [para 5.1.1–5.1.4]

In 2007, the JMLSG issued revised guidance notes setting out how authorised firms should manage their risk in terms of ML and terrorist financing. This affected how almost every authorised firm deals with its customers. The most recent guidance notes reflected the changes introduced under the ML Regulations 2007.

The guidance notes:

- require that firms take a risk-based and proportionate approach to ML prevention;
- simplify the identity verification requirements for many customer types;
- allow for greater reliance on identification verification carried out by other firms.

The JMLSG's 2007 guidance sets out advice on the identification requirement for all types of customers (Part I). It also gives sector-specific guidance for various types of firm (Part II).

In addition, the latest version of the guidance notes:

- introduced some new or revised definitions, including beneficial owners and PEPs;
- set out the customer due diligence (CDD)measures to be applied in various circumstances and stated that CDD should be applied on a risk-based approach;
- set out the extent to which reliance may be placed on the CDD work of other regulated firms;
- set out situations when **simplified CDD** measures may be applied;
- stated that **enhanced due diligence** must be applied in higher-risk situations – for example, on individuals who are PEPs, on the basis that these people may be more vulnerable or susceptible to corruption; in non-face-to-face situations; and in connection with correspondent banking.

Senior management of FCA-regulated firms must appoint an appropriately qualified senior member of staff who will have overall responsibility for the maintenance of the firm's AML systems and controls.

Firms must also have an AML policy statement in place; this provides a framework to the firm and its staff, and must identify named individuals and functions responsible for implementing particular aspects of the policy. The policy must also set out how senior management undertakes its assessment of the ML and TF risks the firm faces, and how these risks are to be managed.

The policy statement should include such matters as the following:

**Guiding principles:**

1. Customers' identities need to be satisfactorily verified before the firm accepts them.
2. A commitment to the firm **knowing its customers** appropriately – both at acceptance and throughout the business relationship by taking appropriate steps to verify a customer's identity and business.
3. Staff need adequate training and need to be made aware of the law and their obligations.
4. Recognition of the importance of staff promptly reporting their suspicions internally.

**Risk mitigation approach:**

1. A summary of the firm's approach to assessing and managing its ML and TF risk.
2. Allocation of responsibilities to specific persons and functions.
3. A summary of the firm's procedures for carrying out appropriate identification and monitoring checks on the basis of their risk-based approach.
4. A summary of the appropriate monitoring arrangements in place to ensure that the firm's policies and procedures are being carried out.

## 3.4.1 The Joint Money Laundering Steering Group's (JMLSG) Guidance on Know Your Customer (KYC)

Chapter 5 of the JMLSG Guidance explains that the requirement to conduct customer due diligence (CDD) derives from the ML Regulations 2007. The requirements are there for two broad reasons:

- to help the firm be satisfied that the customers know who they say they are and that there are no legal reasons preventing the relationship;
- to assist law enforcement.

The CDD requirements should be applied by firms having regard to the risks associated with different types of business relationship. There are three aspects to CDD at the outset of a new business relationship:

- identify the customer – obtain the customer's name, address and date of birth; for non-personal customers the beneficial owners must be identified;
- obtain verification of the customer's identity – conduct additional checks to verify the information;
- obtain information about the intended nature of the business relationship.

This is **standard due diligence**, and Chapter 5 of the JMLSG notes gives practical guidance to the due diligence required for different types of customer. For personal customers, standard verification requirements may be satisfied by the production of a valid passport or photocard driving licence. For non-personal customers, such as companies, partnerships and clubs, it will be necessary to conduct checks on public registers such as Companies House.

**Enhanced due diligence** is where the firm conducts more checks than for standard cases. This is obligatory in three circumstances:

- if the client is a **PEP**;
- if the client is not physically present (non-face-to-face cases); and
- in respect of a correspondent banking relationship.

But the firm may choose to conduct enhanced due diligence for any case where this is deemed necessary.

**Simplified due diligence** means not having to conduct due diligence at all, if the customer falls into one of the following types:

- certain other regulated financial services firms;
- listed companies;
- beneficial owners of pooled accounts held by notaries or legal professionals;
- UK public authorities;
- community institutions;
- certain products/arrangements where the risk of them being used for ML is inherently low: life assurance, e-money products, pension funds and child trust funds (CTFs).

The Regulatory Framework Relating to Financial Crime

If simplified due diligence does not apply, then **satisfactory identification evidence** for the customer should be obtained, and verified, as soon as is reasonably practicable after first contact between the firm and the customer. If there is a delay between the forming of the business relationship and the verification of the customer's identity (eg, in the case of non-face-to-face business) firms' risk management procedures should limit the extent of the relationship. They could do this, for example, by placing restrictions on the transactions the customer can enter into, or on the transfer of funds, until verification is complete.

If a firm cannot satisfactorily verify a customer's identity, it should not proceed with the business relationship, and should consider whether this should cause it to make a report to NCA. If it is simply the case that the customer cannot produce the correct documents or information, the firm may consider whether there is any other way it can satisfy itself as to their identity.

The chapter also deals with KYC requirements in the context of multipartite relationships, eg, where one firm introduces a customer to another, or where more than one firm is involved in providing the service to the customer. In such cases, a firm may rely on the due diligence conducted by another regulated firm.

Regardless of the type of due diligence conducted at outset, in all cases the firm must conduct ongoing monitoring of the business relationship, and this is considered next.

## 3.5 The Money Laundering Reporting Officer (MLRO) and the Nominated Officer

### Learning Objective

8.3 Apply the main concepts, legal requirements and regulations to the prevention of money laundering:

8.3.6 Senior Management Arrangements, Systems and Controls Sourcebook [SYSC] role of the money laundering reporting officer, nominated officer and the compliance function (SYSC 3.2.6, 3.2.6 (A)–(J), 3.2.7 (FCA/PRA), 3.2.8 and 6.3 and the systems and controls that firms are expected to implement)

8.3.7 The importance of ongoing monitoring of business relationships and being able to recognise a suspicious transaction, and the requirement for staff to report to the MLRO and for the firm to report to the National Crime Agency

8.3.8 Understand the duty of firms to report suspicious transactions [SUP 15.10.2]

Under POCA 2002, it is an offence to fail to disclose a suspicion of ML. Obviously, this requires the staff at financial services firms to be aware of what constitutes a suspicion, and there is a requirement that staff must be trained to recognise and deal with what may be a ML transaction. Firms are also required to ensure that business relationships are understood and monitored sufficiently well that their staff will recognise patterns of activity which are not in keeping with the customer's anticipated profile.

The disclosure of suspicions is made, ultimately, to the legal authorities, namely NCA; however, disclosure goes through two stages. First, the employee with a suspicion should disclose that suspicion within the firm to the MLRO – a required controlled function. It is the MLRO who reviews matters, and decides whether the suspicion should be passed on to NCA.

It is important to appreciate that, by reporting to the MLRO, the employee with the suspicion has fulfilled their responsibilities under the law – they have disclosed their suspicions. Similarly, by reporting to NCA, the MLRO has fulfilled their responsibilities under the law.

The main part of the FCA's Handbook which relates to the MLRO is the SYSC Sourcebook. As an approved person, the MLRO is subject to the approved persons' regime. The MLRO is primarily responsible for ensuring a firm adequately trains staff in knowing and understanding the regulatory requirements and how to recognise and deal with suspicious transactions.

### 3.5.1 MLRO or Nominated Officer?

Under the FCA rules, all firms (except for sole traders, general insurance firms and mortgage intermediaries) must appoint an MLRO with responsibility for oversight of its compliance with the FCA's rules on systems and controls against ML.

The ML Regulations require all affected firms to appoint a **nominated officer** to be responsible for receiving internal ML disclosures from staff members, and to make external reports to NCA when necessary. The nominated officer is also responsible for receiving internal disclosures under POCA and the Terrorism Act 2000.

Although the obligations of the MLRO under the FCA requirements are different from those of the nominated officer under POCA, the Terrorism Act and the ML Regulations 2007, in practice, the same person tends to carry on both roles – and is usually known as the MLRO.

### 3.5.2 The FCA's Principles-Based Approach to Money Laundering Prevention

The SYSC requirements place obligations on firms' senior management to ensure that they have systems and controls in place which are appropriate to the business for the prevention of ML and TF. The JMLSG guidance notes aid firms in interpreting and dealing with these obligations in the context of their specific types of business.

In order to determine the arrangements and controls needed by a firm for these purposes, its senior management needs to have carried out a risk assessment. This should consider such factors as:

- the nature of the firm's products and services;
- the nature of its client base and geographical location; and
- the ways in which these may leave the firm open to abuse by criminals.

# The Regulatory Framework Relating to Financial Crime

Previous changes made to the controls environment requirements relating to ML require firms to establish and maintain effective systems and controls for compliance with the various requirements and standards under the regulatory system and for countering the risk that the firm might be used to further financial crime. Firms are required to ensure that their systems and controls enable them to identify, assess, monitor and manage ML risk. They must carry out regular assessments of the adequacy of these systems and controls.

**ML risk is the risk that a firm may be used to launder dirty money.**

Failure by a firm to manage this risk effectively will increase the risk to society of crime and terrorism. When considering whether a breach of its rules on systems and controls against ML has occurred, the FCA will look to see if the firm has followed relevant provisions in the guidance for the UK financial sector provided by the JMLSG.

In identifying its ML risk, and in establishing its systems and controls, a firm should consider a range of factors, including:

- its customer, product and activity profiles;
- its distribution channels;
- the complexity and volume of its transactions;
- its processes and systems; and
- its operating environment.

A firm should ensure that the systems and controls include appropriate:

- training for its employees in relation to ML prevention;
- provision of information to its governing body and senior management, including a report at least annually by the firm's MLRO on the operation and effectiveness of those systems and controls;
- documentation of its risk management policies and risk profile in relation to ML;
- measures to ensure that ML risk is taken into account in its day-to-day operation and also with the development of new products, the taking on of new customers, and changes in its business profile.

A firm must also appoint an MLRO, who is responsible for receiving and assessing internal suspicion reports, and determining – after a proper investigation – whether to report them on to NCA.

The firm must ensure that its MLRO has an appropriate level of authority and independence within the firm and access to resources and information sufficient to enable them to carry out their responsibilities. The MLRO acts as a central point for all activity within the firm relating to AML and should be based in the UK.

Each authorised firm must give a director or senior manager (who may also be the MLRO) overall responsibility for the establishment and maintenance of effective AML systems and controls. Depending on the nature, scale and complexity of its business, it may be appropriate for a firm to have a separate compliance function. This function may be heavily involved in monitoring the firm's compliance with its AML procedures. The organisation and responsibilities of a compliance function should be documented. A compliance function should be staffed by an appropriate number of competent staff who are sufficiently independent to perform their duties. It should be adequately resourced and should have unrestricted access to the firm's relevant records.

### 3.5.3 Reporting of Suspicions

The SUP Manual states that FCA-authorised investment firms and credit institutions which arrange or execute a transaction with or for a client in a qualifying investment, and which have **reasonable grounds** to suspect that the transaction might constitute market abuse, must promptly notify the FCA. Qualifying investments are those admitted to trading on a prescribed market (SUP 15.10.2).

Strictly, this obligation extends only to executed transactions and not to unexecuted orders – but a firm may bring a suspicious order to trade to the FCA's attention voluntarily. The provisions require that firms decide on a case-by-case basis whether there are reasonable grounds for suspecting that a transaction involves market abuse, taking into account the circumstances. Further, Principle 11 of the Principles for Businesses requires that a firm disclose to the FCA everything of which the FCA would reasonably expect notice; and many firms (or rather, their employees) interpret this as giving them grounds to report unexecuted transactions as well.

## 3.6 The National Crime Agency (NCA)

The NCA will tackle organised crime, defend the UK's borders, fight fraud and cybercrime, and protect children and young people. The first details of plans to create this NCA appeared in the *'Policing in the 21st Century'* consultation, which was held in 2010. That consultation set out the need to create a powerful new body of operational crime fighters, including a border police command, which would be led by a senior chief constable and would harness and build on the intelligence, analytical and enforcement capabilities of the SOCA and the Child Exploitation and Online Protection Centre (CEOP).

The NCA will be a powerful body of operational crime fighters, led by a senior chief constable and accountable to the Home Secretary. The NCA will produce and maintain the national threat picture for serious, organised and complex crime, which all other agencies will work to. Using this agreed intelligence picture, the NCA will task and co-ordinate the police and other law enforcement agencies, underpinned by the new strategic policing requirement.

Organised crime is increasingly globalised and IT-enabled, a trend inevitably accelerating with society's dependence on the internet. Organised criminals operate their own self-regulated market for cybercrime goods and services, including stolen data, malicious software, technical infrastructure and money laundering; and they operate on an industrial scale. As more data is acquired, stored and shared, technologies advance and more of our government services and commerce are provided online so the risk increases.

Although there are a number of definitions of cybercrime, the one utilised by SOCA and its partners is as follows:

Cybercrimes are those crimes committed, in full or in part, through the use of information communication technology (ICT) devices, such as computers or other computer-enabled tools, including mobile or 'smart' phones. Cybercrimes can be defined in two ways:

The Regulatory Framework Relating to Financial Crime

- **Pure cybercrimes** (or computer-dependent crimes) – where a criminal act can only be committed through the use of computers or other ICT devices. In these cases the devices are both the tool for committing the crime and target of the crime. For instance, the harvesting of online bank account details using malware, the hacking of a website through Structured Query Language (SQL) injection, hacking of networks to steal sensitive data or distributed denial of service attacks on websites or infrastructure.
- **Cyber-enabled crimes** are those that may be committed without ICT devices, but are changed by use of ICT in terms of scale and reach. This can comprise a wide range of criminal activities, including, but not limited to, online fraud; theft or sexual offending and where the devices are used to organise or arrange crimes.

The multi-agency response to cybercrime, involving SOCA, the police and national and international partners, continues to target the perpetrators of cybercrime and helps to protect the UK against the threat and education of users to operate online more safely.

Nonetheless all users need to be vigilant against the cybercrime threat, and should take sensible and practical precautions such as maintaining up-to-date internet security software (including anti-virus software) and other protections.

The seventh, and final, annual report from SOCA, ahead of the organisation being subsumed into the NCA, outlined several areas in which the organisation helped tackle cyber threats. This included the deployment of cyber liaison officers in key locations overseas, which has led to new and improved partnerships, better leverage, increased intelligence-sharing and more effective operational responses. The success of these partnerships was evident in several takedowns, including a joint investigation into an individual believed to be laundering up to £1 million online led to two arrests for money laundering and cyber-related fraud offences. In addition, as part of a global 'day of action' 36 website domains used to sell compromised credit card data and data from 26 e-commerce type platforms known as automated vending carts (AVCs) were seized by the US Department of Justice working with SOCA. The AVCs allowed criminals to sell large quantities of stolen data quickly and easily. Visitors trying to access these sites were directed to a page indicating that the web domain was under the control of law enforcement.

The NCA will also have its own specialist capabilities, including for surveillance, fraud and threat-to-life situations. These will be used by the NCA itself and will be available to the police and other agencies.

The NCA will become fully functional by December 2013, with some key elements becoming operational sooner.

# 3.7 Terrorist Financing (TF)

### Learning Objective

8.4 Apply the main concepts, legal requirements and regulations relating to the prevention of terrorism financing:

8.4.1 Activities regarded as terrorism in the UK (Terrorism Act 2000 Part 1), the obligations on regulated firms under the Counter-Terrorism Act 2008 (money laundering of terrorist funds) (Part 5 Section 62 and s.7 part 1–7), the Anti-Terrorism Crime & Security Act 2001 Schedule 2 Part 3 (Disclosure of Information) and sanction list for terrorist activities

8.4.2 Preventative measures in respect of terrorist financing, the essential differences between laundering the proceeds of crime and the financing of terrorist acts (JMLSG Guidance 2007 paras 1.38–1.39, Preface 9), and the interaction between the rules of FCA, PRA and the Terrorism Act 2000 and the JMLSG Guidance regarding terrorism
[JMLSG Guidance 2011]

## 3.7.1 The Definition of Terrorism

In light of the **war against terrorism**, legislation in the form of the Terrorism Act 2000 has defined what amounts to terrorism.

Terrorism is the use or threat of action when it:

- involves serious violence against a person or serious damage to property;
- endangers a person's life, other than the person committing the action;
- creates serious risk to the health or safety of the public (or a section of the public);
- is designed seriously to interfere or disrupt an electronic system;
- is designed to influence the government or intimidate the public (or a section of the public);
- is made for the purpose of advancing a political, religious or ideological cause.

## 3.7.2 Anti-Terrorism Legislation and Guidance

Many of the requirements of anti-terrorism legislation are similar to the AML provisions encountered in Section 3.3 of this chapter. A person commits an offence if he enters into, or becomes concerned with, an arrangement that facilitates the retention or control of terrorist property by concealment, removal from the jurisdiction, transfer to nominees or in any other way. The person may have a defence if he can prove that he did not know, and had no reasonable cause to suspect, that the arrangement related to terrorist property.

There is a duty to report suspicions and it is an offence to fail to report when there are reasonable grounds to have a suspicion. The Terrorism Act 2000 and Anti-Terrorism Crime Security Act 2001 specify that a failure to report is liable to a term of up to five years in jail, plus a fine.

The Counter-Terrorism Act (CTA) became law on 26 November 2008, adding further to the government's armoury of legislation to tackle terrorism. Of particular interest is Schedule 7, which gives new powers to the Treasury to issue **directions** to firms in the financial sector.

In summary, directions can be given to individual firms; to firms that fit a particular description; or to the sector as a whole, concerning individuals or institutions who are doing business or are resident in a particular non-EEA country; or regarding the government in that country. Directions can relate to CDD and ongoing monitoring, systematic reporting on transactions and business relationships and limiting or ceasing business.

- **CDD and monitoring** – the provisions are broadly similar to the requirements already imposed under the ML Regulations. However, the Treasury is now able, for example, to direct that CDD be undertaken again or completed before entering into a business relationship (where it might otherwise be conducted in parallel), or that enhanced measures be carried out. It may also direct that specific activity monitoring be carried out.
- **Systematic reporting** – until now, reporting orders have only been available to law enforcement and must be obtained through the courts. Under the CTA, the Treasury itself can now require information to be provided concerning business relationships and transactions involving the specified person(s), on a one-off or periodic basis.
- **Limiting or ceasing business** – the Treasury's powers under the present ML Regulations (Regulation 18) are limited to where the Financial Action Task Force (FATF) has applied counter measures. The CTA powers are more flexible and allow directions to be imposed in a wider range of situations (see below).

Under CTA, the Treasury may issue directions when one or more of the following are met:

- The FATF has advised that countermeasures should be applied to a country (as per the ML Regulations).
- The Treasury reasonably believes that ML/TF activities are being carried on in the country, by its government or by persons resident/incorporated there, which pose a significant threat to the UK's national interests.
- The Treasury reasonably believes that the country is developing or producing nuclear weapons, including chemical ones, or doing anything to facilitate that, and poses a significant threat to the UK's national interests.

While directions to individual firms will be served upon them, it is not yet clear how orders that apply to specified types of firm or the whole sector (which will require secondary legislation each time) will be publicised. It may or may not be via the sanctions mechanism or something similar – this issue is still being clarified with the Treasury.

## 3.7.3 The Relationship between Money Laundering (ML), Terrorist Financing (TF) and other Financial Crime

Although the ML regulations focus on firms' obligations in relation to ML prevention, POCA updated and reformed the **obligation to report** to cover involvement with any criminal property, and the Terrorism Act extended this to cover terrorist property.

From a practical perspective, therefore, firms should consider how best they should assess and manage their overall exposure to financial crime. This does not mean that the prevention of fraud, market abuse, ML and TF must be addressed by a single function within a firm; there will, however, need to be close liaison between those responsible for each activity.

Because terrorist groups can have links with other criminal activities, there is inevitably some overlap between AML provisions and TF acts. However, there are two major difficulties when TF compared with other ML activities:

- Often, only quite small sums of money are required to commit terrorist acts.
- If legitimate funds are used to fund terrorist activities, it is difficult to identify when the funds become **terrorist funds**.

Financial services firms need to be as careful in ensuring compliance with the anti-terrorist and TF legislation (including the Terrorism Act 2000), as they are with the FCA rules on ML issues and the JMLSG guidance notes.

The Terrorism Act requires a court to take account of such approved industry guidance when considering whether a person within the financial sector has failed to report under that Act. The ML regulations also provide that a court must take account of similar industry guidance in determining whether a person or institution within the regulated sector has complied with any of the requirements of the ML regulations.

# 4. The Model Code for Directors

### Learning Objective

8.6.1 Understand the main purpose and provisions of the FCA's Model Code in relation to share dealing by directors and other persons discharging managerial responsibilities, including: closed periods; chairman's approval; no short-term dealing

The FCA fulfils the role of the UKLA. This means that it is the competent authority to set the requirements for shares or other instruments to be **listed**. Listing allows, for example, a company to have its shares traded on an RIE, such as the LSE.

As part of its listing rules, the UKLA has produced the **Model Code** (LR9 Annex 1). Listed companies must comply with the Model Code (or stricter requirements, if they wish), restricting the ability of their senior managers and officers to deal in the company's securities.

The Model Code thus guides directors and senior employees of listed companies on how to deal in the shares of the company they work for, without falling foul of the insider dealing or market abuse regimes.

The Regulatory Framework Relating to Financial Crime

Broadly, the Model Code requires directors of a listed company (and certain other people with access to inside information) to seek clearance before buying or selling shares. Normally, it is the chairman of the company who gives this clearance. If the chairman is seeking permission, the decision will be made by the chief executive officer (CEO); if chairman and CEO are the same, then the decision will be made by the board.

The Model Code also specifies that directors should not deal during the **closed period** – the 60 days leading up to the publication of the company's full-year or half-year accounts, and 30 days leading up to the publication of any quarterly accounts – and they should not deal in the company's shares on **short-term considerations**.

The following dealings are not subject to the provisions of this code:

* undertakings or elections to take up entitlements under a rights issue or other offer (including an offer of securities of the company in lieu of a cash dividend);
* allowing entitlements to lapse under a rights issue or other offer (including an offer of securities of the company in lieu of a cash dividend);
* the sale of sufficient entitlements nil-paid to take up the balance of the entitlements under a rights issue;
* undertakings to accept, or the acceptance of, a takeover offer;
* dealing where the beneficial interest in the relevant security of the company does not change;
* transactions conducted between a person discharging managerial responsibilities and their spouse, civil partner, child or step-child (within the meaning of Section 96B(2) of the Act);
* transfers of shares arising out of the operation of an employees' share scheme into a savings scheme investing in securities of the company;
* with the exception of a disposal of securities of the company received by a restricted person as a participant, dealings in connection with employees' share schemes;
* the cancellation or surrender of an option under an employees' share scheme;
* transfers of the securities of the company by an independent trustee of an employees' share scheme to a beneficiary who is not a restricted person;
* transfers of securities of the company already held by means of a matched sale and purchase into a saving scheme or into a pension scheme in which the restricted person is a participant or beneficiary;
* an investment by a restricted person in a scheme or arrangement where the assets of the scheme (other than a scheme investing only in the securities of the company) or arrangement are invested at the discretion of a third party;
* a dealing by a restricted person in the units of an AUT or in shares in an OEIC;
* *bona fide* gifts to a restricted person by a third party.

# 5. The Disclosure and Transparency Rules

### Learning Objective

8.7.1 Apply the disclosure and transparency rules [DTR 2.1.3, 2.6.1] as they relate to: disclosure and control of inside information by issuers; transactions by persons discharging managerial responsibilities and their connected persons

The disclosure and transparency rules are contained in the FCA's Disclosure and Transparency Rules (DTR) Sourcebook. The rules apply to issuers of securities on certain markets.

The aim of the disclosure rules is, in part, to implement the requirements of the MAD, and to make provisions to ensure that information relating to publicly listed securities is properly handled and disseminated. In particular, it aims to:

- promote prompt and fair disclosure of relevant information to the market;
- set out some specific sets of circumstances in which an issuer can delay the public disclosure of inside information; and
- set out requirements to ensure that such information is kept confidential in order to protect investors and prevent insider dealing.

Among other things, the rules require that an issuer establishes effective arrangements to deny access to inside information to anyone other than those who require it for the exercise of their functions within the issuer.

The aim of the transparency rules, in part, is to implement the requirements of the Transparency Directive (TD) and to ensure there is adequate transparency of and access to information in the UK financial markets.

## 5.1 Continuing Obligations

The continuing obligations are contained in the FCA's Listing Rules and the DTR Sourcebook. They govern the conduct of directors of listed companies and the disclosure of information necessary to protect investors, maintain an orderly market and ensure that investors are treated fairly. In addition, the DTRs contain overarching requirements which relate to the timely and accurate dissemination of inside information.

## 5.2 The Requirement to Disclose Inside Information

The first main requirement of the continuing obligations is the timely disclosure of all relevant information. A listed company has a general duty to disclose all information necessary to apprise investors of the company's position and to avoid a false market in its shares. This reinforces Section 89–92 of the FSMA, which makes it a criminal offence to conceal information dishonestly in order to create a false market in the company's shares.

The Regulatory Framework Relating to Financial Crime

In addition, a company should announce details of any new major or significant developments in its activities which are not known to the public but which may, when known, significantly affect its share price and affect a reasonable investor's decision. This is referred to as **inside information**.

An additional requirement is the equal treatment of all shareholders. This ensures that shareholders receive relevant inside information in the same way at the same time. All regulatory disclosures required must therefore be disclosed to a regulatory information service (RIS) as soon as possible, prior to being disclosed to third parties. An RIS is a firm that has been approved by the FCA to disseminate regulatory announcements to the market on behalf of listed companies. Once an announcement is sent to the RIS, the company's obligation is met. The RIS is then required to release the announcement to the markets through its links with secondary information providers such as data providers, newswires and the news media.

A company that provides inside information via an RIS must also make the information available on its own website by the close of the business day following the day of the RIS announcement. A company must ensure that such inside information is notified to an RIS before or simultaneously with, publication of such information on its own website.

In addition, the company must take reasonable care, without prejudice to its obligations in the UK under the FCA's Listing Rules, to ensure that the disclosure of inside information to the public is synchronised as closely as possible in all jurisdictions in which it has:

- financial instruments admitted to trading on a regulated market;
- requested admission to trading of its financial instruments on a regulated market;
- financial instruments listed on any other overseas stock exchange.

## 5.3    Secrecy and Confidentiality

The general principle of equal treatment of all shareholders is the requirement to prevent leaks of price-sensitive information. This particularly relates to developments or matters in the course of negotiation, when (apart from advisers) there must be no selective dissemination of information, and matters in the course of negotiation must be kept confidential.

## 5.4    Delaying Disclosure of Inside Information

An issuer may, under its own responsibility, delay the public disclosure of inside information, so as not to prejudice its legitimate interests providing that:

- such omission is not likely to mislead the public;
- any person receiving the information owes the issuer a duty of confidentiality, regardless of whether such duty is based on law, regulations, articles of association or contract; and
- the company is able to ensure the confidentiality of that information.

Delaying disclosure of inside information will not always mislead the public, although a developing situation should be monitored so that if circumstances change an immediate disclosure can be made.

Investors understand that some information must be kept confidential until developments are at a stage when an announcement can be made without prejudicing the legitimate interests of the company.

## 5.5 The Control of Inside Information

Companies must establish effective arrangements to deny access to inside information to persons other than those who require it for the exercise of their functions within the company. A company must have measures in place that enable public disclosure to be made via an RIS as soon as possible, in case it is unable to ensure the confidentiality of the relevant inside information.

If an issuer is relying on the rules on delaying disclosure of inside information, as noted in Section 5.4, it should prepare a holding announcement to be disclosed in the event of an actual or likely breach of confidence.

## 5.6 Insider Lists

A company must ensure that it, and persons acting on its behalf or on its account, draw up a list of those persons working for them, under a contract of employment or otherwise, who have access to inside information relating directly or indirectly to the issuer, whether on a regular or occasional basis.

If so requested, an issuer must provide to the FCA as soon as possible an insider list that has been drawn up in accordance with DTR 2.8.1 R.

Every insider list must contain the following information:

- the identity of each person having access to inside information;
- the reason why such person is on the insider list;
- the date on which the insider list was created and updated.

An insider list must be promptly updated:

- when there is a change in the reason why a person is already on the list;
- when any person who is not already on the list is provided with access to inside information;
- to indicate the date on which a person already on the list no longer has access to inside information.

Companies must also ensure that every insider list prepared by it, or by persons acting on its account or on its behalf, is kept for at least five years from the date on which it is drawn up or updated, whichever is the latest. The company, and not its advisers or agents, is ultimately responsible for the maintenance of insider lists.

Further, the company must, so as to ensure compliance with its requirements to draw up an insider list (DTR 2.8.1), maintain a list of its own employees that have access to inside information and its principal contacts at any other firm or company acting on its behalf or on its account with whom it has had direct contact and who also have access to inside information about it.

The Regulatory Framework Relating to Financial Crime

Companies must take the necessary measures to ensure that their employees with access to inside information acknowledge the legal and regulatory duties entailed (including dealing restrictions in relation to the issuer's financial instruments) and are aware of the sanctions attaching to the misuse or improper circulation of such information.

# 6. The Data Protection Act (DPA)

## Learning Objective

8.8 Apply the main concepts, legal requirements and regulations relating to data protection:

8.8.1 The eight principles of the Data Protection Act 1998

8.8.2 Notification of data controllers with the Information Commissioner

8.8.3 Record-keeping requirements of FCA-regulated firms [DPA Schedule 1, Part 1 & COBS]

8.8.4 Data security implications for firms and individuals

The Data Protection Act (DPA) 1998 provides for the way in which personal data must be dealt with in order to protect the rights of the persons concerned. Personal data relates to living individuals who can be identified by that data.

Any firm determining the way personal data is held and processed is a data controller and is, therefore, responsible for compliance with the DPA; all data controllers must be registered with the ICO. A data processor is any person processing data on behalf of the data controller.

The DPA lays down eight **principles**, which must be complied with. These are that:

1. personal data shall be processed fairly and lawfully;
2. personal data shall be obtained for one or more specified and lawful purposes, and shall not be further processed in any manner that is incompatible with those purposes;
3. personal data shall be adequate, relevant and not excessive in relation to the purpose or purposes for which it is processed;
4. personal data shall be accurate and, where necessary, kept up-to-date;
5. personal data shall not be kept for longer than is necessary for its purpose or purposes;
6. personal data shall be processed in accordance with the rights of the subject under the Act;
7. appropriate technical and organisational measures shall be taken against unauthorised or unlawful processing of personal data, and against accidental loss or destruction of, or damage to the personal data;
8. personal data shall not be transferred to a country or territory outside the EEA, unless that country or territory ensures an adequate level of protection in relation to the processing of personal data.

Clearly, these principles of data protection apply to personal data maintained by financial services firms (who often have a duty to **know their customers**) and to the personal data maintained by the FCA itself (in relation to its approved persons regime).

In addition, firms should have regard for the provisions of this Act when considering their record-retention policies. The FCA imposes a number of record-keeping requirements, including, for example, in connection with T&C records for employees. See Section 6.2.

The ICO now has the authority and power to fine investment firms that do not comply with its requirements in respect of data security.

## 6.1 The Information Commissioner office (ICO)

The ICO's mission is *'to uphold information rights in the public interest, promoting openness by public bodies and data privacy for individuals'*.

New legislation available to the ICO has changed the approach to and understanding of data protection by firms. Tougher enforcement penalties for breaches (civil penalty of up to £500,000), can lead to:

- reputation damage;
- a blow to consumer loyalty;
- customer disengagement.

In addition, breaches of data protection can now also lead to criminal prosecution, potentially resulting in unlimited fines.

The ICO has stated that it will only use its new powers in specific circumstances. These are serious contraventions of data protection principles by a data controller, and when the contravention was of a kind likely to cause substantial damage or substantial distress and was either deliberate, or the data controller knew or ought to have known that there was a risk that the contravention would occur but failed to take reasonable steps to prevent the contravention.

Factors impacting the ICO decision to impose a financial penalty include:

- the nature of the personal data involved;
- the duration and extent of the contravention;
- the number of individuals actually or potentially affected;
- the importance, value, degree, amount or extent of the breach;
- the public importance (ie, in the case of a security breach);
- whether the contravention was deliberate and or premeditated;
- whether the data controller was aware of and did not follow relevant advice;
- whether there were inadequate procedures, policies, processes and practices in place.

Factors impacting the ICO decision **not** to impose a financial penalty include whether the:

- data controller has already complied with requirements of another regulatory body;
- contravention was caused by circumstances outside the direct control of the data controller.

The ability for the ICO to impose financial penalties is new territory. Therefore it will provide further guidance based on actual precedents. But it has indicated that it is not looking to impose many financial penalties. The ICO may still serve an enforcement notice if it is satisfied that a data controller has contravened or is contravening any of the data protection principles.

## 6.2 Record-Keeping Requirements

A firm must arrange for orderly records to be kept of its business and internal organisation, including all services and transactions undertaken by it. A firm must retain all records in relation to MiFID business for a period of at least five years. In relation to non-MiFID business, the record-keeping requirement is three years.

The FCA's Conduct of Business Sourcebook has detailed record-keeping requirements relating to specific activities undertaken by firms, such as:

- **COBS 2.3 (Inducements)** – fee, commission or non-monetary benefit [COBS 2.3.1(2)(b)].
- **COBS 3.8 (Client categorisation)** – standard form notice to client and agreements and client categorisation [COBS 3.8.2(i)].
- **COBS 4.11 (Communicating with clients, including financial promotions)** – financial promotion, telemarketing scripts and compliance of financial promotions [COBS 4.11.1 and 4.11.2].
- **COBS 8.1 (Client agreements)** – client agreements [COBS 8.1.4].
- **COBS 9.5 (Suitability including basic advice)** – suitability [COBS 9.5.1].
- **COBS 10.7 (Appropriateness for non-advised services)** – appropriateness [COBS 10.7.1].
- **COBS 11.5 (Dealing and managing)** – client orders, client orders and decisions to deal in portfolio management, client orders [COBS 11.5.1–11.5.3].
- **COBS 11.6 (Dealing and managing)** – prior and periodic disclosure – use of dealing commission [COBS 11.6.19].
- **COBS 11.7 (Dealing and managing)** – personal account dealing [COBS 11.7.4].
- **COBS 16.2 (Reporting information to clients)** – confirmation to clients and periodic statements [COBS 16.2.7 and 16.3.11].

## 6.3 Regulatory Developments – European Commission (EC) proposals for a new Data Protection Regulation

*(The following will not be tested in the exam, but candidates should be aware of the future developments.)*

In 2012 the EC published proposals for a comprehensive and significant reform of the existing EU data protection framework. There were two proposals:

1. a regulation that sets forth the general data protection framework and is intended to replace the current Data Protection Directive; and
2. a directive that applies to the processing of personal data by police and judicial authorities in criminal matters.

The EU Commissioner for Justice, Fundamental Rights and Citizenship and Vice-President of the Commission, identified the following key goals of the proposed reform in a press release to:

- update and modernise the existing EU data protection rules in light of technological developments to address, among other things, online privacy, in order to improve the protection of personal data processed both inside and outside the EU;
- address the protection of personal data processed by law enforcement and judicial authorities;
- give individuals more control over their personal data and facilitate access to and transfer of such data;

- harmonize data protection rules across the EU by establishing a *'strong, clear, and uniform data protection framework'* with a single set of data protection rules and a single national data protection authority (ie, the national data protection authority of the EU member state where the company has its **main establishment** as defined in the General Data Protection Regulation);
- boost the EU digital economy and foster economic growth, innovation and job creation in the EU.

# 7. Whistleblowing

## Learning Objective

8.9.1 Understand the legal and regulatory basis for whistleblowing [SYSC 18.1.2, 18.2.3]

The Public Interest Disclosure Act 1998 (PIDA), which came into force on 2 July 1999, introduced legislation to protect persons from retaliation if they inform regulatory authorities of concerns that might come to their attention at their place of work; this is generally referred to as **whistleblowing**.

The FCA, SYSC 18, reminds firms of PIDA and provides guidance to authorised firms as to how they might want to adopt internal procedures to facilitate whistleblowing as part of an effective risk-management system.

The PIDA makes any clause or term in an agreement between a worker and his employer void if it precludes the worker from making a **protected disclosure** (sometimes known as **blowing the whistle**). A protected disclosure is one, made in good faith, where information is revealed by a worker that shows that one of the following has been, is being, or is likely to be committed:

- a criminal offence;
- a failure to comply with any legal obligation;
- a miscarriage of justice;
- the putting of the health and safety of an individual in danger;
- damage to the environment;
- deliberate concealment of any of the above.

It is irrelevant whether any of the above occurred in the UK or elsewhere, or whether the law is the law of the UK or any other country.

Firms are encouraged to consider adopting (and encouraged to invite their appointed representatives or, where applicable, their tied agents to consider adopting) appropriate internal procedures which will encourage workers with concerns to blow the whistle internally about matters which are relevant to the functions of the FCA.

Smaller firms may choose not to have as extensive procedures in place as larger firms. For example, smaller firms may not need written procedures. The following is a list of things that larger and smaller firms may want to do.

The Regulatory Framework Relating to Financial Crime

For **larger firms**, appropriate internal procedures include:

- a clear statement that the firm takes failures seriously;
- an indication of what is regarded as a failure;
- respect for the confidentiality of workers who raise concerns, if they wish this;
- an assurance that, if a protected disclosure has been made, the firm will take all reasonable steps to ensure that no person under its control engages in victimisation;
- the opportunity to raise concerns outside the line management structure, such as with the compliance director, internal auditor or company secretary;
- penalties for making false and malicious allegations;
- an indication of the proper way in which concerns may be raised outside the firm, if necessary;
- providing access to an external body such as an independent charity for advice;
- making whistleblowing procedures accessible to the staff of key contractors.

For **smaller firms**, appropriate internal procedures include:

- telling workers that the firm takes failures seriously and explaining how wrongdoing affects the organisation;
- telling workers what conduct is regarded as failure;
- telling workers who raise concerns that their confidentiality will be respected, if they wish this;
- making it clear that concerned workers will be supported and protected from reprisals;
- nominating a senior officer as an alternative route to line management and telling workers how they can contact that individual in confidence;
- making it clear that false and malicious allegations will be penalised by the firm;
- telling workers how they can properly blow the whistle outside the firm if necessary;
- providing access to an external body such as an independent charity for advice; and
- encouraging managers to be open to concerns.

Firms should also consider telling workers (through the firm's internal procedures, or by means of an information sheet available from the FCA's website, or by some other means) that they can blow the whistle to the FCA, as the regulator prescribed in respect of financial services and markets matters under PIDA.

# 8. Financial Crime Prevention

### Learning Objective

8.10 The FCA's approach to financial crime prevention:

8.10.1 Understand how the FCA's approach to financial crime prevention upholds ethical principles and high standards of professional practice as reflected in the Financial Crime Guide

8.10.2 Understand how the FCA's approach to financial crime prevention supports good corporate governance and business risk management

The financial crisis exposed significant shortcomings in the governance and risk management across numerous firms. Although poor governance was only one of many factors that contributed to the financial crisis, it was an important one.

It is now incumbent on the FCA to take action on these issues. So, just as it is taking action on a range of fronts in its response to the crisis – from capital and liquidity, right through to asking questions about the very nature of the financial system – it is also going to have to address issues around governance and the culture within firms.

In doing this, it recognises that its regulatory approach before the crisis underestimated the importance of governance, but it is committed to putting that right.

This work is within its overall programme to improve regulation, and is part of the **more intensive supervisory** approach.

The FCA now has a much greater focus on making judgements, for example, about individuals performing key roles and the sustainability of business models of firms. The FCA has stated that it cannot simply rely on monitoring systems and controls or assuming that firms' senior management are necessarily always best placed to make these judgements alone. But improving regulation and the outcomes for firms and consumers is not just about moving the regulatory telescope. The FCA also needs to change the focus and look more closely at behaviour and culture in firms, particularly ensuring that good culture and behaviour in firms are being:

- driven by senior management; and
- reinforced by effective corporate governance and the role of the boards.

Of course, part of changing behaviour and culture is about looking at the incentives on offer.

Why is effective governance important? In broad terms, it enables a firm's board and executive to work together to deliver a firm's agreed strategy. In particular, it is about managing the risks the firm faces.

Good governance enables the board to share a clear understanding of the firm's risk appetite and to establish a robust control framework to manage that risk effectively across the business, with effective oversight and challenge along the way. This is what the FCA is keen to find happening within firms.

## 8.1 The Integrity aspects behind the Laws on Combating Financial Crime

The various laws and FCA regulations in the area of financial crime are there to support efforts to combat ML, TF, fraud and other financial crime.

An example follows of the dilemmas which can arise.

### Case Study: Creative Accounting

***Servicing the requirements of a valuable client requires creative accounting to recover your firm's costs fully.***

You are the chief executive of a small regional finance company which has a good track record of providing financial support to facilitate local infrastructure developments aimed at helping the local community. Before committing financial assistance, your company always researches such developments very thoroughly in order to minimise the risk of default and has developed a good reputation as a responsible lender, and strong supporter of the region in which it operates.

Because of the nature of the project, which also involves significant public funding, you have been advised that reimbursement of your research costs may be available from Ruination, a public body which exists to encourage financial investment and support in the region. On enquiring further into the nature of this reimbursement, you learn that the daily rate payable is substantially below the economic cost of having members of your team research the viability of the development project. Ruination will pay a centrally imposed standard rate of £1,000 per day, plus reasonable expenses, whereas your firm's internal cost of assigning an appropriate team to this exercise is £2,000 per day.

On discussing this matter with your relationship manager he tells you that he has been speaking with a contact at Ruination who has indicated, informally, that it would be quite relaxed if your firm simply charged for a sufficient number of days to cover your costs, effectively inflating the size of the claim. Additionally, this contact has indicated that Ruination's daily reimbursement rate is based upon a five-hour working day, compared with your firm's normal requirement for its employees to work a seven-hour day.

Your firm enjoys a good reputation, which you wish to retain. You wish to assist with the financing, subject to the viability study. In contemplating making claims for reimbursement based on an inflated number of days, you are concerned that you may risk future reputational damage or accusations of fraud if it becomes public knowledge.

## 8.2 FCA Financial Crime Guide: A Guide for Firms

In April 2013 the FCA published two documents on *Financial Crime as A Guide for Firms* – Part 1 is titled *A Firms Guide to Preventing Financial Crime* and Part 2 is called *Financial Crime Thematic Reviews*.

This Guide consolidates FCA guidance on financial crime. It does not contain rules and its contents are not binding. It provides guidance to firms on steps they can take to reduce their financial crime risk and aims to enhance understanding of FCA expectations and help firms to assess the adequacy of their financial crime systems and controls and remedy deficiencies.

An aim of the Guide is to help firms adopt a more effective, risk-based and outcomes-focused approach to mitigating financial crime risk.

The Guide provides practical examples, but not the only way, in which firms might comply with applicable rules and requirements.

Part 1 is divided into the following sections:

- financial crime systems and controls;
- money laundering and terrorist financing;
- fraud;
- data security;
- bribery and corruption;
- sanctions and asset freezes.

Part 2 is divided into 14 sections, listing all of the thematic work that the UK regulator (including the FSA and the FCA) have undertaken since 2006. In each section the FCA provides examples of good and poor practice – by way of guidance to firms.

# 9. The Bribery Act 2010

## Learning Objective

8.5 Apply the main concepts, legal requirements and guidance relating to the prevention of bribery and corruption

8.5.1 The offences of bribery contrary to sections 1–7 Bribery Act 2010

## 9.1 The Bribery Act 2010

The Bribery Act 2010 received Royal Assent on 8 April 2010. It creates a new offence which can be committed by commercial organisations, which fail to prevent persons associated with them from committing bribery on their behalf.

It is a full defence for an organisation to prove that, despite a particular case of bribery it nevertheless had adequate procedures in place to prevent persons associated with it from bribing. Section 9 of the Act requires the Secretary of State to publish guidance about procedures which commercial organisations can put in place to prevent persons associated with them from bribing.

Bribery undermines democracy and the rule of law and poses very serious threats to sustained economic progress in developing and emerging economies and to the proper operation of free markets more generally. The Bribery Act 2010 is intended to respond to these threats and to the extremely broad range of ways that bribery can be committed. It does this by providing robust offences, and enhanced sentencing powers for the courts, raising the maximum sentence for bribery committed by an individual from seven to ten years' imprisonment.

308

The Act contains two general offences covering the offering, promising or giving of a bribe (active bribery) and the requesting, agreeing to receive or accepting of a bribe (passive bribery) in Sections 1 and 2 respectively. It also sets out two further offences which specifically address commercial bribery. Section 6 of the Act creates an offence relating to bribery of a foreign public official in order to obtain or retain business or an advantage in the conduct of business, and Section 7 creates a new form of corporate liability for failing to prevent bribery on behalf of a commercial organisation.

Section 12 of the Act provides that the courts have jurisdiction over the Sections 1, 2 or 6 offences committed in the UK, but they also have jurisdiction over offences committed outside the UK if the person committing them has a close connection with the UK by virtue of being a British national or ordinarily resident in the UK, a body incorporated in the UK or a Scottish partnership.

However, as regards Section 7, the requirement of a close connection with the UK does not apply. Section 7(3) makes clear that a commercial organisation can be liable for conduct amounting to a Section 1 or 6 offence on the part of a person who is neither a UK national or resident in the UK, nor a body incorporated or formed in the UK. In addition, Section 12(5) provides that it does not matter whether the acts or omissions which form part of the Section 7 offence take part in the UK or elsewhere. So, providing that the organisation is incorporated or formed in the UK, or that the organisation carries on a business or part of a business in the UK (wherever in the world it may be incorporated or formed), then UK courts have jurisdiction.

## 9.2 General Bribery Offences (Sections 1–7)

### 9.2.1 Sections 1–5

**Section 1** of the Act (offences of bribing another person) makes it an offence for a person ('P') to offer, promise or give a financial or other advantage to another person in one of two cases:

- **Case 1** applies where P intends the advantage to bring about the improper performance by another person of a relevant function or activity or to reward such improper performance.
- **Case 2** applies where P knows or believes that the acceptance of the advantage offered, promised or given in itself constitutes the improper performance of a relevant function or activity.

**Section 2** of the Bribery Act relates to offences relating to being bribed. A person is guilty of an offence if they request, agree to receive or accept a financial or other advantage intending that, in consequence, a relevant function or activity should be performed improperly by that person (or another person).

**Improper performance** is defined at **Sections 3** (functions or activity to which bribe relates), **4** (improper performance to which bribe relates) and **5** (expectation test). In summary, this means performance which amounts to a breach of an expectation that a person will act in good faith, impartially, or in accordance with a position of trust. The offence applies to bribery relating to any function of a public nature, connected with a business, performed in the course of a person's employment or performed on behalf of a company or another body of persons. Therefore, bribery in both the public and private sectors is covered.

For the purposes of deciding whether a function or activity has been performed improperly the test of what is expected is a test of what a reasonable person in the UK would expect in relation to the performance of that function or activity. If the performance of the function or activity is not subject to UK law (for example, it takes place in a country outside UK jurisdiction) then any local custom or practice must be disregarded – unless permitted or required by the written law applicable to that particular country. **Written law** means any written constitution, provision made by or under legislation applicable to the country concerned or any judicial decision evidenced in published written sources.

By way of illustration, in order to proceed with a case under Section 1, based on an allegation that hospitality was intended as a bribe, the prosecution will need to show that the hospitality was intended to induce conduct that amounts to a breach of an expectation that a person will act in good faith, impartially, or in accordance with a position of trust. This is judged by what a reasonable person in the UK thought. So, for example, an invitation to foreign clients to attend a Six Nations rugby match at Twickenham, as part of a public relations exercise designed to cement good relations or enhance knowledge in the organisation's field, is extremely unlikely to engage Section 1, as there is unlikely to be evidence of an intention to induce improper performance of a relevant function.

## 9.2.2 Section 6 (Bribery of Foreign Public Officials)

Section 6 creates a stand-alone offence of bribery of a foreign public official. The offence is committed if a person offers, promises or gives a financial or other advantage to a foreign public official with the intention of influencing the official in the performance of their official functions. The person offering, promising or giving the advantage must also intend to obtain or retain business or an advantage in the conduct of business by doing so. However, the offence is not committed if the official is permitted or required by the applicable written law to be influenced by the advantage.

A **foreign public official** includes officials, whether elected or appointed, who hold a legislative, administrative or judicial position of any kind in a country or territory outside the UK. It also includes any person who performs public functions in any branch of the national, local or municipal government of such a country or territory or who exercises a public function for any public agency or public enterprise of such a country or territory, such as professionals working for public health agencies and officers exercising public functions in state-owned enterprises. Foreign public officials can also be an officials or agents of a public international organisation, such as the United Nations (UN) or the World Bank.

Sections 1 and 6 can capture the same conduct but do so in different ways. The policy that underpins the offence at Section 6 is the need to prohibit the influencing of decision-making in the context of publicly funded business opportunities by the inducement of personal enrichment of foreign public officials or others at the official's request, assent or acquiescence.

Such activity is very likely to involve conduct which amounts to **improper performance** of a relevant function or activity to which Section 1 applies, but, unlike Section 1, Section 6 does not require proof of it or an intention to induce it. This is because the exact nature of the functions of persons regarded as foreign public officials is often very difficult to ascertain with any accuracy, and the securing of evidence will often be reliant on the co-operation of the state any such officials serve. To require the prosecution to rely entirely on Section 1 would amount to a very significant deficiency in the ability of the legislation to address this particular mischief.

The Regulatory Framework Relating to Financial Crime

That said, it is not the government's intention to criminalise behaviour if no such mischief occurs, but merely to formulate the offence to take account of the evidential difficulties referred to above. In view of its wide scope, and its role in the new form of corporate liability in Section 7, the government offers the following further explanation of issues arising from the formulation of Section 6.

### 9.2.3 Hospitality, Promotional, and Other Business Expenditure

Bona fide hospitality and promotional, or other business expenditure which seeks to improve the image of a commercial organisation, better present products and services, or establish cordial relations, is recognised as an established and important part of doing business and it is not the intention of the Act to criminalise such behaviour. The government does not intend the Act to prohibit reasonable and proportionate hospitality and promotional or other similar business expenditure intended for these purposes. It is, however, clear that hospitality and promotional or other similar business expenditure can be employed as bribes.

In order to amount to a bribe under Section 6 there must be an intention for a financial or other advantage to influence the official in his official role and thereby secure business or a business advantage. In this regard, it may be in some circumstances that hospitality or promotional expenditure in the form of travel and accommodation costs does not even amount to a **financial or other advantage** to the relevant official, because it is a cost that would otherwise be borne by the relevant foreign government rather than the official himself.

### 9.2.4 Section 7 (Failure of Commercial Organisations to Prevent Bribery)

A commercial organisation is liable to prosecution if a person associated with it bribes another person, intending to obtain or retain business or an advantage in the conduct of business for that organisation. The commercial organisation will have a full defence if it can show that, despite a particular case of bribery, it nevertheless had adequate procedures in place to prevent persons associated with it from bribing. In accordance with established case law, the standard of proof which the commercial organisation will need to discharge in order to prove the defence, in the event it was prosecuted, is the balance of probabilities.

Only a **relevant commercial organisation** can commit an offence under Section 7 of the Bribery Act. A relevant commercial organisation is defined at Section 7(5) as a body or partnership incorporated or formed in the UK, irrespective of where it carries on a business, or an incorporated body or partnership which carries on a business or part of a business in the UK, irrespective of the place of incorporation or formation. The key concept here is that of an organisation which **carries on a business**. The courts will be the final arbiter as to whether an organisation carries on a business in the UK, taking into account the particular facts in individual cases.

A commercial organisation is liable under Section 7 if a person **associated** with it bribes another person intending to obtain or retain business or a business advantage for the organisation. A person associated with a commercial organisation is defined at Section 8 as a person who **performs services** for or on behalf of the organisation. This person can be an individual or an incorporated or unincorporated body. Section 8 provides that the capacity in which a person performs services for or on behalf of the organisation does not matter, so employees (who are presumed to be performing services for their employer), agents and subsidiaries are included. Section 8(4), however, makes it clear that the question as to whether a person is performing services for an organisation is to be determined by reference to all the relevant circumstances and not merely by reference to the nature of the relationship between that person and the organisation. The concept of a person who **performs services for or on behalf of the organisation** is intended to give Section 7 broad scope, so as to embrace the whole range of persons connected to an organisation who might be capable of committing bribery on the organisation's behalf.

This broad scope means that contractors could be **associated** persons to the extent that they are performing services for or on behalf of a commercial organisation. Also, if a supplier can properly be said to be performing services for a commercial organisation rather than simply acting as the seller of goods, it may also be an **associated** person.

## 9.3 Adequate Procedures as Defence against the Offence of Bribery – Ministry of Justice Guidance

### Learning Objective

8.5.2 The role of 'adequate procedures' in affording a defence to the offence of a commercial organisation failing to prevent bribery

8.5.3 Guidance on adequate procedures issued by the Ministry of Justice (Section 7 & 9 Bribery Act 2010)

Section 9 of the Act states that the Secretary of State must publish guidance about procedures that relevant organisations can put in place to prevent persons associated with them from bribing.

In 2011 the Ministry of Justice published guidance titled *Guidance about Procedures which Relevant Commercial Organisations can put into place to Prevent Persons Associated with them from Bribing (Section 9 of the Bribery Act 2010)*.

The government considers that procedures put in place by commercial organisations wishing to prevent bribery being committed on their behalf should be informed by six principles. These are set out below. Commentary and guidance on what procedures the application of the principles may produce accompanies each principle in the Ministry of Justice guidance.

These principles are not prescriptive. They are intended to be flexible and outcomes-focused, allowing for the huge variety of circumstances that commercial organisations find themselves in. Small organisations will, for example, face different challenges from those faced by large multinational enterprises. Accordingly, the detail of how organisations might apply these principles, taken as a whole, will vary, but the outcome should always be robust and effective anti-bribery procedures.

312

As set out in more detail below, bribery prevention procedures should be proportionate to risk. Although commercial organisations with entirely domestic operations may require bribery prevention procedures, as a general proposition they will face lower risks of bribery on their behalf by associated persons than the risks that operate in foreign markets. In any event, procedures put in place to mitigate domestic bribery risks are likely to be similar to, if not the same as, those designed to mitigate those associated with foreign markets.

## The Principles

- **Principle 1 – Proportionate procedures** – a commercial organisation's procedures to prevent bribery by persons associated with it are proportionate to the bribery risks it faces and to the nature, scale and complexity of the commercial organisation's activities. They are also clear, practical, accessible, effectively implemented and enforced.
- **Principle 2 – Top-level commitment** – the top-level management of a commercial organisation (be it a board of directors, the owners or any other equivalent body or person) is committed to preventing bribery by persons associated with it. It fosters a culture within the organisation in which bribery is never accepted.
- **Principle 3 – Risk assessment** – the commercial organisation assesses the nature and extent of its exposure to potential external and internal risks of bribery on its behalf by persons associated with it. The assessment is periodic, informed and documented.
- **Principle 4 – Due diligence** – the commercial organisation applies due diligence procedures, taking a proportionate and risk-based approach, in respect of persons who perform or will perform services for or on behalf of the organisation, in order to mitigate identified bribery risks.
- **Principle 5 – Communication (including training)** – the commercial organisation seeks to ensure that its bribery prevention policies and procedures are embedded and understood throughout the organisation through internal and external communication, including training, that is proportionate to the risks it faces.
- **Principle 6 – Monitoring and review** – the commercial organisation monitors and reviews procedures designed to prevent bribery by persons associated with it and makes improvements where necessary.

A commercial organisation's procedures to prevent bribery by associated persons should be proportionate to the bribery risks it faces and to the nature, scale and complexity of the commercial organisation's activities. They should also be clear, practical, accessible, effectively implemented and enforced.

The term **procedures** is used in the Ministry of Justice guidance to embrace both bribery prevention policies and the procedures which implement them. Policies articulate a commercial organisation's anti-bribery stance, show how it will be maintained and help to create an anti-bribery culture. They are therefore a necessary measure in the prevention of bribery, but they will not achieve that objective unless they are properly implemented.

Adequate bribery prevention procedures ought to be proportionate to the bribery risks that the organisation faces. An initial assessment of risk across the organisation is therefore a necessary first step. To a certain extent the level of risk will be linked to the size of the organisation and the nature and complexity of its business, but size will not be the only determining factor. Some small organisations can face quite significant risks, and will need more extensive procedures than their counterparts facing limited risks. However, small organisations are unlikely to need procedures that are as extensive as those of a large multinational organisation.

Bribery prevention procedures may be stand-alone or form part of wider guidance, for example on recruitment or on managing a tender process in public procurement. Whatever the chosen model, the procedures should seek to ensure there is a practical and realistic means of achieving the organisation's stated anti-bribery policy objectives across all of the organisation's functions.

Commercial organisations' bribery prevention policies are likely to include certain common elements, such as a:

- commitment to bribery prevention (principle 2);
- general approach to mitigation of specific bribery risks, such as those arising from the conduct of intermediaries and agents, or those associated with hospitality and promotional expenditure, facilitation payments or political and charitable donations or contributions (principle 3);
- overview of its strategy to implement its bribery prevention policies.

## Case Study

***The overseas operations centre of your bank makes a mistake to the detriment of your customer. The mistake can be speedily rectified by paying a third party, but your bank declines to do so. The mistake is rectified and you are concerned that the customer himself has made an illegal payment.***

Elephant Bank operates a global custodian business and its major operational centre is based in Asia. Manesh is one of Elephant's clients and is a successful businessman who has built up a substantial import-export business from his base in Asia, where he is domiciled. He is also a valued client of Elephant Private Bank's London office, where his relationship manager is Jonathan.

As part of its services to its clients, Elephant Bank files any necessary tax papers with the relevant authorities and it does so for Manesh, after having sent him the form which states his tax liability and requires his signature. Elephant files the return and makes a payment equivalent to nearly £1 million on behalf of Manesh, to cover his outstanding tax liability.

Two days after filing the return, a custody manager in Elephant's Asia office receives an angry phone call from Jonathan, saying that Manesh's current account has been overdrawn to the extent of £800,000 as a result of a £1 million payment made by the Asia office and charged to the London office. The Asia custody manager locates the paperwork and sees that there is an error in the figures, in which a tax liability of £93,000 has been typed as £930,000. However the customer (Manesh) has signed the form, on which he acknowledged the amount outstanding and authorised the bank to make the payment to the debit of his account.

The custody manager, in an effort to resolve the matter, contacts the tax office to try to obtain an immediate refund of the overpayment, but is told that there is an enormous backlog of work and that repayments are almost impossible to obtain in a hurry. The normal time for the process is between nine months and a year. However, the tax official says that there is a special expediting service, but it is expensive and is run through an external agency, and he provides a telephone number. The custody manager phones the number and is told that this will cost £20,000.

Jonathan, on being told this news, says that it looks as though this expediting fee is simply a series of bribes to people in the tax office, and payment would clearly be illegal. The custody manager remains silent at this point and Jonathan says that he will try to arrange an alternative method of providing redress to the customer, whom he points out was a contributor to the problem.

Jonathan's controller agrees that because of the shared blame for this problem, the bank will allow an overdraft for the customer at the bank's notional cost of funds which is determined to be 4%. When Jonathan tells him this, Manesh says that he sees no reason why he should pay and there must be some action that Elephant can take. He also says that he wonders whether Elephant really values him as a customer if they expect him to pay for their mistake. Jonathan then mentions to Manesh what he was told about the expediting service, but adds that this service appears to be based on bribing a number of people, which quite clearly would be illegal.

Manesh says that he would not be a party to any form of bribery, but what is bribery to Jonathan is simply an incentive payment in his country – 'Just like the City bonus payments!' he jokes. Although he is clearly not happy, Manesh concludes the conversation by saying that his cousin has a friend who works in the Department of Revenue and will see if he can help.

Jonathan is surprised when the next communication that he receives is not from Manesh but Elephant's Asia custody manager, advising that, presumably thanks to the efficiency of the expediting service, the Manesh overpayment will be repaid next week. However, before making payment to Manesh's account, because of the amount, it will have to be authorised by the compliance team, who will require an explanation.

Jonathan expresses surprise, saying that he understood that the expediting service was simply bribery and that he had agreed with the custody manager that there was no way that the bank would be involved in it. The manager agrees and says that he has not instructed the agent, but he assumes that someone must have.

Jonathan's main feeling is one of relief, as Manesh's liability will now be repaid, which will get his controller off his back. However, subsequently he wonders whether Manesh may have instigated the expediting payments/bribery, whether that could cause problems for the bank and what, if anything he should do about it. But then Jonathan thinks that maybe Manesh did in fact approach his cousin's friend who was able to arrange a repayment, and if the bank suggests to Manesh that he may have been involved in something illegal when he has not, that could be enormously damaging to both the bank as well as Jonathan's career prospects.

This is a situation which is fraught with possible legal pitfalls resulting from anti-corruption legislation and therefore one might ask why Jonathan should choose to keep quiet. He has not been involved in any of the discussions outside the bank, other than with his customer, and, if he has a suspicion that Manesh is the link in this particular chain, Jonathan might question whether he is someone whom Elephant actually wants as a customer. Manesh's home jurisdiction does not condone bribery or facilitation payments.

The fact that the possible activity took place overseas is not a reason for ignoring the incident because Elephant Bank is incorporated in the UK, which means that the Bribery Act will cover Elephant Bank's staff and agents worldwide.

The most appropriate response for Jonathan must be to consider the transaction against the tests of openness, honesty, transparency and fairness, where it is found wanting. This is a situation where discussion with a third party in the bank should be one's initial action, in order to help form a considered view of the matter, as a result of which the correct way forward is likely to be very much clearer. Therefore a report to his compliance department should be Jonathan's immediate response.

He should also discuss with the customer the implications of the UK Bribery Act and the difficulties that it may cause him if he makes any payments that may be classed as bribery and explain to him the implications for the bank and the potential impact that it could have on the banking relationship.

## Summary of this Chapter

You should have an understanding and knowledge of the following after reading this chapter:

- The market abuse regime:
    - the statutory offence
    - the purpose of the FCA's Code of Market Conduct;
    - Code of Market Conduct Offences;
    - the concept of the regular user and accepted market practices;
    - the enforcement regime, as provided by the FSMA;
    - statutory exceptions to market abuse – safe harbours;
    - relation with Section 89–92 and insider dealing legislation;
    - consequences to the market of market abuse.
- Misleading statement and practices:
    - offences and defences;
    - insider dealing;
    - what is inside information;
    - offences;
    - instruments;
    - defences – general and special;
    - prosecutions powers.
- ML and terrorist financing:
    - legislation – ML Regulations 2007/POCA 2002;
    - the three stages of ML;
    - five offences under POCA;
    - requirements placed on firms under the ML Regulations 2007;
    - the role, purpose and effects of the JMLSG;
    - the role and purpose of the MLRO;
    - the purpose and process for reporting of suspicious transactions;
    - the role of the NCA.
- The Model Code for Directors.
- Disclosure and transparency rules:

The Regulatory Framework Relating to Financial Crime

- ○ requirement to disclose inside information;
- ○ control of inside information/insider lists.
- The Data Protection Act:
  - ○ the role of the ICO.
- Record-keeping requirements.
- Whistleblowing:
  - ○ purpose.
- The Bribery Act 2010:
  - ○ general offences (Sections 1–7);
  - ○ adequate procedures as defence against the offence of bribery;
  - ○ six principles.
- FCAs approach to financial crime prevention, as contained in their financial crime guide.

# End of Chapter Questions

Think of an answer for each question and refer to the appropriate section for confirmation.

1. What is market abuse?
   *Answer reference: Section 1.1*

2. What is the purpose of the FCA's Code of Market Conduct?
   *Answer reference: Sections 1.2, 1.3*

3. What are accepted market practices?
   *Answer reference: Section 1.4.1*

4. What is a safe harbour and when may it be used?
   *Answer reference: Section 1.6*

5. What is the purpose and objective of Sections 89–95 of the Financial Services Act 2012?
   *Answer reference: Section 1.9*

6. What is defined as inside information?
   *Answer reference: Section 2.1*

7. What financial instruments are caught by the CJA?
   *Answer reference: Section 2.3*

8. What are the general and special defences against the allegation of insider dealing?
   *Answer reference: Section 2.4*

9. What is the layering stage of money laundering?
   *Answer reference: Section 3.2*

10. What are the offences established by POCA 2002?
    *Answer reference: Section 3.3*

11. What is the purpose and status of JMLSG guidance?
    *Answer reference: Section 3.4*

12. What duty do firms have to report suspicious client activity?
    *Answer reference: Section 3.5.3*

13. What is the purpose and aim of the model code?
    *Answer reference: Section 4*

14. What are the disclosure rules and to whom do they apply?
    *Answer reference: Section 5*

# The Regulatory Framework Relating to Financial Crime

15. What is the purpose and aim of the PIDA Act and why is it important to financial services firms?
   *Answer reference: Section 7*

16. Looking at the case study, what considerations or tools allow you to judge whether a course of action is ethical?
   *Answer reference: Section 8.1*

17. What is the main purpose of the Bribery Act 2010?
   *Answer reference: Section 9*

# Chapter Nine
# Complaints and Redress

1. **Eligible Complaints** — 323
2. **Complaints Procedures and Process** — 324
3. **Complaints and Dispute Resolution** — 328
4. **The Financial Services Compensation Scheme (FSCS)** — 330
5. **Professional Integrity when Handling Customer Complaints** — 331

**This syllabus area will provide approximately 3 of the 80 examination questions**

Complaints and Redress

In this chapter you will gain an understanding of:

- Who is eligible to make a complaint against a firm.
- Complaints procedures and processes of firms.
- The role and purpose of the Financial Ombudsman Service (FOS) and the framework under which the FCA can be alerted to super-complaints and mass-detriment references.
- The role and purpose of the Financial Services Compensation Scheme (FSCS).
- The limits to the amount of compensation which the FSCS will pay to eligible claimants.

# 1. Eligible Complaints

**Learning Objective**

9.1.1    Apply the criteria for a complainant to be eligible to lodge a complaint [DISP 2.2]

## 1.1    The Purpose of the Rules

It is almost inevitable that customers will raise complaints against a firm; sometimes these complaints will be valid and sometimes they will not. The FCA requires authorised firms to deal with complaints from **eligible** complainants (who are generally regarded as more vulnerable than some other potential complainants) promptly and fairly.

A complaint may only be dealt with under the FOS if it is brought by, or on behalf of, an eligible complainant. A complaint may be brought on behalf of an eligible complainant (or a deceased person who would have been an eligible complainant) by a person authorised by the eligible complainant or authorised by law. It is immaterial whether the person authorised to act on behalf of an eligible complainant is himself an eligible complainant.

## 1.2    Eligible Complainants

Firms must have in place, and follow, internal complaints procedures for eligible complainants which embrace the following (as long as they are classified as retail clients):

- a consumer (a retail and a professional client – any natural person acting for purposes outside of their trade, business or profession);
- an enterprise with fewer than ten employees and turnover or annual balance sheet not exceeding £2 million (a **micro-enterprise**) at the time the complaint is raised;
- charities with an annual income of less than £1 million at the time the complaint is raised; or
- a trustee of a trust with a net asset value of less than £1 million at the time the complaint is raised.

Eligible counterparties (ECPs) are not eligible complainants. An eligible complainant must be one of the above types of retail or professional client and must be a customer, have been a customer, or be a potential customer of the firm against whom they have a complaint.

323

Since 1 November 2007 certain complaints provisions (the complaints-handling and complaints record rules) have been disapplied for all eligible complainants who are not also **retail clients** under MiFID, so as not to impose obligations that are **super-equivalent** – more onerous than those that MiFID requires – in the UK.

# 2. Complaints Procedures and Process

### Learning Objective

9.2.1 Apply the procedures that a firm must implement and follow to handle customer complaints [DISP 1.2.1/3, 1.3.3, 1.4.1, 1.6.1/2/5, 1.9.1, 1.10.1]

9.6.1 Apply appropriate ethical standards and professional integrity when handling customer complaints

## 2.1 Procedures

The FCA requires firms to have appropriate written procedures for handling expressions of dissatisfaction from eligible complainants. However, a firm is permitted to apply these procedures to other complainants as well, if it chooses.

These procedures should be followed regardless of whether the complaint is oral or written, and whether the complaint is justified or not, as long as it relates to the firm's provision of (or failure to provide) a financial service.

These internal complaints-handling procedures should provide for:

- receiving complaints;
- responding to complaints;
- appropriately investigating complaints; and
- notifying complainants of their right to go to the FOS where relevant.

As you might expect, firms' processes for complaints-handling is a key area of focus of the FCA's **TCF** initiative.

The TCF chapter of the FCA's DISP Sourcebook contains rules and guidance on how respondents should deal promptly and fairly with complaints, in respect of business carried on from establishments in the UK or by certain branches of firms in the EEA. It is also relevant to those who may wish to make a complaint or refer it to the FOS.

Complaints and Redress

It is the firms' responsibility to ensure that they instil professional and ethical standards within their staff when dealing with customer complaints, so as to be seen to be complying with the spirit of TCF. It is down to individual firms as to how they ensure that the level of integrity is upheld for staff dealing with complaints. But, senior management with the firm, who are approved persons, are responsible for putting in place adequate systems and controls and assessing the appropriateness of those controls on an ongoing basis.

To aid consumer awareness of the protections offered by the provisions in the TCF chapter of the DISP Sourcebook, firms must publish appropriate summary details of their internal process for dealing with complaints promptly and fairly; they must refer eligible complainants in writing to the availability of these summary details at, or immediately after, the point of sale and provide such summary details in writing on request and when acknowledging a complaint.

Firms are required to have effective and transparent procedures for the reasonable and prompt handling of all complaints. In respect of complaints that do not relate to MiFID business, firms must put in place appropriate management controls and take reasonable steps to ensure that when handling complaints they identify and remedy any recurring of systemic problems, for example, by:

- analysing the causes of individual complaints so as to identify root causes common to different types of complaint;
- considering whether such root causes may also affect other processes or products, including those not directly complained of; and
- correcting, where reasonable to do so, such root causes.

## 2.2    Stages and Timings

The regulations set certain minimum time periods and requirements which must be observed when a firm receives a complaint. These should be reflected in a firm's internal complaints-handling procedures.

Once a firm has received a complaint, it must investigate competently, diligently and impartially, obtaining additional information as necessary. It must assess the subject matter of the complaint fairly, consistently and promptly, and decide:

- whether the complaint should be upheld; and
- what remedial action or redress (or both) may be appropriate and, if appropriate, whether it has reasonable grounds to be satisfied that another firm may be solely or jointly responsible for the matter alleged in the complaint.

Taking into account all relevant factors, firms should offer redress or remedial action when they decide this is appropriate. They should explain to the complainant promptly, and in a way that is fair, clear and not misleading, their assessment of the complaint, their decision on it and any offer of remedial action or redress. Firms should comply promptly with any offer of remedial action or redress accepted by the complainant.

On receipt of a complaint, firms must send the complainant a prompt, written acknowledgement providing early reassurance that they have received the complaint and are dealing with it. In addition, firms must keep the complainant informed thereafter of the progress of the measures being taken for the complaint's resolution.

325

Factors that may be relevant in the assessment of a complaint include the following:

- All the evidence available and the particular circumstances of the complaint.
- Similarities with other complaints received by the respondent.
- Relevant guidance published by the FCA, other regulators, the FOS or former schemes.
- Appropriate analysis of decisions by the FOS concerning similar complaints received by the respondent.

Firms must, by the end of **eight weeks** after their receipt of the complaint, send the complainant a final response, which accepts the complaint, and, if appropriate, offers redress or remedial action, or offers redress or remedial action without accepting the complaint, or rejects the complaint and gives reasons for doing so. In this case, they should enclose a copy of the FOS standard explanatory leaflet and inform the complainant that if they remain dissatisfied with the respondent's response they may refer the complaint to the FOS within six months.

Alternatively they must provide a written response which explains why they are not in a position to make a final response and indicates when they expect to be able to provide one. They must inform the complainant that they may now refer the complaint to the FOS, enclosing a copy of the FOS standard explanatory leaflet.

The requirement placed on a firm regarding providing a final, or other, response within eight weeks does not apply if the complainant has already indicated, in writing, acceptance of a response by the firm, providing that the firm's response informed the complainant of the ultimate availability of the FOS if they remain dissatisfied with the firm's response.

From 1 September 2012 firms are required to appoint a senior manager to consider the root causes for complaints and to review FOS decisions.

## 2.3 Record-Keeping and Reporting

Records must be kept in relation to complaints, both for FCA-monitoring purposes and to enable the firm to co-operate fully with the FOS, if necessary. These records should include:

- the name of the complainant;
- the substance of the complaint; and
- details of any correspondence between the firm and the complainant, including details of any redress offered by the firm.

Firms must provide the FCA with twice-yearly reports on complaints, covering the following:

- the total number of complaints received by the firm, broken down into categories and generic product types;
- the total number of complaints closed by the firm within four weeks or less of receipt, within four to eight weeks of receipt, and more than eight weeks after receipt;
- the total number of complaints outstanding at the end of the period;
- the total number of complaints that the firm knows have been referred to, and accepted by, the FOS in the reporting period;
- the total amount of redress paid in respect of complaints during the reporting period.

Complaints are considered closed when the firm has sent a final response, or when the complainant has indicated, in writing, that he accepts an earlier response by the firm. If the firm adopts the two-stage approach, a complaint is considered closed if the complainant has not responded to the written response within eight weeks.

## 2.4    Regulation

### 2.4.1    Transparency as a Regulatory Tool: Publication of Complaints Data

The FCA is in favour of using transparency as a regulatory tool to help achieve its objectives; it stated *'Disclosure meets the FCA's standards of economy, efficiency and effectiveness'*.

Firms are required to publish information on how they handle complaints (to help people see how firms are performing and to help drive up complaints-handling standards across the industry). In addition, firms that receive 500 or more complaints in a six-month period have to publish the following information twice a year:

- how many complaints they have opened and closed;
- the percentage closed within eight weeks; and
- the percentage of complaints upheld.

Firms will need to present this information by five product areas: banking, home finance, general insurance and pure protection, life and pensions, and investments.

The FCA will then use this information to publish a twice-yearly consolidated list of complaints data covering all affected firms.

# 3. Complaints and Dispute Resolution

**Learning Objective**

9.3.1 Understand the activities to which compulsory jurisdiction applies (DISP 2.3)

9.4.1 Understand the role of the Financial Ombudsman Service (FOS) (DISP Complaints Sourcebook – Dispute Resolution: Complaints: Introduction), and the awards and directions that can be made by the Ombudsman (DISP 3.7.2/4, 3.7.11)

9.4.2 Understand the framework under which the FCA can be alerted to super-complaints and mass detriment references

## 3.1 The Role of the Financial Ombudsman Service (FOS)

Under the provisions of the FSMA, the then UK regulator (FSA) was given the power to make rules relating to the handling of complaints (outlined in Section 2), and an independent body was established to administer and operate a dispute resolution scheme.

The dispute resolution scheme is the FOS, and the body that operates it is the Financial Ombudsman Service Limited (FOSL). The FOS is designed to resolve complaints about financial services firms quickly and with minimum formality. Importantly, it is free to complainants, which removes the deterrent effect of legal costs.

## 3.2 FOS Awards

The FOS can require a firm to pay over money as a result of a complaint. This monetary award against the firm will be an amount which the FOS considers to be fair compensation; however, the sum cannot exceed £150,000 (the rules changed from 1 January 2012: the previous amount that could be awarded was £100,000). If the decision is made to make a monetary award, the FOS can award compensation for financial loss, pain and suffering, damage to reputation and distress or inconvenience.

If the FOS finds in a complainant's favour, it can also award an amount that covers some, or all, of the costs which were reasonably incurred by the complainant in respect of the complaint.

The FOS can also provide a direction against the firm, requiring it to take such steps in relation to the complainant as it considers just and appropriate.

Firms must comply promptly with any award or direction made by the FOS, and with any settlement which it agrees at an earlier stage of the procedures.

## 3.3 Compulsory versus Voluntary Jurisdictions (VJs)

The FOS comprises two jurisdictions:

1. **Compulsory jurisdiction** – this extends to complaints from eligible complainants against FCA-authorised firms in relation to their regulated activities (and any ancillary activities) which the firm is unable to resolve to the satisfaction of the complainant within the timescales outlined above in Section 2.2.
2. **Voluntary jurisdiction** (VJ) – this covers complaints which are not within the compulsory jurisdiction. Currently, the following can be considered under VJ:
   - lending on mortgages by non-FCA-authorised firms;
   - other specified lending activity;
   - providing payments on plastic cards (excluding store cards);
   - accepting deposits and providing general insurance if the service was provided from elsewhere within the EEA but was directed at the UK.

It is important to appreciate that firms can choose to utilise the VJ, but must accept the compulsory jurisdiction, if it applies, for eligible complainants. Those firms choosing to use the VJ are known as **VJ participants**. The FCA has stated that certain complaints which do not fall within the compulsory jurisdiction can be considered under the VJ.

## 3.4 Super-Complaints and Mass-Detriment References

Certain consumer organisations will be able to make what are known as **super-complaints**. The aim is to provide consumer bodies with a way of raising competition and consumer issues with the FCA. This approach is modelled on a similar process that already operates with the Office of Fair Trading (OFT).

The FCA will look at the issues raised in the super-complaint and publish a response within 90 days, setting out how they have dealt with the query and whether they have decided to take any action.

Mass-detriment is defined as a large scale damage, harm or loss to consumers.

# 4. The Financial Services Compensation Scheme (FSCS)

### Learning Objective

9.5.1 Apply the rules of the Financial Services Compensation Scheme in respect of each category of protected claim [COMP 10.2.1/3 (FCA/PRA)]

## 4.1 The Role and Purpose of the FSCS

The Financial Services Compensation Scheme (FSCS) has been established to pay compensation to eligible claimants in the event of a default by an authorised person. Eligible claimants are broadly the less knowledgeable clients of the firm, and the default is typically the firm suffering insolvency. It is essentially an insurance policy that is paid for by all authorised firms and provides protection to some clients in the event of a firm's collapse.

Eligible claimants are certain persons who have a **protected claim** against an authorised person who is in default. This includes most clients of the defaulting firm, except:

- other authorised firms;
- overseas financial institutions;
- supranational institutions, governments and central administrative authorities;
- provincial, regional, local and municipal authorities; and
- large companies or large mutual associations.

The protected claims could relate to money on deposit with a bank (**protected deposits**), or claims on contracts of insurance (**protected contracts of insurance**), or in connection with **protected investment business**. Protected investment business is designated investment business carried on from the UK, or any claims arising from the holder of CIS units against the manager or trustee of an AUT, or the ACD or depositary of an ICVC.

Therefore, in order to receive compensation, the person making the claim must be an eligible claimant and he must have a protected claim against an authorised firm that is in default. The precise amount of compensation that is payable depends upon the amount of money lost by the claimant and the type of protected claim.

## 4.2 Compensation Payable

There are limits to the amount of compensation which the FSCS will pay to eligible claimants:

- For protected insurance (long-term insurance contract) – 90% of the claim.
- For protected compulsory insurance (general insurance contract) – 100% of the claim.
- For protected non-compulsory insurance (ie, other general insurance) – 90% of the claim.

The FSCS rules were increased in respect of the limit for deposits up to £85,000 on 1 January 2011. The limit of £85,000 is for each customer, so joint accounts are guaranteed up to £170,000. The previous limit was £50,000 per person.

The FCA is considering whether accounts with different banks that are owned by the same parent company should be covered. Currently, customers are covered only for one account under each banking licence, so if they have accounts with banks that are owned by the same parent company then they will only have a total of £85,000 guaranteed. An example of this confusion is that Halifax and Bank of Scotland only have one banking licence, meaning a customer is only covered once up to £85,000, whereas NatWest and RBS have separate banking licences, meaning cover applies to both savings accounts held separately with NatWest and RBS up to the full amount.

The changes to the compensation payable for **protected investment business** came into effect on 1 January 2010. This means that the compensation limit for investments and home finance advice is £50,000 (the previous limit for protected investment business was 100% for the first £30,000 and then 90% of the next £20,000 – so the maximum compensation payable was £48,000).

## 5. Professional Integrity when Handling Customer Complaints

### Learning Objective

9.6.1 Apply appropriate ethical standards and professional integrity when handling customer complaints

There are clear FCA rules and published best practice as to how the regulator expects customer complaints to be handled, which is on their merits and by ensuring that the customer is treated fairly. Additionally, they should be handled by a person independent of the matter complained of.

However, there are various other pressures on the firm or on its employees that may result in unethical practices being followed. Here is an example which gives food for thought.

## Case Study

***A conversation is overheard between staff, suggesting that flagrant breaches of procedure are the norm in their office. What would you do?***

It has been a successful week for Katy. As a potential junior manager for a nationwide retail investment firm, she was chosen to attend the firm's national seminar week, in anticipation of a forthcoming promotional opportunity, for which she is short-listed.

The seminar was held in a luxury country house hotel whose clientele included the type of customer which the firm aimed to attract. On the last day after the end of the formal part of the seminar, Katy chose to take a drink onto the public terrace rather than remain in the reception room set aside for the firm, which was becoming noisy with the end-of-seminar spirit. On the terrace she noticed two other employees, easily identifiable by their name badges and seminar bags emblazoned with the company logo. Talking in a loud and animated way, they were probably not the best advert for the firm, but, after all, it was the end of a hard week.

Katy did not join them but sat within earshot; in fact, it would have been difficult not to hear them. When their conversation came round to the complaints procedures workshop held earlier that day, she became fully aware of what they were saying and began to listen intently. Their attitude was that the approved policies were all very well in theory, but the reality in their branch was very different. Their established practice was to use a range of stalling tactics and low offers of compensation unless the customer threatened to escalate the complaint, and they reckoned that they were saving hundreds of pounds towards their targets by this approach.

Dismayed by what she heard, Katy quietly got up and walked away. However, the more she thought about it, the more concerned she became. On the one hand she had heard, in a public place, employees of the firm bragging about breaking the rules; on the other hand, with her promotion pending, why should she risk making a fuss? After all, who would know? She had no hard evidence, nor would she be able to get any.

---

We all know that any evidence of breaches of rules and principles should be reported and that the decision rests with individuals to do so. However, firms have a joint responsibility to help their staff to recognise when they are being faced with a dilemma and to help them to respond in an appropriate way.

## Summary of this Chapter

You should have an understanding and knowledge of the following after reading this chapter:

- The purpose of the dispute resolution rules.
- Who is eligible to make a complaint, and why.
- Complaints procedures for firms, and the internal processes that they must have in place (TCF):
  - stages and timings;
  - record-keeping and reporting of complaints to the regulator;
  - transparency as a regulatory tool.
- The role and purpose of the FOS:
  - how much the FOS can award against firms;
  - the two types of jurisdictions – compulsory and voluntary.
- The role and purpose of the FSCS:
  - who is eligible;
  - compensation limits/types of investments.

# End of Chapter Questions

Think of an answer for each question and refer to the appropriate section for confirmation.

1. What is a complaint?
   *Answer reference: Sections 1.1, 1.2*

2. Why must firms have complaints procedures and processes?
   *Answer reference: Sections 1.1, 2.1*

3. What is an eligible complainant?
   *Answer reference: Section 1.2*

4. How must a firm publicise its complaints-handling procedures?
   *Answer reference: Section 2.1*

5. What are the record-keeping requirements in relation to complaint-handling?
   *Answer reference: Section 2.3*

6. What is the role of the FOS?
   *Answer reference: Section 3.1*

7. In addition to costs, what is the maximum monetary award the FOS can compel a firm to pay to a complainant?
   *Answer reference: Section 3.2*

8. What is the difference between compulsory jurisdiction and voluntary jurisdiction?
   *Answer reference: Section 3.3*

9. What is the role of the FSCS?
   *Answer reference: Section 4.1*

10. Who are normally excluded from claiming compensation from the FSCS?
    *Answer reference: Section 4.1*

11. What compensation is available under the FSCS for protected deposits?
    *Answer reference: Section 4.2*

12. Looking at the case study, what considerations or tools allow you to judge whether a course of action is ethical?
    *Answer reference: Section 5*

13. If a complaint relates to a lack of ethical behaviour, could this amount to a breach of the FCA rules or principles? If so, why?
    *Answer reference: Whole Chapter*

# Chapter Ten
# FCA Conduct of Business Fair Treatment and Client Money Protection

1. General Provisions and Application of Conduct of Business Sourcebook (COBS) — 337
2. The Financial Promotion Rules — 344
3. Client Categorisation — 353
4. Fair Treatment – Accepting Customers — 358
5. Conflicts of Interest — 367
6. Fair Treatment — 374
7. Advising and Selling — 381
8. Client Assets — 390
9. Client Interaction — 396

**This syllabus area will provide approximately 17 of the 80 examination questions**

FCA Conduct of Business Fair Treatment and Client Money Protection

# 1. General Provisions and Application of Conduct of Business Sourcebook (COBS)

**Learning Objective**

10.1 FCA Conduct of Business Sourcebook:

10.1.1 Understand the main FCA principles, rules and requirements relating to conduct of business: firms subject to the FCA Conduct of Business Sourcebook [COBS 1.1.1–1.1.3, 1 Annex 1, Part 3 Section 3 (FCA/PRA)]; activities which are subject to the FCA Conduct of Business Sourcebook including eligible counterparty business and transactions between regulated market participants [COBS 1.1.1–1.1.3, Annex 1, Part 1(1) (FCA/PRA) & (4)]; impact of location on firms/ activities of the application of the FCA Conduct of Business Sourcebook: permanent place of business in UK [COBS 1.1.1–1.1.3 & Annex 1, Part 2 (FCA/PRA) & Part 3 (1–3) (FCA 1-3/PRA 1–2 only)]

The **Conduct of Business Sourcebook (COBS)** is contained within the business standards block of the FCA Handbook. It came into force on 1 November 2007.

The aim of COBS is to move the regulatory approach towards a better focus on outcomes rather than compliance with detailed and prescriptive rules. It also implements the provisions of the MiFID that relate to conduct of business.

## 1.1 Firms and Activities Subject to COBS

### 1.1.1 Firms Subject to COBS

The **general application** rule states that firms are subject to the COBS Sourcebook if they carry on any of a range of activities from an establishment maintained by them or their appointed representative in the UK.

Some COBS rules are modified or disapplied for specific circumstances, for example:

- transitional modifications because of the change from the old regime to the new one;
- based on a firm's location; or
- based on the firm's activities.

### 1.1.2 Activities Subject to COBS

The activities that are covered are:

- designated investment business;
- long-term insurance business in relation to life policies; and
- activities relating to the above.

337

Under MiFID, the **client classification rules** were changed. As a result, firms may find that COBS rules apply to some of their activities when previously they did not – because some of their clients now fit into different categories, and are entitled to the different levels of protection that go with these categories. For example, a characteristic of some of the COBS rules introduced by MiFID is that they extend protection from retail clients only, to professional clients.

### 1.1.3 Eligible Counterparties (ECPs)

Certain of the COBS rules are disapplied for specific types of activity.

For example, a range of COBS rules are disapplied, in certain cases, for firms carrying on **eligible counterparty business**. These include:

- a large part of **COBS 2** – the conduct of business obligations;
- much of **COBS 4** – communicating with clients (including financial promotions);
- **COBS 6.1** – provision of information about the firm, its services and its remuneration;
- **COBS 8** – client agreements;
- **COBS 10** – appropriateness (for non-advised services);
- certain parts of **COBS 11** – best execution, client order handling and the use of dealing commission;
- parts of **COBS 12** – labelling of non-independent research;
- **COBS 14.3** – information relating to designated investments; and
- **COBS 16** – reporting requirements to clients.

### 1.1.4 The Impact of Location

As explained above, COBS applies to a firm carrying on the following activities from an establishment maintained by it in the UK, or from an establishment maintained by its appointed representative in the UK. This is called the **general application** and it is modified depending on the firm's location and activities. For example:

- The rules in COBS that derive from MiFID apply to UK MiFID firms carrying on MiFID business from a UK establishment. They also apply to the MiFID business of a UK MiFID firm carried on from an establishment in another EEA state, but only if that business is not carried on within the territory of that state.
- The rules in COBS that derive from MiFID apply to an EEA MiFID investment firm carrying out MiFID business from an establishment in, and within the territory of, the UK.
- The rules on investment research and personal transactions apply on a home state basis.

## 1.2 Electronic Media

### Learning Objective

10.2 Electronic Media:

10.2.1 Apply the provisions of the FCA Conduct of Business Sourcebook regarding electronic media (Glossary definitions of durable medium and website conditions) and the recording of voice conversations and electronic communications requirements (COBS 11.8)

Increasingly, firms and their customers communicate and transact business electronically. The FCA rules have adapted to reflect this. In particular, if the rules refer to information being transmitted or provided in a **durable medium**, this means one of the following:

- Paper.
- Any instrument which lets the recipient store the information so that he can access it for future reference, for an appropriate time and on an unchanged basis. It includes storage on a PC but excludes internet sites, unless they meet the requirement for storage and retrieval. So, for example, information conveyed on a website page will not automatically meet the requirements for a durable medium.

With specific reference to website conditions, the FCA requires that:

- If information is provided by means of a website, that provision must be appropriate to the context in which the business between the firm and the client is (or is to be) carried on. That is, there must be evidence that the client has regular access to the internet. Evidence could, for example, be by them providing their email address to carry on that business.
- The client must specifically consent to having information provided to them in that form.
- They must be notified electronically of the website address, and the place on it where the information can be accessed.
- The information must be up to date.
- It must be accessible continuously by way of that website for such a period of time as the client may reasonably need to inspect it.

### 1.2.1 Recording Voice Conversations and Electronic Communication Requirements

Electronic communications include those made by means of fax, email, and instant messaging, as well as telephone conversations made using **firm-provided** mobile phones.

Firms are required to take reasonable steps to record relevant telephone conversations and keep a copy of relevant electronic confirmations which use equipment provided, sanctioned or permitted by the firm for the purpose of carrying out the activities referred to.

A firm must take reasonable steps to prevent relevant telephone conversations and electronic communications on privately owned equipment that the firm is unable to copy.

Records must be kept for at least six months.

The rules on the recording of voice conversations and electronic communications apply to a firm which carries out any of the following activities:

- receiving client orders;
- executing client orders;
- arranging for client orders to be executed;
- carrying out transactions on behalf of the firm, or another person in the firm's group, and which are part of the firm's trading activities or of another person in the firm's group;
- executing orders that result from decisions by the firm to deal on behalf of its client;
- placing orders with other entities for execution that result from decisions by the firm to deal on behalf of its client.

The rules apply to the extent that the activities relate to:

- qualifying investments admitted to trading on a prescribed market;
- qualifying investments in respect of which a request for admission to trading on such a market has been made; and
- investments which are related to such qualifying investments.

Who do the new rules not apply to?

- Activities carried out between operators, or between operators and depositaries, of the same CIS.
- Corporate finance business.
- Corporate treasury functions.
- A discretionary investment manager, if the telephone call is made with a firm that they believe is subject to the recording obligations (COBS 11.8.5).

For the purpose of the rules, a relevant conversation or communication is either between an employee or contractor of the firm with a:

- client, or when acting on behalf of a client, with another person, which concludes an agreement by the firm to carry out the activities referred to above as principal or as agent;
- professional client or an eligible counterparty.

The rules do not include conversations or communications made by investment analysts, retail financial advisers and persons carrying on back office functions, nor general conversations or communications about market conditions.

# 1.3 Inducements

### Learning Objective

10.3 Rules applying to all firms communicating with clients (COBS 4.1, 4.2.1–4):

10.3.2 Inducements rules (COBS 2.3.1/2, 2.3.10–16) and the use of dealing commission, including what benefits can be supplied/obtained under such agreements (COBS 11.6); Rules, guidance and evidential provisions regarding reliance on others (COBS 2.4.4/6/7)

The inducements rules should be seen as a **payment rule** as they prohibit any payment, unless expressly permitted. The rules on inducements apply to firms carrying on designated investment business which is MiFID business as well non-MiFID business. The rules only apply to professional clients and retail clients; therefore, investment firms undertaking ECP business will not be subject to the detailed inducement provisions.

In relation to MiFID business, firms are prohibited from paying or accepting any fees or commissions, or providing or receiving non-monetary benefits, other than:

- fees, commissions or non-monetary benefits paid to or by the client, or someone on his behalf (eg, management fees);
- proper fees which are necessary for the provision of the service (eg, custody costs, legal fees, settlement fees) and which cannot, by their nature, give rise to conflicts; or
- fees, commissions or non-monetary benefits paid to or by a third party (or someone on their behalf).

These are permissible only if they:

- do not impair compliance with the firm's duty to act in the client's best interests;
- are designed to enhance the quality of the service to the client; and
- are disclosed in accordance with set standards prior to the provisions of the service to the client.

Firms can satisfy their disclosure obligations under these rules if they:

- disclose the essential arrangements for such payments/benefits in summary form;
- undertake to their client that further details will be disclosed on request; and
- do, in fact, give such details on request.

Firms must also keep full records of such payments/benefits made to other firms, for all MiFID business. The inducements provisions have not been fully implemented for non-MiFID firms/business. In relation to third-party payments, these firms will only have to comply with the **does not impair compliance test**; the other two tests (disclosure and enhancement) do not apply. Retail non-MiFID business for the sale of packaged products is subject to the disclosure requirements of the inducement provisions.

The extension of the provision does not, however, expect firms to disclose details of reasonable non-monetary benefits for non-MiFID business.

The EC has confirmed that it will be looking at inducements as part of its review of MiFID (refer to Chapter 5 for more details).

## 1.4 The Use of Dealing Commissions

Owing to the implementation of MiFID, there were changes to the use of dealing commission provisions. Firstly, a link was established between the inducement provisions and the use of dealing commission provisions, whereby investment managers complying with these requirements must now also comply with the rules on inducements. Previously there was a carve-out from the inducements provisions. Secondly, the requirement for investment managers to provide **prior disclosure** now forms part of the **summary form** disclosure requirement under the inducements provisions.

When an investment manager executes customer orders that relate to certain designated investments (eg, shares, warrants, certificates representing certain securities, options and rights to, or interests in, investments of shares) it is not permitted to use client-dealing commissions, generated from dealing on behalf of its clients, to purchase goods or services, unless those goods or services relate to execution services or provisions of research.

These commission agreements are only allowed for goods or services that assist the recipient firm in providing a better service to its customers.

The rules state that an investment manager must not execute customer orders through a broker or another person and pass on the charges to its customers, unless the investment manager has reasonable grounds to be satisfied that the goods and services in return for the charges are:

- related to the execution of trades on behalf of the investment manager's customers;
- comprise the provision of research; and
- will reasonably assist the investment manager in providing services to its customers and do not (and is not likely to) impact the investment manager's duty to act in the best interests of its customers.

When the goods or services relate to the execution of trades, an investment manager should have reasonable grounds to be satisfied that the requirements are met if the goods or services are:

- linked to the arranging and conclusion of a specific investment transaction, or series of related transactions; and
- provided between the point at which the investment manager makes an investment or trading decision and the point at which the investment transaction, or series of transactions, is concluded.

When the goods or services relate to the provision of research, an investment manager should have reasonable grounds to be satisfied that the requirements are met if the research:

- is capable of adding value to the investment or trading decisions by providing new insight that informs the investment manager when making such decisions;
- whatever output it takes, represents original thought in the critical and careful consideration and assessment of new existing facts, and does not merely repeat or repackage what has been presented before;
- has intellectual rigour and doesn't merely state what is commonplace or self-evident; and
- involves analysis or manipulation of data to reach meaningful conclusions.

FCA Conduct of Business Fair Treatment and Client Money Protection

Examples of goods and services that relate to execution trades, or the provision of research that the FCA does not regard as meeting the requirements, include:

- valuation or portfolio measurement services;
- computer hardware;
- connectivity services, such as electronic networks and dedicated telephone lines;
- seminar fees;
- subscription for publications;
- travel, accommodation or entertainment costs;
- order and execution management systems;
- office administration software, such as word processing or accounting programmes;
- membership fees to professional associations;
- the purchase or rental of standard office equipment or ancillary facilities;
- employee salaries;
- direct money payments;
- corporate access services;
- publicly available information; and
- custody services (other than incidental to the execution of trades).

Furthermore, the investment manager should not enter into any arrangements that could compromise its ability to comply with its best execution obligations. This includes the investment manager not passing on any costs greater than those charged by the broker and the investment manager making a fair assessment of the charge where the relevant good or service being offered/received is not distinctly priced.

An investment manager that enters into arrangements under this section must make adequate **prior disclosure** to customers concerning the receipt of goods or services that relate to the execution of trades or the provision of research. This prior disclosure should form part of the summary form disclosure under the rule on inducements.

If an investment manager enters into arrangements in accordance with the rule on the use of dealing commission, it must, in a timely manner, make adequate **periodic disclosure** to its customer of the arrangements entered into. Adequate prior and periodic disclosure under this section must include details of the goods or services that relate to the execution of trades and, whenever appropriate, separately identify the details of the goods or services that are attributable to the provision of research.

An investment manager must make a periodic disclosure to its customers at least once a year.

An investment manager must make a record of each prior and periodic disclosure it makes to its customer in accordance with this section and must maintain each record for at least five years from the date on which it is provided.

## 1.5    Reliance on Others

If a firm carrying on MiFID business receives an instruction to provide investment or ancillary services for a client through another firm, and that other firm is a MiFID firm or is an investment firm authorised in another EEA state, and subject to equivalent regulations, then the firm can rely on:

- information relayed about the client to it by the third-party firm; and
- recommendations that have been provided by the third-party firm.

If a firm relies on information provided by a third party, this information should be given in writing. In additional guidance, the FCA states that it will generally be reasonable for a firm to rely on information provided to it in writing by an unconnected authorised person, or a professional firm, unless it is aware, or ought reasonably to be aware, of anything that would give it reasonable grounds to question the accuracy of that information.

# 2. The Financial Promotion Rules

## 2.1 The Application of the Rules on Communicating with Clients

**Learning Objective**

10.4 The requirements of the financial promotion rules:

10.4.1 Understand the purpose and application of the financial promotion rules and the relationship with Principles 6 and 7 (COBS 4.1)

10.4.2 Apply the financial promotion rules and firms' responsibilities for appointed representatives (COBS 3.2.1(4), 4.1)

10.4.3 Apply the types of communication addressed by COBS 4 including the methods of communication

A **financial promotion** is an invitation or an inducement to engage in investment activity. The term, therefore, describes most forms and methods of marketing financial services. It covers traditional advertising, most website content, telephone sales campaigns and face-to-face meetings.

The **financial promotion rules** apply to firms communicating with clients regarding their designated investment business, and communicating or approving a financial promotion, other than:

- for qualifying credit, a home purchase plan or a home reversion plan;
- promotion for a non-investment insurance contract; or
- the promotion of an unregulated CIS which the firm is not permitted to approve.

They also apply to communications to authorised professional firms in accordance with COBS 18 (Specialist Regimes).

In general, these rules apply to a firm which carries on business with, or communicates a financial promotion to, a client in the UK (including when this is done from an establishment overseas), except that they do not apply to communications made to persons inside the UK by EEA firms.

The majority of these rules do not apply when the client is an ECP.

FCA Conduct of Business Fair Treatment and Client Money Protection

Firms must ensure that financial promotions which they communicate or approve, and which are addressed to clients, are clearly identifiable as such.

This rule does not apply to a third-party prospectus in respect of MiFID (or equivalent third-country) business. There are some exceptions in respect of non-MiFID business, including prospectus advertisements, image advertising, non-retail communicating and deposits.

The methods of communication contemplated include:

- **direct offer financial promotions** (these are promotions that make an offer to any person to enter into an agreement and include a form of response or specify the manner of responding);
- **cold calls and other unwritten promotions**.

Firms must ensure that if they provide information about designated investment business, or issue/approve a financial promotion that is likely to be received by a retail client, they adhere to certain rules. These rules state that:

- the firm's name is included on the communication;
- the information is accurate and does not emphasise potential benefits, without also giving fair and prominent indication of any relevant risks;
- it is sufficient for, and presented in a way likely to be understood by, the **average** member of the group at whom it is directed or by whom it is likely to be received;
- it does not disguise, diminish or obscure important items, statements or warnings.

If comparisons are made, they must be meaningful and presented in a fair and balanced way. For MiFID business, the data sources for the comparisons must be cited, as must any key facts and assumptions used.

If tax treatment is mentioned, firms must explain that this depends on the individual circumstances of each client and that it may be subject to change. Information included in financial promotions must be consistent with that given in the course of carrying on business.

These rules are disapplied for third-party prospectuses and image advertising. For non-MiFID businesses they are also disapplied for excluded communications.

## 2.1.1 The Purpose of the Rules

The purpose of the financial promotion rules is to ensure that such promotions are identified as such, and that they are fair, clear and not misleading. The financial promotion rules are consistent with Principles 6 and 7 of the FCA's Principles for Businesses where a firm must pay due regard to:

- **Principle 6** – the interests of its customers and treat them fairly.
- **Principle 7** – the information needs of its clients and communicate information to them in a way which is clear, fair and not misleading.

Section 21 of the FSMA imposes a restriction on the communication of financial promotions by unauthorised persons. An individual (including a firm) must not communicate a financial promotion unless:

- they are an authorised person; or
- the content of the financial promotion is approved by an authorised person.

The penalty for a breach of Section 21 of the FSMA is two years in jail and an unlimited fine.

## 2.1.2 Fair, Clear and Not Misleading

### Learning Objective

10.3 Rules applying to all firms communicating with clients (COBS 4.1, 4.2.4–4):

10.3.1 Apply the main FCA principles, rules and requirements relating to: the conduct of designated investment business: financial promotions; territorial scope; fair, clear and not misleading communications

Principle 7 requires firms to communicate to clients in a way which is clear, fair and not misleading. There are also specific rule requirements. The rule and requirements of **fair, clear and not misleading** apply to communications by firms to a client in relation to:

- designated investment business other than a third-party prospectus;
- financial promotion communicated by the firm that is not an excluded communication (that takes advantage of specified exemptions (See Section 2.2 below)), a non-retail communication or a third-party prospectus; and
- a financial promotion approved by the firm.

Firms' compliance with the requirements of the fair, clear and not misleading rules should be appropriate and proportionate and take account of the means of communication, and what information the communication is intended to convey. So, for example, communications aimed at professional clients may not need to include all the same information as those aimed at retail clients.

In connection with communications which are financial promotions, firms should ensure that:

- those which deal with products or services where a client's capital may be at risk make this clear;
- those quoting yields give a balanced impression of both the short-term and long-term prospects for the investment;
- if an investment product is, or service charges are, complex, or if the firm may receive more than one element of remuneration, this is communicated fairly, clearly and in a manner which is not misleading and which takes into account the information needs of the recipients;
- the FCA is named as the firm's regulator and that any communication refers to matters not regulated by the FCA (making it clear that those matters are not regulated by the FCA);
- those relating to packaged or stakeholder products not produced by the firm itself give a fair, clear and non-misleading impression of the producer or manager of the product.

FCA guidance advises that firms may wish to take account of the Code of Conduct for the Advertising of Interest-Bearing Accounts, produced by the BBA and the Building Societies Association (BSA), when they are drafting financial promotions for deposit accounts.

# FCA Conduct of Business Fair Treatment and Client Money Protection

### 2.1.3 FCA Finalised Guidance on Prominence

In September 2011, the then UK regulator (the FSA) published its finalised guidance on prominence, the aim being to capture emerging concerns and, where necessary, to clarify their expectations of firms.

Prominence of relevant information plays a key role in ensuring that a communication is clear, fair and not misleading. As a consequence, a number of requirements for financial promotions within COBS relate to prominence.

The FCA defines prominence as *'the state of being easily seen'*, ie, in terms of a statement within a financial promotion and likely to be seen by virtue of its size or position.

The FCA's general rule in communicating with retail clients requires firms to ensure that information does not emphasise any potential benefits, without giving a fair and prominent indication of any relevant risks. It must also not disguise, diminish or obscure important items.

### 2.1.4 Powers provided by the Financial Services Act 2012

The Act provided the FCA with new powers that enables it to ban misleading financial promotions, which allows the FCA to remove promotions immediately from the market or prevent them being used in the first place, without going through the enforcement process.

The FCA has stated that the use of this new power will be determined by the specific promotion and not used against the firm as a whole. It can be used on its own or before the FCA takes enforcement action against a firm. It will work separately for the FCA's general disciplinary powers, which it will use when firms fail to comply with the rules and their overall systems and approach are poor.

How the financial promotions power will work:

1. The FCA will give a direction to an authorised firm to remove its own financial promotion or one it approves on behalf of an unauthorised firm, setting out its reasons for banning it.
2. Firms can make representations to the FCA if they think they are making the wrong decision.
3. The FCA will decide whether to confirm, amend or revoke the direction. If it is confirmed, the FCA will publish it, along with a copy of the promotion and the reasons behind the decision.

Following the third step, firms will be able to refer the matter to the Upper Tribunal if the FCA decides not to revoke the direction.

The promotions that the FCA will use the power for will not only be the worst cases; they will not always measure harm to consumers in terms of actual or potential financial loss. The FCA will also consider financial promotions that adversely affect consumers' ability to make informed choices and secure the best deal for themselves.

### 2.1.5 Appointed Representatives

The COBS rules also apply to firms in relation to the relevant activities carried on for them by their appointed representatives.

In particular, firms must ensure that they comply with the COBS rules when they communicate financial promotions via their appointed representatives.

Refer to Chapter 7, Section 4.4, for more details on appointed representatives.

## 2.2 Exemptions to the Financial Promotion Rules

### Learning Objective

10.4 The requirements of the financial promotion rules:

10.4.4 Understand the main exemptions to the financial promotion rules and the existence of the financial promotions order (COBS 4.8)

The financial promotion rules are disapplied in certain cases, notably for excluded communications.

These are communications which are:

- exempt under the financial promotion order (FPO). This is an order which makes certain sorts of promotion exempt from the regime if it is communicated by an unauthorised person, or originates outside the UK and cannot have an effect within the UK;
- from outside the UK, and would be exempt under the FPO if the office from which they are communicated were a separate unauthorised person (even though it is not);
- subject to (or exempted from) the Takeover Code, or similar rules in another EEA state;
- personal quotes or illustration forms;
- one-off promotions that are not cold calls.

The exemption for excluded communications will not generally apply in relation to MiFID business.

## 2.3 Approval of Financial Promotions

### Learning Objective

10.4 The requirements of the financial promotion rules:

10.4.5 Apply the rules on approving and communicating financial promotions and compliance with the financial promotions rules [COBS 4.10 + SYSC 3 & 4 (FCA/PRA)]

The COBS rules on approval of financial promotions complement requirements under SYSC. SYSC 3 and SYSC 4 require that a firm which communicates with a client, in relation to designated investment business, or which communicates or approves a financial promotion, puts in place systems and controls or policies and procedures in order to comply with the rules on financial promotions.

# FCA Conduct of Business Fair Treatment and Client Money Protection

COBS states that, before an authorised firm approves a financial promotion for communication by an unauthorised person, it must confirm that it complies with the financial promotion rules. If, later, it becomes aware that the financial promotion no longer complies, it must withdraw its approval and notify anyone it knows to be relying on that approval as soon as is reasonably practicable.

Firms may not authorise financial promotions to be made in the course of personal visits, telephone conversations or other interactive dialogue.

If a firm approves a financial promotion for which any of the financial promotion rules are disapplied, it must do so on the terms that its approval is limited to those circumstances.

## 2.3.1 Firms Relying on Promotions Approved by Another Party

In relation to non-MiFID business only, a firm is not in breach of the rules if it communicates a financial promotion that has been produced by another party and:

- takes reasonable care to establish that another authorised firm has confirmed that the promotion complies with the rules;
- takes reasonable care that it communicates it only to the type of recipient it was intended for at the time of the confirmation;
- as far as it is (or should be) aware, the promotion has not ceased to be fair, clear and not misleading and the promotion has not been withdrawn.

## 2.4    Direct Offer or Invitations

### Learning Objective

10.4    The requirements of the financial promotion rules:

10.4.6    Apply the rules relating to the compilation of direct offer and non-real time financial promotions including the relationship with FCA Principles and the requirements in relation to past, simulated past and future performance (COBS 4.1; 4.6; 4.7.1–4)

**Direct offer** promotions – those making a direct offer or invitation, such as in a newspaper, trade magazine or mailed directly – likely to be received by a retail client must contain:

- prescribed information about the firm and its services;
- when relevant, prescribed information about the management of the client's investments;
- prescribed information about the safekeeping of client investments and money;
- prescribed information about costs and charges;
- prescribed information about the nature and risks of any relevant designated investments; when an investment is the subject of a public offer, any prospectus published in accordance with the Prospectus Directive must be made available;

349

- if a designated investment combines two or more investments or services, so as to result in greater risk than the risks associated with the components singly, an adequate description of those components and how that increase in risk arises;
- if a designated investment incorporates a third-party guarantee, enough detail for the client to make a fair assessment of it.

The above need not be included, however, if the client would have to refer to another document containing that information in order to respond to the offer.

## 2.4.1 Past, Simulated Past and Future Performance

### Past Performance

Firms must ensure that information, including indications of past performance, is such that:

- the past performance indication is not the most prominent feature;
- it covers at least the immediately preceding five years, or the whole period that the investment has been offered/the financial index has been established/the service has been provided if this is less than five years. In any event, it must show complete 12-month periods;
- reference periods and sources are clearly shown;
- there is a clear and prominent warning that the data/figures are historic and are not a reliable indicator for future performance;
- if the figures are in a currency other than that of the EEA state in which the client is resident, that the currency is stated and there is a warning about the possible effects of currency fluctuations;
- if the performance is cited **gross**, that the effect of commissions, fees and other charges is disclosed.

### Simulated Past Performance

If firms give figures based on simulated (ie, notional, not having taken place in reality) past performance because the product or service does not have a track record, a firm must ensure that the simulated past performance figures:

- relate to an investment or index;
- are based on actual past performance of one or more investments/indices which are the same as, or underlie, the investments being simulated;
- meet the rules set out above on past performance (except for the statement that they relate to that investment's past performance, since they don't);
- contain a prominent warning that they relate to simulated past performance and that past performance is no guide to future performance.

### Future Performance

Firms must ensure that information containing an indication of the possible future performance of relevant business, a relevant investment, a structured deposit, or a financial index:

- is not based on, and does not refer to, simulated past performance;
- is based on reasonable assumptions supported by objective data;
- if it is based on gross performance, discloses the effects of commissions, fees or other charges;
- contains a prominent warning that such forecasts are not reliable indicators of future performance.

## 2.4.2 Unwritten Promotions, Cold Calling and Overseas Persons

### Unwritten Promotions

A firm must not initiate an unwritten promotion to a particular person outside its premises, unless the individual doing so:

- does so at an appropriate time of day;
- identifies himself and his firm at the outset and makes the reason for the contact clear;
- gets clarification of whether the client would like to continue with the communication or terminate it (and does so if requested); and
- gives the client a contact point, if an appointment is arranged with them.

### Cold Calling

Cold calling is the practice of authorised persons or exempt persons contacting people without a prior appointment with a view to communicating a financial promotion to them.

Firms must not cold call unless:

- the recipient has an existing client relationship with the firm and would envisage receiving such a call; or
- the call relates to a generally marketable packaged product which is neither a higher-volatility fund, nor a life policy linked to such a fund; or
- it relates to a **controlled activity** relating to a limited range of investments, including deposits and readily realisable investments other than warrants or generally marketable non-geared packaged products.

### Overseas Persons

Firms are not permitted to communicate or approve financial promotions for overseas firms, unless the promotion sets out which firm has approved/communicated it, and (if relevant) explains:

- that the rules for the protection of investors will not apply;
- the extent that the UK compensation scheme arrangements will be available (and if they will not, that fact); and
- if the communicator wishes to do so, the details of any overseas compensation/deposit protection scheme applicable.

The firm must not communicate/approve the promotion unless it has no doubt that the overseas firm will deal with its UK retail clients honestly and reliably.

## 2.5 Ethical Considerations

### Learning Objective

10.4 The requirements of the financial promotion rules:

10.4.7 Understand the ethical implications of issuing misleading financial promotions

There are extensive FCA rules on financial promotions in Sections 2.1–2.4, but there are other matters or aspects requiring consideration which are subjective and require the application of integrity and ethical judgement.

An example follows which will help you to think about this.

### Case Study

***You are concerned that a product designed by your firm for distribution to retail customers via a third party is riskier than it appears, and the risks have not been fully considered.***

You work within an investment bank in structured product design. Currently the bank is working on a product code named Lemming that will be labelled in the name of a major insurance group and sold and distributed through their sales force. Only in the small print will your bank's connection be disclosed.

The product will offer a highly attractive, fixed rate of interest over the next five years, but there is the possibility of leveraged capital erosion should the stock market have fallen by more than 30% at the end of the five-year term.

The insurance company is now planning a major sales campaign which will be directed towards retail investors who are currently dissatisfied with the low rates available on ordinary bank deposits. Ahead of the launch, the insurance company has asked you to review some of the promotional material to check its factual accuracy, and you are concerned to note that the advertising suggests that the product is available to general retail investors.

Your marketing director has convinced the board on the benefits of this link and stressed the point that sales process and documentation are to be left entirely to the insurance company, although you are unaware of any internal discussion on the intrinsic merits or risks arising from this process. You believe that discussion has focused exclusively on the ability to generate revenue and foster strong links and establish a new distribution channel through the insurance company. The launch of this product is now close and will be a high-profile event, being the first of a planned series.

You remain concerned that the potential risks are not being addressed at a senior level and that your marketing director's eagerness to launch the product has prevented adequate consideration being given to the reputational and financial risk to the bank, should the worst case scenario occur.

There appears to have been no consideration within your company of the merits or risks of the approach whereby the sales process/documentation has been left entirely to the insurance company.

FCA Conduct of Business Fair Treatment and Client Money Protection

There are two distinct considerations in determining appropriate responses to this situation. The first is the impact upon your employer if the proposed course of action is implemented without further discussion; the second is what you might do about it.

On the face of it, the situation might be held to be quite straightforward, in that your bank has sold a product to another professional organisation on a principal-to-principal basis and any subsequent promotion, distribution and sale is the sole responsibility of the intermediary.

In its promotion of TCF, the then regulator (the FSA) suggested that the responsibilities of product originators cannot be compartmentalised and, increasingly, originators must have due regard for the likely end purchasers of their products. The FCA is continuing the work that the FSA started.

Additionally, there must be a strong possibility, particularly against the background of TCF, that, in the event of the retail product's not living up to consumer expectations, aggrieved investors will, either singly or en bloc, seek financial redress against all parties associated with the construction and distribution of the product.

Under those circumstances, the cost to the originator's reputation, even if it is able to defend itself successfully against the retail purchasers' actions, is likely to include the spotlight of publicity being turned upon the organisation in a way that it would probably prefer to avoid. The old theatrical adage that all publicity is good publicity does not apply in the financial services industry.

# 3. Client Categorisation

## Learning Objective

10.5 Understand the main FCA principles, rules and requirements relating to:

10.5.1 Client categorisation (eligible counterparties/professional/retail) (COBS 3.1–3.6)

10.5.2 Notification to clients of their categorisation (COBS 3.3)

10.5.3 Requirements for clients electing to be professional clients and eligible counterparties, together with those wishing higher level of protection (COBS 3.5–3.9, 3.6.4–7)

A firm is required to categorise its clients if it is carrying on designated investment business. MiFID laid down rules as to how client categorisation has to be carried out for MiFID business. For non-MiFID business, the FCA uses the same client categorisation terminology, but the rules on how the categories must be applied are modified in some cases.

When a firm provides a mix of MiFID and non-MiFID services, it must categorise clients in accordance with the MiFID requirements, unless the MiFID business is conducted separately from the non-MiFID business.

So, for example, if a firm were to advise a client on the relative merits of investing in a CIS (advice which would fall within the scope of MiFID), and also on a life policy (which would not), it should use the MiFID client categorisation.

## 3.1 The Definition of a Client

COBS defines a client as someone to whom a firm provides, intends to provide or has provided a service in the course of carrying on a regulated activity and, in the case of MiFID or equivalent third-country business, anything which is an **ancillary service**. This was discussed in Chapter 5.

The term includes potential clients. In addition, in relation to the financial promotions rules, it includes a person to whom a financial promotion is communicated, or is likely to be communicated.

Clients of a firm's appointed representative or tied agent are regarded as clients of the firm.

## 3.2 The Client Categories

Under COBS, clients may be categorised as:

- retail clients;
- professional clients; or
- ECPs.

The importance of the categorisation is that it determines what regulatory protections the client will be given because certain of the rules are applied only to particular categories of client. Retail clients get the most regulatory protection and ECPs get the least.

A **retail client** is any client who is not a professional client or an ECP. The term **customer** means retail clients and professional clients.

**Professional clients** may be either elective professional clients, or per se professional clients. An elective professional client is one who has chosen to be treated as such.

**Per se professional clients** are, generally, those which fall into any of the following categories – unless they are an ECP, or are categorised differently under other specific provisions.

- An entity required to be authorised or regulated to operate in the financial markets. This includes:
    - a credit institution;
    - an investment firm;
    - any other authorised or regulated financial institution;
    - an insurance company;
    - a CIS or the management company of such a scheme;
    - a pension fund or the management company of a pension fund;
    - a commodity or commodity derivatives dealer;
    - a local;
    - any other institutional investor.

354

# FCA Conduct of Business Fair Treatment and Client Money Protection

- **Large undertakings** – companies whose balance sheet, turnover or own funds meet certain levels, specifically:
  - For MiFID and equivalent third-country business, undertakings that meet any two of the following size requirements on a company basis:
    - a balance sheet total of €20 million;
    - a net turnover of €40 million;
    - own funds of €2 million.
  - For other (non-MiFID) business, large undertakings are:
    - a company whose called-up share capital or net assets are, or have at any time in the past two years been, at least £5 million, or currency equivalent (or any company whose holding companies/subsidiaries meet this test);
    - a company which meets (or which the holding companies/subsidiaries meet) any two of the following criteria: a balance sheet total of €12.5 million; a net turnover of €25 million; an average of 250 employees during the year;
    - a partnership or unincorporated association whose net assets are, or have at any time in the past two years been, at least £5 million, or currency equivalent. In the case of limited partnerships, this should be calculated without deducting any loans owing to the partners;
    - a trustee of a trust (other than certain types of pension scheme, dealt with in the next bullet point) which has, or has at any time in the past two years had, assets of at least £10 million;
    - a trustee of an occupational pension scheme or a small self-administered scheme, or the trustee/operator of a personal pension or stakeholder pension scheme, if the scheme has, or has at any time in the past two years had: at least 50 members; and assets under management of at least £10 million.
    - a local or public authority.

The list of per se professional clients also includes:

- governments, certain public bodies, central banks, international/supranational institutions and similar; and
- institutional investors whose main business is investment in financial instruments.

COBS contains a list with the types of clients which can be classified as **ECPs**.

Each of the following is an ECP (per se). This includes an entity that is not from an EEA state that is equivalent to any of the following (unless and to the extent it is given a different categorisation under COBS 3):

*[The list below is, to a certain extent, identical to the per se professional client listed earlier in this section. However, the ECP category is narrower as it does not include large undertakings.]*

- a credit institution;
- an investment firm;
- another financial institution authorised or regulated under the EC legislation or the national law of an EEA state (that includes regulated institutions in the securities, banking and insurance sectors);
- an insurance company;
- a CIS authorised under the UCITS Directive or its management company;
- a pension fund or its management company;
- a national government or its corresponding office, including a public body that deals with the public debt;

- a supranational organisation;
- a central bank;
- an undertaking exempted from the application of MiFID under either Article 2(1)(k) (certain own account dealers in commodities or commodity derivatives) or Article 2(1)(l) (locals) of MiFID.

A client can only be categorised as an ECP for the following three types of business:

- executing orders; and/or
- dealing on own account; and/or
- receiving and transmitting orders.

This means that if the same ECP wants to engage in other types of business, such as investment management or investment advice for example, it will have to be classified as a per se professional client.

As explained earlier, many of the COBS rules do not apply when the client is an ECP; the result of this is that the ECP will not benefit from the protections afforded by these rules. Having said that, the majority of ECPs are large firms, who are very familiar with the financial markets, or are themselves large players in the financial markets and do not need such protections anyway. Some ECPs, however, would rather have more protections by voluntarily asking to opt-down a client category and become professional clients.

## 3.3 Agents

When a firm knows that someone to whom it is providing services (A) is acting as the agent of another person (B), then it should regard A as its client.

This is not the case when the firm has agreed in writing with A that it should treat B as its client instead, or if the involvement of A in the arrangement is mainly for the purpose of reducing the firm's duties to B; in this case, B should be treated as the client in any case.

## 3.4 Notifications of Client Classification

New clients must be notified of how the firm has classified them. They must also, before services are provided, advise the clients of their rights to request recategorisation and of any limits in their protections that arise from this.

### 3.4.1 Policies, Procedures and Records

A firm must implement appropriate written internal policies and procedures to categorise its clients. A firm must make a record of the form of each notice provided and each agreement entered into. This record must be made at the time that the standard form is first used and retained for the relevant period after the firm ceases to carry on business with clients who were provided with that form.

FCA Conduct of Business Fair Treatment and Client Money Protection

# 3.5 Recategorising Clients

## 3.5.1 Elective Professional Clients

A retail client may be treated as an elective professional client, both for MiFID and non-MiFID business, only if:

- the firm has assessed its expertise, experience and knowledge and believes it can make its own investment decisions and understands the risks involved (this is called the **qualitative test**); and
- any **two** of the following are true (this is called the **quantitative test**);
    - the client carried out, on average, ten significantly sized transactions on the relevant market in each of the past four quarters;
    - the size of the client's financial portfolio exceeds €500,000 (defined as including cash deposits and financial instruments);
    - the client works, or has worked, as a professional in the financial services sector for at least a year on a basis which requires knowledge of the transactions envisaged;
- the firm must follow certain procedures, including giving a clear written warning to the client of the lost protections, to which the client must agree in writing. In particular, the client must state in writing to the firm that it wishes to be treated as a professional client, either generally or in respect of a particular service or transaction or type of transaction or product.

For MiFID business, a client may be treated as an elective professional client if it meets both the qualitative test **and** the quantitative test.

If a firm becomes aware that a client no longer fulfils the initial conditions that justified categorisation as an elective professional client, the firm must take appropriate action. If the appropriate action involves re-categorising the client as a retail client, the firm must notify that client of its new categorisation.

## 3.5.2 Elective Eligible Counterparties (ECPs)

A professional client may be treated as an elective eligible counterparty if it is a company and it is:

- a per se professional client (other than one which is only a professional client because it is an institutional investor); or
- it asks to be treated as such and is already an elective professional client (but only for the services for which it could be treated as a professional client); and
- it expressly agrees with the firm to be treated as an ECP.

## 3.5.3 Recategorising Clients and Providing Higher Levels of Protection

Firms must allow professional clients and ECPs to request recategorisation so as to benefit from the higher protections afforded to retail clients or professional clients (as applicable).

In addition, firms can treat:

- per se professional clients as retail clients; and
- ECPs as professional or retail clients on their own initiative as well as at the client's request.

Recategorisation may be carried out for a client on:

- a general basis; or
- more specific terms; for example, in relation to a single transaction only.

A firm can therefore classify a client under a different client classification for different financial instruments that it may trade/undertake transactions in. However, this will mean complex internal arrangements for firms; this is why most firms will classify a client just once for all financial instruments that it may undertake transactions in.

# 4. Fair Treatment – Accepting Customers

## Learning Objective

10.6.1 Understand the main FCA principles and requirements relating to the fair treatment of customers: FCA's Principles for Businesses (PRIN 1.1.1 (FCA/PRA)/2, 1.1.7 & 2.1.1 (FCA/PRA)); FCA's six consumer outcomes (corporate culture; marketing; clear information; suitability of advice; fair product expectations; absence of post-sale barriers); interaction with SYSC and the requirements for senior management to review management information (SYSC 4.1.1 (FCA/PRA)); importance of the fiduciary relationship and the responsibilities of professional advisers towards clients; requirements for fair agreements & the FCA's ability to enforce unfair contract terms legislation (UNFCOG 1.1, 1.3 & 1.4); FCA requirement for a conflicts management policy (SYSC 10.1.10/11/12 (FCA/PRA))

10.7.1 Understand the main FCA principles, rules and requirements relating to client take-on processes, agreements and disclosures: timing, order and medium in which client disclosures may be made, including requirements on electronic media; disclosure of service provision, costs and associated charges and terms of business; client agreements for designated investment business (COBS 8.1.1–8.1.3); interpreting the different information requirements and responsibilities between managing investments and execution-only services (COBS 6.1.6); requirements of disclosure information – compensation scheme, complaints eligibility, status information, permanent place of business, voice recording

As seen in Chapter 7, the FCA Handbook includes 11 key Principles for Businesses (the Principles), which authorised firms must observe. The Principles apply with respect to the carrying on of regulated activities, activities that constitute dealing in investments as principal, ancillary activities in relation to designated investment business, home finance activity, insurance mediation activity and accepting deposits, as well as the communication and approval of financial promotions.

If a firm breaches any of the Principles which apply to it, it will be liable to disciplinary sanctions. However, the onus will be on the FCA to show that the firm has been at fault. The FCA is continuing the work that the then regulator (the FSA) started in pursuing a TCF initiative to encourage firms to adopt a more ethical frame of mind within the industry, leading to more ethical behaviour at every stage of a firm's relationship with its customers.

To recap, the 11 Principles for Businesses are:

1. Integrity.
2. Skill, care and diligence.
3. Management and control.
4. Financial prudence.
5. Market conduct.
6. Customers' interests
7. Communication with clients.
8. Conflicts of interest.
9. Customers: relationships of trust.
10. Clients' assets.
11. Relations with regulators.

# 4.1 Treating Customers Fairly (TCF)

It should be apparent from reading the above that a general theme of overriding **fair play** runs through the Principles. This is coupled with a recognition that there is often an information imbalance between the firm and its customers (since the firm is usually more expert in its products and services than its customers).

This theme is reinforced through the FCA's **TCF** initiative. This was launched by the then regulator (the FSA) in response to some work it undertook in 2000–01, to look at what a **fair deal** for customers should actually mean. At the time, this was mainly considered in the context of post-sales relationships. The initiative has since been widened to encompass all parts of the customer relationship.

While the initiative has given new emphasis to the fair treatment of customers, and in particular a focus on getting the right outcomes for them, the FCA is at pains to remind firms that **fair treatment** has always been one of its Principles for Businesses – it is embedded in Principle 6 above – and that the TCF agenda is really no more than a clearer way of focusing firms' attention on what really matters.

The FCA has defined six **consumer outcomes** to explain to firms what it believes TCF should do for its consumers:

1. Consumers can be confident that they are dealing with firms where the fair treatment of customers is central to the corporate culture.
2. Products and services marketed and sold in the retail market are designed to meet the needs of identified consumer groups and are targeted accordingly.
3. Consumers are provided with clear information and are kept appropriately informed before, during and after the point-of-sale.
4. When consumers receive advice, the advice is suitable and takes account of their circumstances.
5. Consumers are provided with products that perform as firms have led them to expect, and the associated service is both of an acceptable standard and as they have been led to expect.
6. Consumers do not face unreasonable post-sale barriers imposed by firms to change product, switch provider, submit a claim or make a complaint.

To help firms, the FCA has published illustrative examples of each of the outcomes on its website. By March 2008, firms were obliged to have completed the **implementation stage** of their TCF work – that is, to have reviewed their internal arrangements, assessed any gaps in what they were doing, and started to take remedial steps. Those firms that did not meet this deadline were subject to increased supervisory attention and possible enforcement action.

Firms were obliged to have appropriate management information (MI) arrangements in place to enable them to monitor their own TCF performance, and be able to demonstrate that this activity had borne fruit, and that they could show, through their own MI, that they were in fact treating their customers fairly at all stages of the relationship.

In addition, these efforts were underpinned when MiFID came into force on 1 November 2007. A new, general obligation was imposed on firms that '... *all firms act honestly, fairly and professionally, and in accordance with the best interests of the client*'.

The MiFID requirement was implemented in the UK through its inclusion in the FCA's revised Conduct of Business rules (COBS). It may not appear to differ markedly from the overall impact of the Principles – and indeed if firms comply with all the Principles, they should not, in general, have much difficulty in complying with COBS. However, there are some differences in specific areas.

### 4.1.1 Requirement for Fair Agreements

The requirement for a client agreement applies to designated investment business carried on for retail clients and professional clients in relation to MiFID or equivalent third-country business. It also applies to ancillary services, to MiFID business or equivalent third country-business.

It does not apply to insurance firms issuing life policies as principal.

Firms must, in good time, **before** a retail client is bound by any agreement relating to designated investment business or ancillary services or before the provision of those services, whichever is earlier, provide that client with:

- the terms of any such agreement; and
- the information about the firm and its services relating to that agreement or those services required by COBS 6.1.4 (information about a firm and its services), including authorised communications, conflicts of interest and the firm's authorised status.

Firms must provide the agreement and information in durable medium or via a website, where the website conditions are satisfied.

A firm may provide the agreement and the information immediately after the client is bound by any such agreement only in the following circumstances:

- The firm was unable to comply with the requirement to provide the agreement in good time prior to the carrying out of investment business for the client, due to the agreement concluding using a means of distance communication which prevented the firm from doing so.
- If the rule on voice telephone communications (COBS 5.1.12 – distance marketing disclosures rules) does not otherwise apply, the firm complies with that rule in relation to a service that the firm is providing to that client.

FCA Conduct of Business Fair Treatment and Client Money Protection

A firm must establish a record that includes the agreement between itself and a client which sets out the rights and obligations of the parties, and the other terms on which it will provide services to the client. The records must be maintained for at least the longer of:

- five years;
- the duration of the relationship with the client; or
- in the case of a records relating to pensions transfers, pension opt-outs or additional voluntary contributions to a private pension/pension contract from an occupational pension scheme, indefinitely.

Firms should also consider other COBS rules (such as fair, clear and not misleading, disclosure of information and distance communications) when considering their approach to client agreements.

## 4.1.2 Information Requirements Relating to the Nature and Risks of Investments

Firms carrying on MiFID business, or equivalent third-country business, must provide clients with appropriate information in a comprehensible form about:

- the firm and its services;
- designated investments and proposed investment strategies, including appropriate guidance on, and warnings of, risks associated with investments in those designated investments or in respect of particular investment strategies;
- an explanation of leverage and its effects, and the risk of losing the entire investment;
- volatility of the price and any limitations on the available market for such investments;
- if the client has entered into contingent liability transactions, that they might assume additional obligations additional to the cost of acquiring the investments;
- margin requirements or similar obligations applicable to certain investments;
- execution venues;
- costs and associated charges.

This information means that the client is reasonably able to understand the nature and risks of the service and of the specific type of designated investments that are being offered and to take investment decisions on an informed basis.

Firms carrying on non-MiFID business with or for a retail client in relation to derivatives, warrants or stock lending activity must also provide the information quoted above.

## 4.1.3 Information about the Firm

A firm must provide a retail client with the following general information, if relevant:

- The name and address of the firm, contact details necessary to enable the client to communicate effectively with the firm.
- In respect of MiFID business or equivalent third-country business, the languages in which the client may communicate with the firm and receive documents and other information from the firm.
- The methods of communication to be used between the firm and the client, including those for the sending and receiving of orders.

361

- A statement of the fact that the firm is authorised and the name and contact details of the competent authority that has authorised it.
- If the firm is acting through an appointed representative or, where applicable, a tied agent, a statement of this fact specifying in which EEA state the appointed representative or tied agent is registered.
- The nature, frequency and timing of the reports on the performance of the service to be provided by the firm to the client in accordance with the rules on reporting to clients on the provision of services [COBS 16].
- In the case of a common platform firm (a firm subject to either MiFID or the CRD), a description, which may be provided in summary form, of the firm's conflicts of interest policy (and at any time that the client requests it, further details of the conflicts of interest policy) and for non-MiFID business carried on for clients when a material interest or conflict of interest may or may not arise, the manner in which the firm will ensure fair treatment of the client.

### 4.1.4 Information Requirements Relating to Managing Investments

A firm that manages investments for a client must establish an appropriate method of evaluation and comparison, such as a meaningful benchmark, based on the investment objectives of the client and the types of investment included in the client's portfolio, to enable the client to assess the firm's performance.

If a firm proposes to manage investments for a retail client, the firm must provide the client with the following information, if applicable:

- information on the method and frequency of valuation of the investments in the client's portfolio;
- details of any delegation of the discretionary management of all or part of investments or funds in the client's portfolio;
- specification of any benchmark against which performance of the portfolio will be compared;
- the types of investment that may be included and the types of transaction that may be carried out, including any limits;
- objectives, the level of risk to be reflected in the manager's exercise of discretion, and any specific constraints on that discretion.

### 4.1.5 Information on Safeguarding Investments/Money

Firms holding client money or investments for retail clients, subject to the MiFID custody/client money rules (as applicable), also have to provide the following information, where it is appropriate:

1. that the investments/money may be held by a third party on the firm's behalf;
2. what the firm's responsibility is for any acts/omissions of that third party;
3. what will happen if the third party becomes insolvent;
4. if the investments cannot be separately designated in the country in which they are held by a third party, what this means for the client and what the risks are;
5. that the investments are subject to the laws of a non-EEA jurisdiction and what this means for their rights over them;
6. a summary of the steps the firm has taken to protect the client money/investments, including details of any relevant investor compensation scheme or deposit guarantee scheme;

FCA Conduct of Business Fair Treatment and Client Money Protection

7.  if the money or investments are subject to any security interest, lien or right of set-off, this fact and the terms of it;
8.  full and clear information, in a durable medium, in **good time** before entering into securities financing transactions using their investments, about what the firm's obligations are with regard to those investments and what the risks might be.

Firms holding money or designated investments for **professional clients** must provide them with the information in points 5 and 7 above.

## 4.1.6 Disclosure of Costs

Firms must provide their retail clients with information on the costs and charges to which they will be subject, including (where applicable) the following:

- the total price to be paid, including all related fees, commissions, charges and expenses and any taxes payable via the firm;
- if these cannot be indicated at the time, the basis on which they will be calculated so that the client can verify them;
- the commissions charged by the firm must be itemised separately in every case;
- if the above are to be paid in a foreign currency, what currency is involved and the conversion rates and costs;
- where other costs and taxes not paid or imposed by the firm could be applicable, the fact that this is so;
- how the above items are to be paid/levied;
- information about compensation schemes.

### Timing of Disclosure

Information to clients should be provided in good time before the provision of designated investment business or ancillary services. Alternatively, the firm may provide the information immediately after the provision of designated investment business or ancillary services if:

a.  at the request of the client, the agreement was concluded using a means of distance communication which prevented the firm from providing the information before the provision of a designated investment business or ancillary services; and
b.  the firm complies with the rule on voice telephone communications, which applies to services provided to consumers (ie, the firm should treat the retail client as a **consumer**).

### Medium of Disclosure

The firm must provide the information in a **durable medium**. This can be a paper or any instrument which enables the recipient to store information addressed personally to him in a way accessible for future reference for a period of time adequate for the purposes of the information.

The instrument should also allow the unchanged reproduction of the information stored. In particular, the term durable medium covers floppy disks, CD-ROMs, DVDs and hard drives or personal computers on which electronic email is stored. It excludes internet sites, unless such sites meet the criteria specified above (ie, unless it enables the recipient to store information addressed personally to him in a way accessible for future reference for a period of time adequate for the purposes of the information).

363

The firm can also provide this information via a website, providing that the website conditions are satisfied. The website conditions are as follows:

1. There is evidence that the client has regular access to the internet, such as the provision by the client of an email address for the purposes of the carrying on of that business.
2. The client must specifically consent to the provision of that information in that form.
3. The client must be notified electronically of the address of the website, and the place on the website where the information may be accessed.
4. The information must be up-to-date.
5. The information must be accessible continuously by means of that website for such period of time as the client may reasonably need to inspect it.

## Keeping the Client Up-to-Date

A firm must notify a client in good time about any material change to the information provided which is relevant to a service that the firm is providing to that client. This notification must be in a durable medium if the information to which it relates was given in a durable medium.

## Existing Clients

A firm does not need to treat each of several transactions in respect of the same type of financial instrument as a new or different service. This means that it does not need to comply with the disclosure rules in relation to each transaction. The firm should, however, ensure that the client has received all relevant information in relation to a subsequent transaction, such as details of product charges that differ from those disclosed in respect of a previous transaction.

## Compensation Information

A firm, which carries on MiFID business, must make available to the client, who has used or intends to use those services, the information necessary for the identification of the compensation scheme or any other investor compensation scheme of which the firm is a member, or any alternative arrangement provided for in accordance with the investor compensation scheme. The information must include the amount and scope of the cover offered by the compensation scheme and any rules laid down by another EEA state, if relevant. If the client so requests, the firm must provide information concerning the conditions governing compensation and the formalities which must be completed to obtain compensation. This information must be provided in a durable medium or via a website if the website conditions are satisfied.

## 4.2 The Retail Distribution Review (RDR)

### Learning Objective

10.7.2 Understand the requirements for an adviser to a retail client to be remunerated only by adviser charges in relation to any personal recommendation or related service

10.8.2 Understand the requirements for a firm making a personal recommendation to be independent or restricted

### 4.2.1 Adviser Charging

In 2009 the then regulator (FSA) published a consultation paper and proposals for implementing the RDR. The regulator was seeking to:

- improve the clarity with which firms describe their services to consumers;
- address the potential for adviser remuneration to distort consumer outcomes; and
- increase the professional standards of advisers.

Restricted advice is where an adviser can only recommend certain products, product providers or both. Therefore, they might only offer products from one company, or just one type of product. They could also focus on one particular market.

The regulator issued its feedback and policy statement, together with final rules on adviser remuneration and improving clarity for consumers about advice services, in March 2010. The rules on adviser charging became effective on 1 January 2013.

The approach for implementing the RDR means that it applies to advised sales for a defined range of retail products, but does not apply to non-advised business – such as execution-only and discretionary. However, firms that carry out discretionary management and provide advice as part of that service will be caught by the RDR requirements.

The requirements widened the scope of investment products that can be advised within the scope of the regime for retail investment products. The range of instruments available for advice within the regime is wider than the current packaged product regime. Notably, advisers can now provide a personal recommendation on investment trusts shares, not just a regular savings scheme, as well as unauthorised collective investment trust schemes.

Advisers who are not independent, ie, do not select instruments from the whole of the market, will be classified as restricted. They must describe this restricted service to consumers, with a short description to help consumers understand the service that is being provided to them.

Advisers cannot be remunerated from the product provider when making a personal recommendation to a consumer. They must charge the consumer for the advice and service that they are providing. It is for the adviser and the consumer to agree the charge, prior to the service being provided by the adviser.

The adviser is prohibited from receiving trail commission on any new business carried out with consumers, including existing clients, as of 1 January 2013. But the adviser can receive trail commission on advice provided before 31 December 2012 on **legacy business**.

A client can pay the adviser separately for the services, or the charge for the service can be deducted from the amount that is being invested.

The adviser charging rules in COBS 6.2A (Describing advice services) state that a firm must not hold itself out to a retail client as acting independently unless the only personal recommendations in relation to retail investment products it offers to that retail client are based on a comprehensive and fair analysis of the relevant market and are unbiased and unrestricted.

A firm must disclose in writing to a retail client, in good time before the provisions of its services in respect of a personal recommendation or basic advice in relation to a retail investment product, whether the advice will be independent advice or restricted advice.

A firm that provides independent advice in respect of a relevant market that does not include all retail investment products must include in its disclosure to the retail client an explanation of that market – including the types of retail investment products which constitute that market. If a firm provides restricted advice, its disclosure must explain the nature of the restriction. If a firm provides both independent advice and restricted advice, the disclosure must clearly explain the different nature of the independent advice and restricted advice services.

Disclosure must be made in a durable medium or through a website. A firm is able to provide the disclosure by using a services and costs disclosure document or a combined initial disclosure document.

If a firm provides restricted advice and engages in spoken interaction with a retail client, the firm must disclose orally in good time before the provision of its services in respect of a personal recommendation that it provides restricted advice and the nature of that restriction.

In January 2014 the FCA published finalised guidance relating to supervising retail investment advice: *Inducements and Conflicts of Interest*.

The FCA undertook a review on how effective the RDR rules and requirements were being adhered to by firms. The review looked to see if firms were undermining the objectives of the RDR. They assessed whether advisory firms were soliciting payments for entering into service or distribution agreements; agreements that could lead them to channel business to particular providers and affect the advice given to clients. Additionally providers were making these payments to secure distribution of their products.

The FCA identified certain practices that caused them some concerns, in particular the creation of conflicts of interest which could result in firms not acting in their customers' best interest.

The review identified certain practices where there was the potential for influencing personal recommendations and instances of conflicts of interest around receiving payments from providers.

FCA Conduct of Business Fair Treatment and Client Money Protection

# 5. Conflicts of Interest

## Learning Objective

10.6.1 Understand the main FCA principles and requirements relating to the fair treatment of customers: FCA requirement for a conflicts management policy (SYSC 10.1.10/11/12)

10.6.3 Understand the application and purpose of the principles and rules on conflict of interest; the rules on identifying conflicts and types of conflicts; the rules on recording and managing conflicts; and the rule on disclosure of conflicts (PRIN 2.1.1 Principle 8, SYSC 10.1.1–10.1.9 (FCA/PRA))

The FCA requires that all UK-based firms properly identify and correctly manage actual and potential conflicts of interest that arise within all their business areas. Compliance with the FCA rules on conflicts of interest is one of the ways in which firms seek to ensure that customers are treated fairly and that conflicts of interest are identified and managed effectively.

The conflicts of interest rules are derived from MiFID. The detailed provisions in Articles 21 and 22 of the Level 2 Implementing Directive sit under the general requirement in Articles 18 and 19(1) of MiFID for firms to act honestly, fairly and professionally in accordance with the best interests of their clients.

The conflicts of interest rules reflect the FCA's Principles for Businesses, Principle 8 – Conflicts of Interest, under which firms must manage conflicts of interest fairly, both between themselves and client and between clients.

The rules on conflicts of interest are contained in SYSC. They apply to both common platform firms (those subject to the CRD or MiFID) in respect of regulated business and of ancillary services which constitute MiFID business, as well as non-MiFID firms and business.

The requirements of SYSC conflicts of interest provisions will only apply when a service is provided by a firm. The status of the client to whom the service is provided (a retail client, a professional client or an ECP) is irrelevant for this purpose.

They require that firms take all reasonable steps to identify conflicts of interest between:

- the firm, including its managers, employees, appointed representatives/tied agents and parties connected by way of control and a client of the firm; and
- one client of the firm and another.

Firms under these obligations should, inter alia:

- maintain (and apply) effective organisational and administrative arrangements, designed to prevent conflicts of interest from adversely affecting the interests of their clients;
- for those producing **externally facing** investment research, have appropriate information controls and barriers to stop information from these research activities flowing to the rest of the firm's business (for example, this might include Chinese walls/information barriers);

367

- if a specific conflict cannot be managed away, ensure that the general or specific nature of it is disclosed (as appropriate to the circumstances). Note that disclosure should be used only as a last resort;
- prepare, maintain and implement an effective conflicts policy;
- provide retail clients and potential retail clients with a description of that policy; and
- keep records of those of its activities when a conflict has arisen.

Principle 8 of the Principles for Businesses states *'A firm must manage conflicts of interest fairly, both between itself and its customers and between a customer and another client'*. Therefore, Principle 8 requires that authorised firms ensure that when conflicts of interest do materialise, they manage the conflicts to ensure that customers are treated fairly.

## 5.1 Types of Conflict

For the purpose of identifying the types of conflict of interest that arise, or may arise, in the course of the firm providing a service and whose existence may entail a material risk of damage to the interest of a client, firms must take into account, as a minimum, whether the firm, or a person directly or indirectly linked by control to the firm:

- is likely to make a financial gain, or avoid a financial loss, at the expense of the client;
- has an interest in the outcome of a service provided to the client, or of a transaction carried out on behalf of the client, which is different to the client's interest in that outcome;
- has a financial or other incentive to favour the interest of another client or group of clients over the interest of the client;
- carries on the same business as the client;
- receives, or will receive, from a person other than the client an inducement in relation to a service provided to the client, in the form of monies, goods or services, other than the standard commission or fee for that service.

The conflict of interest may arise if the firm, or person, carries on a regulated activity or ancillary activity or provides ancillary services or engages in other activities.

For non-common platform firms, ie, those not subject to either the CRD or MiFID, the above requirements must be taken as being guidance rather than a rule, other than when the firm produces, or arranges the production of, investment research in accordance with COBS 12.2 (investment research) or produces or disseminates non-independent research in accordance with COBS 12.3 (non-independent research).

## 5.2 Recording of Conflicts

Common platform firms must keep and regularly update a record of the kinds of services or activity carried out by, or on behalf of, the firm in which a conflict of interest entailing a material risk of damage to the interest of one or more clients has arisen or, in the case of an ongoing service or activity, may arise.

## 5.3 Conflicts of Interest Policies

Firms are required to have in place (and apply) an effective conflicts of interest policy, that is set out in writing and is appropriate to the size and organisation of the firm and the nature, scale and complexity of its business. The rules do not prescribe how the policy should be structured, so large and complex firms may have more detailed policies than smaller firms.

SYSC requires that the policy should be designed to ensure that all of a firm's relevant persons, who are engaged in activities which involve a conflict of interest with material risk of damage to client interests, carry on those activities with a level of independence. The policy should record the circumstances which constitute or may give rise to a conflict of interest and whether they have been identified as having the potential to impact on the firm's business. The policy should detail how these conflicts are to be managed, specify the procedures that are to be followed, and the measures adopted in order to manage them.

If a firm is a member of a group, the policy should take into account any potential conflicts arising from the structure/business activities of other members of that group.

Measures that a firm might wish to consider in drawing up its conflicts of interest policy in relation to the management of an offering of securities include the following:

- At an early stage, agreeing with its corporate finance client relevant aspects of the offering process, such as the process the firm proposes to follow in order to determine:
  - what recommendations it will make about allocations for the offering;
  - how the target investor group will be identified;
  - how recommendations on allocation and pricing will be prepared;
  - whether the firm might place securities with its investment clients or with its own proprietary book, or with an associate, and how conflicts arising might be managed;
  - agreeing allocation and pricing objectives with the corporate finance client; inviting the corporate finance client to participate actively in the allocation process; making the initial recommendation.
- For allocation to retail clients of the firm as a single block and not on a named basis: having internal arrangements under which senior personnel responsible for providing services to retail clients approve the allocation.
- The initial allocation recommendations for allocation to retail clients of the firm; and disclosing to the issuer details of the allocations actually made.

## 5.4 Managing Conflicts

A firm must maintain and operate effective organisational administrative arrangements to ensure that it is taking all reasonable steps to prevent conflicts of interest arising as defined in SYSC 10.1.3 from constituting or giving rise to a material risk of damage to the interests of its clients.

Firms will require the following processes and procedures in order to manage conflicts of interest to ensure the fair treatment of clients (SYSC 10.2):

- information barriers, such as reporting lines;
- remuneration structures;

- segregation of duties;
- policy of independence.

The procedures and measures provided for must:

- be designed to ensure that relevant persons, engaged in different business activities involving a conflict of interest of the kind specified above, carry on those activities at a level of independence appropriate to the size and activities of the common platform firm and of the group to which it belongs, and to the materiality of the risk of damage to the interests of clients;
- include such of the following as are necessary and appropriate for the common platform firm to ensure the requisite degree of independence:
    - effective procedures to prevent or control the exchange of information between relevant persons engaged in activities involving a risk of a conflict of interest if the exchange of that information may harm the interests of one or more clients;
    - the separate supervision of relevant persons whose principal functions involve carrying out activities on behalf of, or providing services to, clients whose interests may conflict, or who otherwise represent different interests that may conflict, including those of the firm;
    - the removal of any direct link between the remuneration of relevant persons principally engaged in one activity and the remuneration of, or revenues generated by, different relevant persons principally engaged in another activity, when a conflict of interest may arise in relation to those activities;
    - measures to prevent or limit any person from exercising inappropriate influence over the way in which a relevant person carries out services or activities;
    - measures to prevent or control the simultaneous or sequential involvement of a relevant person in separate services or activities when such involvement may impair the proper management of conflicts of interest.

If the adoption or the practice of one or more of those measures and procedures does not ensure the requisite level of independence, a common platform firm must adopt such alternative or additional measures and procedures as are necessary and appropriate.

## 5.4.1 Chinese Walls

Chinese wall is the term given to arrangements made by a firm such that, in order to manage conflicts of interest, information held by an employee in one part of the business must be withheld from (or, if this is not possible, at least not used by) the people with, or for, whom he acts in another part of the business.

SYSC requires that if a firm establishes and maintains a Chinese wall, it must:

- withhold or not use the information held;
- for that purpose, permit its employees in one part of the business to withhold the information from those employed in another part of the business, but only to the extent that at least one of those parts of the business is carrying on regulated activities, or another activity carried on in connection with a regulated activity;
- take reasonable steps to ensure that these arrangements remain effective and are adequately monitored.

# FCA Conduct of Business Fair Treatment and Client Money Protection

**Example of a Chinese Wall in Operation**

When a common platform firm establishes and maintains a Chinese wall, it allows the persons on one side of the wall, eg, corporate finance, to withhold information from persons on the other side of the wall, eg, the equity research/market-making arm, but only to the extent that one of the parts involves carrying on regulated activities, ancillary activities or MiFID ancillary services.

The effect of the Chinese wall rule is that the corporate finance department may have plans for a company that will change the valuation of that company's shares. The equity research/market-making arm on the other side of the wall should have no knowledge of these plans; consequently, the inability to pass this knowledge on to clients is not seen as a failure of duty to their clients.

A firm will, therefore, not be guilty of the offences of market manipulation (Section 89-92 of the Financial Services Act 2012) or market abuse (Section 118 FSMA) or be liable to a lawsuit under Section 150 (FSMA) when the failure arises from the operation of a Chinese wall.

## 5.5 Disclosing Conflicts

When the arrangements that a firm puts in place to manage potential conflicts of interest are not sufficient to ensure, with reasonable confidence, that the risk of damage to the interest of a client will be prevented, the firm must clearly disclose the general nature and/or source of conflicts of interest to the client before undertaking business for/on behalf of the client.

Disclosure must be made in a durable medium and include sufficient detail, taking into account the nature of the client, to enable that client to take an informed decision with respect to the service in the context of which the conflict of interest arises.

Common platform firms should aim to identify and manage the conflicts of interest arising in relation to their various business lines and, when applicable, their group's activities, under a comprehensive conflicts of interest policy. The disclosure of conflicts of interest should not exempt firms from the obligation to maintain and operate effective organisational and administrative arrangements under SYSC 10.1.3.

While disclosure of specific conflicts of interest is required under SYSC 10.1.8, an over-reliance on disclosure without adequate consideration as to how conflicts may appropriately be managed is not permitted.

Therefore, the disclosure of a conflict of interest should be undertaken as a last resort if the firm's internal controls (managing conflicts) will not satisfy the risk of material damage to the client's best interests.

# 5.6 Conflicts of Interest in Relation to Investment Research

### learning objectives

10.6.4 Know the rules on managing conflict in connection with investment research and research recommendations (COBS 12.1.2, 12.2.1/3/5/10, 12.3.1–4, 12.4.1/4/5/6/7/9/10/15/16/17) and the rules on Chinese walls [SYSC 10.2 (FCA/PRA)]

In general, the conflicts management rules on the production and dissemination of investment research apply to all firms. The requirements for certain disclosures in connection with research recommendations are derived from the MAD. → Market Abuse Directive.

### Measures and Arrangements

If a common platform firm produces investment research, it must implement all the measures for managing conflicts of interest set out in SYSC 10.1.11 in relation to the financial analysts involved in producing research, and other relevant persons, if their interests may conflict with those to whom it is disseminated.

Firms must have in place arrangements designed to ensure that the following conditions are satisfied:

- Financial analysts and other relevant persons, who know the likely timing and content of investment research which is not yet publicly available or available to clients and which cannot be inferred from information that is so available, cannot undertake personal transactions, or trade for others, until the recipient of the investment research has had a reasonable opportunity to act on it. However, there are certain exceptions, such as the receipt of an instruction from an execution-only client or a market maker acting in good faith:
- in cases not covered by the above, they cannot undertake personal account transactions without prior approval from the firm's compliance or legal department and then only in exceptional circumstances;
- the firm and any person involved in the production of research must not accept inducements from those with a material interest in the subject matter of the research;
- they may not promise issuers favourable research coverage;
- none of the issuers, relevant persons other than financial analysts, or anyone else may be allowed to review draft investment research which includes a recommendation or target price, other than to verify compliance with the firm's legal obligations.

A firm which disseminates investment research produced by another person to its clients is exempt from the above requirements if the following criteria are met:

- the person (firm) that produces the investment research is not a member of the group to which the firm belongs;
- the firm does not substantially alter the recommendation within the investment research;
- the firm does not present the investment research as having been produced by itself;
- the firm itself verifies that the producer of the investment research is itself subject to the requirements in COBS 12.2.3 and 12.2.5 (as noted above) in relation to the production of investment research, or has established a policy setting such requirements.

Some conflict management rules are disapplied to the extent that a firm produces **non-independent research** labelled as a marketing communication.

## Required Disclosures

If a firm produces investment research, it must make the following disclosure requirements in the context of conflicts of interest:

- All of its relationships and circumstances that may reasonably be expected to impair the objectivity of the research recommendation.
- When the disclosure would be disproportionate in relation to the length of the research recommendation, the firm must make clear and prominent reference to such a place where disclosures can be directly and easily accessed by the public.
- Major shareholdings that exist between it, on the one hand, and the relevant issuer (the subject of the investment research recommendation) on the other hand, including at least:
  - shareholdings exceeding 5% of the total issued share capital held by the firm or affiliated company;
  - shareholdings exceeding 5% of the total issued share capital of the firm or any affiliated company held by the relevant issuer.
- Any other financial interests held by the firm or any affiliated company in relation to the relevant issuer which are significant in relation to the research recommendation.
- If applicable, a statement that the firm or any affiliated company is party to any other agreement with the relevant issues relating to the provision of investment banking services.
- In general terms, the effective organisational and administrative arrangements set up within the firm for the prevention of avoidance of conflicts of interest with respect to research recommendations, including information barriers.

## Application of Conflicts of Interest to Non-Common Platform Firms when producing Investment Research or Non-Independent Research

The rules relating to:

- types of conflict – SYSC 10.1.4 (Section 3.5.1);
- records of conflicts – SYSC 10.1.6 (Section 3.5.2);
- conflicts of interest policies – SYSC 10.1.10 (Section 3.6);

also apply to a firm which is not a common platform firm when it produces, or arranges for the production of, investment research that is intended for, or likely to be subsequently disseminated to, clients of the firm or to the public in accordance with COBS 12.2 (investment research) and when it produces or disseminates non-independent research in accordance with COBS 12.3 (non-independent research).

# 6. Fair Treatment

### Learning Objective

10.6.2 Understand the FCA Conduct of Business Rules relating to fair treatment of customers: communication to clients and the additional requirements relating to retail clients (COBS 4.1; 4.5); provision of dealing confirmations and periodic statements to customers (COBS 16.1–16.3); ability to ensure and demonstrate the fair treatment of customer dealing, taking into account personal account dealing policy, client order management policy, concepts of best and timely execution, churning and switching (COBS 9.3, 11)

The rules on dealing and managing (aside from those on personal account dealing) apply generally to authorised firms; there are some variations in application, depending on the nature of business and location of the firm:

- certain provisions (those marked in the FCA Handbook with an EU) apply to non-MiFID firms as if they were rules;
- the rules on the use of dealing commissions (see Section 1.4) apply to a firm that is acting as an investment manager.

The rules on personal account dealing (see Section 6.6) apply to the designated investment business of an authorised firm, in relation to the activities it carries on from an establishment in the UK. These rules:

- also apply to passported activities carried on by a UK MiFID investment firm from a branch in another EEA state;
- do not apply to the UK branch of an EEA MiFID firm in relation to its MiFID business.

## 6.1 Communicating with Retail Clients

Firms must ensure that if they provide information about designated investment business, or issue/approve a financial promotion that is likely to be received by a retail client, they adhere to certain rules. These rules state that:

- its name is included on the communication;
- the information is accurate and does not emphasise potential benefits, without also giving fair and prominent indication of any relevant risks;
- the information is sufficient for, and presented in a way likely to be understood by, the **average** member of the group at whom it is directed or by whom it is likely to be received;
- the information does not disguise, diminish or obscure important items, statements or warnings.

If comparisons are made, they must be meaningful and presented in a fair and balanced way. For MiFID business, the data sources for the comparisons must be cited, as must any key facts and assumptions used.

If tax treatment is mentioned, firms must explain that this depends on the individual circumstances of each client and that it may be subject to change.

Information included in financial promotions must be consistent with that given in the course of carrying on business. These rules are disapplied for third-party prospectuses and image advertising. For non-MiFID businesses they are also disapplied for excluded communications.

## 6.2 Confirmation of Transactions and Periodic Statements

### 6.2.1 Transaction Reporting

Firms are required to ensure that clients receive adequate reports on the services they provide to them. These must include any associated costs.

If a firm (other than one managing investments) carries out an order for a client, it must:

- provide the essential information on it, promptly, and in a durable medium;
- provide clients with information about the status of their orders on request; and
- for retail clients, send a notice confirming the deal details as soon as possible (but no later than on the next business day); when the confirmation is received from a third party, the firm must pass the details on no later than the business day following receipt.

If the firm is managing investments, it need not do so if the same details are already being sent to the client by another person.

For non-MiFID business only, there are some exceptions to the above rules and requirements, namely if the client has confirmed that confirmations need not be sent either in general or in specified circumstances.

Firms must keep copies of all confirmations sent to clients:

- for MiFID business, for at least five years from the date of dispatch;
- for other business, for at least three years from the date of dispatch.

For the purpose of calculating the unit price in the trade confirmation information, if the order is executed in tranches, firms may supply clients with the information about the price of each tranche or the average price.

### 6.2.2 Periodic Reporting

Firms managing investments on behalf of clients must provide them with a periodic statement in a durable medium, unless these are provided by another party. For retail clients, this must be at least six-monthly, with the following exceptions:

- the client may request statements three-monthly instead;
- if the client receives deal-by-deal confirmations, and certain higher-risk investments are excluded, the statement may be sent every 12 months;
- if the client has authorised that their portfolio be leveraged, the statement must be provided monthly.

A firm must make and retain a copy of any periodic statement:

- for MiFID business, for a period of at least five years;
- for other business, for a period of at least three years.

If firms manage investments for clients, or operate certain types of account for them which include uncovered open positions in a contingent liability transaction, they must report any losses over a pre-agreed limit to the client. They must do so by the end of the business day on which the limit is breached; if this happens on a non-business day, they must do so by the end of the next business day.

For the purpose of this section, a contingent liability transaction is one that involves any actual or potential liability for the client that exceeds the cost of acquiring the instrument. For the purpose of calculating the unit price in the trade confirmation information or periodic information, if the order is executed in tranches, firms may supply clients with the information about the price of each tranche or the average price.

## 6.3 The Requirement for Best Execution

The rules on best execution apply to MiFID and non-MiFID firms and business. However, there is an exemption from the requirements for firms acting in the capacity of an operator of a regulated collective scheme when purchasing or selling units/shares in that scheme.

The best execution rules under COBS require firms to execute orders on the terms that are most favourable to their client. Broadly, they apply if a firm owes contractual or agency obligations to its client and is acting on behalf of that client.

Specifically, they require that firms take all reasonable steps to obtain, when executing orders, the best possible result for their clients, taking into account the **execution factors**. These factors are price, costs, speed, likelihood of execution and settlement, size, nature or any other consideration relevant to the execution of an order. The relative importance of each factor will depend on the following criteria and characteristics:

- the client, including how he is categorised;
- the client order;
- the financial instruments involved; and
- the execution venues to which that order could be directed.

Best execution is not merely how to achieve the best price. Any of the other factors mentioned above should be considered and, depending on the criteria or characteristics, could be given precedence. For some transactions, for example, the likelihood of execution could be given precedence over the speed of execution. In other transactions, the direct and/or implicit execution costs of a particular venue could be so high, as to be given precedence over the price of the instrument on this venue.

The obligation to take all reasonable steps to obtain the best possible results for its clients applies to a firm which owes contractual or agency obligations to the client. The obligation to deliver the best possible result when executing client orders applies in relation to all types of financial instruments.

Given the differences in the structures of financial instruments, it may be difficult to identify and apply a uniform standard of, and procedure for, best execution that will be effective and appropriate for all classes of instruments. Therefore, best execution obligations should be applied in a manner that takes into account all the different circumstances associated with the particular types of financial instruments.

### 6.3.1 The Role of Price

For retail clients, firms must take account of the total consideration for the transaction, ie, the price of the financial instrument and the costs relating to execution, including all expenses directly related to it such as execution venue fees, clearing and settlement fees, and any fees paid to third parties.

### 6.3.2 Best Execution Venues

When a firm could execute the client's order on more than one execution venue, the firm must take into account both its own costs and the costs of the relevant venues in assessing which will give the best outcome. Its own commissions should not allow it to discriminate unfairly between execution venues, and a firm should not charge a different commission or spread to clients for execution in different venues, if that difference does not reflect actual differences in the cost to the firm of executing on those venues.

### 6.3.3 Order Execution Policies

Firms are required to establish an order execution policy to enable them to obtain the best possible results for their clients. For each class of financial instrument the firm deals in, this must include information about the different execution venues where the firm executes its client orders, and the factors that will affect the choice of venue used. Furthermore, the policy must include those venues that enable the firm consistently to obtain the best possible result for its clients.

Firms must give their clients appropriate information about their execution policies; this needs to be more detailed for retail clients. Firms must obtain their clients' prior consent to their order execution policies (although this may be tacit).

Firms must review their order execution policies whenever a material event occurs, but at least annually, and must notify clients of any material changes to their order execution arrangements or execution policy. However, the FCA does not define the term **material change**.

### 6.3.4 Specific Client Instructions

Whenever a firm receives a specific instruction from a client, it must execute the order as instructed. It will be deemed to have satisfied its obligation to obtain the best possible result if it follows such specific instructions (even if an alternative means of executing the order would have given a better result).

Firms should not induce clients to instruct an order in a particular way, by expressly indicating or implicitly suggesting the content of the instruction to the client, if they know that any instruction to the client will have the likely effect of preventing it from obtaining the best possible result for the client.

## 6.3.5 Compliance with Policies, and the Obligations on Portfolio Managers and Firms Receiving/Transmitting Orders

Firms must monitor the effectiveness of their execution arrangements and policies to identify and (if need be) correct any deficiencies.

In addition they must be able to demonstrate to their clients, on request, that they have executed their orders in accordance with their execution policy. → CIS - Disclosure 2

**Portfolio managers** must act in their clients' best interests when placing orders for them, on the basis of the firm's investment decisions.

**Firms receiving and transmitting orders** for clients must also act in their client's best interests when transmitting those orders to other parties (eg, brokers) to execute. This means taking account of the execution factors listed above (unless the client has given specific instructions, in which case these must be followed). Portfolio managers, and receivers/transmitters of orders, must also maintain order execution policies, but need not get client consent to them.

The policy must identify, in respect of each class of instruments, the entities with which the orders are placed or to which they transmit orders for execution. The entities must have execution arrangements that enable the firm to comply with its obligations under the best execution requirements when it places an order with, or transmits an order to, that entity for execution.

## 6.3.6 Client Order Handling

Firms must apply procedures and arrangements which provide for the prompt, fair and expeditious execution of client orders, relative to the other orders or trading interests of the firm. This rule is also consistent with the need for firms to avoid conflicts of interest, if possible.

In particular, these should allow comparable client orders to be executed in the order in which they are received.

Firms should ensure that:

- executed client orders are promptly and accurately recorded and allocated;
- comparable orders are executed sequentially and promptly, unless this is impracticable or client interests require otherwise;
- retail clients are informed of any material difficulty in the prompt execution of their order, promptly on the firm becoming aware of this;
- if the firm is responsible for overseeing or arranging settlement, that the assets or money are delivered promptly and correctly.

Firms must not misuse information relating to client orders, and must also take steps to prevent its abuse (for example, in order to profit by dealing for its own account).
↓
Front Running.

## 6.4    Aggregation and Allocation

Firms must aggregate their own-account deals with those of a client, or aggregate two or more clients' deals, only if:

- this is unlikely to disadvantage any of the aggregated clients;
- the fact that aggregation may work to their disadvantage is disclosed to the clients;
- an order allocation policy has been established which provides (in sufficiently precise terms) for the fair allocation of transactions. This must cover how volume and price of orders will affect allocation; it must also cover how partial allocations will be dealt with.

When an aggregated order is only partly executed, the firm must then allocate the various trades in order with this allocation policy.

When firms have own-account deals in an aggregated order along with those of clients, they must not allocate them in a way which is detrimental to the clients.

In particular, a firm must allocate the client orders in priority over its own, unless it can show that without the inclusion of its own order, less favourable terms would have been obtained. In these circumstances, it may allocate the deals proportionately.

The firm's order allocation policy must incorporate procedures preventing the reallocation of own-account orders aggregated with client orders in a way detrimental to a client.

## 6.5    Client Limit Orders

Unless the client instructs otherwise, a firm which receives a client limit order for shares listed on a regulated market, and which cannot immediately execute it under the prevailing market conditions, must make the limit order public (in a manner easily accessible to other market participants) immediately so that it can be executed as soon as possible. It need not do so, however, for orders over normal market size.

It may do this by:

- transmitting the order to a regulated market or MTF operating an order book trading system; or
- ensuring the order is made public and can be easily executed as soon as market conditions allow.

## 6.6    The Personal Account Dealing Rules

### 6.6.1    Application and Purpose

The personal account dealing rules apply to firms that conduct designated investment business. These rules require firms to establish, implement and maintain adequate arrangements aimed at preventing certain activities when:

- these activities may give rise to conflicts of interest;
- the individual involved in these activities has access to inside information, as defined in MAD;
- the individual involved in these activities has access to other confidential information relating to clients or transactions with or for clients.

The arrangements should aim to prevent the following activities:

1. Entering into a personal transaction that is: contrary to MAD; involves misuse or improper disclosure of confidential information; or conflicts with the firm's duties to a customer.
2. Improperly advising or procuring that anyone else enters into a transaction that (if it had been done by the employee themselves) would have fallen foul of point 1 above or of a **relevant provision**.
3. Improperly disclosing information or opinion, if they know, or should know, that the person to whom they have disclosed it is likely to enter into a transaction that (if it had been done by the employee themselves) would have fallen foul of point 1 above or of a relevant provision, or to encourage someone else to do so.

The relevant provisions are:

- the rules on personal account transactions undertaken by financial analysts contained elsewhere in COBS (we have already looked at these rules in Section 5.6 of this chapter);
- the rules on the misuse of information relating to pending client orders (which we have also looked at in Section 6.3.6 of this chapter).

Firms must keep records of all personal transactions notified to them, and of any authorisation or prohibition made in connection with them.

### 6.6.2 Compliance with, and Exceptions to, the Personal Account Dealing Rules

The arrangements must ensure that the affected employees are aware of the restrictions on personal transactions, and of the firm's procedures in this regard. They must be such that the firm is informed promptly of any such personal transaction, either by notification of it, or some other procedure enabling the firm to identify it.

When outsourcing takes place, the arrangements must be such that the outsourcee must maintain a record of personal transactions undertaken by any relevant person, and provide this record to the firm promptly on request.

The rules on personal account dealing are disapplied for:

- deals under a discretionary management service, if there is no prior communication between the portfolio manager and the relevant person (or any other person for whose account the transaction is being executed) about the deal;
- deals in units/shares in certain classes of fund, if the relevant person (and any other person for whom the deals are effected) is not involved in the management of the fund.

## 6.7 Churning and Switching

Churning is the activity of dealing overly frequently for a client, in order to generate additional fees/commissions for the firm. It is relevant when, for example, a firm manages a client's portfolio on a discretionary basis. Switching is the activity of selling one investment and replacing it with another.

The FCA's guidance on churning and switching is contained in the COBS rules on suitability. It states that, in the context of assessing suitability, a series of transactions that look **suitable** in isolation may not be suitable if the recommendations/trading decisions to make them are so frequent as to be detrimental to the client.

It also states that firms should bear the client's investment strategy in mind when determining how frequently to deal for him.

# 7. Advising and Selling

## Learning Objective

10.8.1 Understand the main FCA principles, rules and requirements relating to the provision of investment advice and product disclosure: assessment of client suitability requirements (COBS 9.1.1–9.1.4; 9.2.1–7; 9.3.1); difference in requirements between professional and retail clients and the timing of suitability reports (COBS 9.2.8; 9.4.1–3); obligations for assessing appropriateness and circumstances not necessary (COBS 10.2; 10.4–10.6); cancellation and withdrawal rights (COBS 15.1.1; 15.2.1; 15.2.3; 15.2.5; 15.3.1; 15.3.2)

## 7.1 Application of the Rules on Suitability

The COBS rules on the suitability requirements apply when firms:

- make personal recommendations relating to designated investments;
- manage investments.

There are specific rules relating to the provision of **basic advice** (personal recommendations on stakeholder products); firms may, if they choose, apply those rules instead of the more general rules on suitability when advising on stakeholder products.

For non-MiFID business, the rules only apply for:

- retail clients; or
- if the firm is managing the assets of an occupational, stakeholder or personal pension scheme.

## 7.2 The Requirement to Assess Suitability, Timing and Content of a Suitability Report

The suitability rules exist to ensure that firms take reasonable steps to ensure that personal recommendations (or decisions to trade) are suitable for their clients' needs.

When a firm makes a personal recommendation, or is managing a client's investments, it should obtain the necessary information regarding the client's:

- knowledge and experience in the investment field, relevant to the specific type of designated investment business;
- financial situation; and
- investment objectives,

so that it enables the firm to make the recommendations, or take the decisions, which are suitable for the client.

A firm must provide a retail client with a suitability report if it makes a personal recommendation to the client, if the client:

- acquires a holding in, or sells all or part of a holding in:
    - a regulated CIS;
    - an investment trust, either directly or through an investment trust savings scheme;
    - an investment trust where the shares are to be held in an individual savings account (ISA) which has been promoted as the means for investing in one or more specific investment trusts; or
- buys, sells, surrenders, converts or cancels rights under, or suspends contributions to, a personal pension scheme or a stakeholder pension scheme; or
- elects to make income withdrawals or purchase a short-term annuity; or
- enters into a pension transfer or pension opt-out.

A firm must also provide a suitability report if it makes a personal recommendation in connection with a life assurance policy.

There are some exceptions to the requirement to provide a suitability report:

- if a firm, acting as investment manager for a retail client, makes a personal recommendation in connection with a regulated CIS;
- if the client is habitually resident outside the EEA and is not present in the UK at the time of acknowledging consent to the proposal form to which the personal recommendation relates;
- if the personal recommendation is made by a friendly society in connection with a **small life policy** sold by it, with a premium not exceeding £50 a year or (if payable weekly) £1 a week;
- if the personal recommendation is to increase a regular premium to an existing contract; or
- if it is to invest additional single premiums or single contributions to an existing packaged product, to which a single premium or single contribution has previously been paid.

In terms of timing, a suitability report must be provided:

- in connection with a life policy, before the contract is concluded, unless the necessary information is provided orally, or cover is required immediately (in which case the report must be provided in a durable medium immediately after the contract is concluded); or
- in connection with a personal pension scheme or a stakeholder pension, where the cancellation rules apply, within 14 days of concluding the contract; or
- in any other case, when, or as soon as possible after, the transaction is effected or executed.

FCA Conduct of Business Fair Treatment and Client Money Protection

The suitability report must, at least, specify the client's demands and needs, explain any possible disadvantages of the transaction for the client and why the firm has concluded that the recommended transaction is suitable for the client, having due regard to the information provided by the client.

If the transaction is the sale of a life policy by telephone, and the only contact between the firm and client before the contract is concluded is by telephone, then the suitability report must:

- comply with the Distance Marketing Directive (DMD) rules;
- be provided immediately after conclusion of the contract; and
- be in a durable medium.

In respect of timing, a suitability report must be provided when, or as soon as possible after, the transaction is effected or executed in respect of professional clients.

## 7.3    Information Required to make a Suitability Assessment

In order to make a suitability assessment, a firm should establish, and take account of, the client's:

- knowledge and experience of investment relevant to the specific type of designated investment or service;
- investment objectives; and
- level of investment risk that they can bear financially that is consistent with their investment objectives.

In order to do so, a firm should gather enough information from its client to understand the **essential facts** about them. It must have a reasonable basis to believe that (bearing in mind its nature) the service or transaction:

- meets their investment objectives;
- carries a level of investment risk that they can bear financially; and
- carries risks that they have the experience and knowledge to understand.

In terms of assessing the client's knowledge and experience, the firm should gather information on:

- the types of service/transaction/investment with which they are familiar;
- the nature, volume, frequency and period of their involvement in such transactions/investments; and
- their level of education, profession or relevant former profession.

Firms must not discourage clients from providing this information (for example, because it would rule a particular transaction out and result in a loss of business to the firm). They are entitled to rely on the information the client provides, unless it is manifestly out-of-date, inaccurate or incomplete.

If a firm does not obtain the information it needs to assess suitability in this way, it must not make a personal recommendation to the client or take a decision to trade for them.

383

### 7.3.1 Assessing Suitability – Professional Clients

A firm is entitled to assume that a client classified as a professional client in respect of MiFID or equivalent third-country business, for certain products, transactions or services, has the necessary experience and knowledge in that area, and that the client is able financially to bear any related investment risks consistent with his investment objectives.

## 7.4 The Application of the Rules on Appropriateness (Non-Advised Sales)

The rules on non-advised sales apply to a range of MiFID (and some non-MiFID) investment services which do not involve advice or discretionary portfolio management. Specifically, they apply to:

- firms providing MiFID investment services other than the provision of personal recommendations or the managing of investments;
- firms arranging deals, or dealing, in warrants and derivatives for retail clients, when the firm is, or should be, aware that the client's application or order is in response to a direct offer financial promotion;
- firms which assess appropriateness on behalf of other MiFID firms.

When a firm provides one of the above services, it must ask the client for information about his knowledge and experience in the investment field of the specific type of product or service offered or demanded so that it can assess whether the product/service is appropriate.

In assessing appropriateness, the firm:

- must determine whether the client has the experience and knowledge to understand the risks involved;
- may assume that a client classified as a professional client for certain services/products has the necessary knowledge and experience in that field for which it is classified as a professional client.

In terms of a client's knowledge and experience, a firm should obtain information (to the extent appropriate to the circumstances) on:

- the types of service/transaction/investment with which he is familiar;
- the nature, volume, frequency and period of his involvement in such transactions/investments;
- his level of education, profession or relevant former profession.

The firm must not discourage a client from providing this information. A firm is entitled to rely on information provided by a client unless it is aware that the information is out-of-date, inaccurate or incomplete. A firm can use information it already has in its possession. A firm may satisfy itself that a client's knowledge alone is sufficient for them to understand the risk involved in a product or service.

When reasonable, a firm may infer knowledge from experience.

# 7.5 Circumstances when Assessment is Unnecessary

Firms are not required to ask clients to provide information or assess appropriateness if:

- the service is execution-only or, for the receipt and transmission of client orders, in relation to particular financial instruments (see below) and at the client's initiative; and
- the client has been clearly informed that the firm is not required to do so in this particular case, and that they will, therefore, not get the benefit of the protection under the rules on assessing suitability; and
- the firm complies with its obligations regarding conflicts of interest. Principle 8 of the Principles for Businesses states that *'a firm must manage conflicts of interest fairly, both between itself and its customers and between a customer and another client'*.

The particular financial instruments are:

- shares listed on a regulated market or an equivalent third-country market;
- money market instruments, bonds or other forms of securitised debt (providing that they do not have embedded derivatives);
- holdings in UCITS funds; and
- other investments meeting a definition of **non-complex** investments.

A financial instrument is **non-complex** if:

- it is not a derivative;
- there is sufficient liquidity in it;
- it does not involve liability for the client that exceeds the cost of acquiring the investment; and
- it is publicly available and comprehensive information is available on it.

Firms do not need to reassess appropriateness each time if a client is engaged in a series of similar transactions or services, but they must do so before beginning to provide the service. If a client was engaged in a course of dealings of this type before 1 November 2007, the firm may assume that he has the necessary experience and knowledge to understand the risks. This does not mean, however, that the other criteria may necessarily be deemed to have been met.

# 7.6 The Obligation to Warn Clients

If a firm believes, based on the above assessment, that the product or service contemplated is not appropriate for the client, it must warn them of that fact. It may do so in a standardised format.

Further, if the client declines to provide the information the firm needs to assess appropriateness, the firm must warn them that it will then be unable to assess the product/service's appropriateness for them (and again it may do so in standard format). If the client then asks the firm to proceed regardless, it is up to the firm to decide whether to do so based on the circumstances.

## 7.7 Product Disclosure – Key Investor Information Documents (KIIDs) and Key Features Documents (KFDs)

### 7.7.1 KIIDs

For each UCITS scheme that an authorised fund manager (AFM) manages, it must produce a key investor information document (KIID).

The KIID must be fair, clear, not misleading and be consistent with relevant parts of the prospectus.

KIIDs must include appropriate information about the essential characteristics of the UCITS scheme, which is to be provided to investors so that they are reasonably able to understand the nature and risks of the investment product being offered to them, and therefore make investment decisions on an informed basis.

In addition, it must provide information on the following essential elements in respect of the UCITS scheme:

a. identification of the scheme;
b. a short description of its investment objectives and investment policy;
c. past performance presentation or, where relevant, performance scenarios;
d. costs and associated charges; and
e. risk/reward profile of the investment, including appropriate guidance and warnings in relation to the risks associated with investments in the scheme.

### 7.7.2 KFDs

The rules on product disclosure requires that a firm prepares a disclosure document in good time before it needs to, in respect of:

- each package product;
- cash deposit ISAs;
- cash deposit CTFs;
- a key features illustration for each packaged product to produces.

KIIDs cover the terms and features of a product in a prescribed level of detail.

The exceptions are:

- where another firm has agreed to prepare such a document;
- KIIDs are not needed for certain types of schemes, or in some cases if the information is already provided in enough detail in another document;
- there are some specific rules for reinsurance and pure protection insurance contracts.

Firms must provide particular information on the nature and risks of designated investments to clients for whom they undertake MiFID business. They must also do so for retail clients in relation to certain other business.

# 7.8 Cancellation and Rights to Withdraw

The rules on cancellation apply to:

- most firms providing retail financial products based on designated investments or deposits; and
- firms entering into distance contracts with consumers, relating to deposits or designated investments.

They are intended to ensure that clients entering into the relevant range of transactions have the opportunity to reconsider, within a certain period of time, and to cancel the transaction. If a consumer does so, the effect is that he withdraws from the contract and it is terminated.

For example, should a client who receives a cancellation notice in respect of an advised purchase of an authorised unit trust or OEIC wish to exercise their right to cancel, they must do so within 14 days.

Another example is that the cancellation rights period for a life and pensions contract is 30 days.

If cancellation rights apply, firms must tell the consumer of their rights in good time before (or if that is not possible, immediately after) the consumer is bound by the contract, and they must do so in a durable medium. They must tell the consumer of:

- the existence of the cancellation/withdrawal right;
- its duration;
- the conditions for exercising it (including information on any amount the consumer may have to pay);
- what happens if they do not exercise it; and
- practical details of how to exercise it, including the address to which he must send any notification.

A firm need not do this if the consumer is already receiving similar information from it, or another person, under the COBS rules (distance marketing disclosures rules and providing product information).

Cancellation rights do not apply to clients who have discretionary managed portfolios.

The record-keeping retention period is:

- indefinitely for pension transfers, pension opt-out or free-standing additional voluntary contribution (FSAVCs);
- at least five years in relation to a life policy, pension contract, personal pension scheme or stakeholder pension scheme;
- at least three years in any other case.

# 7.9 Advice on Retail Investment Products

Since 1 January 2013 the following have been classified as retail investment products:

- life policies;
- units in an authorised or unauthorised CIS (ie, OEICs or unit trusts);
- stakeholder pension schemes;
- personal pension schemes;

- interests in investment trusts (ie, regular savings schemes);
- securities in investment trusts;
- any other designated investments which offer exposure to underlying financial assets in a packaged form which modifies that exposure when compared with a direct holding in the financial asset;
- structured capital-at-risk products.

## 7.10 Recent Regulatory Publications

### 7.10.1 FCA Finalised Guidance – Assessing Suitability (Establishing the Risk a Customer is Willing and Able to Take and Making a Suitable Investment Selection)

In March 2011 the then UK regulator (the FSA) published finalised guidance to help firms with their suitability requirements.

It was noted that, out of a sample of investment files assessed as unsuitable, over half of these were assessed as unsuitable on the grounds that the investment selection failed to meet the risk that the customer was willing and able to take. This level of failure in this area was deemed unacceptable by the regulator. It took, and continues to take, tough action to address these failings with individual firms.

Prompted by these results and its ongoing concerns in this area, and to help firms and trade bodies to tackle the issues, the regulator issued finalised guidance that looks at:

- how firms establish and check the level of investment risk that retail customers are willing and able to take (in the wider context of the overall suitability assessment);
- the potential causes of failures to provide investment selections that meet the risk a customer is willing and able to take; and
- the role played by risk-profiling and asset-allocation tools, as well as the providers of these tools.

The work in this area has identified some common approaches that can lead to an inadequate assessment of the risk a customer is willing and able to take.

- Although most advisers and investment managers consider a customer's attitude to risk when assessing suitability, many fail to take appropriate account of his capacity for loss.
- If firms use a questionnaire to collect information from customers, the regulator was concerned that these often use poor question and answer options, have over-sensitive scoring or attribute inappropriate weighting to answers. Such flaws can result in inappropriate conflation or interpretation of customer responses.
- The regulator saw examples of firms failing to have a robust process to identify customers that are best suited to placing their money in cash deposits because they are unwilling or unable to accept the risk of loss of capital.

It was concluded that a firm should ensure that, in particular:

- it has a robust process for assessing the risk a customer is willing and able to take, including:
  - assessing a customer's capacity for loss;
  - identifying customers that are best suited to placing their money in cash deposits because they are unwilling or unable to accept the risk of loss of capital;

# FCA Conduct of Business Fair Treatment and Client Money Protection

- appropriately interpreting customer responses to questions and not attributing inappropriate weight to certain answers;
- tools, where used, are fit for purpose and any limitations recognised and mitigated;
- any questions and answers that are used to establish the risk a customer is willing and able to take, and descriptions used to check this, are fair, clear and not misleading;
- it has a robust and flexible process for ensuring investment selections are suitable, given a customer's investment objectives and financial situation (including the risk they are willing and able to take) as well as their knowledge and experience;
- it understands the nature and risks of products or assets selected for customers; and
- it engages customers in a suitability assessment process (including risk-profiling) which acts in the best interests of those customers.

## 7.10.2 Dear CEO Letter – Wealth Management Review

In 2011 the then UK regulator (the FSA) undertook a review of the suitability of client portfolios in a sample of firms in the wealth management industry. It identified significant, widespread failings, which it was concerned might also be prevalent in firms outside the sample. The purpose of the **Dear CEO** letter was to explain the issues that they identified and for firms to consider whether they meet – and can demonstrate that they meet – the suitability requirements.

The key focus of the review was to assess suitability of client portfolios against documented client information, which includes, but is not limited to, the client's knowledge and experience, financial situation and investment objectives.

Several key areas of concern arose from the review, particularly the inability of firms to demonstrate that client portfolios and/or portfolio holdings were suitable.

For example, the regulator evidenced an inability to demonstrate suitability because of:

- an absence of basic KYC information;
- out-of-date KYC information;
- inadequate risk-profiling;
- some firms not implementing MiFID client classification requirements;
- the lack of a record of clients' financial situation (assets, source and extent of income, financial commitments); and,
- the failure to obtain sufficient (or any) information on client knowledge, experience and objectives.

Risk of unsuitability due – in summary – to:

- inconsistencies between portfolios and the client's attitude to risk; and
- inconsistencies between portfolios and the client's investment objective, investment horizon and/ or agreed mandate.

The regulator also had concerns that firms were not taking reasonable care to organise and control their affairs responsibly and effectively, using adequate risk management systems.

Firms were required to respond to the 'Dear CEO' letter acknowledging that they had read and understood the content of the letter and considered its implications for their firm.

The regulator also stated that in order for firms to satisfy themselves that they are currently meeting the suitability requirements and to mitigate the risk of future non-compliance, it expected that firms would consider the client information contained in their client files and whether it is likely to satisfy their obligations regarding customers' desired investment portfolios.

In addition, the regulator hinted at what firms should be doing in terms of KYC and investment suitability by stating that firms may want to consider the following in relation to suitability:

- sampling a meaningful number of client files;
- assessing whether files have relevant, meaningful, accurate and up-to-date client information;
- the depth, breadth and quality of client information; and
- whether the client portfolios, and the current holdings in client portfolios, are suitable, based on the documented client information held.

Following the review of 2011 the then regulator (FSA) continued with its work regarding this work and also took enforcement action against some firms.

# 8. Client Assets

## 8.1 The Purpose of the Client Money and Custody Rules

### Learning Objective

5.4.1 Understand the key internal and external mechanisms within firms that support the regulatory framework: client money oversight function

10.9 Client assets protection:

10.9.1 Understand the principles of client money segregation, holding assets in trust and the requirements for senior management systems, controls and oversight over client money and custody assets (CASS 1A.2.7 & 1A.3.1)

The rules relating to the custody and safeguarding of client money and client assets are contained in CASS. They exist to ensure that firms take adequate steps to protect those client assets for which they are responsible. Within CASS, the requirement to segregate client money from a firm's own money is aimed at ensuring that, if the firm fails, money will not be used to repay its creditors. Usually this is done by ensuring that it is placed promptly in a separately designated client money account with a bank and ensuring that the bank treats it as separate from the firm's own.

CASS, in general, applies to every firm, with some specific exemptions. It applies directly in respect of activities conducted with, or for, all categories of client, ie, retail clients, professional clients and ECPs.

**CASS 6** contains the custody rules that apply when a firm holds financial instruments for a client in the course of MiFID business and when it is safeguarding and administering investments in the course of non-MiFID business.

390

FCA Conduct of Business Fair Treatment and Client Money Protection

**CASS 7** (client money and distribution rules) applies to an MiFID investment firm either when:

- it holds client money in the course of its MiFID business; or
- in the course of investment business that is non-MiFID business in respect of any investment agreement entered into, or to be entered into with or for a client;
- it holds money in respect of which CASS 5 (client money: insurance mediation activity) applies and the firm elects to apply the provisions of CASS 7.

Firms must, when holding safe custody assets belonging to clients, make adequate arrangements so as to safeguard clients' ownership rights, especially in the event of the firm's insolvency and to prevent the use of safe custody assets belonging to a client on the firm's own account, except with the client's express consent. Firms must also introduce adequate organisational arrangements to minimise the risk of loss or diminution of client's safe custody assets. Firms must take the necessary steps to ensure that client money deposited in accordance with the requirement of CASS 7.4.1 (depositing client money) is held in an account or accounts identified separately from any accounts used to hold money belonging to the firm.

**CASS 7.4.1** – a firm, on receiving any client money, must promptly place this money into one or more accounts opened with any of the following: a central bank; a Banking Consolidation Directive (BCD) credit institution; a bank authorised in a third country; a qualifying money market fund.

There are a number of circumstances when the client money rules do not apply, for example if money is held in connection with a delivery versus payment (DVP) transaction (unless the DVP does not occur by the close of business on the third business day following the date of payment of a delivery obligation) or where it becomes due and payable to the firm. Banks holding monies as deposits with themselves are also exempted.

In 2009 the FSA published a consultation (CP10/9 Enhancing the Client Assets Sourcebook (CASS)) proposing a number of policies to enhance the protections offered by CASS in response to issues highlighted by the global financial crisis and a number of insolvency appointments – most notably that relating to the insolvency of Lehman Brothers International (Europe) (LBIE). Although the UK client asset regime has performed relatively well in facilitating the early return of client assets and money (compared with some overseas jurisdictions), the failure of LBIE and the financial crisis in general highlighted a number of issues relating to existing market practices.

By introducing new rules, the regulator aimed to enhance standards of client protection in the UK, as well as market confidence and financial stability.

The new requirements focused on the following

- **Re-hypothecation** – the process where a borrower pledges collateral to secure a debt or a borrower, as a condition precedent to a loan. In financial markets, mainly in prime-broking, the collateral pledged by clients as collateral for its own borrowing is used by investment firms. The collapse of Lehman Brothers raised this issue.
- **Increased reporting to clients** – the FCA requires daily reporting on client money and assets holdings to all prime brokerage clients. This means that clients know exactly what is happening to their assets, what transactions have been completed and, if relevant, which and how many of their assets have been re-hypothecated.

- **Holding client money with group banks** – restricting the placement of client money deposits held in client bank accounts within a group to 20%. This limits the amount by which a client is exposed to group credit risk. The rules state that an entity is a relevant group entity if it is a BCD credit institution, a bank authorised in a third-country, a qualified money market fund or the entity operating or managing a qualifying money market fund and a member of the same group as the firm.
- **Prohibiting the use of general liens in custodial agreements** – the FCA considers it unacceptable that a client's assets held with a custodian were subject to a lien exercised because of the debt of a completely unrelated group entity to the relevant custodian. This emerged as part of the Lehman insolvency and contributed to significant delays in the insolvency practitioners' ability to recover assets from deposits not under their direct control.
- **Creating a new controlled function with specific responsibility for client money and assets** – a senior individual within the firm should be responsible for oversight and protection of client assets and money. Proportionate to the size of the firm, this should be one named individual who may be interviewed for the post and who will hold an FCA significant influence controlled function.
- **Introducing a client money and assets return (CMAR)** – this return is reviewed and authorised on a monthly basis for medium-large firms and twice a year for small firms. This provides the FCA with an overview of firm-specific CASS positions and an overview of UK firms' CASS holdings, and enables the FCA to make regulated interventions on a firm-specific or thematic basis.

## 8.2 Due Diligence and the Establishment of Client Bank Accounts

### Learning Objective

10.9 Client asset protection:

10.9.2 Understand the processes for the establishment of client bank and custody accounts: importance of due diligence and statutory trust status of client bank accounts: the mitigation of counterparty and settlement risks and risks arising from overseas investment activity

Firms that do not deposit client money with a central bank must exercise all due skill, care and diligence in the selection, appointment and periodic review of the credit institution, bank or qualifying money market fund where the money is deposited, and in the arrangements for the holding of this money.

Firms must make a record of the grounds upon which they satisfy themselves as to the appropriateness of their selection of a credit institution, a bank or a qualifying money market fund. The firm must make the record on the date it makes the selection and must keep it from the date of such selection until five years after the firm ceases to use the third party to hold client money.

# 8.3 The Requirement to Reconcile

### Learning Objective

10.9 Client asset protection:

10.9.2 Understand the processes for the establishment of client bank and custody accounts: importance of due diligence and statutory trust status of client bank accounts: the mitigation of counterparty and settlement risks and risks arising from overseas investment activity

10.9.3 Understand the CASS client money and custody rules and the client money reconciliation including the timing, identification, resolution and reporting of discrepancies (CASS 6.2.1–3, 6.5.4–13, 7.3.1–2, 7.4.11, 7.6.9–16, 7.7.1–2)

## 8.3.1 Reconciliation of Client Assets

A firm must keep such records and accounts as necessary to enable it, at any time and without delay, to distinguish safe custody assets held for one client from safe custody assets held for any other client, and from the firm's own assets.

CASS 6.5 sets out the obligations of firms to perform **internal** and **external** reconciliations. Broadly, reconciliations should be made **as often as necessary** to ensure the accuracy of a firm's records and accounts, between its internal accounts and records and those of any third parties by whom those safe custody assets are held. If possible, they should be done by someone who has not been involved in the production or maintenance of the records that are being reconciled.

If the reconciliation shows a discrepancy, the firm must make good (or provide the equivalent of) any shortfall for which it is responsible. If another person is responsible, the firm should take reasonable steps to resolve the position with that person.

Firms must inform the FCA without delay of any failure to comply with the reconciliation requirements, including reconciliation discrepancies and making good any such differences.

## 8.3.2 The Reconciliation of Client Money

A firm must keep such records and accounts as necessary to enable it at any time and without delay to distinguish client money held for one client from client money held for any other client, and from its own money.

CASS 7.6 sets out the obligations of firms to perform internal and external reconciliations.

## Internal Client Money Reconciliations

As explained in CASS 7.6.6 G, in complying with its obligations under CASS 7.6.2 R (records and accounts), and where relevant SYSC 4.1.1 R (general organisational requirements) and SYSC 6.1.1 R (compliance), firms should carry out internal reconciliations of records and accounts of client money the firm holds in client bank accounts and client transaction accounts. The FCA considers the following method of reconciliation to be appropriate for these purposes (the standard method of internal client money reconciliation).

- Each business day, a firm that adopts the normal approach should check whether its client money resource, being the aggregate balance on the firm's client bank accounts, as at the close of business on the previous business day, was at least equal to the client money requirement as at the close of business on that day.
- Each business day, a firm that adopts the alternative approach should ensure that its client money resource, being the aggregate balance on the firm's client bank accounts, as at the close of business on that business day is at least equal to the client money requirement as at the close of business on the previous business day. No excess or shortfall should arise when adopting the alternative approach.

For the purposes of performing its reconciliations of records and accounts, a firm should use the values contained in its accounting records, for example its cash book, rather than values contained in statements received.

If a reconciliation shows a discrepancy, the firm must investigate to identify the reason for the discrepancy and ensure that either any shortfall is paid into the client bank account or any excess is withdrawn from the client bank account by close of business on the day the reconciliation is performed.

## External Client Money Reconciliations

This means cross-checking the internal client money accounts against the records of third parties (eg, banks) with whom client money is held. Firms must perform external reconciliations as often as is necessary, and as soon as reasonably practicable after the date to which the reconciliation relates.

If there is a discrepancy, the firm must investigate and correct it as soon as possible. If it cannot do so, and the firm should be holding a greater amount of client money, it must pay its own money into the client bank account pending resolution of the discrepancy, which it must correct as soon as possible.

If a firm has not complied with these requirements, or is for some reason unable to comply in a material aspect with a particular requirement, it must inform the FCA in writing.

The FCA believes that an adequate method of reconciling client money balances with external records is as follows:

- a reconciliation of a client bank account as recorded by the firm with the statement issued by the bank (or other form of confirmation issued by the bank);
- a reconciliation of the balance on each client transaction account as recorded by the firm, with the balance of that account as set out in the statement (or other form of confirmation) issued by the person with whom the account is held.

## 8.4 The Exemptions from CASS

### Learning Objective

10.9    Client asset protection:

10.9.4    Apply the rules relating to the application and exemption from the requirements of the CASS rules [CASS 1.2.3–4, 6.1.1–6, 7.1.1–12]

CASS does not apply to, *inter alia*:

- investment companies with variable capital ICVCs;
- incoming EEA firms other than insurers, for their passported activities;
- UCITS qualifying schemes;
- a credit institution (eg, a bank) under the BCD, in relation to deposits held with itself;
- coins held for the value of their metal;
- money transferred under **title transfer collateral arrangements**;
- money held in connection with a DVP transaction (unless payment does not occur after three business days);
- money due and payable to the firm;
- if a firm carries on business in its name but on behalf of the client when that is required by the nature of the transaction and the client is in agreement; or
- the custody rules [CASS 6] do not apply if a client transfers full ownership of a safe custody asset to a firm for the purpose of securing or otherwise covering present or future, actual contingent or prospective obligations.

Specific rules within CASS may be disapplied depending on the nature of a firm's activities; the details are set out within the individual rules.

## 8.5 Regulatory Developments

Under the EMIR changes were made to the CASS rules. EMIR is a European regulation and is directly applicable to CCPs and their clearing members in the UK. Under EMIR, when a CCP determines that a clearing member firm is in default, the client transactions (or positions) the clearing members hold in client accounts at the CCP, and the margin supporting those transactions in the same accounts, may be transferred to another client account held by a back-up clearing member. In addition, in the event of a clearing member going into default, EMIR requires that the CCP return any balance of its clients' collateral from the failed clearing member's client account at the CCP directly to the clients or back to the failed clearing member for the account of its clients.

Under CASS rules the failure of a firm triggers a primary pooling event (PPE), whereby the firm's client money is pooled for distribution, including any amount payable by a CCP to a client transaction account. To ensure compliance with EMIR requirements, CASS was amended so that client money that is held by a clearing member firm in a client transaction account at a CCP is excluded from the pooling and distribution triggered by a PPE.

# 9. Client Interaction

## 9.1 Communication

**Learning Objective**

10.10 Client interaction:

10.10.1 Understand the skills necessary to listen and communicate professionally, and to adapt to individual needs and capabilities within a diverse customer base

10.10.2 Understand the skills necessary to: elicit, confirm and record client information relevant to the investment advisory process; assess and analyse clients' needs and circumstances; reach a shared conclusion and make appropriate recommendations

It is the firm's responsibility to ensure that each adviser has the skills to communicate clearly and effectively both orally and in writing. New advisers receive training in communications skills in accordance with each firm's policy and culture; putting it into practice is important but sometimes tricky for some key reasons:

- People come from diverse backgrounds and develop their own **map of the world** which is reflected in how each of us uses and interprets language and information. This can lead to misunderstandings that we may not even be aware of.
- If one person seeks another's professional opinion, there is invariably some scope for power imbalance. Client and adviser each possess different knowledge of equal relevance, but the client's perception of an adviser as **expert** can increase this imbalance. Despite confidentiality underpinning the agreement, new clients in particular can be understandably anxious or cautious about parting with personal or sensitive information to someone whom they do not yet know. Hence they tend to rely on their perception of an adviser's expertise as a proxy for personal trust. Occasionally, this can prevent a client from being sufficiently confident to clarify their own thoughts or question something they have been told.
- We cannot **not influence**. Doing or saying nothing can affect an outcome just as much as behaving more proactively. In an interview situation, the spoken word accounts for less than 10% of what is communicated. Body language is automatically interpreted according to the observer's perception, and hence the listener may reach potentially inaccurate or irrelevant conclusions, without the speaker even being aware of it. This applies equally to advisers and clients.
- Clients differ enormously in how they relate to money and their impressions of what they are capable of earning, saving and spending. Their attitude to risk may differ in general (some people are more or less cautious than average) and in specific contexts; for example, a client who enjoys terrifying fairground experiences may adopt a highly risk-averse approach to finances. Clients come from diverse backgrounds in terms of education, social background, ethnicity, language fluency, age and outlook. Professional advisers need to safeguard against stereotyping or assuming anything about a client which has not been appropriately elicited and evidenced.

## Example

Next time you are in an environment where you can observe someone you have never met, notice the assumptions that you form about them.

How did you reach your conclusions?

The role of a professional adviser includes the ability to work with people from diverse backgrounds in a respectful and genuinely helpful manner, and this requires the flexibility to modify our natural approach in order to **meet the client halfway** while also keeping to a businesslike agenda.

The structure of a face-to-face meeting contains a number of important **boundaries**, which are there to protect and serve the interests of the client and the adviser, especially if the client is paying a time-based fee. There should be an explicit, agreed **agenda** which should fit within a reasonable **time limit**. The advisory role is also an important type of boundary, because it requires objectivity to perform the work well. The opposite might be an intimate friendship, where emotional subjectivity features more prominently. It is the adviser's responsibility to reinstate boundaries of time, agreed agenda and professionalism if it becomes apparent that these are unravelling. This protects against the **slippery slope** of poor practice and consequent risks. Experienced advisers are skilled in communicating the nature and purpose of these boundaries with appropriate sensitivity and firmness. **Contracting** with clients is the way in which these boundaries are established, and it is imperative to adhere to an appropriate procedure in this regard.

**Meeting the client halfway** takes place within these boundaries, ensuring that clients can engage with the adviser and the process without feeling intimidated, judged, confused or unheard, and that there is full and shared understanding concerning information, roles and responsibilities. The most obvious way of achieving this is to **pace the client** by aligning your use of language and the pace at which you operate to the client, rather than automatically expecting every client to adjust to you. Listening to someone talking reveals the speed at which they absorb and process information, the simplicity or complexity of their language, and the focus of their attention. Even slightly modifying your rate of speech and/or style of language and actively noticing what interests them can help increase understanding in both directions. In written communication, pacing is achieved by incorporating some of the client's language, where appropriate, into correspondence.

An important part of meeting any client halfway is to **explain or present information in a way that clients can understand**: avoiding industry jargon as far as possible, pacing the client's capacity to understand and fully explaining any new piece of terminology. In written communications, it may be possible to ask a colleague to review a letter or email from the client's perspective.

Although an adviser's job is ultimately to provide advice, the quality of advice rests on the quality of information elicited from the client, only some of which is objective or factual, such as date of birth. Much of the information forming the basis of financial advice is more subjective, such as attitude to risk. It helps to have a fact-finding questionnaire with a series of questions; however, many clients experience a degree of anxiety when initially discussing personal finances and some of the questions may require more time to answer than imagined, because they may never have thought about them before. **Giving the client time to think through and fully express their responses** reassures clients that they are being taken seriously, and it reduces the risk that anxious or inexperienced clients **rush** their answers to some of the bigger questions.

How questions are asked matters a good deal in terms of the quality of information elicited. The three most common types of questions can all be used either effectively or unhelpfully, depending on context:

- **Closed questions** contain an embedded assumption, demand a **yes or no** response, and in doing so they close out the potential for another answer to emerge. For example, 'Do you want to retire at 60?' may lead a client to conclude that only one retirement age is possible. Closed questions are best used on a limited basis.
- **Open questions** minimise assumptions and leave the window open for clients to express their own views, leading to better quality information. 'Do you have a retirement age in mind?' offers the client greater freedom and accuracy of response.
- **Either/or question**s are sometimes known as **double binds** because they offer only two alternatives. These questions can be highly manipulative. An unscrupulous adviser may ask, *'Would you prefer fund A or fund B?'* where either could generate more commission than average for the adviser, and the client is tricked into accepting one of them in the absence of wider choice. Effectively, double binds offer false choice and should be avoided wherever possible.

When the information has been collected, it is vital to ensure that the adviser and client have shared their perceptions, in order to minimise the risk of misperception or misinformation. This can be achieved in a number of ways:

- **Paraphrasing** – summarising information in one's own words, verbally or in writing, in order to check essential facts or understanding. This can be important where a lengthy discussion may have yielded a lot of detail and the adviser needs to ensure that the salient facts have been captured: *'So the important aspects for me to bear in mind here are as follows…'*
- **Clarifying** – checking for accuracy of fact or interpretation where there may otherwise be scope for doubt and hence inaccuracy. Clarifying is a form of summarising which is preceded by a question such as *'Do you mind clarifying…Can I just check whether I have this right?'* This serves as an important final check, while letting the client know that you are prepared to listen again if necessary.
- **Asking the client to confirm their understanding**, in their own words. This is very important if the adviser has explained concepts or information which may be new or difficult to grasp. While an expert may be fluent in the meaning of terminology such as **short sale** or **sub-prime**, clients may struggle or merely pretend to understand. Clearly this is not about **examining** their financial wisdom, but rather about ensuring that they have grasped salient facts.

Finally, memory is now known to be more fallible than many people are willing to accept. **Keeping accurate notes or recordings of meetings and interviews** is an important adjunct to maintaining an accurate picture on which to base recommendations and ultimately decisions.

## 9.2 Professional and Best Practice

### Learning Objective

10.10 Client interaction:

10.10.3 Apply relevant principles, rules and sound judgment in working within the scope of authorisation, professional competence and job description

10.10.4 Apply relevant principles, rules and sound judgment when monitoring and reviewing clients' plans and circumstances, taking into account relevant changes

This manual has provided a detailed and thorough overview of the regulations, regulatory guidance, ethical and professional principles and should enable an adviser to practise competently and with integrity within the scope of their authorised role and job description. It is incumbent on members of any profession to maintain their knowledge and expertise through regular CPD; therefore this examination is an important foundation stone in the building of a career in finance.

It is beyond the scope of this workbook to explore the framework for financial advice in terms of the steps typically undertaken to provide an advisory service to clients. However, it is important to keep in mind that the **foundation stone** of this module sits at the heart of the fiduciary obligations to clients and how these are implemented.

One of the key aspects of an advisory role is that clients can differ in how they make use of professional advice. Some clients may only require a very brief and focused service, while others may require a professional adviser over a lengthy period of time. Each deserves similar levels of professionalism, respect and care. Maintaining high standards over time, every time, also requires methods of working that can appropriately support and move with change.

Best practice is about working beyond minimal compliance or having an armchair understanding of ethics. It is about being motivated by excellence, in such a way that personal qualities such as positive motivation and self-discipline lead to better client outcomes and greater career satisfaction for their advisers.

Examples of best practice include:

- Maintaining objectivity: forming evidence-based conclusions, minimising personal assumptions, and strong self-management (of time, emotions and own preferences).
- Ensuring that you fully explain the basis of your recommendations, both in terms of how they are suitable in relation to what the client has asked for, and their attitude to risk and any other constraints.
- Explaining to new clients the process, roles and responsibilities, and limits of service provision.
- Ensuring that your recommendations are individually tailored according to the clients' own preferences, needs and attitude to risk.
- Being systematic; for example, undertaking regular reviews of high risk products, and keeping accurate, up-to-date records.
- Keeping up-to-date: for example, monitoring information on a regular basis to identify any trends, or having a **watch list** of investments that you have already researched yourself.

- Understanding products and investments well enough to be able to explain them to a wide variety of clients.
- Keeping a calendar of review or key dates, and helping to develop productive meetings with clients by setting a shared agenda.
- Paying attention to client concerns before they become urgent issues.
- Presenting a balanced explanation of products – advantages and drawbacks – especially if there are potential suitability issues.
- Telling them **what it is, not what it isn't**. Presenting concepts in ways that are easy for clients to comprehend. Helping clients to become more knowledgeable about their finances.

By now, you should also be able to identify the kinds of inappropriate action (including inaction) to avoid and the **slippery slope** of consequences: rule breaches, unethical practice, poor professionalism or indeed any combination with ramifications not just for the individual adviser, but also for the firm.

## 9.3 The Consequences of Unethical Behaviour

### Learning Objective

10.10 Client interaction:

10.10.5 Apply an understanding of the potential outcomes of unethical sales practices, investment activity, abuse of bankruptcy and other unethical practice in terms of multiple and systemic risks, reputational risk and damage to public confidence

Finally, we will look at the interaction of sales targets, bonus structures and even the need for a person to keep their job by achieving targets, which can lead to unethical sales practices.

An example follows.

### Case Study

***A new customer presents a tempting opportunity for an adviser to achieve his sales target and win a valuable incentive.***

A private bank offers a range of its own investment products exclusively to its clients, who are mainly high net worth individuals living in the UK. It positions itself as a high-quality holistic adviser and devotes considerable resources to maintaining a well-trained, competent sales force. It prides itself on its exclusivity, the quality of its advisers and the fact that it offers innovative investment products to its private clients.

The bank's compliance department has, in conjunction with senior management and the product development team, imposed relatively tight restrictions on the sale of these funds, as they only have quarterly liquidity, and they are valued only after any sales or purchases have been made.

Advisers have to demonstrate that any proposed investment does not exceed a certain proportion of the client's overall investments, and also to demonstrate that the potential client has alternative liquidity available in the event that they may not be able to realise their investment.

# FCA Conduct of Business Fair Treatment and Client Money Protection

As demand for these funds has increased, more and more pressure has been applied by the bank's advisers, and by the product development team, to relax the restrictions; over time they have been loosened. Now, the bank's senior management, convinced that hedge funds sales are a way to encourage clients to stay with the firm and also to provide a good source of upfront income to the firm, is demanding more and more sales from the bank's advisers.

Advisers' compensation has always taken the form of a salary- and performance-related bonus but, following a recent takeover, everyone has been re-papered. The incentive structure has been changed to a lower basic but higher results-based compensation and there is a suspicion amongst some observers and staff that this has led to a lowering of standards.

The bank's management now uses competitions and league tables to incentivise its employees, by naming and shaming those advisers who are not reaching their targets. The advisers who make the biggest sales are rewarded with high-profile weekend breaks; those who fail to make their targets are publicly identified.

Following the introduction of the incentives, advisers have sought to put more and more of their clients' money into the funds and capacity has been reached in several of the existing funds. As a result, the bank's product development team has created more and more funds, with increasingly esoteric strategies, and the bank's compliance department is expected to relax the guidelines for clients' exposure to hedge funds.

The advisers, faced with another competition that will see ten of them sent on an all-expenses paid trip to the Monaco Grand Prix, and with an eye on the league table that has just been published on the bank's intranet, are preparing to promote the bank's BRIC long/short fund to their private clients.

One adviser has been with the bank for five years and has always been considered to be in the top half of the performance table. He has been told by his manager that he is expected to put £10 million of client money into the new fund.

Although a number of his existing clients have purchased every fund that has been launched to date, currently he is struggling to make his target and his manager has expressed disappointment, telling him that the bank expects more, adding that he is letting down the whole team.

The bank's senior management believes that it is on to a winner with its hedge funds, and the parent company is delighted with the income that the bank is now providing. How can they stop themselves from getting carried away with this strategy, if indeed they should?

## The Dilemma

- The adviser goes to a meeting with a new potential client, who has a substantial inheritance of £2 million to invest, but apparently has little investment knowledge, and he considers it unlikely that the client would say no to a persuasive argument. He is keen to win a place on the trip to Monaco and has the presentation for the BRIC long/short fund on his laptop.
- He meets the customer and his preconceptions regarding his investment knowledge are confirmed when the customer says that he has heard a lot about hedge funds, and friends have told him that they are the way to make money, so he wants to invest heavily in them.
- This could be just what he needs to help him on his way to Monaco.
- What should he do?

In September 2012 the then regulator, the FSA, published a report on the findings of a thematic review into financial incentives for retail sales staff. This report showed that most firms had incentive schemes that were likely to drive mis-selling, without effective controls in place to manage the risks. The report highlighted areas of concern and provided draft guidance for firms that was finalised in January 2013.

The FCA made it clear that it expects firms to:

- consider if their incentive schemes increased the risk of mis-selling and, if so, how
- review whether their governance and controls were adequate, and
- take action to address any inadequacies.

They also said that they would undertake follow-up work to assess how firms had responded, leaving open the possibility to strengthen their rules.

The FCAs intervention to date has resulted in significant change, increased awareness and focus on financial incentives.

The majority of the largest UK based retail banks have either replaced or made significant changes to their incentive schemes to reduce risk to consumers. They have also improved their controls.

Nearly all other firms also appear to have considered their guidance and many have made changes or improvements. The level of engagement and change was less at the smallest firms.

However, there is still work to be done. The FCA estimates that around one in ten of the firms with sales teams had higher-risk incentive scheme features where it appeared they were not managing the risk properly at the time of the FCA's assessment.

The FCA identified common areas where firms may need to do more to manage incentive risks effectively, in particular:

- checking for spikes or trends in the sales patterns of individuals to identify areas of increased risk;
- doing more to monitor poor behaviour in face-to-face sales conversations;
- managing the risks in discretionary incentive schemes and balanced scorecards, including the risk that discretion could be misused;
- monitoring non-advised sales to ensure staff who are incentivised to sell do not give personal recommendations;
- improving oversight of incentives used by appointed representatives;
- recognising that remuneration that is effectively 100% variable pay based on sales increases the risk of mis-selling and managing this risk.

# Summary of this Chapter

You should have an understanding and knowledge of the following after reading this chapter:

- Firms subject to COBS:
  - the importance of location;
  - eligible counterparties.
- The interaction with electronic media.
- Inducements and payments are permitted.
- Using client dealing commissions to purchase services.
- The financial promotions rules:
  - what is permitted;
  - the exclusions and exemptions.
- Client categorisation requirements.
- Conflict of interest:
  - margining and disclosing;
  - in relation to investment research.
- Fair treatment of customers:
  - best execution;
  - churning and switching.
- Advising and selling proactives:
  - suitability and appropriateness.
- Client assets.
- Reporting to clients.

# End of Chapter Questions

Think of an answer for each question and refer to the appropriate section for confirmation.

1. What activities are subject to COBS rules?
   *Answer reference: Section 1.1.2*

2. Are COBS rules disapplied for ECP business?
   *Answer reference: Section 1.1.3*

3. What is the impact of location on the application of the COBS rules?
   *Answer reference: Section 1.1.4*

4. What activities are subject to the recording of telephone lines?
   *Answer reference: Section 1.2.1*

5. What payments are permitted under the inducements rules?
   *Answer reference: Section 1.3*

6. What goods or services are permitted to be supplied under a dealing commission agreement?
   *Answer reference: Section 1.4*

7. What two principles are exemplified by the financial promotion rules?
   *Answer reference: Section 2.1.1*

8. What is the purpose of the financial promotion rules?
   *Answer reference: Section 2.1.1*

9. What types of communication are subject to the fair, clear and not misleading communication rule?
   *Answer reference: Section 2.1.2*

10. Does COBS apply to appointed representatives?
    *Answer reference: Section 2.1.5*

11. What are the main exemptions to the financial promotion rules?
    *Answer reference: Section 2.2*

12. What information must a direct offer contain?
    *Answer reference: Section 2.4*

13. What are eligible counterparties?
    *Answer reference: Section 3.2*

14. What are the notification requirements to a client on their client categorisation?
    *Answer reference: Section 3.4*

## FCA Conduct of Business Fair Treatment and Client Money Protection

15. What are the criteria for opting a retail client up to a professional client status?
   *Answer reference: Section 3.5.1*

17. What are the FCA's new adviser charging rules, and who do they apply to?
   *Answer reference: Section 4.2.1*

18. What is TCF and who does it apply to?
   *Answer reference: Section 4.1*

19. What types of conflicts do firms face?
   *Answer reference: Section 5.1*

20. What should a firm's conflicts policy contain?
   *Answer reference: Section 5.3*

21. What is the purpose of the best execution requirements?
   *Answer reference: Section 6.3*

22. What are the rules on churning and who do they apply to?
   *Answer reference: Section 6.7*

23. When is a firm required to assess suitability on a client?
   *Answer reference: Section 7.2*

24. What information does a firm need in order to assess suitability on a client?
   *Answer reference: Section 7.3*

25. What activities do the rules on appropriateness cover, and when is an assessment not required?
   *Answer reference: Sections 7.4, 7.5*

26. What is the purpose of the client money and custody rules?
   *Answer reference: Section 8.1*

27. To what business activities do the client assets rules not apply?
   *Answer reference: Section 8.4*

28. Looking at the case studies, what considerations or tools allow you to judge whether a course of action is ethical?
   *Answer reference: Section 9*

29. Think of an example where a person acting strictly in accordance with the FCA rules, nevertheless displays a lack of integrity.
   *Answer reference: Whole Chapter*

# Glossary and Abbreviations

# Glossary and Abbreviations

**Aggregation**

Multiple client orders are bulked together and processed as a single order. Customers must be notified of this procedure and its advantages and disadvantages.

**Allocation**

The division of a single aggregated order between two or more investors' accounts.

**Alternative Trading System (ATS)**

See *Multilateral Trading Facility (MTF)*.

**American Depositary Receipt (ADR)**

A negotiable instrument representing rights to a block of shares in (generally) a non-US company; the ADR is an acknowledgement from a bank or trust company that the block of shares is held by it for the account of its client. ADRs are a common means for non-US companies to have their shares traded in the US.

**Anti-Money Laundering (AML)**

See *Money Laundering*.

**Appointed Representative**

An appointed representative can be any type of person (ie, an individual or a company). It/he must be a party to a contract with an authorised person that allows it/him to carry on certain regulated activities – and the authorised person must have accepted responsibility for the conduct of these regulated activities in writing.

**Approved Persons**

Individuals who are approved by the Financial Conduct Authority (FCA) or the Prudential Regulation Authority (PRA) to undertake controlled functions. These individuals are required to comply with the FCA's Statements of Principle for Approved Persons and Code of Practice for Approved Persons.

**Authorisation**

The Financial Services and Markets Act (FSMA 2000) requires firms to obtain authorisation prior to conducting investment business. Authorisation is gained by receiving one or more Part 4A Permissions from the FCA and/or the PRA.

**Bank of England**

The UK's central bank which acts as the government's banker and determines interest rates via its Monetary Policy Committee (MPC).

**Base Rate**

The minimum rate at which banks will lend money to individuals. In the UK, this is set each month by the Monetary Policy Committee (MPC) at the Bank of England.

**Base Requirement**

Part of the financial resource requirement of an authorised firm.

**Best Execution**

Firms take into account not only price factors, but also such issues as costs, speed, likelihood of execution and settlement, and all these in the light of the size and nature of the deal, in determining the means of obtaining the best outcome for a client when executing his deal.

**Capital Adequacy Directive (CAD)**

A European directive that aims to establish uniform capital requirements for both banking firms and non-bank securities firms. See **Capital Requirements Directive (CRD)**.

**Capital Gains Tax (CGT)**

Tax paid on profits realised from selling assets. In the UK there is an annual exemption limit. CGT is paid at the investor's highest marginal tax rate, adjusted for losses and the holding period.

409

### Capital Requirements Directive (CRD)
Formerly known as the Capital Adequacy Directive (CAD), this sets out the financial rules for financial firms. It came into force from 1 January 2007 and applies to banks, building societies and most investment firms. The CRD has been implemented in the UK. The aim of the CRD is to ensure that firms hold adequate financial resources and have adequate systems and controls to prudently manage the business and the associated risks.

### Chinese Walls
Organisational barriers to the flow of information set up in large firms, to prevent the movement of confidential sensitive information between departments and to manage any potential conflicts of interest.

### Churning
Excessive trading by a broker in order to generate commission, regardless of the interests of the customer.

### Client
Individuals or firms that conduct business through an authorised person. Every client is either a customer (retail or professional) or an eligible counterparty.

### Client Assets
Securities or other assets held by a firm on behalf of its clients. The assets have to be kept separate (segregated) from the firm's own assets.

### Code of Practice for Approved Persons
A code established by the FCA/PRA with regard to the behaviour of Approved Persons. Compliance with the code will be an indication of whether or not an Approved Person has complied with the Statement of Principles for Approved Persons.

### Collective Investment Scheme (CIS)
Open-ended funds such as unit trusts and Open-Ended Investment Companies (OEICs), also known as Investment Companies with Variable Capital (ICVCs).

### Common Platform Firm
Firms subject to either of the Capital Requirements Directive (CRD) or the Markets in Financial Instruments Directive (MiFID).

### Compulsory Jurisdiction
The range of activities for which complaints fall compulsorily within the jurisdiction of the Financial Ombudsman Service (FOS).

### Conduct of Business Sourcebook (COBS) Rules
Rules made by the FCA under the Financial Services and Markets Act (FSMA 2000) dealing mainly with the relationship between an authorised firm and its clients.

### Consumer Prices Index (CPI)
Measure of inflation used in the UK economy. See also Harmonised Index of Consumer Prices.

### Contract for Differences (CFDs)
An investment instrument consisting of a contract under which the parties hope to make a profit (or avoid a loss) by reference to movements in the price of an underlying asset. The underlying asset does not change hands.

### Contracts of Insurance
Financial products specified by Part III of the Regulated Activities Order 2001, with two subdivisions: general and long-term insurance contracts.

### Controlled Functions
Certain roles within authorised firms for which the FCA/PRA requires the occupant to be approved (see Approved Persons).

### CREST

A recognised clearing house, CREST was the organisation in the UK that facilitated the clearing and settlement of trades in UK and Irish company shares, particularly in dematerialised form. As of 1 July 2007, CREST changed its operating and legal name to Euroclear UK & Ireland. The term CREST is still used for the clearing and settlement system itself.

### Criminal Justice Act (CJA) 1993

A substantial act which includes provisions relating to insider dealing, including a definition of that offence.

### Customer Function

The Controlled Function conducted by persons who interact with a firm's customers, such as an investment managers or an investment advisers.

### Data Protection Act 1998

Legislation governing how personal data should be held and processed and the rights of access to it.

### Debt Securities

Securities whereby the issuer acknowledges a loan made to it. The term includes instruments such as bonds, gilts, Treasury bills, certificates of deposit (CDs) and commercial paper.

### Defined Benefit (DB) Pension Scheme

Final salary pension which is paid as a percentage of the employee's final salary.

### Defined Contribution (DC) Pension Scheme

Money purchase pension that depends on the contributions made and the investment return. UK personal pensions and US 401(k) programmes are Defined Contribution (DC) schemes.

### Designated Investment Exchange (DIE)

An overseas exchange designated by the **FCA** as meeting certain standards of investor protection in terms of such criteria as market efficiency, transparency and liquidity.

### Designated Professional Body (DPB)

Professional bodies whose members are able to carry on limited financial services business without the need for authorisation from the FCA, providing that the limited financial services offered to clients are incidental to their main business. These are the professional bodies for lawyers, accountants, chartered surveyors, licensed conveyancers and actuaries.

### Directives

Legislation issued by the European Union to its member states requiring them to enact and implement local legislation.

### Directors' Model Code

The Model Code for directors of a listed company. This sets out standards of conduct for these people, adherence to which should avoid their falling foul of insider dealing legislation. For example, it stipulates that a company director should not deal in his company's shares without permission, and may only do so at certain times.

### Disclosure and Transparency Rules (DTR)

An FCA Sourcebook; the rules apply to issuers of securities on certain markets.

The aim of the Disclosure Rules is, in part, to implement the requirements of the Market Abuse Directive (MAD), and to make provisions to ensure that information relating to publicly listed securities is properly handled and disseminated. The aim of the Transparency Rules, in part, is to implement the requirements of the Transparency Directive and to ensure there is adequate transparency of and access to information in the UK financial markets.

### Durable Medium

Paper or any instrument which enables the recipient to store information addressed personally to them in a way accessible for future reference for a period of time adequate for the purposes of the information.

### Eligible Counterparty (ECP)
A client that under the Markets in Financial Instruments Directive (MiFID) client categorisations is either a per se eligible counterparty or an elective eligible counterparty.

### Euroclear UK & Ireland
A recognised clearing house, Euroclear UK & Ireland is the organisation in the UK that facilitates the clearing and settlement of trades in the UK and Irish company shares, particularly in dematerialised form. Prior to 1 July 2007, it was known as CREST.

### European Central Counterparty (EuroCCP)
A UK-incorporated Recognised Clearing House (RCH) regulated by the FCA.

### European Economic Area (EEA)
The EEA is the 28 member states of the European Union plus Norway, Iceland and Liechtenstein.

### Exempt Persons
Firms exempt from the need to be authorised to carry on regulated activities. The term includes bodies such as Recognised Investment Exchanges (RIEs) and Recognised Clearing Houses (RCHs).

### Financial Conduct Authority (FCA)
The Financial Conduct Authority (FCA) replaced the FSA as the body responsible for regulating conduct in retail and wholesale markets; supervising the trading infrastructure that supports those markets and for the prudential regulation of firms not prudentially regulated by the Prudential Regulation Authority (PRA).

### Financial Conduct Authority (FCA) Handbook
The document containing the FCA rules and guidance, with which authorised firms must comply. It is divided into a number of separate sourcebooks covering different subjects.

### Financial Ombudsman Service (FOS)
The body established to investigate and determine the outcome of complaints made by eligible complainants. **FOS** can make awards, when appropriate, up to a maximum of £150,000 plus costs.

### Financial Policy Committee (FPC)
The new regulatory structure in the UK includes the FPC which is part of the Bank of England. Its aim is to identify, monitor and take action to remove or reduce systems risk with a view to protecting and enhancing resilience of the UK financial system.

### Financial Resources Requirement (FRR)
The requirements as to the financial resources held by an FCA/PRA-authorised firm. The FRR is made up of primary and secondary requirements. The primary requirement addresses various standard sets of risks faced by a firm when undertaking business. The secondary requirement is set at the discretion of the FCA/PRA and covers its perception of the firm's additional risk.

### Financial Services Act 2012
The Financial Services Act 2012 is the primary legislation through the government-enacted reforms to the UK financial services regulatory structure. Its main role is to amend the Financial Services and Markets Act 2000 (FSMA) to establish the new regulators and to set out their additional powers. The new Financial Services Bill received Royal Assent on 19 December 2012.

### Financial Services and Markets Act (FSMA 2000)
The legislation that established the financial regulator (the FSA) and empowered it to regulate the financial services industry. The FSA was split in April 2013 – the FCA looks after conduct issues and the PRA looks after prudential issues.

## Financial Services and Markets Tribunal (FSMT)

See *Tax and Chancery Chamber of the Upper Tribunal*.

## Financial Services Authority (FSA)

The agency created by the Financial Services and Markets Act (FSMA 2000) to be the single financial regulator in the UK. In April 2013 it was split into two – the FCA looking after conduct issues and the PRA looking after prudential issues.

## Financial Services Compensation Scheme (FSCS)

Created to provide a safety net for customers in the case of firms that have ceased trading, and cannot meet their obligations to them.

## Financial Skills Partnership (FSP)

An independent, employer-led organisation, established in 2004 to provide strategic leadership for education, training and skills development for financial services, and more recently accountancy and finance, across the UK.

## Fit and Proper

Under the Financial Services and Markets Act (FSMA 2000), every firm conducting investment business must be fit and proper. The Act does not define the term; this is left to the FCA. This is also the minimum standard for becoming and remaining an approved person.

## Forward Rate Agreement (FRA)

An agreement to pay or receive, on an agreed future date, an amount calculated by reference to the difference between a fixed interest rate agreed at the outset, and a reference interest rate actually prevailing on a given future date for a given period.

## Future

A futures contract is a legally binding arrangement by which parties commit to buy/sell a standard quantity and (if applicable) quality of an asset from another party on a specified date in the **future**, but at a price agreed today. Because the price is agreed at the outset, the seller is protected from a fall in the price of the underlying asset in the intervening time period (and vice versa).

## Gilts

UK government securities. They may be for fixed terms or undated (eg, War Loan).

## Gross Domestic Product (GDP)

Measures the amount of goods and services produced each year. **GDP** measures the products made in the UK.

## Gross National Product (GNP)

GNP measures products and services made by UK companies worldwide.

## Harmonised Index of Consumer Prices (HICP)

Modern UK inflation indicator used by the Treasury as the formal yardstick. Also known in UK as Consumer Prices Index (CPI).

## Her Majesty's Revenue & Customs (HMRC)

The government department responsible for the administration and collection of tax in the UK, and the guidance notes on HM Treasury's rules for Individual Savings Accounts (ISAs). HMRC is the result of the merger of two formerly separate departments, Her Majesty's Customs & Excise and the Inland Revenue.

## Home State

The term used for the European Union (EU) country where a financial services firm conducting cross-border business is based.

**Host State**

The term used for a European Union (EU) country in which a financial services firm is doing business from elsewhere.

**Index-Linked Government Bonds**

Some issuers increase the coupon and redemption value in line with an inflation indicator. In the UK, index-linked gilts are linked to the RPIX. US index-linked T-bonds are linked to the Consumer Prices Index (CPI).

**Inside Information**

Information relating to a specific security, or an issuer, which is not publicly known and which would affect the price of the security if it was made public.

**Insider Dealing**

One of several offences created under the Criminal Justice Act (CJA) 1993 which may be committed by an insider in possession of unpublished price-sensitive information if he attempts to deal in affected securities, encourages others to deal, or passes the information on.

**Integration**

The third stage of Money Laundering; integration is the stage at which the laundered funds appear to be of legitimate provenance.

**InterContinentalExchange (ICE) Futures**

Formerly known as the International Petroleum Exchange (IPE). One of six Recognised Investment Exchanges (RIEs), ICE deals in futures for energy products, such as crude oil and gas, and also in new instruments such as carbon emission allowances.

**Investment Company with Variable Capital (ICVC)**

See *Open-Ended Investment Company (OEIC)*.

**Investment Services Directive (ISD)**

See *Markets in Financial Instruments Directive (MiFID)*.

**Joint Money Laundering Steering Group (JMLSG)**

A group whose membership is made up of 17 trade bodies in the financial services industry. The JMLSG has published guidance notes which set out how firms should interpret and implement the Money Laundering Regulations 2007. This guidance is not binding but, where there is a breach, compliance with the guidance is relevant to an enforcement court.

**Know Your Customer (KYC)**

The Money Laundering Regulations 2007 and the Financial Conduct Authority (FCA) Rules requiring firms to take sufficient steps, before taking on a customer, to satisfy themselves of the identity of that customer.

**Layering**

The second stage of Money Laundering, in which money or assets are typically passed through a series of transactions to obscure their true origin.

**LCH.Clearnet**

An independent clearing house which acts as central counterparty for trades executed on Euronext.liffe, the London Metal Exchange (LME) and InterContinental Exchange (ICE) Futures, and for certain trades executed on the London Stock Exchange (LSE). It is a Recognised Clearing House (RCH).

**London Metal Exchange (LME)**

A recognised investment exchange (RIE). It is the market for trading contracts in base metals and some plastics.

**London Stock Exchange (LSE)**

The dominant UK market for trading in securities, especially shares and bonds. The LSE is a Recognised Investment Exchange (RIE).

## Market Abuse

A set of offences introduced under the Financial Services and Markets Act (FSMA 2000), judged against what a regular user would view as a failure to observe required market standards. The offences include abuse of information, misleading the market, and distortion of the market.

## Market Maker

A firm which quotes bid and offer prices for a named list of securities in the market. Such a firm is normally under an obligation to make a price in any security for which it is Market Maker at all times.

## Markets in Financial Instruments Directive (MiFID)

A European Union (EU) directive which replaced the Investment Services Directive (ISD) on 1 November 2007. It allows firms authorised in one member state to provide/offer financial services to customers in another member state, subject to some restrictions.

## Misleading Statement

The term used for false information given about an investment, in order to (or with the effect of) affecting its value – a criminal act under Section 89-92 of the Financial Services Act 2012 and a potential form of market abuse.

## Monetary Policy Committee (MPC)

The committee chaired by the governor of the Bank of England which sets sterling interest rates.

## Money Laundering

The process whereby criminals attempt to conceal the true origins of the proceeds of their criminal activities, and to give them the appearance of legitimacy by introducing them into the mainstream financial system.

## Money Laundering Regulations 2007

The regulations under which authorised firms, and some other businesses, are required to comply with certain administrative obligations in order to prevent their firms/organisation from being used for Money Laundering. The obligations include record-keeping, identification of clients and appointment of a Nominated Officer (NO) to receive suspicion reports, and staff training. Failure to comply may result in a fine and/or imprisonment.

## Money Laundering Reporting Officer (MLRO)

A senior employee who is responsible for assessing internal suspicion reports, and, if these appear justified, reporting those suspicions to the National Crime Agency (NCA).

## Multilateral Trading Facility (MTF)

A system operated by authorised firms which brings together multiple buyers and sellers of securities, but which is not an exchange. Prior to 1 November 2007 (when Markets in Financial Instruments Directive (MiFID) provisions came into force), most MTFs were operated as Alternative Trading Systems (ATSs).

## National Crime Agency (NCA)

The law enforcement agency to which suspicions of money laundering must be reported by a firm's Money Laundering Reporting Officer (MLRO).

## Nominated Officer (NO)

A term for the officer who is required to receive a firm's internal suspicion reports under Proceeds of Crime Act 2002 (POCA), the Terrorism Act and the Money Laundering Regulations; in practice, usually the same individual as the Money Laundering Reporting Officer (MLRO).

## Nominee

The party which, under a legal arrangement, holds assets in its own name on behalf of the true beneficial owner.

**NYSE Euronext Liffe**

A Recognised Investment Exchange (RIE) for Futures and traded Options.

**Open-Ended Investment Company (OEIC)**

A Collective Investment Scheme (CIS) constituted as an open-ended company. This means that its share capital can expand or contract to meet investor supply and demand. It is also referred to as an Investment Company with Variable Capital (ICVC).

**Option**

An option gives the holder the right (but not the obligation) to buy or sell a fixed quantity of an underlying asset on, or before, a specified date in the **future**. There are two basic types of **option** – puts and calls. The holder of a call **option** has the right to buy the underlying asset at a given price. The holder of a put **option** has the right to sell the underlying asset at a given price.

**Part 4A Permission**

The specific activity which an authorised firm is permitted to carry on. It is so called because Part 4A permissions are granted by the Financial Conduct Authority (FCA) and/or the Prudential Regulation Authority (PRA) under Part IV of the Financial Services and Markets Act (FSMA 2000).

**Passporting**

The method by which firms authorised in one European Union (EU) member state are – under the Markets in Financial Instruments Directive (MiFID) – permitted to carry on regulated financial services activities in another state without the need to become fully authorised in that other state.

**Placement**

The first stage of Money Laundering, in which money is introduced into the financial system.

**Principles for Businesses**

11 key principles established by the FCA which must be observed by authorised firms. These principles are detailed in the FCA's Handbook.

**Proceeds of Crime Act 2002 (POCA)**

Legislation which contains, among other things, Anti-Money Laundering provisions.

**Prohibition Order**

An order which may be exercised by the Financial Services Authority (FSA) under powers given to it under Section 56 of the Financial Services and Markets Act (FSMA 2000). Such an order prohibits the individual in connection with whom it is granted from carrying out particular Controlled Functions on the grounds that he is not Fit and Proper.

**Prudential Regulation Authority (PRA)**

The Prudential Regulation Authority (PRA), which is a subsidiary of the Bank of England, is responsible for the prudential regulation of financial firms, including banks, investment banks, building societies and insurance companies.

**Public Interest Disclosure Act (PIDA) 1998**

An act which, among other things, provides protection for employees who, in good faith, disclose suspicions of wrongdoing within an organisation. See also Whistleblowing.

**Recognised Clearing House (RCH)**

A term used to denote those clearing houses recognised by the Financial Conduct Authority (FCA) as providing appropriate standards of protection in the provision of clearing and settlement facilities to certain markets. LCH.Clearnet and Euroclear UK & Ireland are two examples of the five organisations granted this status.

### Recognised Investment Exchange (RIE)

A term used to denote those UK exchanges which operate markets in investments, meeting certain standards set by the Financial Conduct Authority (FCA).

### Recognised Overseas Investment Exchange (ROIE)

An overseas exchange offering membership or providing facilities within the UK, and having been recognised by the Financial Conduct Authority (FCA) as meeting appropriate standards of investor protection.

### Regular User

A hypothetical person regularly using a particular market. It is through the eyes of the Regular User that behaviour is assessed for determining whether it meets the standards required under the legacy offences of the Market Abuse regime.

### Regulated Activities

Activities for which authorisation from the Financial Conduct Authority (FCA) (or exemption from the need for that authorisation) is required. Regulated Activities are defined in relation both to the activities themselves, and to the investments to which they relate.

### Regulated Activities Order 2001 (as amended)

The statutory instrument which defines the range of Regulated Activities.

### Regulatory Decisions Committee (RDC)

A committee of the Financial Conduct Authority (FCA) which is responsible for disciplinary decisions.

### Retail Prices Index (RPI)

Measure of cost of living (inflation) in the UK (usually use RPIx which excludes mortgage interest rates).

### Significant Influence Function (SIF)

Certain functions carried out by directors and other senior personnel. In the Approved Persons regime, these comprise the governing functions, the required Controlled Functions, the systems and controls functions and the significant management functions.

### Stabilisation

The activity of supporting the price of a new issue of securities or bonds in order to minimise the volatility that can sometimes arise with new issues.

### Statements of Principle for Approved Persons

A set of principles established by the Financial Conduct Authority (FCA) with which Approved Persons are required to comply at all times.

### Stock Exchange Trading Service (SETS)

The London Stock Exchange (LSE) electronic order book system for UK blue chip securities.

### Tax and Chancery Chamber of the Upper Tribunal (Upper Tribunal)

The Upper Tribunal took over the role of the Financial Services and Markets Tribunal (FSMT) on 6 April 2010. It is independent of the Financial Conduct Authority (FCA) and is appointed by the government's Ministry of Justice (formerly the Department of Constitutional Affairs).

### Threshold Conditions

The conditions which a firm must meet before the Financial Conduct Authority (FCA) will authorise or continue to authorise it.

### Tipping Off

An offence established under various pieces of Anti-Money Laundering and terrorist financing legislation. It involves disclosing the fact that an investigation is, or is likely to be, under way, if that disclosure may imperil any such investigation.

### Training and Competence (T&C) Sourcebook

Part of the Business Standards block of the Financial Conduct Authority (FCA) Handbook which sets out the FCA's requirements in connection with all staff (but especially in connection with people employed in Controlled Functions). The Sourcebook includes commitments which firms must make in connection with training and competence, including with regard to staff training, maintenance of competence, supervision and record-keeping.

### Transparency Rules

See *Disclosure and Transparency Rules*.

### Treasury

The government department that is responsible for formulating and implementing the government's financial and economic policies. Among other things this means that it is responsible for financial services regulation in the UK.

### Trust

A means of holding assets (legally owned by Trustees) on behalf of underlying beneficial owners. Investment portfolios within a Trust may be professionally managed, eg, charitable Trust, Unit Trust. Governed by the Trustee Act 2000.

### Trustee

A person or organisation who is the legal owner of assets held in Trust for someone else. The Trustee is responsible for safeguarding the assets, complying with the Trust deed and (if the trust is a Unit Trust) overseeing the activities of the Unit Trust's manager.

### UK Listing Authority (UKLA)

Under European Union (EU) regulations each member state must appoint a competent authority for the purpose of listing securities. The competent authority for listing in the UK is the Financial Conduct Authority (FCA); in this capacity, the FCA is called the UK Listing Authority.

### Undertakings for Collective Investment in Transferable Securities (UCITS)

A type of Collective Investment Scheme (CIS) established under the UCITS Directives. These directives are intended to harmonise European Union (EU) member states' laws so as to allow for the marketing of UCITS schemes across EU borders.

### Unit Trust

A form of collective investment constituted under a Trust deed. Unit Trusts are open-ended investments; therefore the underlying value of the assets is always directly represented by the total number of units issued, multiplied by the unit price, less the transaction or management fee charged and any other associated costs. Each fund has a specified investment objective to determine the management aims and limitations.

### Upper Tribunal

See Tax and Chancery Chamber of the Upper Tribunal.

### Warrant

An investment instrument giving the holder the right to buy a set number of the underlying equities at a predetermined price on specified dates, or at any time up to the end of a predetermined time period. **Warrants** are usually issued by companies or by securities houses.

### Whistleblowing

The term used when an individual raises concerns over potential wrongdoing. The Public Interest Disclosure Act 1998 provides some statutory protections for whistleblowers.

# Glossary and Abbreviations

**ABI**
Association of British Insurers

**ACD**
Authorised Corporate Director

**ADR**
American Depositary Receipt

**AIF**
Alternative Investment Fund

**AIFM**
Alternative Investment Fund Manager

**AIFMD**
Alternative Investment Fund Mangers' Directive

**AIM**
Alternative Investment Market

**AMC**
Annual Management Charge

**AMEX**
American Stock Exchange

**AML**
Anti-Money Laundering

**APA**
Approved Publication Arrangement

**APER**
Statements of Principle and Code of Practice for Approved Persons

**APR**
Annual Percentage Rate

**ARROW**
Advanced Risk-Responsive Operating frameWork

**ASPF**
Alternatively Secured Pension Fund

**ASX**
Australian Stock Exchange

**ATS**
Alternative Trading System

**AUT**
Authorised Unit Trust

**AUTH**
Authorisation Sourcebook

**BBA**
British Bankers' Association

**BCBS**
Basel Committee on Banking Supervision

**BCD**
Banking Consolidation Directive

**BIPRU**
Prudential Handbook for Banks, Building Societies and Investment Firms

**BMSA**
Business Model and Strategy Analysis

**BOE**
Bank of England

**BP**
Basis Point

**BRIC**
Brazil, Russia, India and China

**CAD**
Capital Adequacy Directive

**CASS**
Client Assets Sourcebook

**CBRC**
China Banking Regulatory Commission

**CBU**
Conduct of Business Unit

**CC**
Charity Commission

**CCP**
Central Counterparty

**CCX**
Chicago Climate Exchange

**CD**
Certificate of Deposit

**CDD**
Customer Due Diligence

**CEO**
Chief Executive Officer

**CEOP**
Child Exploitation and Online Protection Centre

**CESR**
Committee of European Securities Regulators

**CF**
Controlled Function

**CFD**
Contract For Difference

**CFPB**
Consumer Financial Protection Bureau

**CGT**
Capital Gains Tax

**CII**
Critical Illness Cover

**CIRC**
China Insurance Regulatory Commission

**CIS**
Collective Investment Scheme

**CISI**
Chartered Institute for Securities & Investment

**CJA**
Criminal Justice Act 1993

**CMAR**
Client Money and Assets Return

**CME**
Chicago Mercantile Exchange

**CML**
Council of Mortgage Lenders

**COBS**
Conduct Of Business Sourcebook

**COLL**
Collective Investment Schemes Sourcebook

**COMP**
Compensation Sourcebook

**COND**
Threshold Conditions

**CP**
Consultation Paper

**CPAAOB**
Certified Public Accountants and Auditing Oversight Board

**CPB**
Capital Planning Buffer

**CPD**
Continuing Professional Development

**CPI**
Consumer Prices Index

# Glossary and Abbreviations

**CPS**
Crown Prosecution Service

**CRD**
Capital Requirements Directive

**CRO**
Chief Risk Officer

**CRR**
Capital Requirements Regulations

**CSRC**
China Securities Regulatory Commission

**CTA**
Counter-Terrorism Act

**CTF**
i.     Child Trust Fund
ii.    Counter-Terrorism Financing

**CVA**
Company Voluntary Arrangement

**DEPP**
Decisions Procedure and Penalties Manual

**DIE**
Designated Investment Exchange

DISP

Dispute Resolution: Complaints

**DMD**
Distance Marketing Directive

**DMO**
Debt Management Office

**DPA**
Data Protection Act

**DPB**
Designated Professional Body

**DTCC**
Depository Trust and Clearing Corporation

**DTR**
Disclosure and Transparency Rules

**DVP**
Delivery versus Payment

**DWF**
Discount Window Facility

**DWP**
Department for Work and Pensions

**EAD**
Eligible Assets Directive

**EBA**
European Banking Authority

**EBRD**
European Bank for Reconstruction and Development

**EC**
European Commission

**ECB**
European Central Bank

**ECOFIN**
European Council Of Finance Ministers

**ECON**
Economic and Monetary Affairs

**ECP**
Eligible Counterparty

**EEA**
European Economic Area

**EG**
Enforcement Guide

421

**EIB**
European Investment Bank

**EIOPA**
European Insurance and Occupational Pensions Authority

**EMIR**
European Markets Infrastructure Regulation

**EPOA**
Enduring Power Of Attorney

**ESA**
European Supervisory Authorities

**ESCB**
European System of Central Banks

**ESFS**
European System of Financial Supervision

**ESMA**
European Securities and Markets Authority

**ESRB**
European Systemic Risk Board

**EU**
European Union

**EUROCCP**
European Central Counterparty

**FATF**
Financial Action Task Force

**FCA**
Financial Conduct Authority

**FINRA**
Financial Industry Regulatory Authority

**FIT**
Fit and Proper Test for Approved Persons

**FOF**
Fund Of Funds

**FOS**
Financial Ombudsman Service

**FPC**
Financial Policy Committee

**FPO**
Financial Promotion Order

**FRC**
Financial Reporting Council

**FSA**
Financial Services Authority

**FSAP**
i.   Financial Services Action Plan
ii.  Financial Services Agency (Japan)

**FSAVC**
Freestanding Additional Voluntary Contribution

**FSB**
Financial Stability Board

**FSCS**
Financial Services Compensation Scheme

**FSF**
i.   Financial Stability Forum
ii.  Firm Systematic Framework

**FSMA**
Financial Services and Markets Act (2000)

**FSMT**
Financial Services and Markets Tribunal

**FSP**
Financial Skills Partnership

# Glossary and Abbreviations

**FTSE**
Financial Times Stock Exchange

**FX**
Foreign Exchange

**G20**
Group of 20

**GABRIEL**
GAthering Better Regulatory Information ELectronically

**GDP**
Gross Domestic Product

**GDR**
Global Depositary Receipts

**GEM**
Growth Enterprise Market

**GENPRU**
General Prudential Sourcebook

**GNP**
Gross National Product

**GPP**
Group Personal Pension

**HFT**
High Frequency Trading

**HICP**
Harmonised Index of Consumer Prices

**HKEx**
Hong Kong Exchanges

**HKFE**
Hong Kong Futures Exchange

**HKFR**
Hong Kong Futures Exchange

**HKMA**
Hong Kong Monetary Authority

**HMRC**
Her Majesty's Revenue & Customs

**HMT**
Her Majesty's Treasury

**IBE**
Institute of Business Ethics

**IBRD**
International Bank for Reconstruction and Development

**ICAAP**
Internal Capital Adequacy Assessment Processes

**ICAEW**
Institute of Chartered Accountants of England and Wales

**ICE**
InterContinentalExchange

**ICO**
Information Commissioner

**ICT**
Information Communication Technology

**ICVC**
Investment Company with Variable Capital

**IFA**
Independent Financial Adviser

**IHT**
Inheritance Tax

**ILAA**
Individual Liquidity Adequacy Assessment

**ILAS**
Individual Liquidity Adequacy Standards

**IMF**
International Monetary Fund

**IPAs**
Individual Pension Account

**IPE**
International Petroleum Exchange

**IPI**
Income Protection Insurance

**IPRU-INV**
Interim Prudential (Sourcebook for Investment Business)

**ISA**
Individual Savings Account

**ISD**
Investment Services Directive

**ISDX**
ICAP Securities and Derivatives Exchange

**ISE**
International Securities Exchange

**IT**
Information Technology

**IVA**
Individual Voluntary Arrangement

**JMLSG**
Joint Money Laundering Steering Group

**JSDA**
Japan Securities Dealers Association

**KFD**
Key Features Document

**KYC**
Know Your Customer

**LBIE**
Lehman Brothers International (Europe)

**LCH**
London Clearing House

**LEL**
Lower Earnings Limit

**LIFFE**
London International Financial Futures and Options Exchange

**LLP**
Limited Liability Partnership

**LME**
London Metal Exchange

**LPOA**
Lasting Power of Attorney

**LSE**
London Stock Exchange

**M&A**
Mergers and Acquisitions

**MAD**
Market Abuse Directive

**MAR**
Market Conduct Sourcebook

**MAS**
i.   Money Advice Service
ii.  Monetary Authority of Singapore

**MCOB**
Mortgages and Home Finance Conduct of Business Sourcebook

424

## Glossary and Abbreviations

**MD**
Managing director

**MI**
Management Information

**MiFID**
Markets in Financial Instruments Directive

**MiFIR**
Markets in Financial Instruments Regulation

**ML**
Money Laundering

**MLRO**
Money Laundering Reporting Officer

**MOU**
Memorandum of Understanding

**MPC**
Monetary Policy Committee

**MTF**
Multilateral Trading Facility

**NAO**
National Audit Office

**NASD**
National Association of Securities Dealers

**NASDAQ**
National Association of Securities Dealers Automated Quotations

**NCA**
National Crime Agency

**NCB**
National Central Bank

**NED**
Non-Executive Directors

**NEET**
Not in Education, Employment or Training

**NI**
i. National Insurance
ii. National Income

**NIC**
National Insurance Contribution

**NO**
Nominated Officer

**NS&I**
National Savings and Investments

**NURS**
Non UCITS Retail Scheme

**NYSE**
New York Stock Exchange

**OCC**
Office of the Comptroller of the Currency

**OCI**
Office of the Commissioner of Insurance

**OECD**
Organisation for Economic Co-operation and Development

**OEIC**
Open-Ended Investment Company

**OFT**
Office of Fair Trading

**OMO**
Open Market Operation

**OPG**
Office of the Public Guardian

425

| | |
|---|---|
| **OTC** Over-the-Counter | **PPE** Primary Pooling Event |
| **OTF** Organised Trading Facility | **PPI** Payment Protection Insurance |
| **OTS** Office of Thrift Supervision | **PRA** Prudential Regulation Authority |
| **PA** Personal Assistant | **PRIN** Principles for Businesses |
| **PAYE** Pay As You Earn | **PSNCR** Public Sector Net Cash Requirement |
| **PBOC** People's Bank of China | **QCF** Qualification and Credit Framework |
| **PBU** Prudential Business Unit | **QE** Quantitative Easing |
| **PCAOB** Public Company Accounting Oversight Board | **QIS** Qualified Investor Scheme |
| **PDMR** Person Discharging Management Responsibility | **RAO** Regulated Activities Order |
| **PEP** Politically Exposed Person | **RASFS** Revised Approach to Small Firms Supervision |
| **PERG** Perimeter Guidance | **RBS** Royal Bank of Scotland |
| **PIDA** Public Interest Disclosure Act (1998) | **RCH** Recognised Clearing House |
| **PII** Professional Indemnity Insurance | **RDC** Regulatory Decisions Committee |
| **POA** Power of Attorney | **RDR** Retail Distribution Review |
| **POCA** Proceeds of Crime Act (2002) | **RICS** Royal Institution of Chartered Surveyors |

## Glossary and Abbreviations

**RIE**
Recognised Investment Exchange

**RIS**
Regulatory Information Service

**RNS**
Regulatory New Service

**ROIE**
Recognised Overseas Investment Exchange

**RTGS**
Real-Time Gross Settlement

**S&P**
Standard & Poor's

**S2P**
State Second Pension

**SAR**
Special Administration Regime

**SEC**
Securities and Exchange Commission

**SEHK**
Stock Exchange of Hong Kong

**SEP**
Supervisory Enforcement Programme

**SERPS**
State Earnings-Related Pension Scheme

**SESC**
Securities and Exchange Surveillance Committee

**SFC**
Securities and Futures Commission

**SGX**
Singapore Exchange Securities

**SIC**
Securities Industry Council

**SICAV**
Société d'Investissement à Capital Variable

**SIF**
Significant Influence Function

**SIPP**
Self-Invested Personal Pension

**SIV**
Structured Investment Vehicle

**SME**
Small- and Medium-Sized Enterprises

**SQL**
Structured Query Language

**SOCA**
Serious Organised Crime Agency

**SOCPA**
Serious Organised Crime Police Act 2005

**SPS**
Statements of Professional Standing

**SRA**
Sector Risk Assessment

**SRO**
Self-Regulatory Organisation

**SRR**
Special Resolution Regime

**SSP**
Statutory Sick Pay

**SUP**
Supervision Sourcebook

**SYSC**
Senior Management Arrangements, Systems and Controls Sourcebook

**T&C**
Training and Competence

**TC**
Training and Competence Sourcebook

**TCF**
Treating Customers Fairly

**TD**
Transparency Directive

**TER**
Total Expense Ratio

**TF**
Terrorist Financing

**UCITS**
Undertaking for Collective Investments in Transferable Securities

**UEL**
Upper Earnings Limit

**UKLA**
United Kingdom Listing Authority

**UN**
United Nations

**UNFCOG**
Unfair Contract Terms Regulatory Guide

**VAT**
Value Added Tax

**VJ**
Voluntary Jurisdiction

**WOL**
Whole of Life

**WTO**
World Trade Organisation

# Syllabus Learning Map

# Syllabus Learning Map

| Syllabus Unit/ Element | | Chapter/ Section |
|---|---|---|
| **Element 1** | **The Financial Services Industry**<br>On completion, the candidate will be able to: | **Chapter 1** |
| **1.1** | **Understand the factors that influence the UK financial services industry:** | |
| 1.1.1 | The role of the government in the economy: policy, regulation, taxation and social welfare | 1 |
| 1.1.2 | The role of financial investment in the economy:<br>• primary markets<br>• secondary markets<br>• balance of payments<br>• exchange rates | 2 |
| 1.1.3 | The role and structure of the global financial services industry and its key participants:<br>• UK<br>• Europe<br>• North America<br>• Asia | 3 |
| 1.1.4 | The role of government and central banks in financial markets:<br>• interest rate setting process<br>• money market operations<br>• fiscal and quantitative easing<br>• other interventions | 4 |
| 1.1.5 | The main stages of economic, financial and stock market cycles, including:<br>• national income<br>• global influences<br>• long-term growth trends | 5 |
| 1.1.6 | The impact of global trends:<br>• Globalisation of business, finance and markets<br>• Advances in technology<br>• Regulatory challenges | 6 |

| Syllabus Unit/ Element | | Chapter/ Section |
|---|---|---|
| **Element 2** | **UK Financial Services and Consumer Relationships**<br>On completion, the candidate will be able to: | **Chapter 2** |
| **2.1** | **Understand the main financial risks, needs and priorities of UK consumers:** | |
| 2.1.1 | Balancing, budgeting and managing finances; debt acquisition and accumulation | 1 |

431

| Syllabus Unit/ Element | | Chapter/ Section |
|---|---|---|
| 2.1.2 | Lifestyle changes and their impact on finances. Funding and safeguarding major investments, including:<br>• housing<br>• incapacity<br>• unemployment and unplanned difficulty in earning income<br>• income provision during retirement and old age<br>• taxation | 1 |
| 2.1.3 | Provision for dependants before and after death | 1 |
| **2.2** | **UK Consumers** | |
| 2.2.1 | Understand how the main financial risks, needs and priorities of UK consumers are typically met:<br>• financial planning and financial advice<br>• state benefits<br>• credit finance and management<br>• mortgages<br>• insurance and financial protection<br>• retirement and pension funding<br>• estate and tax planning<br>• savings and investment | 2 |
| **2.3** | **Professional Conduct and Ethical Practice** | |
| 2.3.1 | Understand how professional conduct and ethical practice can directly affect the experience and perception of consumers | 3 |

| Element 3 | UK Contract and Trust Legislation<br>On completion, the candidate will be able to: | Chapter 3 |
|---|---|---|
| **3.1** | **Understand specific legal concepts relevant to financial advice:** | |
| 3.1.1 | Contract, agency and capacity: legal persons – individuals, personal representatives, trustees, companies, limited liability partnerships | 1.1–1.3 |
| 3.1.2 | Powers of attorney and managing the grantor's affairs: wills, intestacy and administration of estates | 1.4 |
| 3.1.3 | Real property, personal property and joint ownership | 1.5 |
| 3.1.4 | Insolvency, receivership and bankruptcy | 1.6 |
| **3.2** | **Main Types of Trust** | |
| 3.2.1 | Understand in outline the main types of trust and their purpose, creation and administration | 2 |
| **3.3** | **Creation of Trusts** | |
| 3.3.1 | Apply knowledge of the creation and administration of trusts | 2 |

| Element 4 | Integrity and Ethics in Professional Practice<br>On completion, the candidate will be able to: | Chapter 4 |
|---|---|---|
| **4.1** | **Professional Ethics** | |
| 4.1.1 | Understand core ethical theories, principles and values | 1.1 |

## Syllabus Learning Map

| Syllabus Unit/ Element | | Chapter/ Section |
|---|---|---|
| 4.1.2 | Understand the differences between ethical values, qualities and behaviours in professional practice contrasted with unethical or unprofessional practice | 1.2 |
| 4.1.3 | Understand the impact of the following when applying an ethical approach within an organisational or team environment:<br>• self-interest<br>• the role of the agent<br>• the role of the stakeholders<br>• the role of the group or team | 1.3 |
| 4.1.4 | Understand the evidence relating to the positive effects of ethical approaches on corporate profitability and sustainability when contrasted with the results of unethical or less ethical practices | 1.4 |
| 4.1.5 | Apply processes to:<br>• create ethical awareness<br>• assess ethical dilemmas<br>• implement ethical decisions | 1.5 |
| **4.2** | **Codes of Ethics and Codes of Conduct** | |
| 4.2.1 | Understand the relationship between ethical principles, the development of regulatory standards and professional codes of conduct | 2.1 |
| 4.2.2 | Understand how decisions and outcomes for the industry, firms, advisers and consumers may be limited by reliance on rule-based compliance, and how ethical behaviour and decision-making can enhance these outcomes | 2.2 |
| 4.2.3 | Apply the Chartered Institute for Securities & Investment's Code of Ethics to professional practice | 2.3 |
| **4.3** | **Understand Key Principles of Professional Integrity** | |
| 4.3.1 | • openness, honesty, transparency and fairness | 3.1 |
| 4.3.2 | • relationship between personal, corporate and societal values | 3.1 |
| 4.3.3 | • commitment to professional ideals and principles extending beyond professional norms | 3.1 |
| **4.4** | **Apply Behaviours that Reflect Professional Integrity:** | |
| 4.4.1 | • commitment and capacity to work to accepted professional values | 3.2 |
| 4.4.2 | • ability to relate professional values to personally held values | 3.2 |
| 4.4.3 | • ability to give a coherent account of beliefs and actions | 3.2 |
| 4.4.4 | • strength of purpose and ability to act on the values | 3.2 |
| **4.5** | **Professional Integrity and Ethics** | |
| 4.5.1 | Understand the meaning of professional integrity and ethics within financial services and how this is typically demonstrated in the:<br>• operation of financial markets and institutions<br>• personal conduct of finance professionals<br>• duties of fiduciaries and agents in financial relationships | 3.3 |

| Syllabus Unit/ Element | | Chapter/ Section |
|---|---|---|
| **Element 5** | **The Regulatory Infrastructure of UK Financial Services**<br>On completion, the candidate will be able to: | **Chapter 5** |
| 5.1 | **Understand the wider structure of UK financial regulation including the responsibilities of the main regulating bodies and the relationship between them:** | |
| 5.1.1 | • Market regulators: the Financial Conduct Authority and the Prudential Regulation Authority | 1 |
| 5.1.2 | • Other regulators: the UK Competition Commission, the Information Commissioner and the Pensions Regulator | 1 |
| 5.1.3 | The relationships and co-ordination between the following:<br>• The Financial Conduct Authority (FCA)<br>• The Prudential Regulation Authority (PRA)<br>• The Financial Ombudsman Scheme (FOS)<br>• Her Majesty's Revenue & Customs (HMRC)<br>• The Financial Services Compensation Scheme (FSCS)<br>• The Financial Policy Committee (FPC)<br>• The Upper Tribunal (Tax and Chancery)<br>• The Bank of England (BOE)<br>• Her Majesty's Treasury (HMT) | 1 |
| 5.2 | **FCA and PRA Regulatory Principles, Statutory Objectives, Structure, Powers and Activities** | |
| 5.2.1 | Understand the strategic and operational objectives, structure, powers and activities of the FCA | 2 |
| 5.2.2 | Understand the strategic and operational objectives, structure, powers and activities of the PRA | 2 |
| 5.2.3 | Understand the 8 regulatory principles | 2 |
| 5.3 | **Understand the scope of authorisation and regulation of the FCA and the PRA under the FSMA (as amended):** | |
| 5.3.1 | • regulation of UK financial markets and exchanges<br>• recognition of overseas exchanges, investment exchanges and clearing houses<br>• UK listing of financial instruments<br>• authorisation of firms, individuals and collective investment schemes | 3.1 |
| 5.3.2 | Principles, rules, guidance and rule-making powers:<br>• regulation and enforcement relating to financial crime and market abuse<br>• supervision, investigations and enforcement | 2 |
| 5.3.3 | National Strategy for Financial Capability and Consumer Support | 3.2 |

# Syllabus Learning Map

| Syllabus Unit/ Element | | Chapter/ Section |
|---|---|---|
| **5.4** | **Support for Regulatory Framework** | |
| 5.4.1 | Understand the key internal and external mechanisms within firms that support the regulatory framework: <br> • senior and executive management <br> • compliance and risk management <br> • finance function <br> • internal and external auditors and legal advisers <br> • CASS oversight function <br> • regulatory reporting | Chapter 7, Section 1.6 <br><br> Chapter 10, Section 8.1 |
| **5.5** | **EU Directives and Regulations** | |
| 5.5.1 | Understand the relevant European Union Directives and Regulations and their impact on the UK Financial Services industry in respect of: <br> • MiFID – passporting within the EEA and home versus host state regulation <br> • UCITS – selling collective investment schemes cross border; Prospective Directive – selling securities cross border <br> • Capital Requirements Directive – firms undertaking investment business <br> • AIFMD – regulation of AIFMD and the promotion of AIF within the EU <br> • EMIR – requirements placed on EEA established counterparties | 4 |

| Element 6 | **FCA and PRA Supervisory Objectives, Principles and Processes** <br> On completion, the candidate will be able to: | Chapter 6 |
|---|---|---|
| **6.1** | **The FCA's Approach to Regulation** | |
| 6.1.1 | Understand the merits and limitations of the FCA's conduct risk, outcomes and principles-based approaches to regulation | 1.1 |
| **6.2** | **Sources of Information** | |
| 6.2.1 | Understand the sources of information on the FCA's and the PRA's supervisory approach, including the annual risk outlook document, speeches and newsletters | 1.1.3 |
| **6.3** | **Understand the FCA's main disciplinary and enforcement powers, and how they are used:** | |
| 6.3.1 | Decision Procedure and Penalties Manual (DEPP) | 2 |
| 6.3.2 | Perimeter Guidance Manual: Authorisation & Regulated Activities (PERG 2) | 2 |
| 6.3.3 | Unauthorised investment business; enforceability of agreements, penalties and defences | 2 |
| 6.3.4 | Powers to require information and carry out investigations (FSMA 2000 s.165 & 167/8 (as amended)) | 2 |
| 6.3.5 | Powers of intervention (products and financial promotions) | 2 |

435

| Syllabus Unit/ Element | | Chapter/ Section |
|---|---|---|
| 6.4 | **Provisions and Guidance** | |
| 6.4.1 | Understand the six types of provisions used by the FCA/PRA in its Handbook and the status of the approved industry guidance | 3 |
| 6.5 | **Understand the purpose and application of the following prudential standards relating to financial services:** | |
| 6.5.1 | General Prudential Sourcebook (GENPRU) | 4.1 |
| 6.5.2 | Prudential Sourcebook for Banks, Building Societies and Investment Firms (BIPRU) | 4.1 |
| 6.5.3 | Capital adequacy and liquidity requirements for certain types of firm IFPRU | 4.1 |
| 6.6 | **Promotion of Fair and Ethical Outcomes** | |
| 6.6.1 | Understand how the FCA's use of outcomes-based regulation, including high-level principles (PRIN), corporate governance, Approved Persons responsibilities and Treating Customers Fairly requirements, is intended to promote fair and ethical outcomes and why this may not always be achieved | 6 |
| 6.7 | **Remuneration Code** | |
| 6.7.1 | Apply the principles and rules of the Remuneration Code (SYSC 19A (FCA/PRA) & C) | 5 |
| 6.8 | **Corporate Governance and Business Risk Management** | |
| 6.8.1 | Understand how the FCA's and PRA's approaches to supervision support corporate governance and business risk management | 1.2 |

| Element 7 | **FCA and PRA Authorisation of Firms and Individuals** On completion, the candidate will be able to: | **Chapter 7** |
|---|---|---|
| | **Authorisation of Firms** | |
| 7.1 | **Understand the purpose and application of the FCA's and PRA's High Level Standards:** | |
| 7.1.1 | Principles for Businesses (PRIN) | 1.1 |
| 7.1.2 | Systems and Controls (SYSC) | 1.6 |
| 7.1.3 | Threshold Conditions (COND) | 1.7 |
| 7.1.4 | Statements of Principle and Code of Practice for Approved Persons (APER) | 1.2 |
| 7.1.5 | The Fit and Proper Test for Approved Persons (FIT) | 1.5 |
| 7.2 | **Apply the main concepts, principles and rules relating to Regulated and Prohibited Activities:** | |
| 7.2.1 | Regulated and prohibited activities (Part II/III of FSMA 2000, Regulated Activities Order 2001) | 2 |
| 7.2.2 | Investments specified in Part III of the Regulated Activities Order | 2 |
| 7.3 | **Apply the main concepts, principles and rules relating to FCA and PRA authorisation:** | |
| 7.3.1 | Related guidance in the Perimeter Guidance Manual (PERG) | 3 |

# Syllabus Learning Map

| Syllabus Unit/ Element | | Chapter/ Section |
|---|---|---|
| 7.3.2 | Authorised Persons, Exempt Persons (PERG 2) and exclusions (FSMA Exemption Order 2001, SI 2001/1201) | 3 |
| 7.3.3 | Purpose, provisions, offences and scope of Permission Notices (SUP) | 3 |
| 7.3.4 | The requirement to act honestly, fairly and professionally (COBS 2.1) | 3 |
| 7.3.5 | Authorisation: conditions and procedures for firms (COND), and process and criteria for obtaining approval of Controllers including fitness and propriety (FIT (FCA/PRA)) | 3 |
| **7.4** | **Record-Keeping and Notifications** | |
| 7.4.1 | Apply the principles and rules relating to record-keeping and notification for regulatory purposes (SYSC 9.1 (FCA/PRA), PRIN 2.1.1(11) (FCA/PRA), SUP (FCA/PRA), Disp 1.9) | 6 |
| | **Approval of Individuals** | |
| **7.5** | **Understand the FCA's and PRA's main regulatory processes and provisions relating to the approval of individuals:** | |
| 7.5.1 | Approval Process | 4.1 |
| 7.5.2 | Approved Persons | 4.2 |
| 7.5.3 | Controlled Functions | 4.2 |
| 7.5.4 | Appointed Representatives | 4.4 |
| | **Training and Competence** | |
| **7.6** | **Apply the concepts, principles and rules relating to Training and Competence including appropriate professionalism:** | |
| 7.6.1 | Systems and controls responsibilities in relation to the competence of employees (SYSC 3.2.13; 14; 5.1.1 (FCA/PRA)) | 5 |
| 7.6.2 | The activities and functions to which the T&C regime applies | 5 |
| 7.6.3 | Measures to demonstrate competence – including those prior to assessment, at assessment, FCA and PRA approval and ongoing through Continuing Professional Development and the need for a Statement of Professional Standing | 5 |
| **7.7** | **Ethical Principles and Professional Conduct** | |
| 7.7.1 | Understand how the FCA's and PRA's approach to the authorisation of firms and approval of individuals upholds ethical principles and high standards of professional conduct<br>• Consumers<br>• Government and regulators<br>• Senior management of a regulated firm<br>• Employees of a regulated firm | 7 |
| **7.8** | **Corporate Governance and Business Management** | |
| 7.8.1 | Understand how the FCA's and PRA's approach to the authorisation of firms and approval of individuals supports good corporate governance and business risk management | 7 |

| Syllabus Unit/ Element | | Chapter/ Section |
|---|---|---|
| **Element 8** | **The Regulatory Framework relating to Financial Crime** <br> On completion, the candidate will be able to: | **Chapter 8** |
| | **Market Abuse** | |
| **8.1** | **Apply the main concepts, legal requirements and regulations relating to the prevention of market abuse:** | |
| 8.1.1 | Statutory offence of market abuse (Financial Services and Markets Act 2000 s.118 (1–8)) | 1.1 |
| 8.1.2 | Status of the FCA's Code of Market Conduct [FSMA 2000 s.119(1)–(3)]; the territorial scope of the legislation and regulation [FSMA 2000 s.118] | 1.2 |
| 8.1.3 | Offences outlined in the Code of Market Conduct [MAR 1.2.2/7, 1.3.1, 1.4.1, 1.5.1, 1.6.1, 1.7.1, 1.8.1, 1.9.1, 1.2.22] | 1.3 |
| 8.1.4 | Concepts of effect rather than intention [MAR 1.2.3] and reasonable regular user [MAR 1.2.20/21] | 1.3 |
| 8.1.5 | Statutory exceptions (safe harbours) to market abuse [MAR 1.10.1–4 (excl. table 1.10.5)] | 1.6 |
| 8.1.6 | The distinction between offences under market abuse, insider dealing (CJA) and under Financial Services Act 2012 s.89–s.95 misleading statements and practices | 1.7 |
| 8.1.7 | Ethical considerations and consequences of Market Abuse in relation to all market participants, clients and the integrity of the market system | 1.8 |
| 8.1.8 | Understand the purpose, provisions, offences and defences of the Financial Services Act 2012 s.89–s.95 – misleading statements and practices | 1.9.1 |
| | **Insider Dealing** | |
| **8.2** | **Apply the main concepts, legal requirements and regulations relating to the prevention of insider dealing:** | |
| 8.2.1 | Definitions of insider, insider dealing and inside information | 2.1 |
| 8.2.2 | Offences described in the legislation and the instruments covered by the Criminal Justice Act 1993 (CJA s.52 + Schedule 2) | 2.2 |
| 8.2.3 | General defences relating to insider dealing (CJA s.53) | 2.4 |
| 8.2.4 | Special defences: market makers acting in good faith, market information and price stabilisation (CJA s.53 and Schedule 1 paras 1–5) | 2.4 |
| 8.2.5 | The FCA's powers to prosecute insider dealing (FSMA s.402 EG 12.7–10) | 2.5 |

# Syllabus Learning Map

| Syllabus Unit/ Element | | Chapter/ Section |
|---|---|---|
| | **Money Laundering** | |
| **8.3** | **Apply the main concepts, legal requirements and regulations relating to the prevention of money laundering:** | |
| 8.3.1 | The terms money laundering, criminal conduct and criminal property the application of money laundering to all crimes [Proceeds of Crime Act 2002 s.340] and the power of the Secretary of State to determine what is relevant criminal conduct | 3 |
| 8.3.2 | The three stages of money laundering | 3.2 |
| 8.3.3 | The key provisions, objectives and interaction between the following legislation and guidance relating to money laundering:<br>• Proceeds of Crime Act 2002 [POCA], as amended by the Serious Organised Crime and Police Act 2005 [SOCPA]: main offences, tipping off, reporting suspicious transactions, and defences<br>• Money Laundering Regulations 2007 (internal controls), which includes obligations on firms for adequate training of individuals on money laundering | 3.3 |
| 8.3.4 | The standards expected by the Joint Money Laundering Steering Group Guidance notes particularly in relation to:<br>• Risk-based approach<br>• Requirements for directors and senior managers to be responsible for money laundering precautions<br>• Need for risk assessment<br>• Need for enhanced due diligence in relation to politically exposed persons [JMLSG 5.5.1–5.5.29]<br>• Need for high-level policy statement<br>• Detailed procedures implementing the firm's risk based approach [JMLSG 1.20, 1.27, 1.40–1.43, 4.17–4.18] | 3.4 |
| 8.3.5 | The money laundering aspects of know your customer (Joint Money Laundering Steering Groups' Guidance for the Financial Sector [Para 5.1.1–5.1.14] | 3.4 |
| 8.3.6 | Senior Management Arrangements, Systems and Controls Sourcebook [SYSC] role of the money laundering reporting officer, nominated officer and the compliance function [SYSC 3.2.6, 3.2.6 (A)–(J), 3.2.7 (FCA/PRA), 3.2.8 and 6.3 and the systems and controls that firms are expected to implement | 3.5 |
| 8.3.7 | The importance of ongoing monitoring of business relationships and being able to recognise a suspicious transaction, and the requirement for staff to report to the MLRO and for the firm to report to the National Crime Agency | 3.5 |
| 8.3.8 | Understand the duty of firms to report suspicious transactions [SUP 15.10.2] | 3.5 |

439

| Syllabus Unit/ Element | | Chapter/ Section |
|---|---|---|
| | **Financing of Terrorism** | |
| 8.4 | Apply the main concepts, legal requirements and regulations relating to the prevention of terrorism financing: | |
| 8.4.1 | Activities regarded as terrorism in the UK [Terrorism Act 2000 Part 1], the obligations on regulated firms under the Counter-Terrorism Act 2008 [money laundering of terrorist funds] [part 5 section 62 and s.7 part 1–7], the Anti-Terrorism Crime & Security Act 2001 Schedule 2 Part 3 [Disclosure of Information] and sanction list for terrorist activities | 3.7 |
| 8.4.2 | Preventative measures in respect of terrorist financing, the essential differences between laundering the proceeds of crime and the financing of terrorist acts [JMLSG Guidance 2007 paras 1.38–1.39, Preface 9], and the interaction between the rules of FCA, PRA and the Terrorism Act 2000 and the JMLSG Guidance regarding terrorism [JMLSG Guidance 2011] | Section 3.7 |
| | **Bribery Act 2010** | |
| 8.5 | Apply the main concepts, legal requirements and guidance relating to the prevention of bribery and corruption: | |
| 8.5.1 | The offences of bribery contrary to sections 1–7 Bribery Act 2010 | Section 9 |
| 8.5.2 | The role of adequate procedures in affording a defence to the offence of a commercial organisation failing to prevent bribery | Section 9.3 |
| 8.5.3 | Guidance on adequate procedures issued by the Ministry of Justice (sections 7 & 9 Bribery Act 2010) | Section 9.3 |
| 8.6 | **Model Code** | |
| 8.6.1 | Understand the main purpose and provisions of the FCA's Model Code in relation to share dealing by directors and other persons discharging managerial responsibilities, including closed periods; chairman's approval; no short-term dealing | Section 4 |
| 8.7 | **Disclosure and Transparency Rules** | |
| 8.7.1 | Apply the Disclosure and Transparency rules [DTR 2.1.3, 2.6.1] as they relate to:<br>• Disclosure and control of inside information by issuers<br>• Transactions by persons discharging managerial responsibilities and their connected persons | Section 5 |
| | **Data Protection** | |
| 8.8 | Apply the main concepts, legal requirements and regulations relating to data protection: | |
| 8.8.1 | The eight principles of the Data Protection Act 1998 | Section 6 |
| 8.8.2 | Notification of data controllers with the Information Commissioner | Section 6 |
| 8.8.3 | Record-keeping requirements of FCA regulated firms [DPA Schedule 1, Part 1 & COBS] | Section 6 |
| 8.8.4 | Data security implications for firms and individuals | Section 6 |

## Syllabus Learning Map

| Syllabus Unit/ Element | | Chapter/ Section |
|---|---|---|
| **8.9** | **Whistleblowing** | |
| 8.9.1 | Understand the legal and regulatory basis for whistleblowing [SYSC 18.1.2, 18.2.3] | Section 7 |
| **8.10** | **The FCA's Approach to Financial Crime Prevention** | |
| 8.10.1 | Understand how the FCA's approach to financial crime prevention upholds ethical principles and high standards of professional practice as reflected in the Financial Crime Guide | Section 8 |
| 8.10.2 | Understand how the FCA's approach to financial crime prevention supports good corporate governance and business risk management | Section 8 |

| Element 9 | Complaints and Redress | Chapter 9 |
|---|---|---|
| | On completion, the candidate will be able to: | |
| **9.1** | **Eligible Complainant** | |
| 9.1.1 | Apply the criteria for a complainant to be eligible to lodge a complaint [DISP 2.2] | 1 |
| **9.2** | **Procedures** | |
| 9.2.1 | Apply the procedures that a firm must implement and follow to handle customer complaints [DISP 1.2.1/3, 1.3.3, 1.4.1, 1.6.1/2/5, 1.9.1, 1.10.1] | 2 |
| **9.3** | **Compulsory Jurisdiction** | |
| 9.3.1 | Understand the activities to which Compulsory Jurisdiction applies (DISP 2.3) | 3 |
| **9.4** | **Complaints and Dispute Resolution** | |
| 9.4.1 | Understand the role of the Financial Ombudsman Service (FOS) [DISP Complaints Sourcebook – Dispute Resolution: Complaints: Introduction], and the awards and directions that can be made by the Ombudsman [DISP 3.7.2/4, 3.7.11] | 3 |
| 9.4.2 | Understand the framework under which the FCA can be alerted to super complaints and mass detriment references | 3 |
| **9.5** | **Financial Services Compensation Scheme** | |
| 9.5.1 | Apply the rules of the Financial Services Compensation Scheme in respect of each category of protected claim [COMP 10.2.1/3 (FCA/ PRA)] | 4 |
| **9.6** | **Ethical Standards and Professional Integrity** | |
| 9.6.1 | Apply appropriate ethical standards and professional integrity when handling customer complaints | 2, 5 |

| Syllabus Unit/ Element | | Chapter/ Section |
|---|---|---|
| **Element 10** | **FCA Conduct of Business – Fair Treatment of Customers, the Provision of Advice & Services, and Client Asset Protection** | **Chapter 10** |
| | On completion, the candidate will be able to: | |
| **10.1** | **Conduct of Business Sourcebook:** | |
| 10.1.1 | Understand the main FCA principles, rules and requirements relating to conduct of business:<br>• firms subject to the FCA Conduct of Business Sourcebook [COBS 1.1.1–1.1.3, 1 Annex 1, Part 3 section 3 (FCA/PRA)]<br>• activities which are subject to the FCA Conduct of Business Sourcebook including Eligible Counterparty Business and transactions between regulated market participants [COBS 1.1.1–1.1.3, Annex 1, Part 1(1) (FCA/PRA) & (4)]<br>• impact of location on firms/activities of the application of the FCA Conduct of Business Sourcebook: permanent place of business in UK [COBS 1.1.1–1.1.3 & Annex 1, Part 2 (FCA/PRA) & Part 3 (1–3) (FCA 1-3/PRA 1-2 only)] | 1 |
| **10.2** | **Electronic Media** | |
| 10.2.1 | Apply the provisions of the FCA Conduct of Business Sourcebook regarding electronic media [glossary definitions of durable medium and website Conditions] and the recording of voice conversations and electronic communications requirements [COBS 11.8] | 1.2 |
| **10.3** | **Rules applying to all firms communicating with clients [COBS 4.1, 4.2.1–4]** | |
| 10.3.1 | Apply the main FCA principles, rules and requirements relating to:<br>• the conduct of designated investment business<br>• financial promotions<br>• territorial scope<br>• fair, clear and not misleading communications | 2.1.2 |
| 10.3.2 | Inducements rules [COBS 2.3.1/2, 2.3.10–16] and the use of dealing commission, including what benefits can be supplied/obtained under such agreements [COBS 11.6]; Rules, guidance and evidential provisions regarding reliance on others [COBS 2.4.4/6/7] | 1.3 |
| **10.4** | **The Requirements of the Financial Promotion Rules** | |
| 10.4.1 | Understand the purpose and application of the financial promotion rules and the relationship with Principles 6 and 7 [COBS 4.1] | 2.1 |
| 10.4.2 | Apply the financial promotion rules and firms' responsibilities for appointed representatives [COBS 3.2.1(4), 4.1] | 2.1 |
| 10.4.3 | Apply the types of communication addressed by COBS 4 including the methods of communication | 2.1 |
| 10.4.4 | Understand the main exemptions to the financial promotion rules and the existence of the Financial Promotions Order [COBS 4.8] | 2.2 |

# Syllabus Learning Map

| Syllabus Unit/ Element | | Chapter/ Section |
|---|---|---|
| 10.4.5 | Apply the rules on approving and communicating financial promotions and compliance with the financial promotions rules [COBS 4.10 + SYSC 3 & 4 (FCA/PRA)] | 2.3 |
| 10.4.6 | Apply the rules relating to the compilation of direct offer and non-real time financial promotions including the relationship with FCA Principles, and the requirements in relation to past, simulated past and future performance [COBS 4.1; 4.6; 4.7.1–4] | 2.4 |
| 10.4.7 | Understand the ethical implications of issuing misleading financial promotions | 2.5 |
| | **Client Categorisation** | |
| **10.5** | **Understand the main FCA principles, rules and requirements relating to:** | |
| 10.5.1 | Client categorisation (eligible counterparties/professional/retail) [COBS 3.1–3.6] | 3 |
| 10.5.2 | Notification to clients of their categorisation [COBS 3.3] | 3 |
| 10.5.3 | Requirements for clients electing to be professional clients & eligible counterparties, together with those wishing higher level of protection [COBS 3.5.3–9; 3.6.4–7] | 3 |
| **10.6** | **Fair Treatment of Customers** | |
| 10.6.1 | Understand the main FCA principles and requirements relating to the fair treatment of customers:<br>• FCA's Principles for Businesses (PRIN 1.1.1 (FCA/PRA)/2, 1.1.7 & 2.1.1 (FCA/PRA))<br>• FCA's six consumer outcomes (corporate culture; marketing; clear information; suitability of advice; fair product expectations; absence of post-sale barriers)<br>• Interaction with SYSC and the requirements for senior management to review management information (SYSC 4.1.1 (FCA/PRA))<br>• Importance of the fiduciary relationship and the responsibilities of professional advisers towards clients<br>• Requirements for fair agreements and the FCA's ability to enforce Unfair Contract Terms legislation (UNFCOG 1.1, 1.3 & 1.4)<br>• FCA requirement for a conflicts management policy (SYSC 10.1.10/11/12 (FCA/PRA)) | 4, 5 |
| 10.6.2 | Understand the FCA Conduct of Business Rules relating to fair treatment of customers:<br>• Communication to clients and the additional requirements relating to retail clients [COBS 4.1; 4.5]<br>• Provision of dealing confirmations and periodic statements to customers [COBS 16.1–16.3]<br>• Ability to ensure and demonstrate the fair treatment of customer dealing, taking into account PA Dealing Policy, Client Order Management Policy, Concepts of Best and Timely Execution, Churning & Switching [COBS 9.3; 11] | 6 |

443

| Syllabus Unit/ Element | | Chapter/ Section |
|---|---|---|
| 10.6.3 | Understand the application and purpose of the principles and rules on conflict of interest; the rules on identifying conflicts and types of conflicts; the rules on recording and managing conflicts; and the rule on disclosure of conflicts [PRIN 2.1.1 Principle 8, SYSC 10.1.1–10.1.9 (FCA/PRA)] | 5 |
| 10.6.4 | Know the rules on managing conflict in connection with investment research and research recommendations [COBS 12.1.2, 12.2.1/3/5/10, 12.3.1–4, 12.4.1/4/5/6/7/9/10/15/16/17] and the rules on Chinese walls [SYSC 10.2 (FCA/PRA)] | 5.6 |
| **10.7** | **Accepting Customers** | |
| 10.7.1 | Understand the main FCA principles, rules and requirements relating to client take-on processes, agreements and disclosures:<br>• timing, order and medium in which client disclosures may be made, including requirements on electronic media<br>• disclosure of service provision, costs and associated charges and terms of business<br>• client agreements for designated investment business [COBS 8.1.1–8.1.3]<br>• interpreting the different information requirements and responsibilities between managing investments and execution-only services [COBS 6.1.6]<br>• requirements of disclosure information – compensation scheme, complaints eligibility, status information, permanent place of business, voice recording | 4 |
| 10.7.2 | Understand the requirements for an adviser to a retail client to be remunerated only by adviser charges in relation to any personal recommendation or related service | 4.2 |
| **10.8** | **Investment Advice and Product Disclosure** | |
| 10.8.1 | Understand the main FCA principles, rules and requirements relating to the provision of investment advice and product disclosure:<br>• assessment of client suitability requirements [COBS 9.1.1–9.1.4; 9.2.1–7; 9.3.1]<br>• difference in requirements between professional and retail clients and the timing of suitability reports [COBS 9.2.8; 9.4.1–3]<br>• obligations for assessing appropriateness and circumstances not necessary [COBS 10.2; 10.4–10.6]<br>• cancellation and withdrawal rights [COBS 15.1.1; 15.2.1; 15.2.3; 15.2.5; 15.3.1; 15.3.2] | 7 |
| 10.8.2 | Understand the requirements for a firm making a personal recommendation to be independent or restricted | 4.2 |

# Syllabus Learning Map

| Syllabus Unit/ Element | | Chapter/ Section |
|---|---|---|
| | **Client Assets Protection** | |
| 10.9.1 | Understand principles of client money segregation, holding assets in trust and the requirements for senior management systems, controls & oversight over client money & custody assets (CASS 1A.2.7 & 1A.3.1): | 8.1 |
| 10.9.2 | Understand the processes for the establishment of client bank and custody accounts: <br> • importance of due diligence <br> • statutory trust status of client bank accounts <br> • the mitigation of counterparty and settlement risks <br> • risks arising from overseas investment activity | 8.2, 8.3 |
| 10.9.3 | Understand the CASS client money and custody rules and the client money reconciliation including the timing, identification, resolution and reporting of discrepancies[CASS6.2.1–3, 6.5.4–13, 7.3.1–2, 7.4.11, 7.6.9–16, 7.7.1–2] | 8.3 |
| 10.9.4 | Apply the rules relating to the application and exemption from the requirements of the CASS rules [CASS 1.2.3–4, 6.1.1–6, 7.1.1–12] | 8.4 |
| **10.10** | **Client Interaction** | |
| 10.10.1 | Understand the skills necessary to listen and communicate professionally, and to adapt to individual needs and capabilities within a diverse customer base | 9.1 |
| 10.10.2 | Understand the skills necessary to: <br> • elicit, confirm and record client information relevant to the investment advisory process <br> • assess and analyse clients' needs and circumstances <br> • reach a shared conclusion and make appropriate recommendations | 9.1 |
| 10.10.3 | Apply relevant principles, rules and sound judgment in working within the scope of authorisation, professional competence and job description | 9.2 |
| 10.10.4 | Apply relevant principles, rules and sound judgment when monitoring and reviewing clients' plans and circumstances, taking into account relevant changes | 9.2 |
| 10.10.5 | Apply an understanding of the potential outcomes of unethical sales practices, investment activity, abuse of bankruptcy and other unethical practice in terms of multiple and systemic risks, reputational risk and damage to public confidence | 9.3 |

445

# Examination Specification

Each examination paper is constructed from a specification that determines the weightings that will be given to each element. The specification is given below.

It is important to note that the numbers quoted may vary slightly from examination to examination as there is some flexibility to ensure that each examination has a consistent level of difficulty. However, the number of questions tested in each element should not change by more than plus or minus 2.

| Element Number | Element | Questions |
|---|---|---|
| 1 | The Financial Services Industry | 2 |
| 2 | UK Financial Services and Customer Relationships | 3 |
| 3 | UK Contract and Trust Legislation | 2 |
| 4 | Integrity & Ethics in Professional Practice | 8 |
| 5 | Regulatory Infrastructure of UK Financial Services | 6 |
| 6 | FCA and PRA Supervisory Objectives, Principles and Processes | 7 |
| 7 | FCA and PRA Authorisation of Firms and Individuals | 14 |
| 8 | The Regulatory Framework relating to Financial Crime | 18 |
| 9 | Complaints and Redress | 3 |
| 10 | FCA Conduct of Business – including fair treatment of customers, the provision of advice and services, and client money protection | 17 |
| **Total** | | **100** |

# CISI Chartered MCSI Membership can work for you...

**Studying for a CISI qualification is hard work and we're sure you're putting in plenty of hours, but don't lose sight of your goal!**

This is just the first step in your career; there is much more to achieve!

The securities and investments industry attracts ambitious and driven individuals. You're probably one yourself and that's great, but on the other hand you're almost certainly surrounded by lots of other people with similar ambitions.

So how can you stay one step ahead during these uncertain times?

**Entry Criteria for Chartered MCSI Membership**

As an ACSI and MCSI candidate, you can upgrade your membership status to Chartered MCSI. There are a number of ways of gaining the CISI Chartered MCSI membership.

A straightforward route requires candidates to have:
- a minimum of one year's ACSI or MCSI membership;
- passed a full Diploma; Certificate in Private Client Investment Advice & Management or Masters in Wealth Management award;
- passed the IntegrityMatters with an A grade; and
- successfully logged and certified 12 months' CPD under the CISI's CPD Scheme.

Alternatively, experienced-based candidates are required to have:
- a minimum of one year's ACSI membership;
- passed the IntegrityMatters with an A grade; and
- successfully logged and certified six years' CPD under the CISI's CPD Scheme.

| **Joining Fee:** | Current Grade of Membership | Grade of Chartership | Upgrade Cost |
|---|---|---|---|
| | ACSI | Chartered MCSI | £75.00 |
| | MCSI | Chartered MCSI | £30.00 |

By belonging to a Chartered professional body, members will benefit from enhanced status in the industry and the wider community. Members will be part of an organisation which holds the respect of government and industry, and can communicate with the public on a whole new level. There will be little doubt in consumers' minds that chartered members of the CISI are highly regarded and qualified professionals and as a consequence will be required to act as such.

The Chartered MCSI designation will provide you with full access to all member benefits, including Professional Refresher where there are currently over 50 modules available on subjects including Behavioural Finance, Cybercrime and Conduct Risk. CISI TV is also available to members, allowing you to catch up on the latest CISI events, whilst earning valuable CPD hours.

# Professional Refresher

**Self-testing elearning modules to refresh your knowledge, meet regulatory and firm requirements, and earn CPD hours.**

Professional Refresher is a training solution to help you remain up-to-date with industry developments, maintain regulatory compliance and demonstrate continuing learning.

This popular online learning tool allows self-administered refresher testing on a variety of topics, including the latest regulatory changes.

There are currently over 50 modules available which address UK and international issues. Modules are reviewed by practitioners frequently and new topics are added to the suite on a regular basis.

**Benefits to firms:**
- Learning and tests can form part of business T&C programme
- Learning and tests kept up to date and accurate by the CISI
- Relevant and useful – devised by industry practitioners
- Access to individual results available as part of management overview facility, 'Super User'
- Records of staff training can be produced for internal use and external audits
- Cost-effective – no additional charge for CISI members
- Available to non-members

**Benefits to individuals:**
- Comprehensive selection of topics across industry sectors
- Modules are frequently reviewed and updated by industry experts
- New topics introduced regularly
- Free for members
- Successfully passed modules are recorded in your CPD log as Active Learning
- Counts as structured learning for RDR purposes
- On completion of a module, a certificate can be printed out for your own records

The full suite of Professional Refresher modules is free to CISI members or £150 for non-members. Modules are also available individually. To view a full list of Professional Refresher modules visit:

### cisi.org/refresher

If you or your firm would like to find out more contact our Client Relationship Management team:
+ 44 20 7645 0670
crm@cisi.org

For more information on our elearning products, contact our Customer Support Centre on +44 20 7645 0777, or visit our website at cisi.org/study

# Professional Refresher

**Free to CISI members**

## Top 5

### Integrity & Ethics
- High Level View
- Ethical Behaviour
- An Ethical Approach
- Compliance vs Ethics

### Anti-Money Laundering
- Introduction to Money Laundering
- UK Legislation and Regulation
- Money Laundering Regulations 2007
- Proceeds of Crime Act 2002
- Terrorist Financing
- Suspicious Activity Reporting
- Money Laundering Reporting Officer
- Sanctions

### Financial Crime
- What is Financial Crime?
- Insider Dealing and Market Abuse Introduction, Legislation, Offences and Rules
- Money Laundering Legislation, Regulations, Financial Sanctions and Reporting Requirements
- Money Laundering and the Role of the MLRO

### Information Security and Data Protection
- Information Security: The Key Issues
- Latest Cybercrime Developments
- The Lessons From High-Profile Cases
- Key Identity Issues: Know Your Customer
- Implementing the Data Protection Act 1998
- The Next Decade: Predictions For The Future

### UK Bribery Act
- Background to the Act
- The Offences
- What the Offences Cover
- When Has an Offence Been Committed
- The Defences Against Charges of Bribery
- The Penalties

## Compliance

### Behavioural Finance
- Background to Behavioural Finance
- Biases and Heuristics
- The Regulator's Perspective
- Implications of Behavioural Finance

### Conduct Risk
- What is Conduct Risk?
- Regulatory Powers
- Managing Conduct Risk
- Treating Customers Fairly
- Practical Application of Conduct Risk

### Conflicts of Interest
- Introduction
- Examples of Conflicts of Interest
- Examples of Enforcement Action
- Policies and Procedures
- Tools to Manage Conflicts of Interest
- Conflict Management Process
- Good Practice

### Risk (an overview)
- Definition of Risk
- Key Risk Categories
- Risk Management Process
- Risk Appetite
- Business Continuity
- Fraud and Theft
- Information Security

### T&C Supervision Essentials
- Who Expects What From Supervisors?
- Techniques for Effective Routine Supervision
- Practical Skills of Guiding and Coaching
- Developing and Assessing New Advisers
- Techniques for Resolving Poor Performance

## Wealth

### Client Assets and Client Money
- Protecting Client Assets and Client Money
- Ring-Fencing Client Assets and Client Money
- Due Diligence of Custodians
- Reconciliations
- Records and Accounts
- CASS Oversight

### Investment Principles and Risk
- Diversification
- Factfind and Risk Profiling
- Investment Management
- Modern Portfolio Theory and Investing Styles
- Direct and Indirect Investments
- Socially Responsible Investment
- Collective Investments
- Investment Trusts
- Dealing in Debt Securities and Equities

### Principles of RDR
- Professionalism – Qualifications
- Professionalism – SPS
- Description of Advice – Part 1
- Description of Advice – Part 2
- Adviser Charging

### Suitability of Client Investments
- Assessing Suitability
- Risk Profiling and Establishing Risk
- Obtaining Customer Information
- Suitable Questions and Answers
- Making Suitable Investment Selections
- Guidance, Reports and Record Keeping

## Operations

### Best Execution
- What Is Best Execution?
- Achieving Best Execution
- Order Execution Policies
- Information to Clients & Client Consent
- Monitoring, the Rules, and Instructions
- Client Order Handling

### Central Clearing
- Background to Central Clearing
- The Risks CCPs Mitigate
- The Events of 2007/08
- Target 2 Securities

### Corporate Actions
- Corporate Structure and Finance
- Life Cycle of an Event
- Mandatory Events
- Voluntary Events

## International

### Dodd-Frank Act
- Background and Purpose
- Creation of New Regulatory Bodies
- Too Big to Fail and the Volcker Rule
- Regulation of Derivatives
- Securitisation
- Credit Rating Agencies

### Foreign Account Tax Compliance Act (FATCA)
- Reporting by US Taxpayers
- Reporting by Foreign Financial Institutions
- Implementation Timeline

### Sovereign Wealth Funds
- Definition and History
- The Major SWFs
- Transparency Issues
- The Future
- Sources

# cisi.org/refresher

## Feedback to the CISI

Have you found this workbook to be a valuable aid to your studies? We would like your views, so please email us at learningresources@cisi.org with any thoughts, ideas or comments.

## Accredited Training Providers

Support for examination students studying for the Chartered Institute for Securities & Investment (CISI) Qualifications is provided by several Accredited Training Providers (ATPs), including Fitch Learning and BPP. The CISI's ATPs offer a range of face-to-face training courses, distance learning programmes, their own learning resources and study packs which have been accredited by the CISI. The CISI works in close collaboration with its ATPs to ensure they are kept informed of changes to CISI examinations so they can build them into their own courses and study packs.

## CISI Workbook Specialists Wanted

### Workbook Authors

Experienced freelance authors with finance experience, and who have published work in their area of specialism, are sought. Responsibilities include:

- Updating workbooks in line with new syllabuses and any industry developments
- Ensuring that the syllabus is fully covered

### Workbook Reviewers

Individuals with a high-level knowledge of the subject area are sought. Responsibilities include:

- Highlighting any inconsistencies against the syllabus
- Assessing the author's interpretation of the workbook

### Workbook Technical Reviewers

Technical reviewers provide a detailed review of the workbook and bring the review comments to the panel. Responsibilities include:

- Cross-checking the workbook against the syllabus
- Ensuring sufficient coverage of each learning objective

### Workbook Proofreaders

Proofreaders are needed to proof workbooks both grammatically and also in terms of the format and layout. Responsibilities include:

- Checking for spelling and grammar mistakes
- Checking for formatting inconsistencies

If you are interested in becoming a CISI external specialist call:
**+44 20 7645 0609**

or email:
**iain.worman@cisi.org**

For bookings, orders, membership and general enquiries please contact our Customer Support Centre on +44 20 7645 0777, or visit our website at cisi.org